GLITCHSCAPES

Julian H. Scaff

ISBN 978-0-692-17372-5

CONTENTS

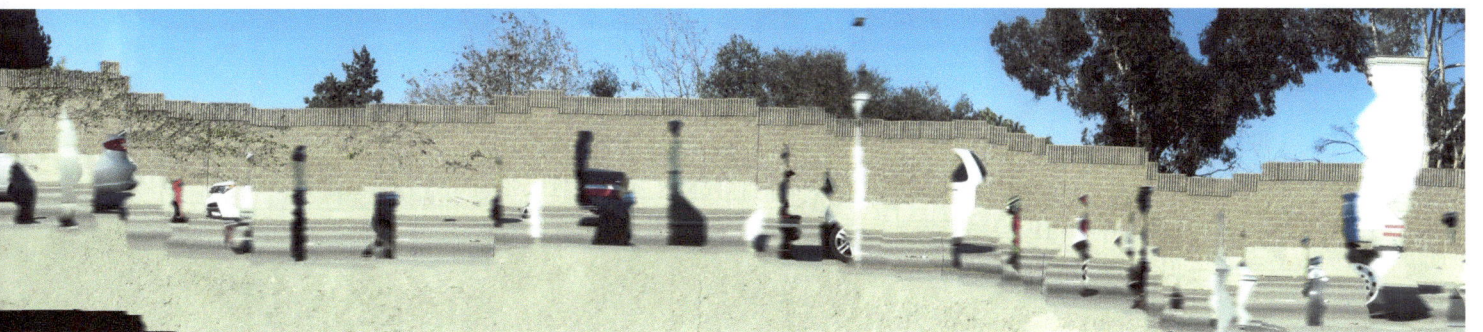

GLITCHSCAPES
The Aesthetics of Panoramic Malfunction

"It's the glitches and twists, I thought, that make this universe unique and compelling. Without flaws, there would be no depth, no substance."
~A.M. Jenkins, *Reposessed*

These glitched panoramic photographs, which I call Glitchscapes, are not manipulated in any way. They appear here exactly as they come out of the camera. It started with a Fujifilm point-and-shoot. I tweaked the panoramic stitching algorithms in the firmware with the help of a Norwegian circuit-bending artist named Arvid who I met while living in the Netherlands. It was a trial and error process that required numerous attempts before the camera would still function but would create photographic glitches when shooting in panorama mode. After about a year and over a hundred Glitchscapes, the Fujifilm camera mysteriously stopped working altogether.

I discovered by accident that I could achieve a remarkably similar effect to the hacked point-and-shoot camera by moving my iPhone camera in a very particular motion while in panorama mode. Unlike the Fujifilm camera, where the glitches were created inside the software, the iPhone Glitchscapes are created external to the camera through motion that breaks the abilities of the algorithms to correctly stitch the images together. The intended iPhone panorama stitching works correctly by moving the camera slowly and in a straight plane. If you move too quickly and/or break the plane of motion, the stitching doesn't work correctly. Through practice, I honed a particular technique to achieve the desired effect, sometimes by performing Tai Chi-style movements with the phone, sometimes by brisk walking, and sometimes by shooting from a car going at a set velocity.

These images reflect both an aesthetic of digital failure—of software glitches—as well as a snapshot of a very particular technology at a very particular point in history. Future generations of digital cameras/phones may indeed "fix" this glitch by speeding up processing power and software stitching, rendering this technique more difficult if not impossible to achieve. With advancements in technology, this effect will become anachronistic, like the Super 8 and PixelVision cameras of the past.

The specific features of a panoramic Glitchscape are distinct to the software embedded In the camera. Unlike an aberration of the lens, a mechanical malfunction of a shutter mechanism, or digital glitches created after the image is captured, the Glitchscape is solely a malfunction of the stitching of multiple images into one, a failure to create a seamless gestalt. Some of the most distinctive results are repeating patterns of very far away objects, the truncating of objects closer to the camera, lines that don't connect, disembodied floating fragments, and the flattening of three dimensional space.

There is a gap in time from when I stopped taking the photos to when I started curating them for this book. As I look back on these images now, they seem less about technology or technique and more about a peculiar way of seeing and remembering. As John Berger wrote in *Understanding a Photograph*, a photograph is neither lie nor truth, but rather "a fleeting, subjective impression." Glitchscapes are like our memories: fragmented and subjective.

I present here a small selection of the images I find most interesting, taken over a 6-year period. I have chosen to arrange them in chronological order because they represent a journey through disjointed time and malfunctioning space during a period in my life when I frequently moved and traveled across three continents. Once my life became less frantic, the need to create these Glitchscapes ceased, not unlike the Fujifilm camera that one day just gave up on glitching. The glitches in images, as in life, both obfuscate and reveal, destroy and create, like the defective architectonics of memory.

Julian H. Scaff

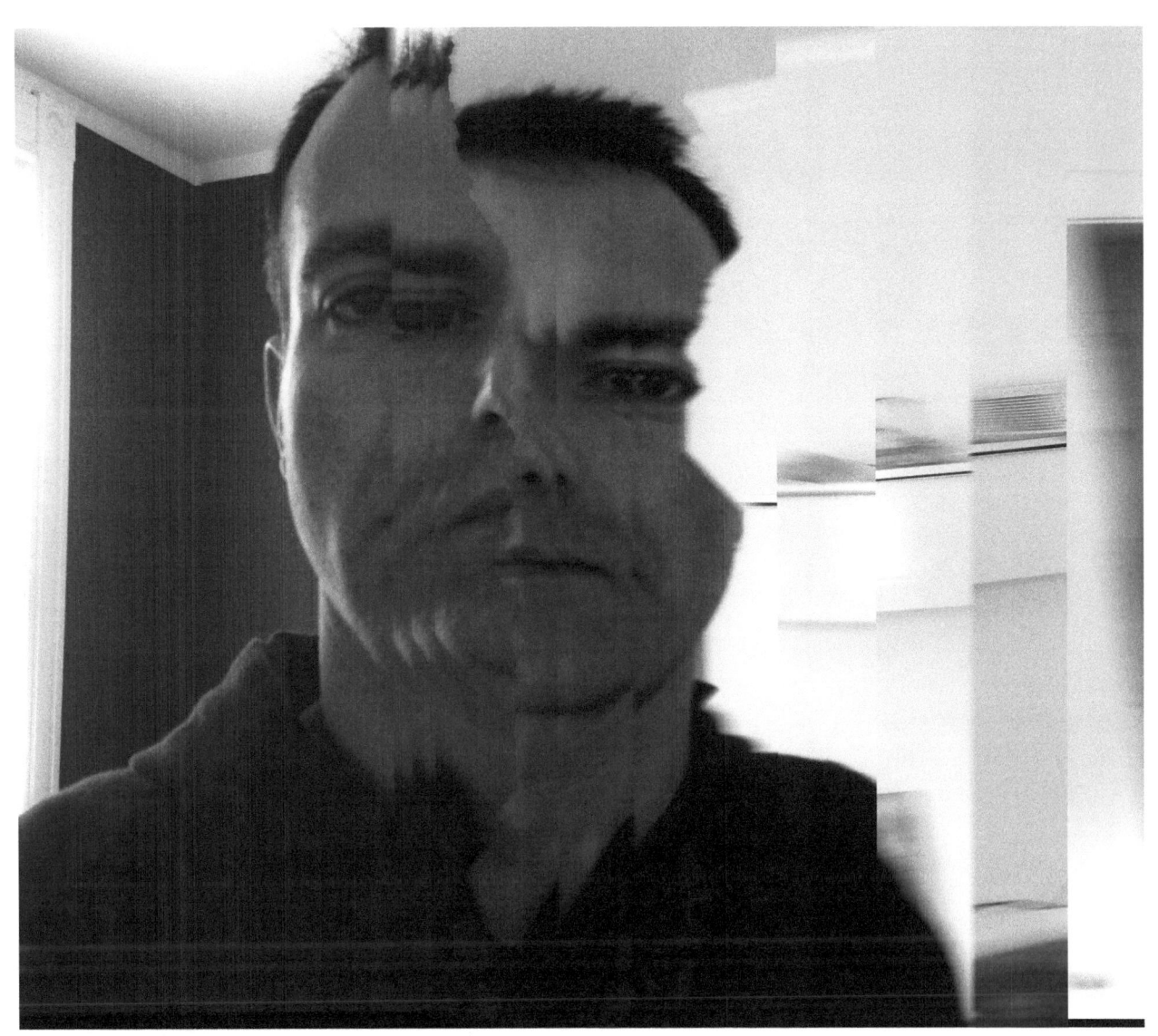

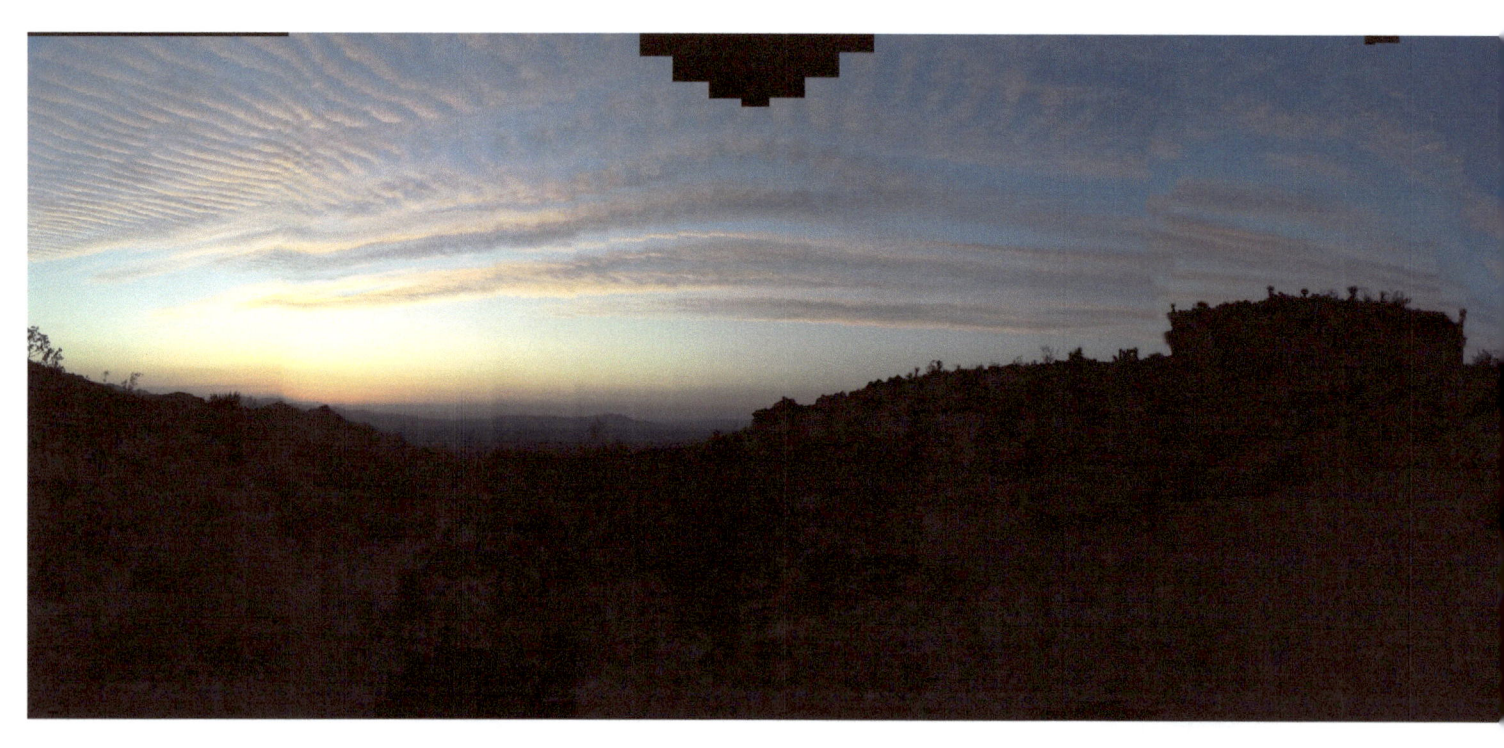

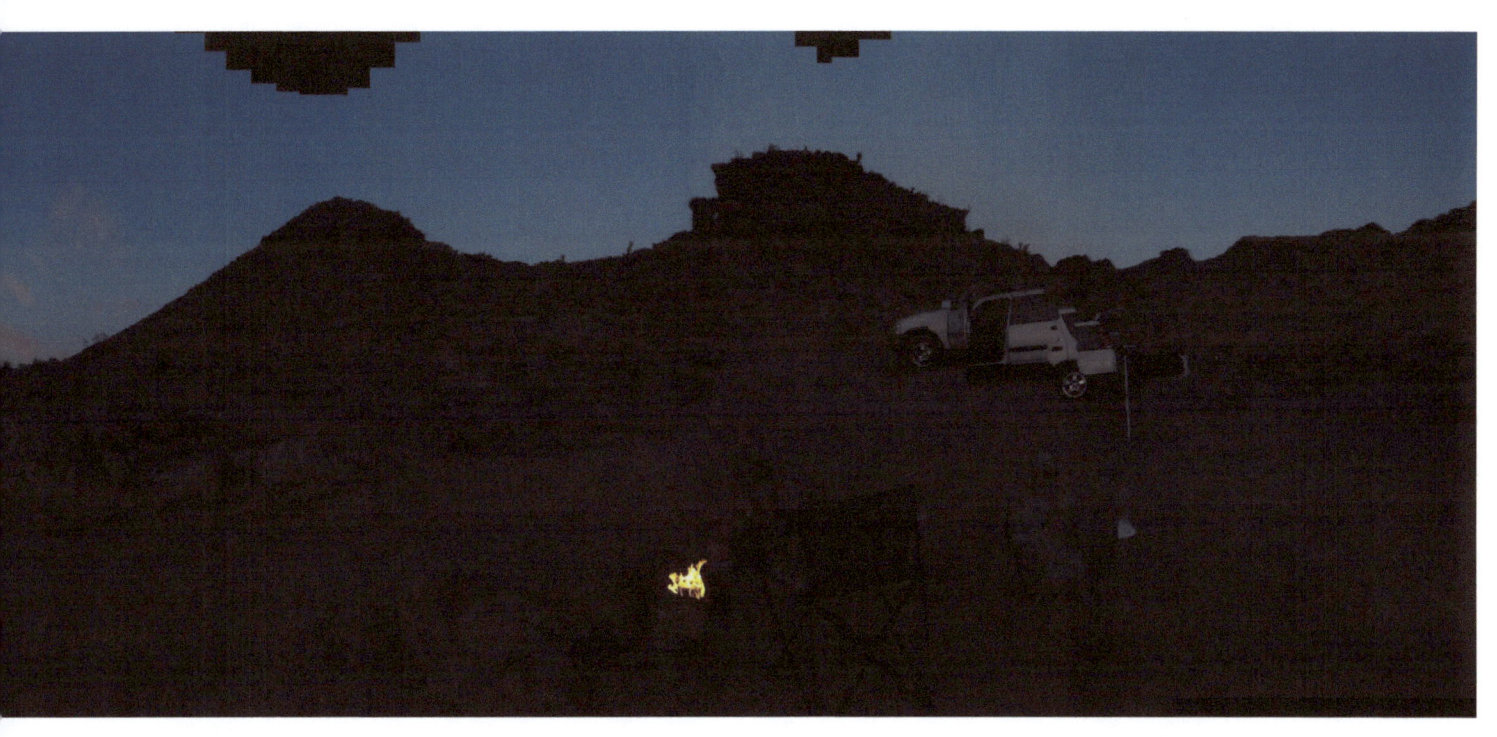

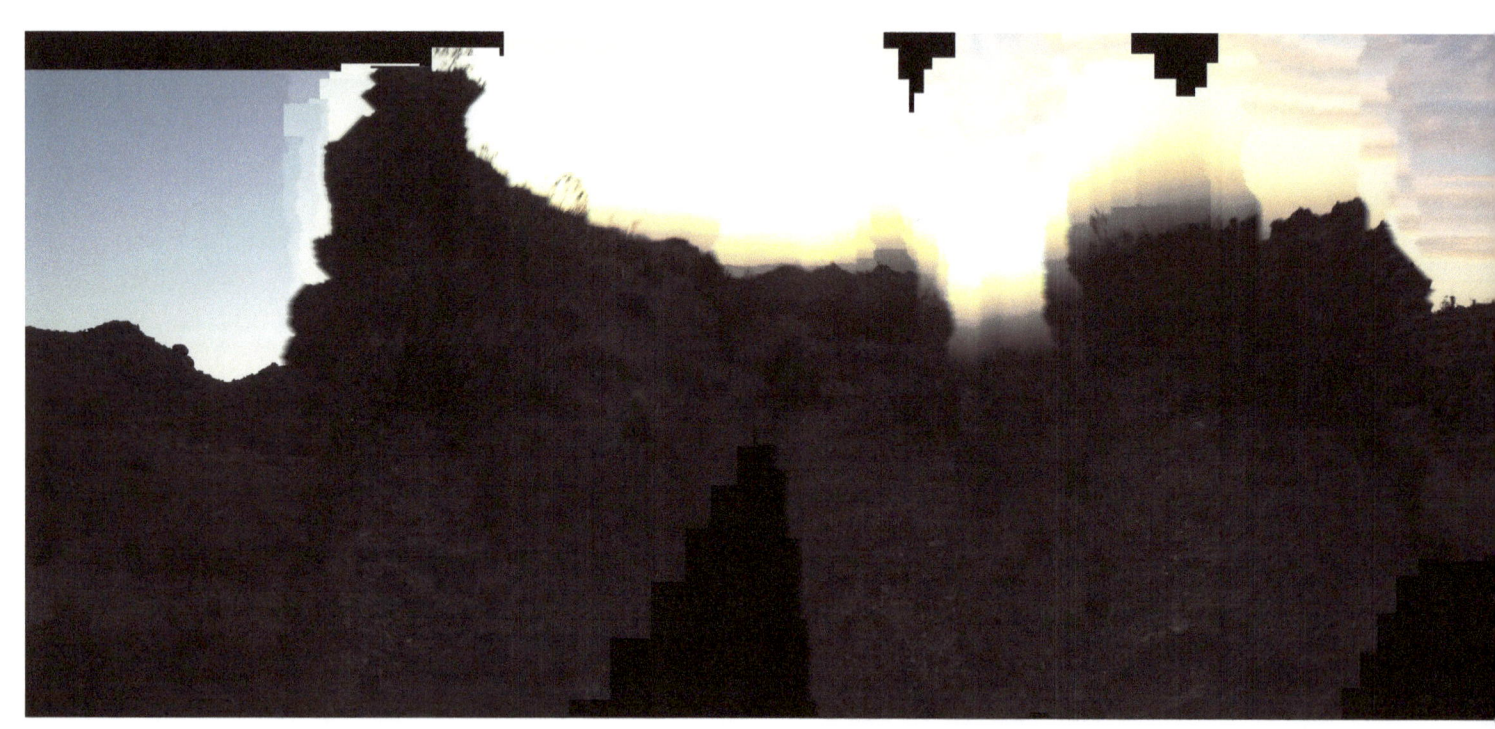

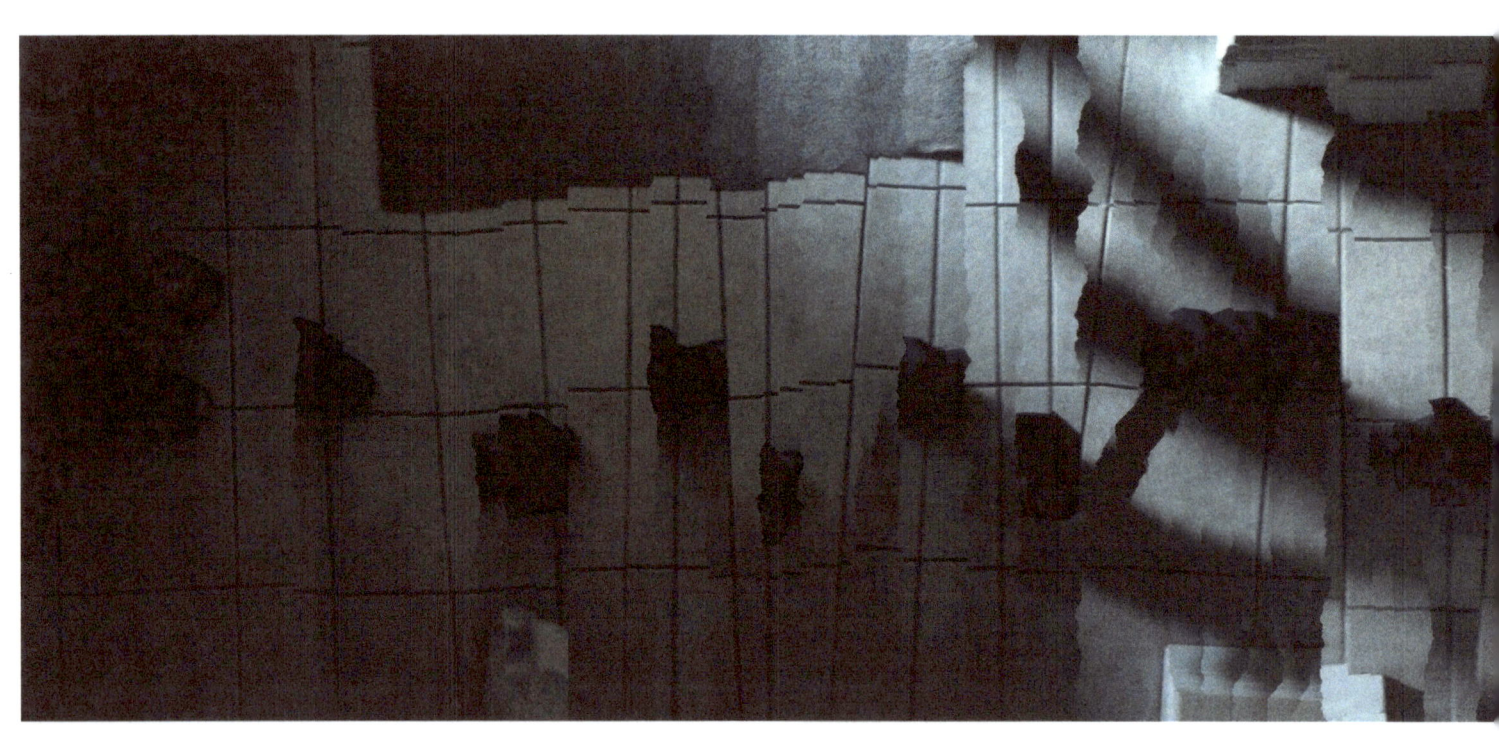

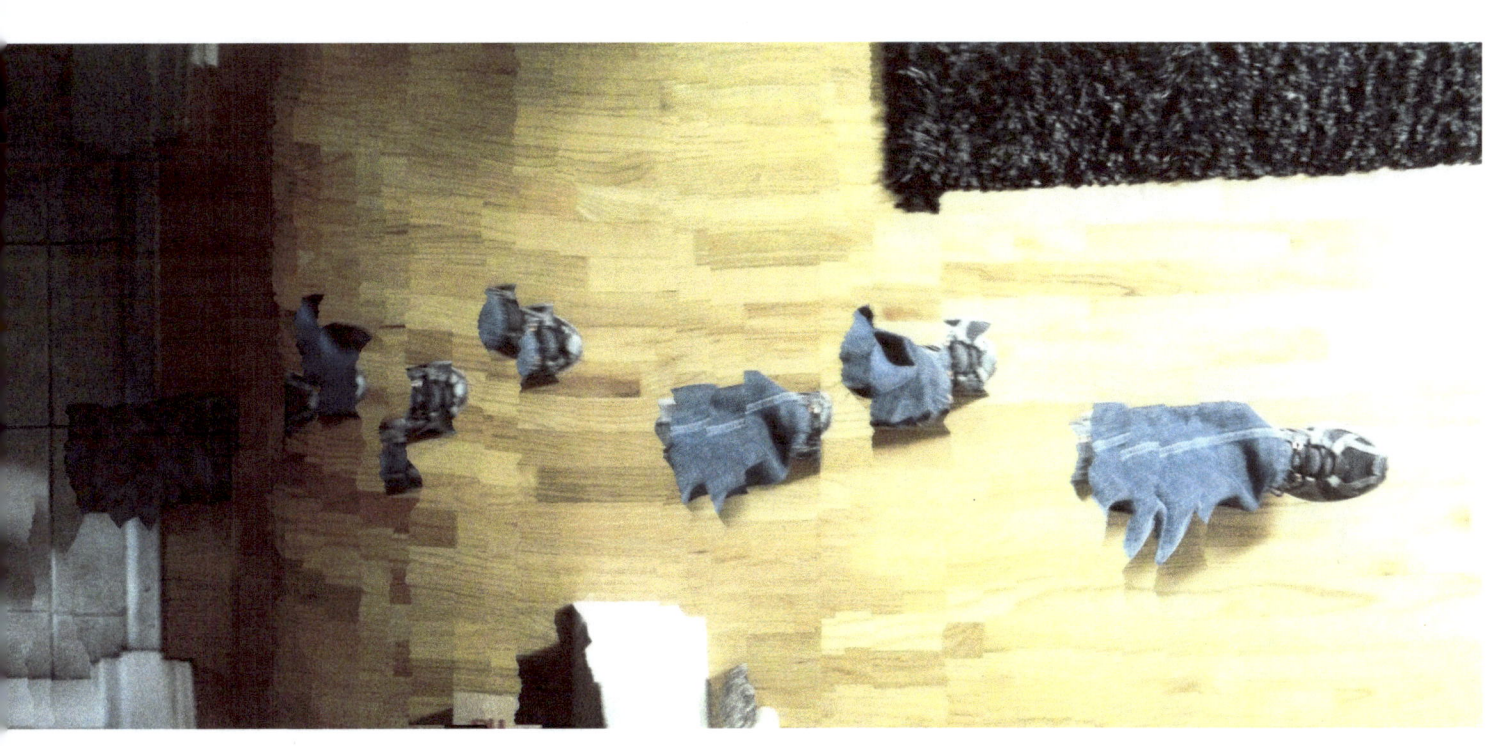

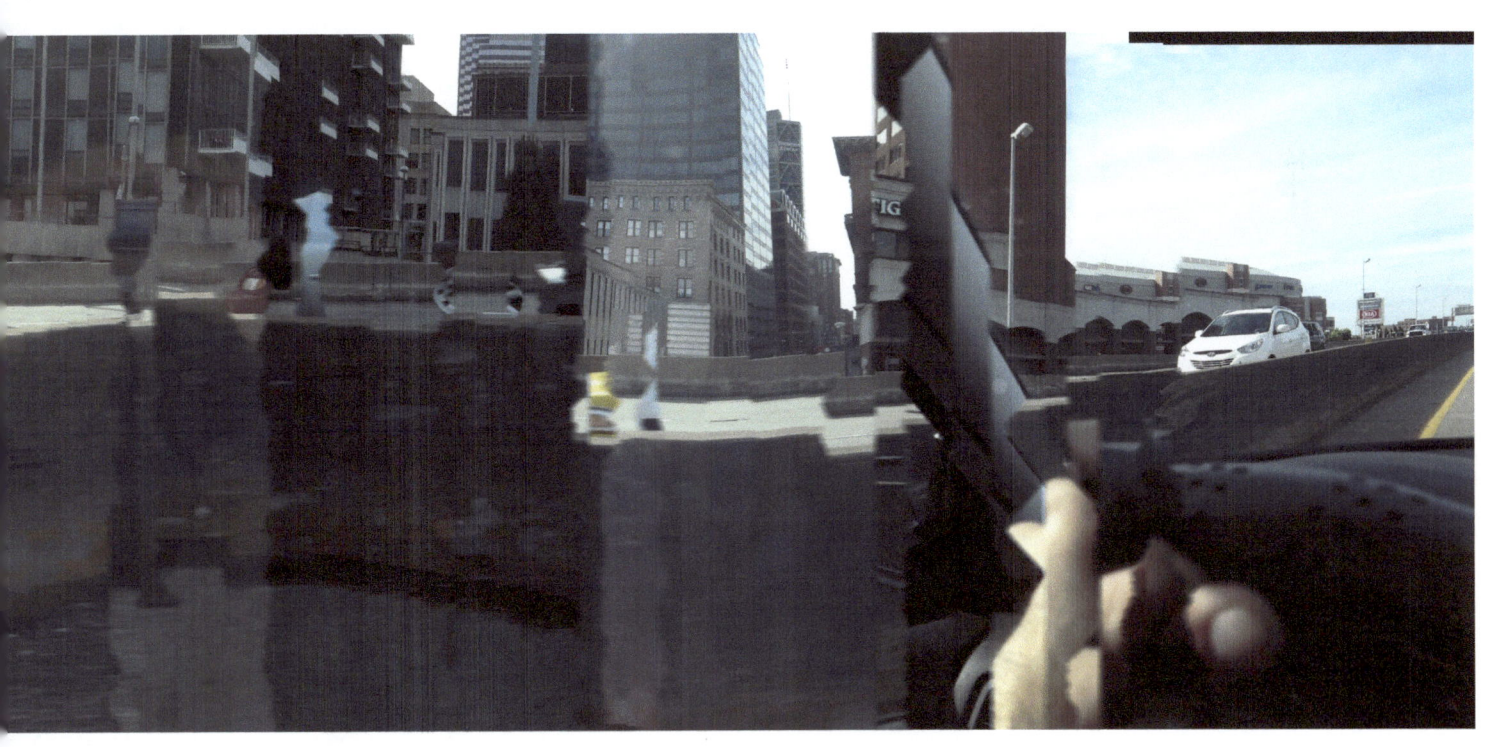

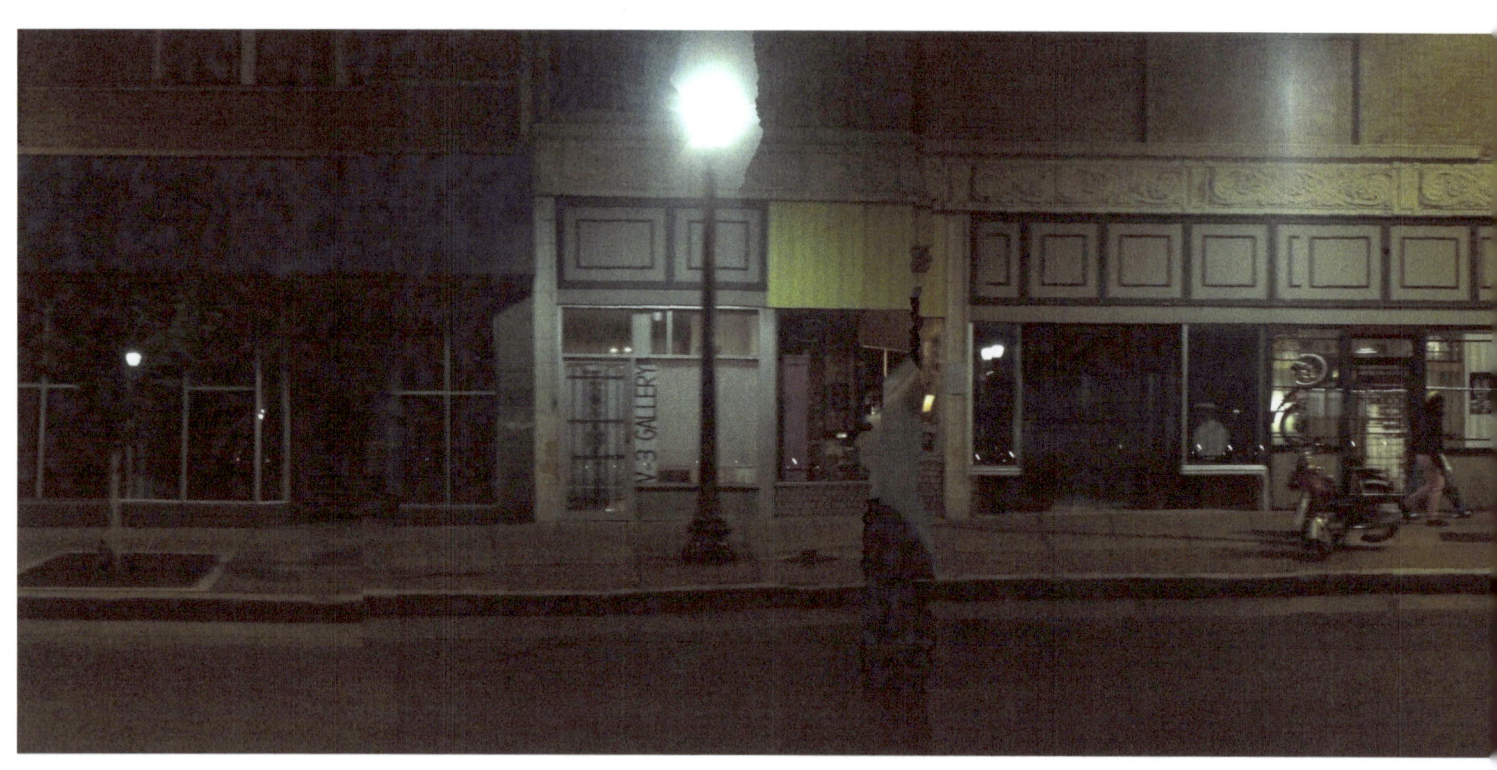

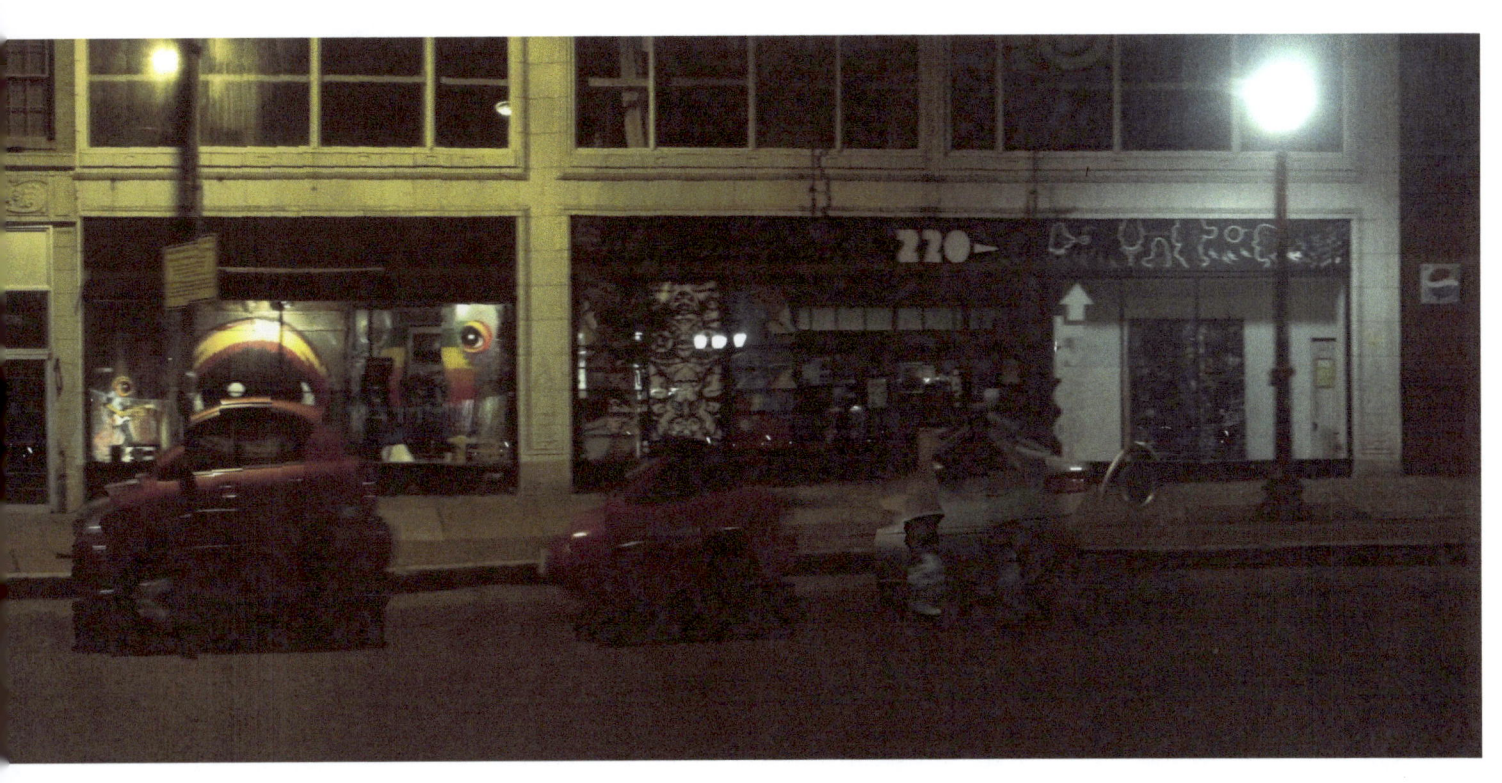

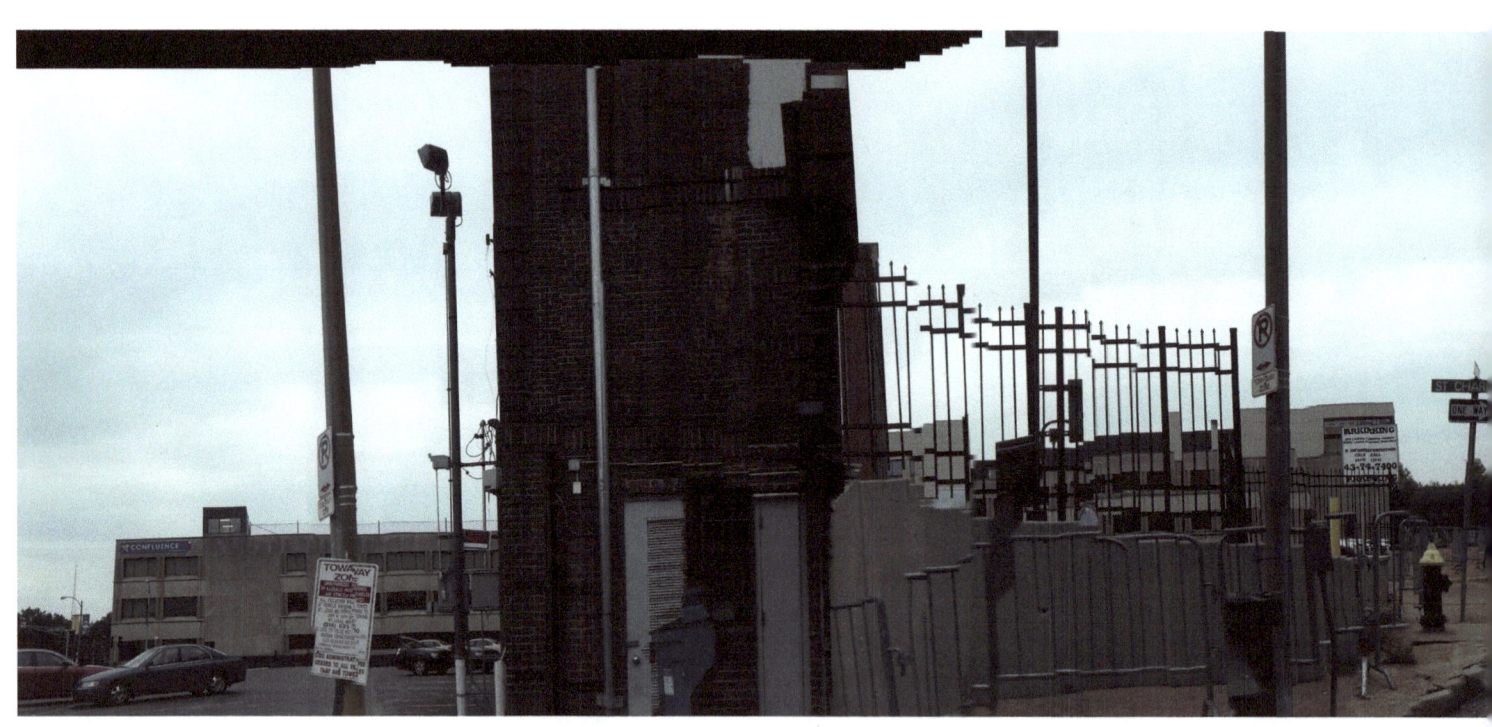

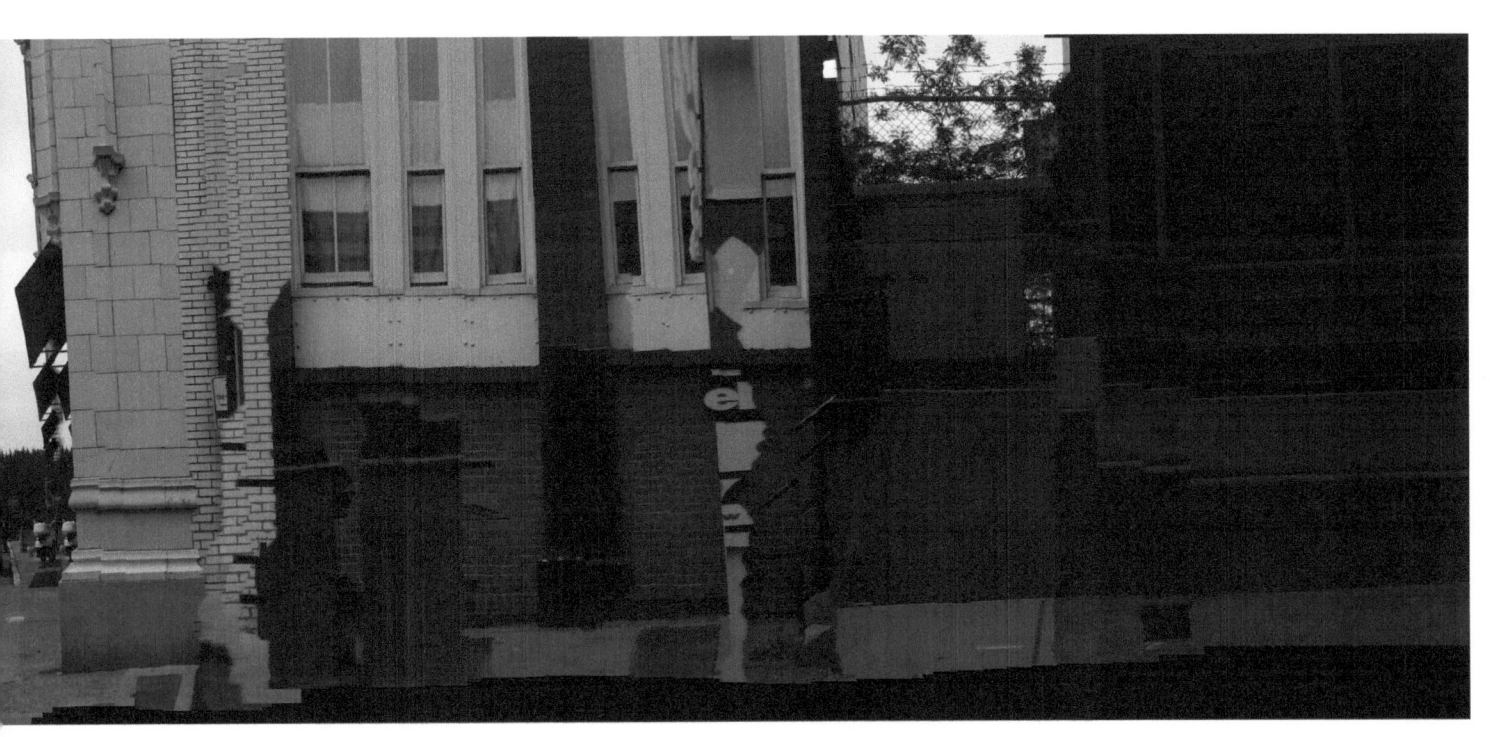

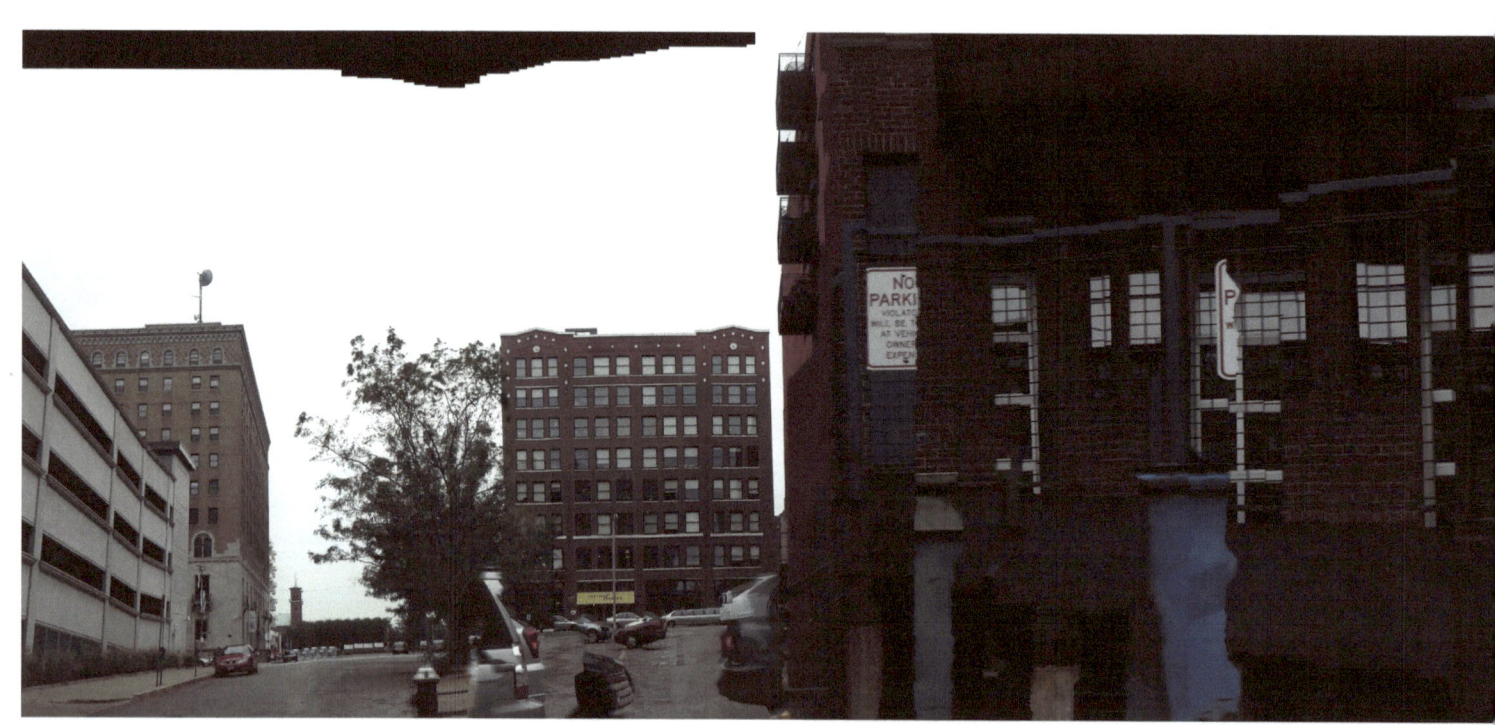

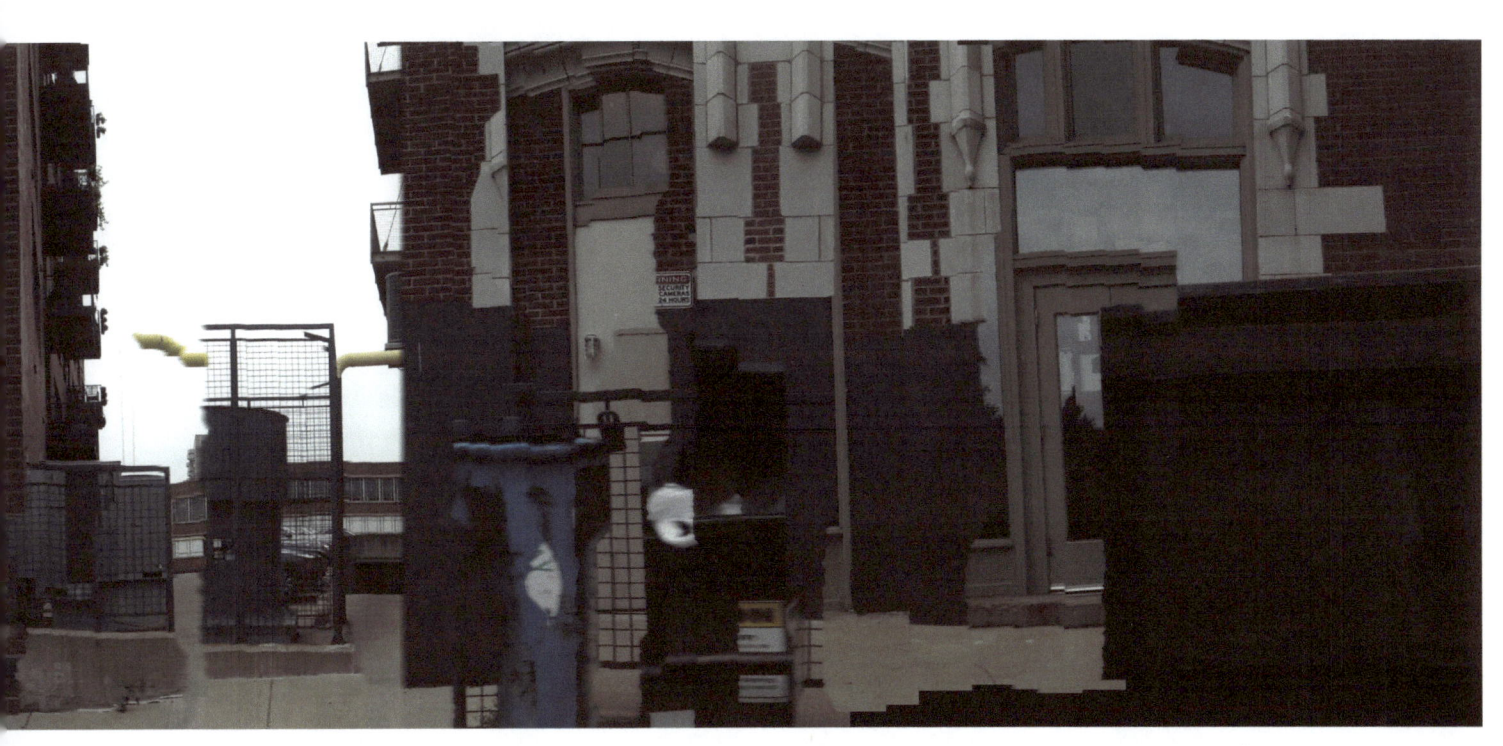

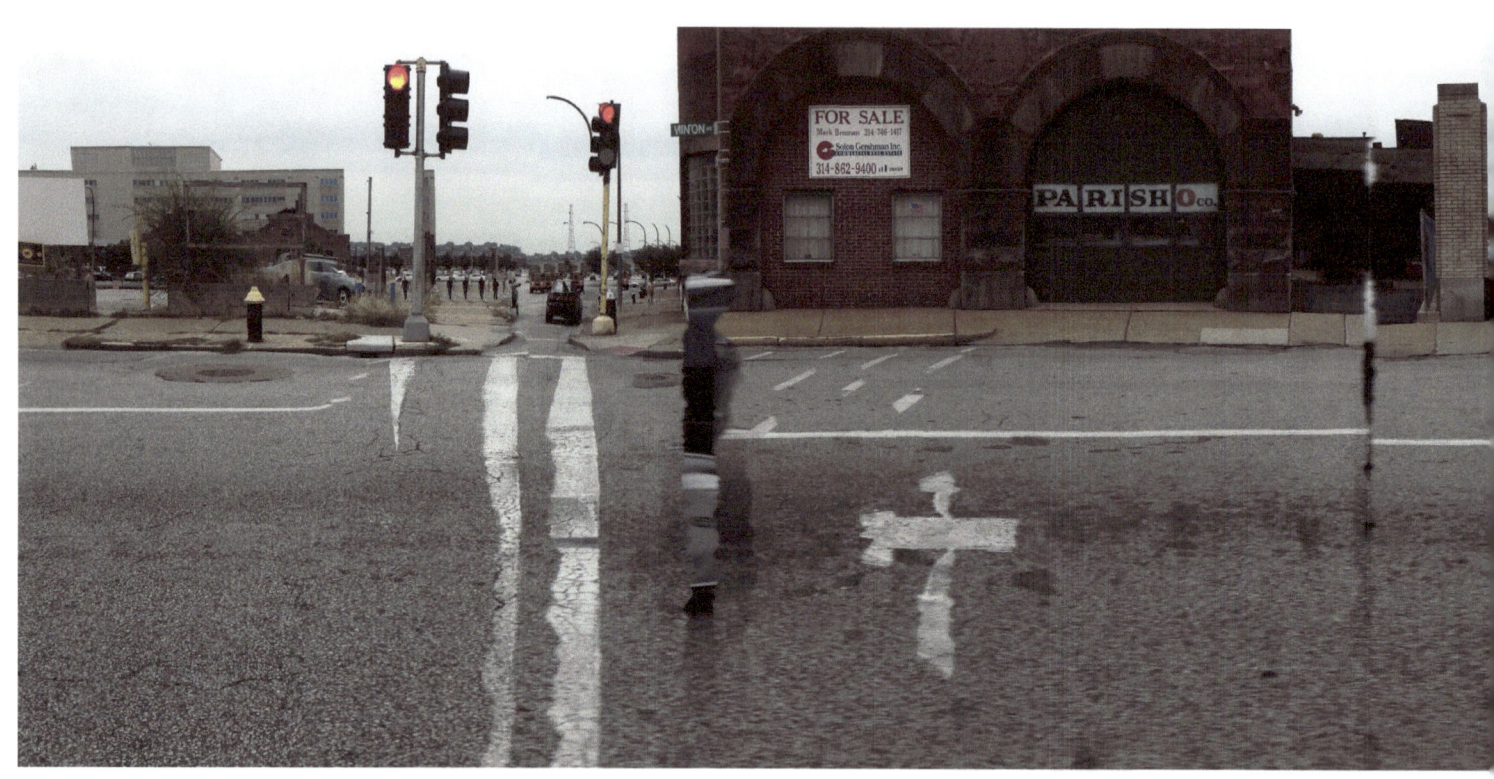

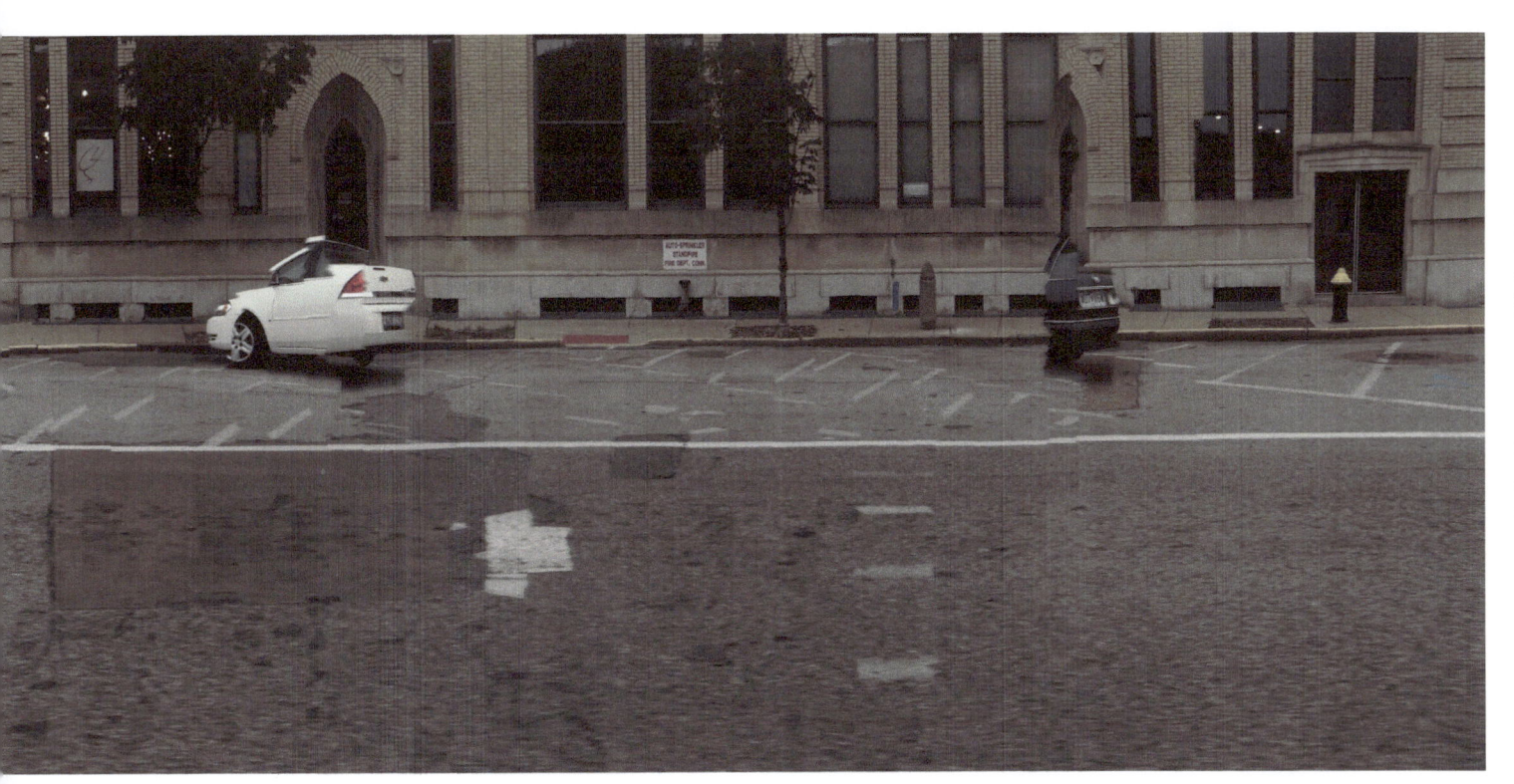

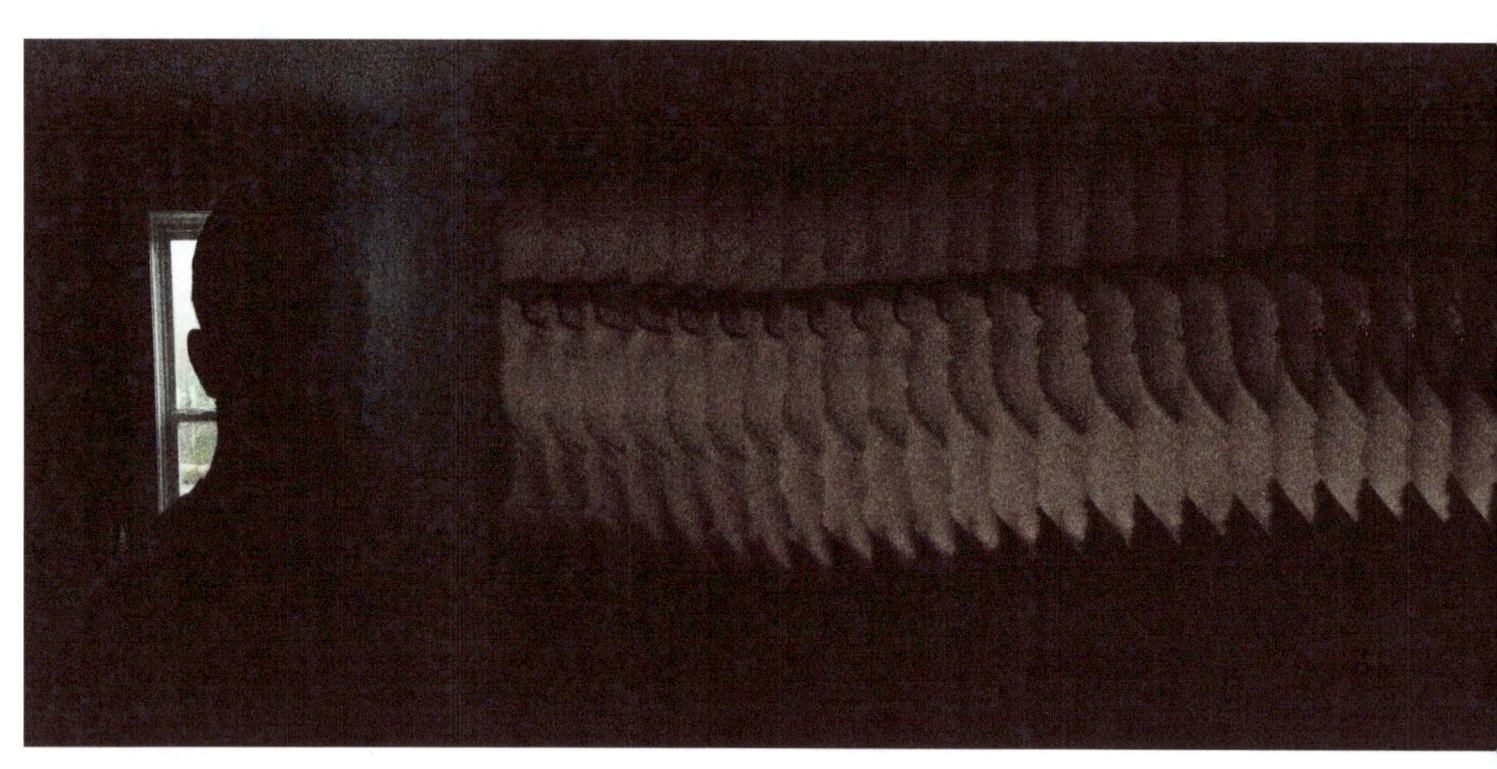

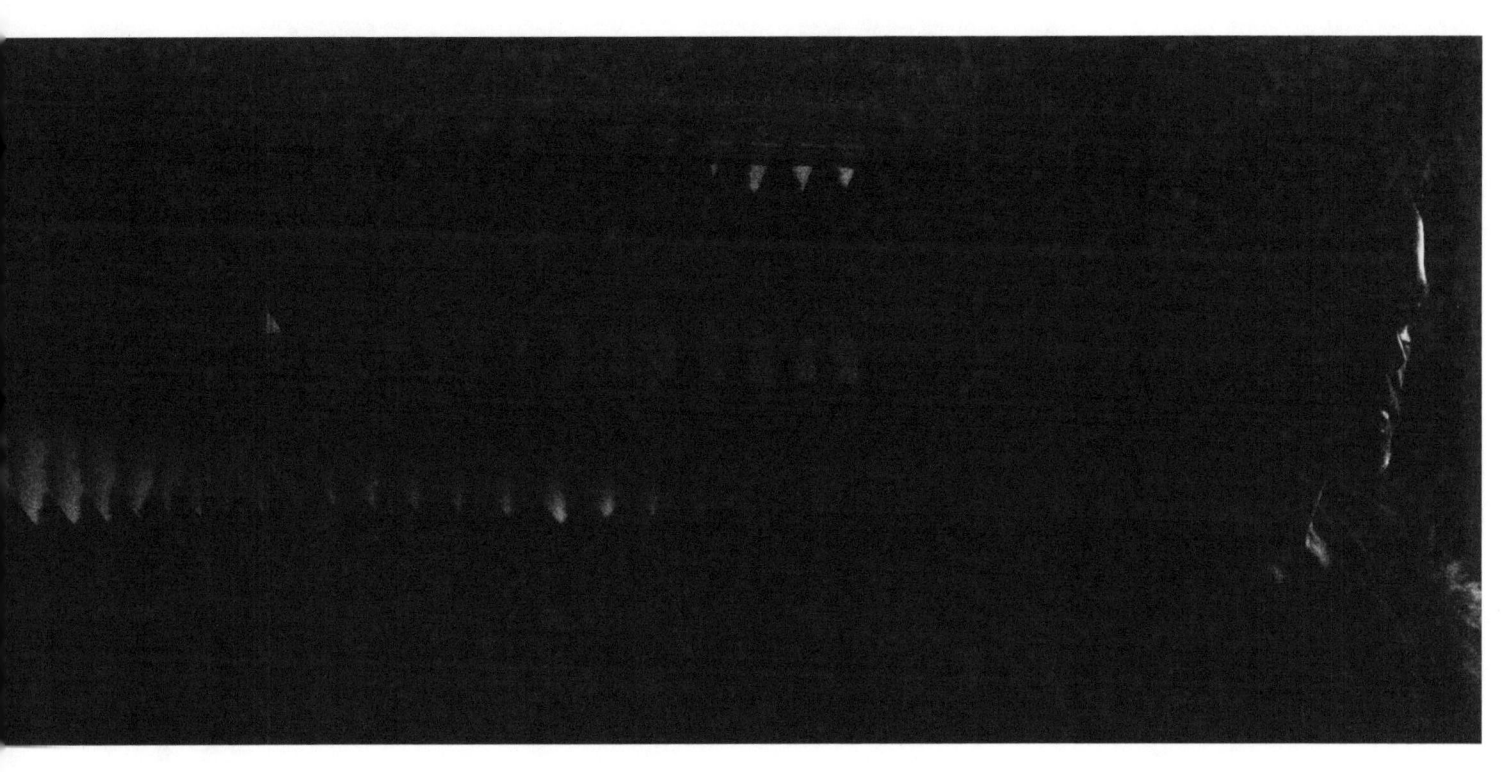

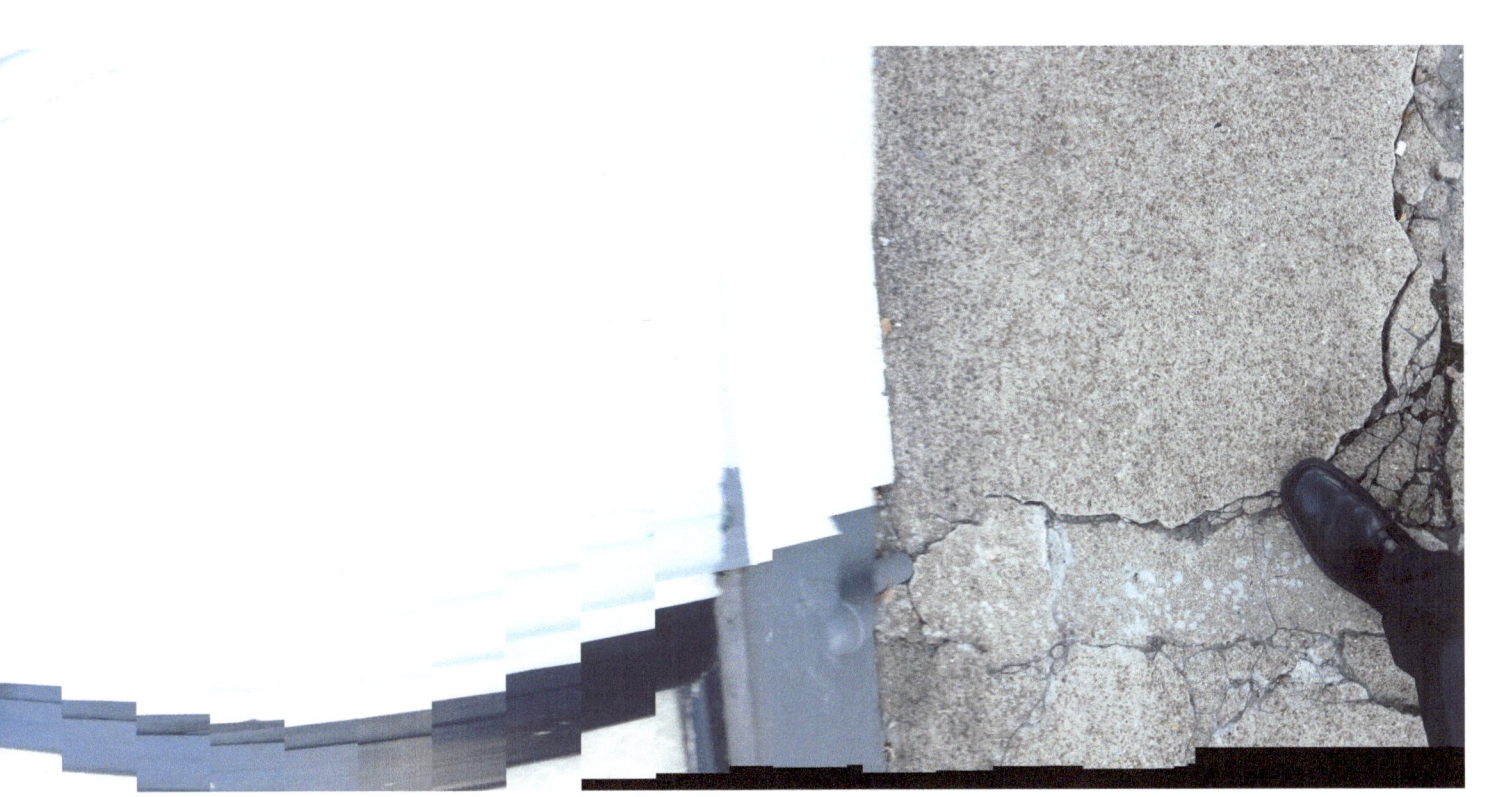

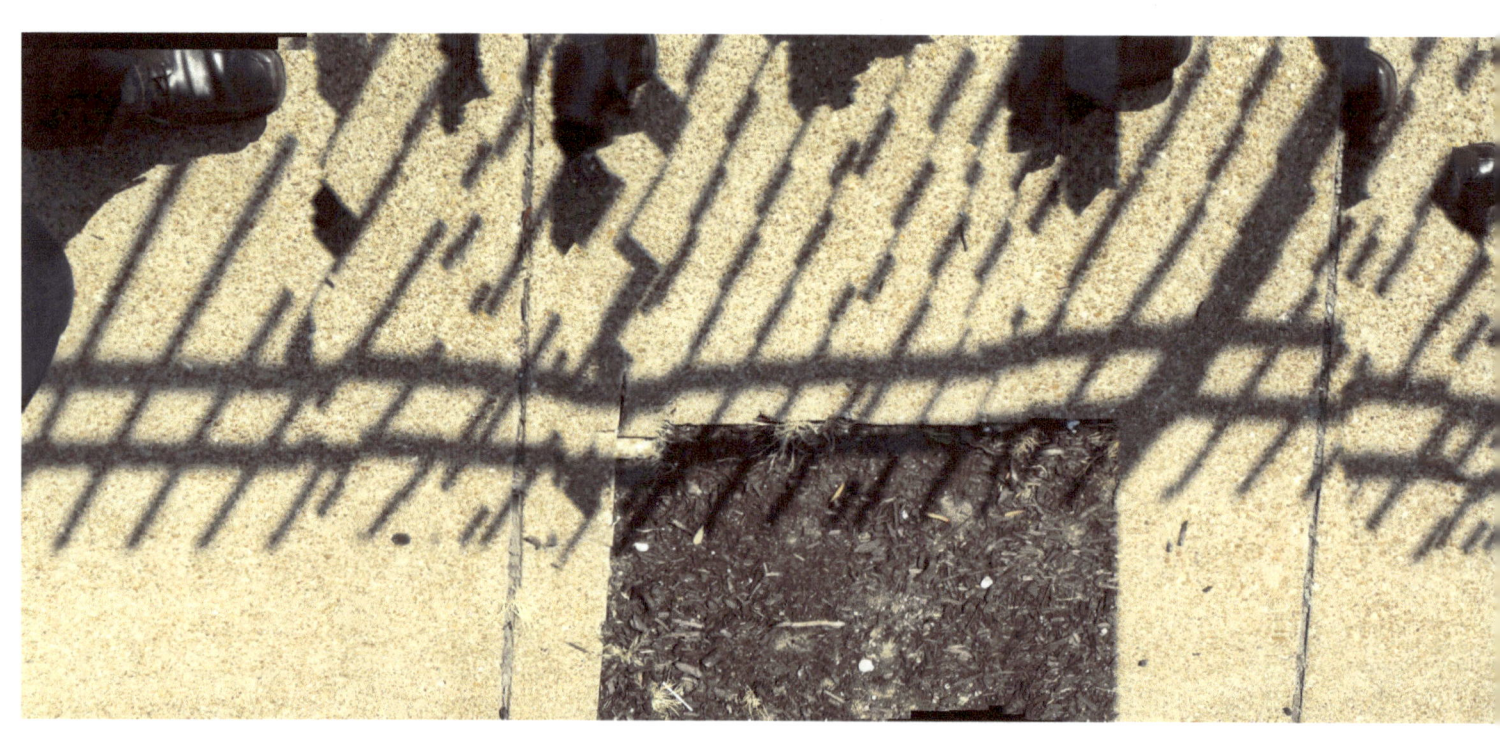

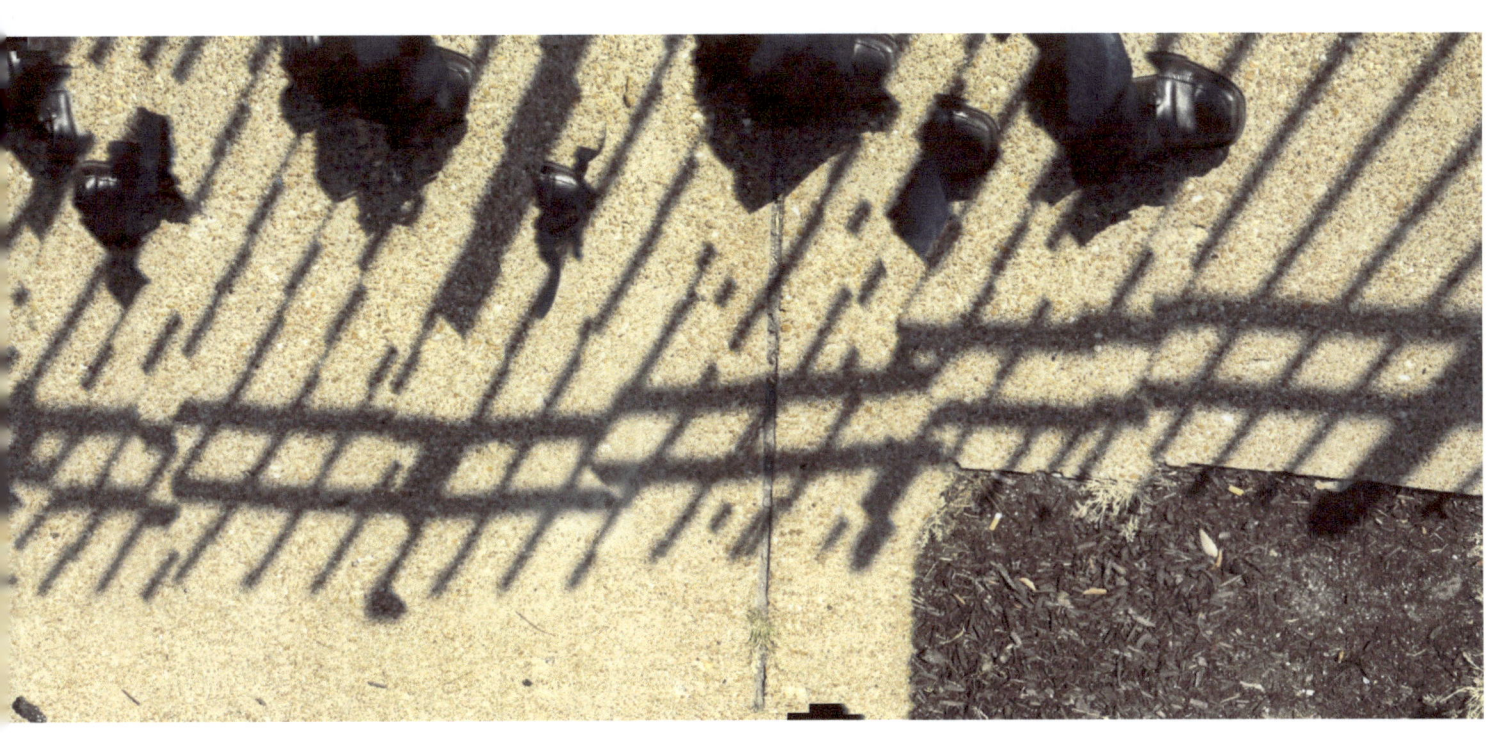

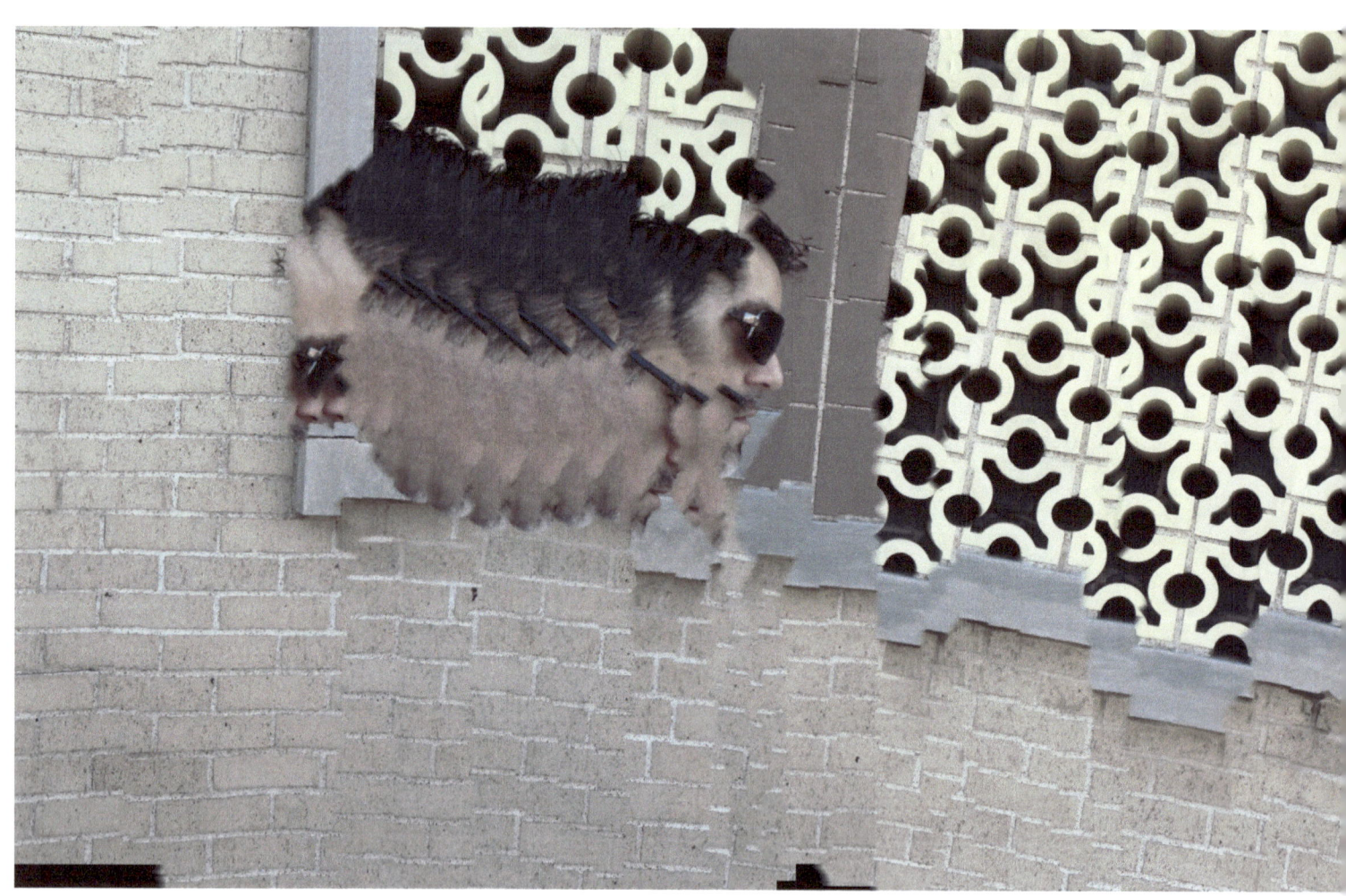

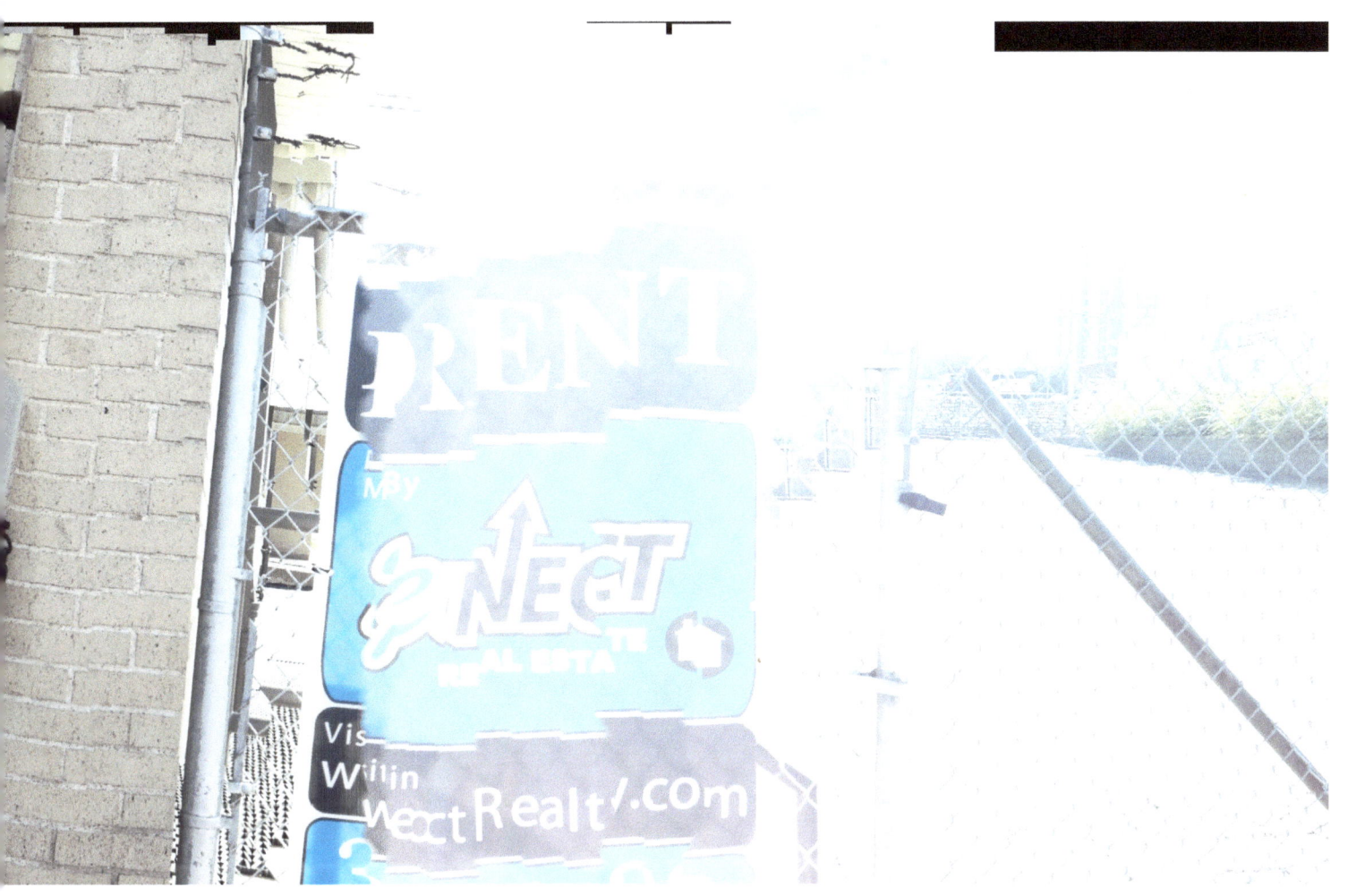

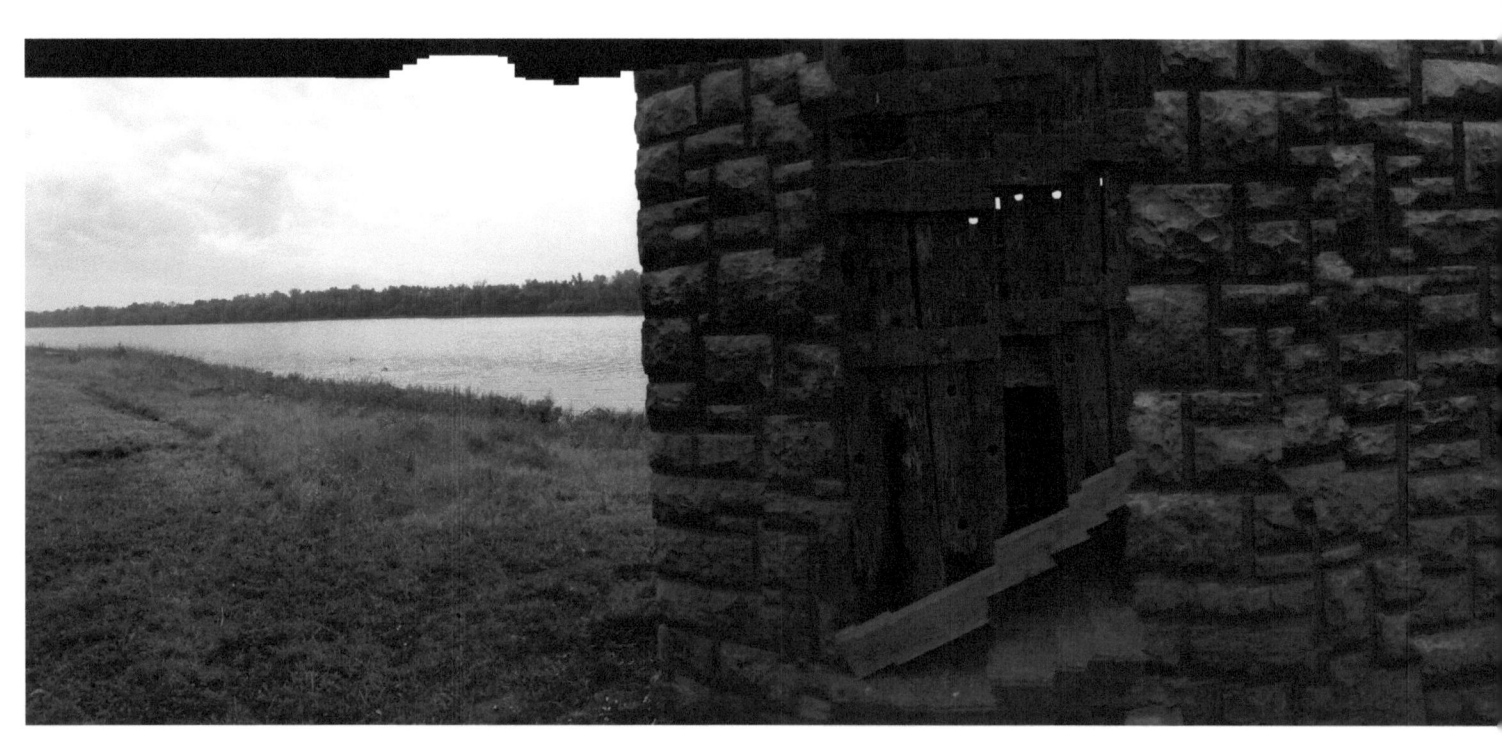

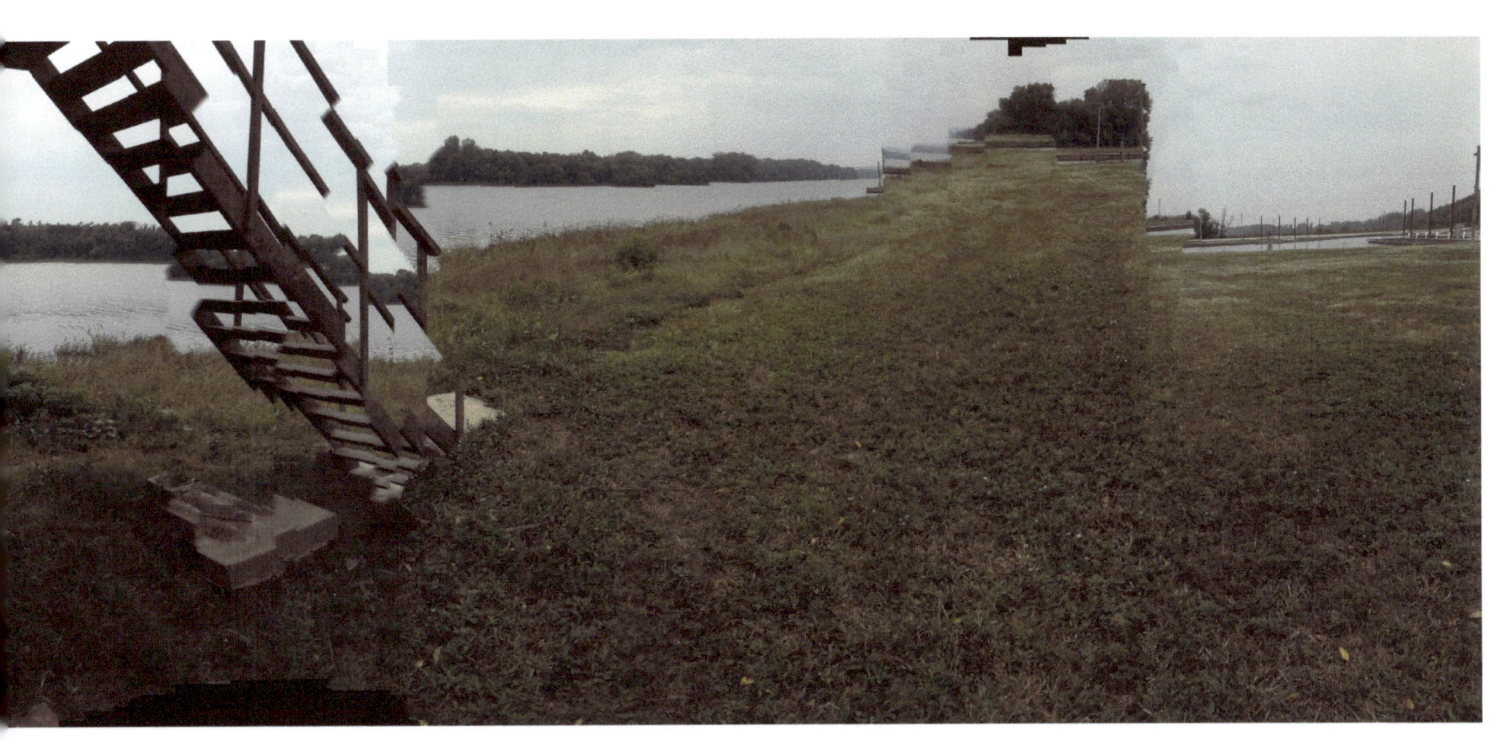

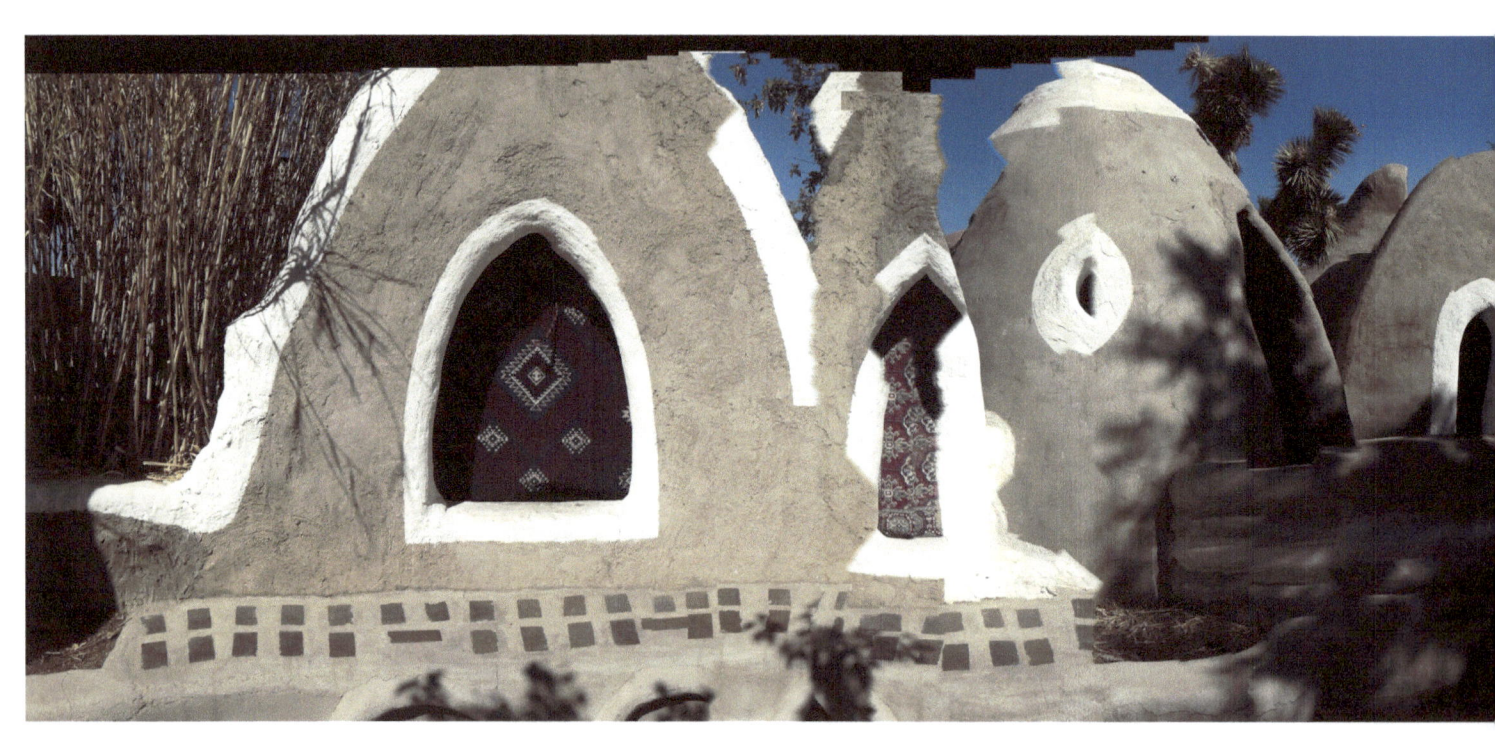

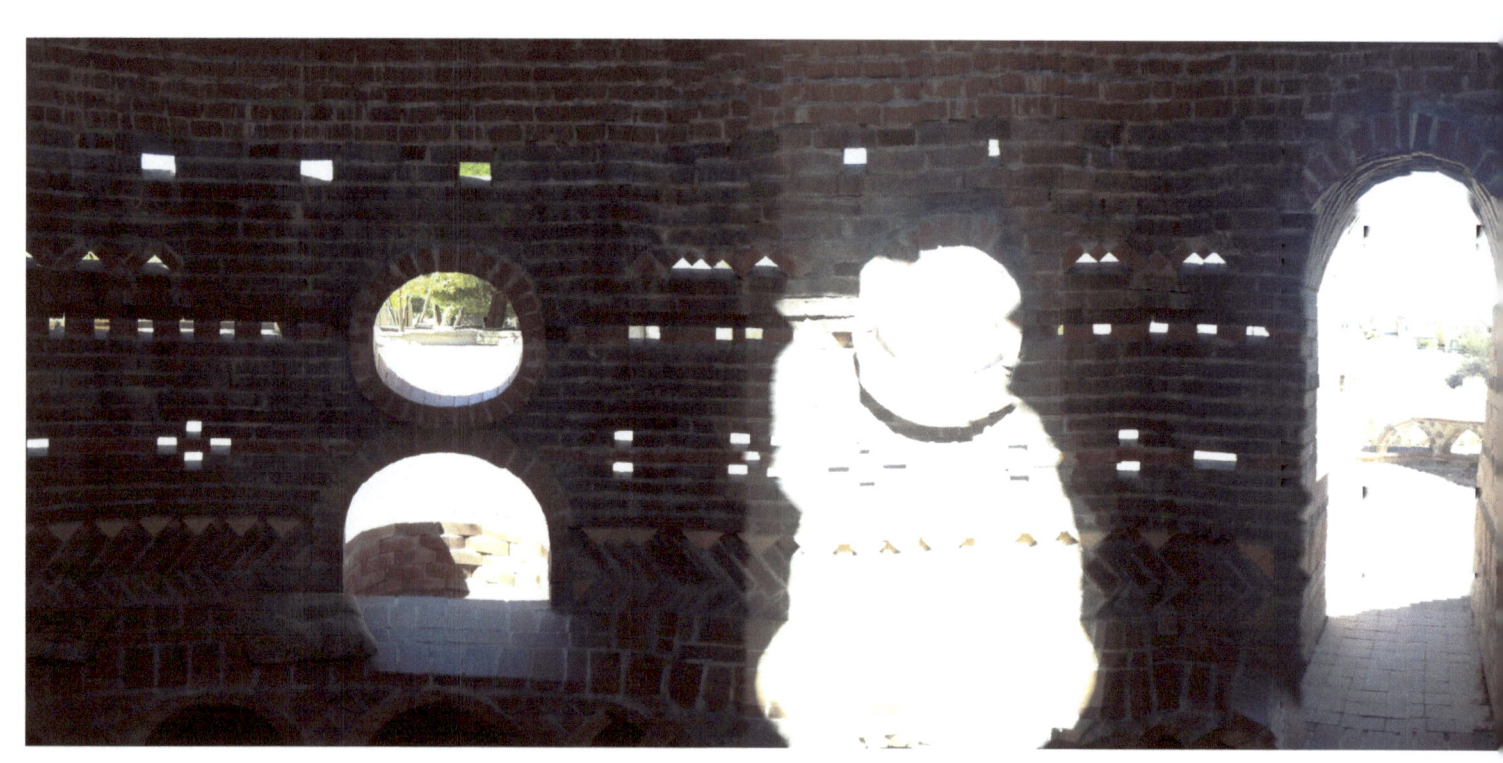

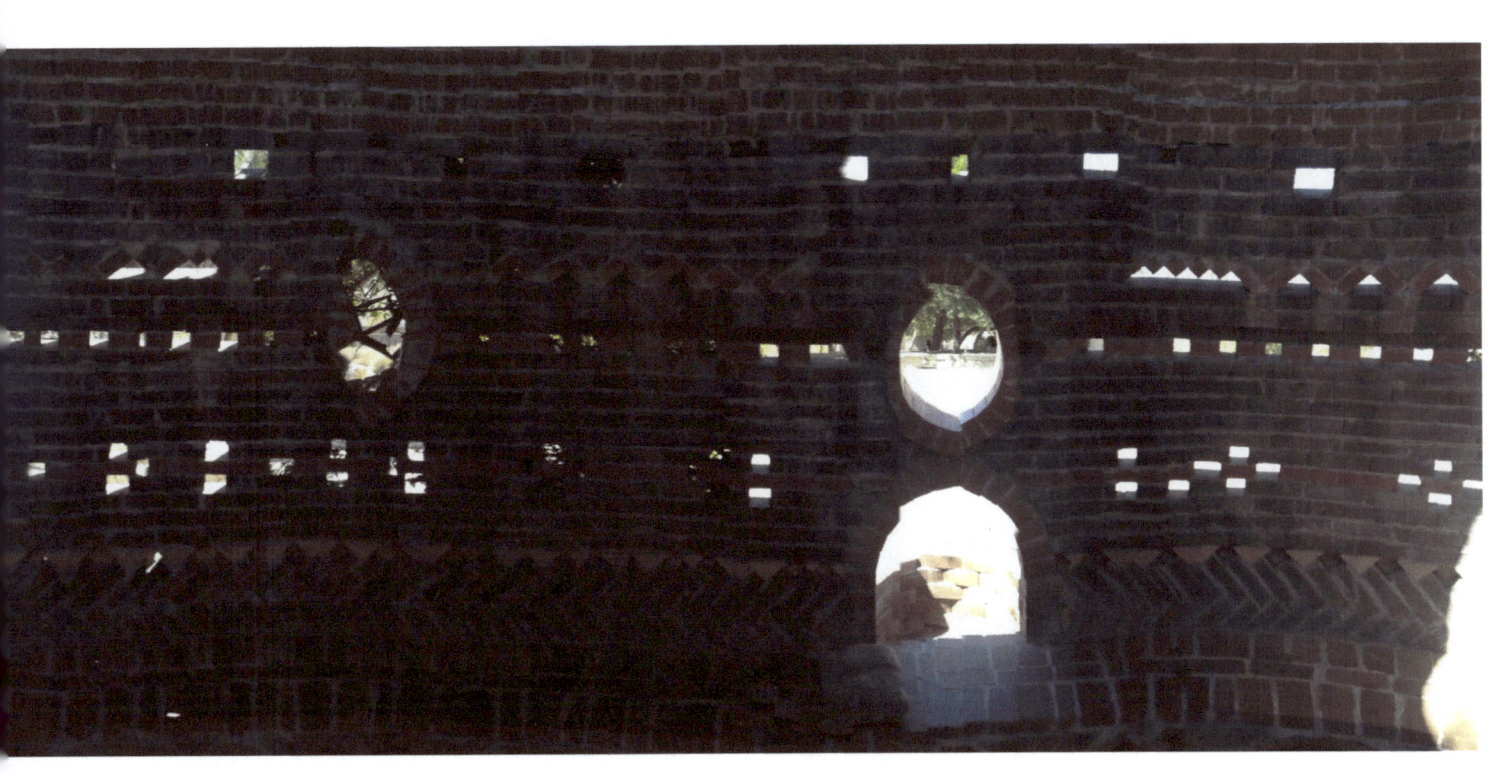

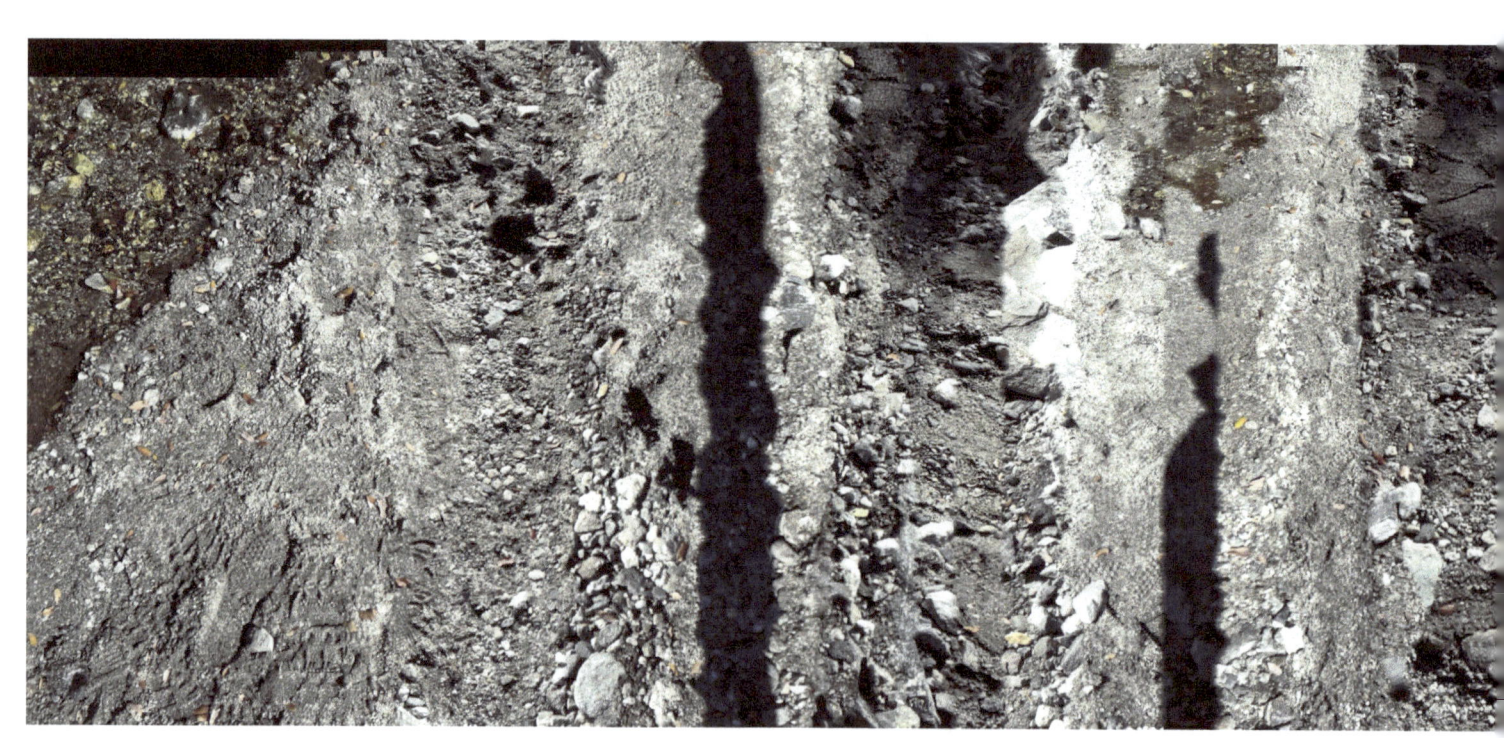

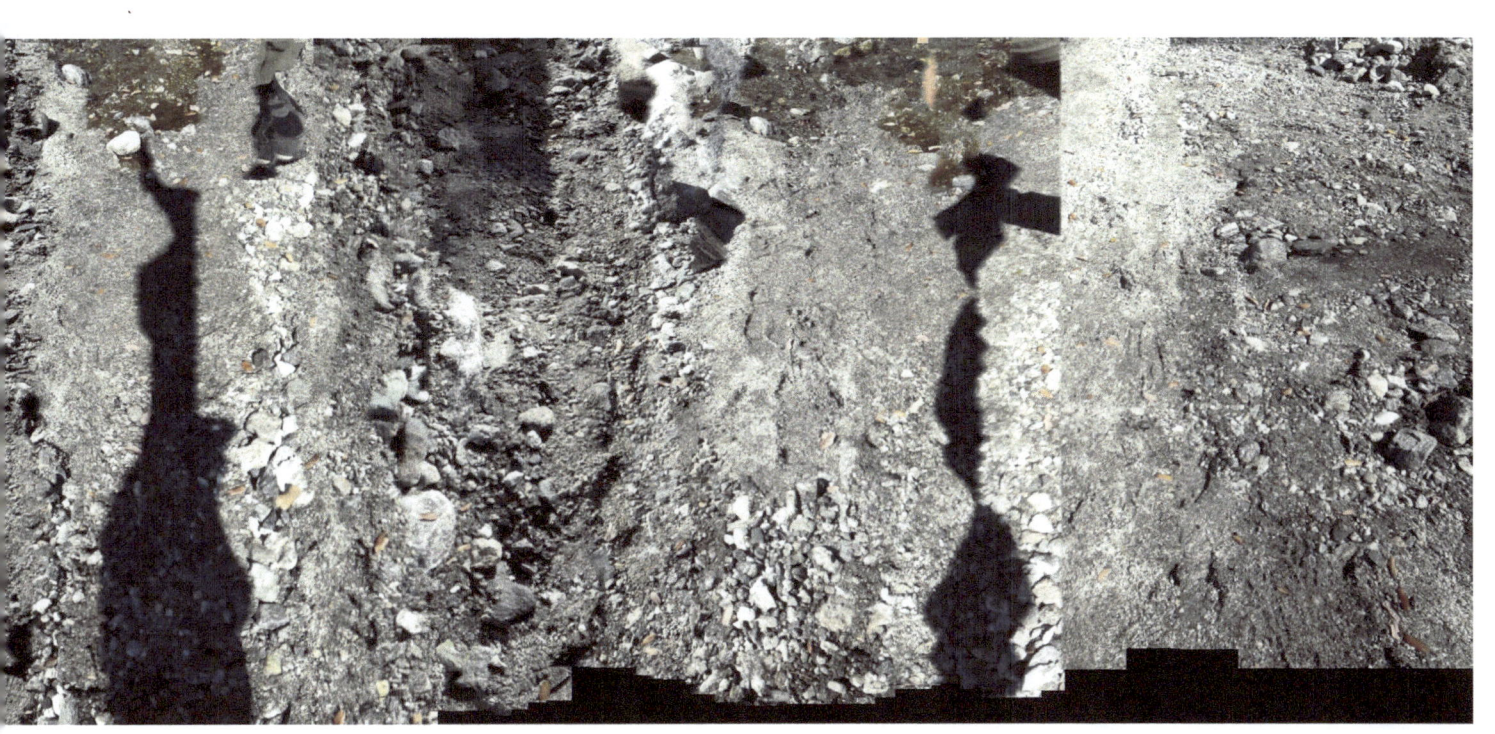

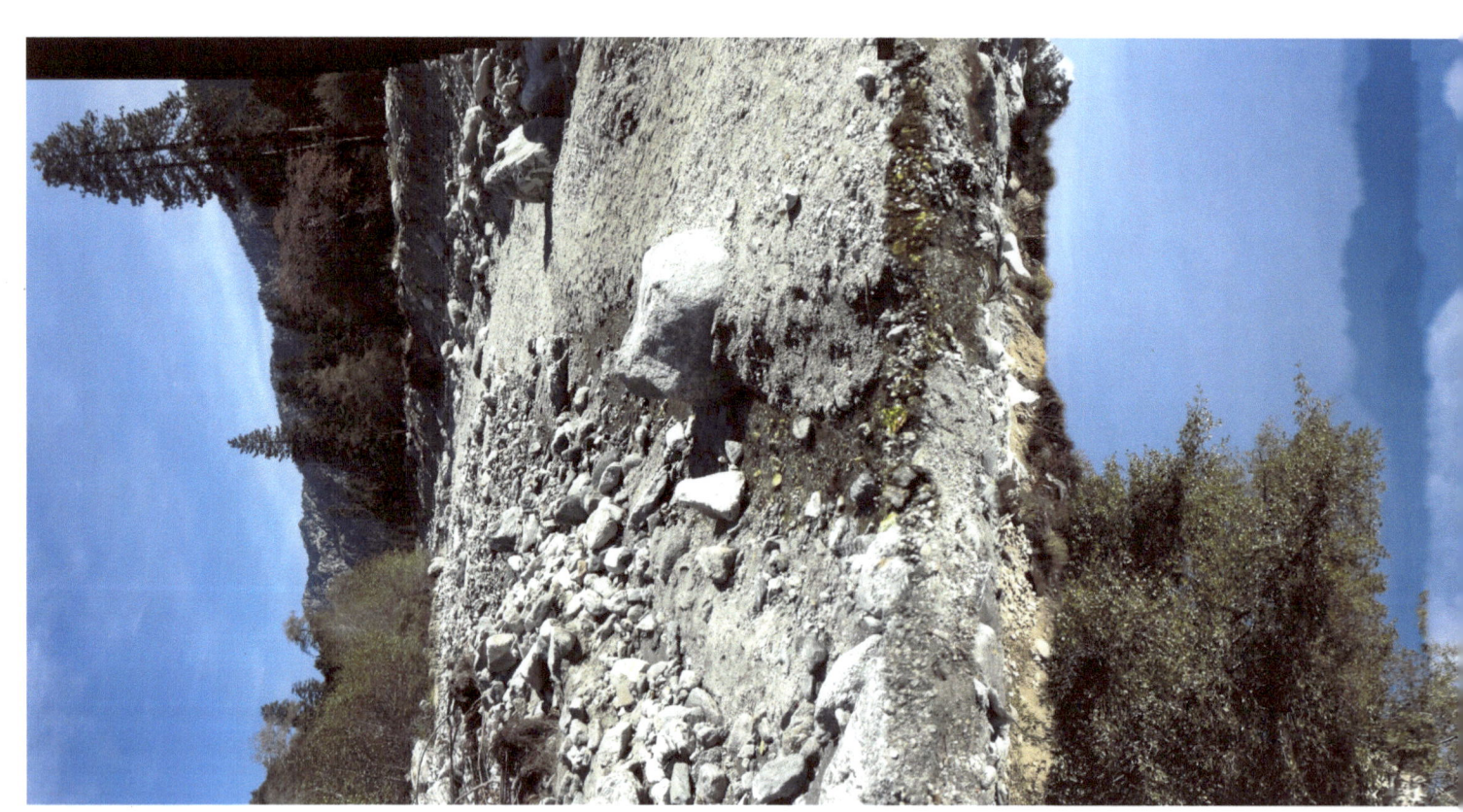

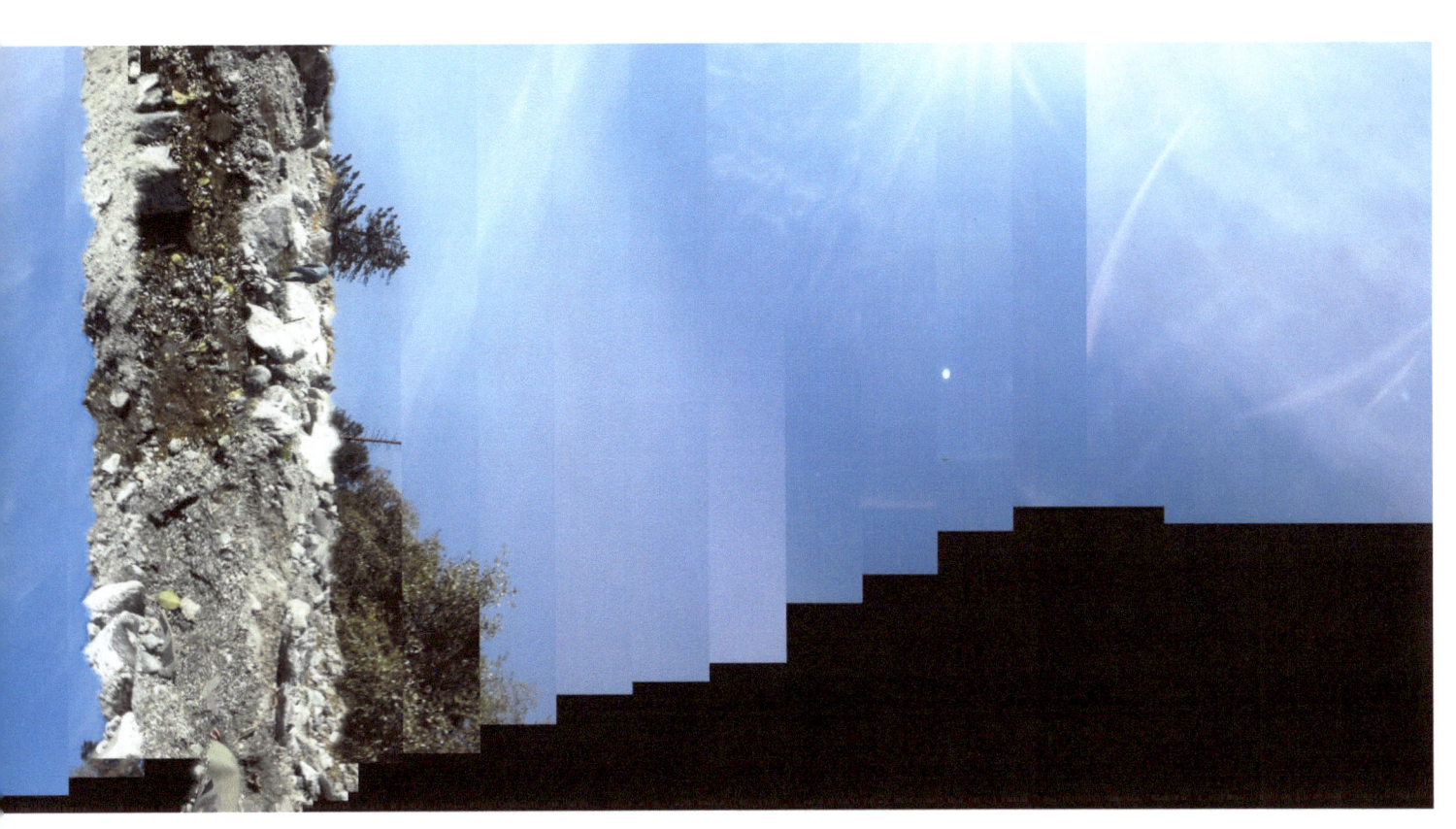

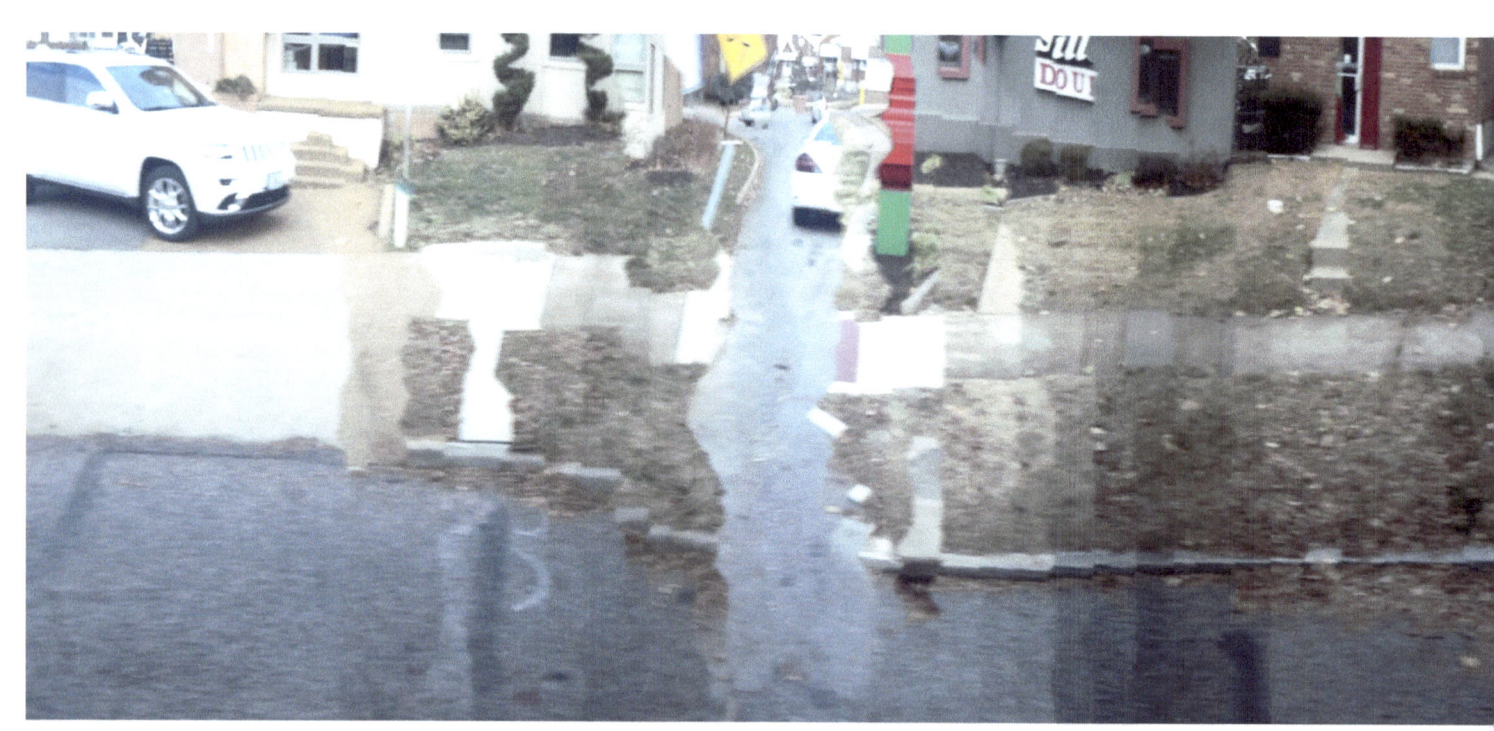

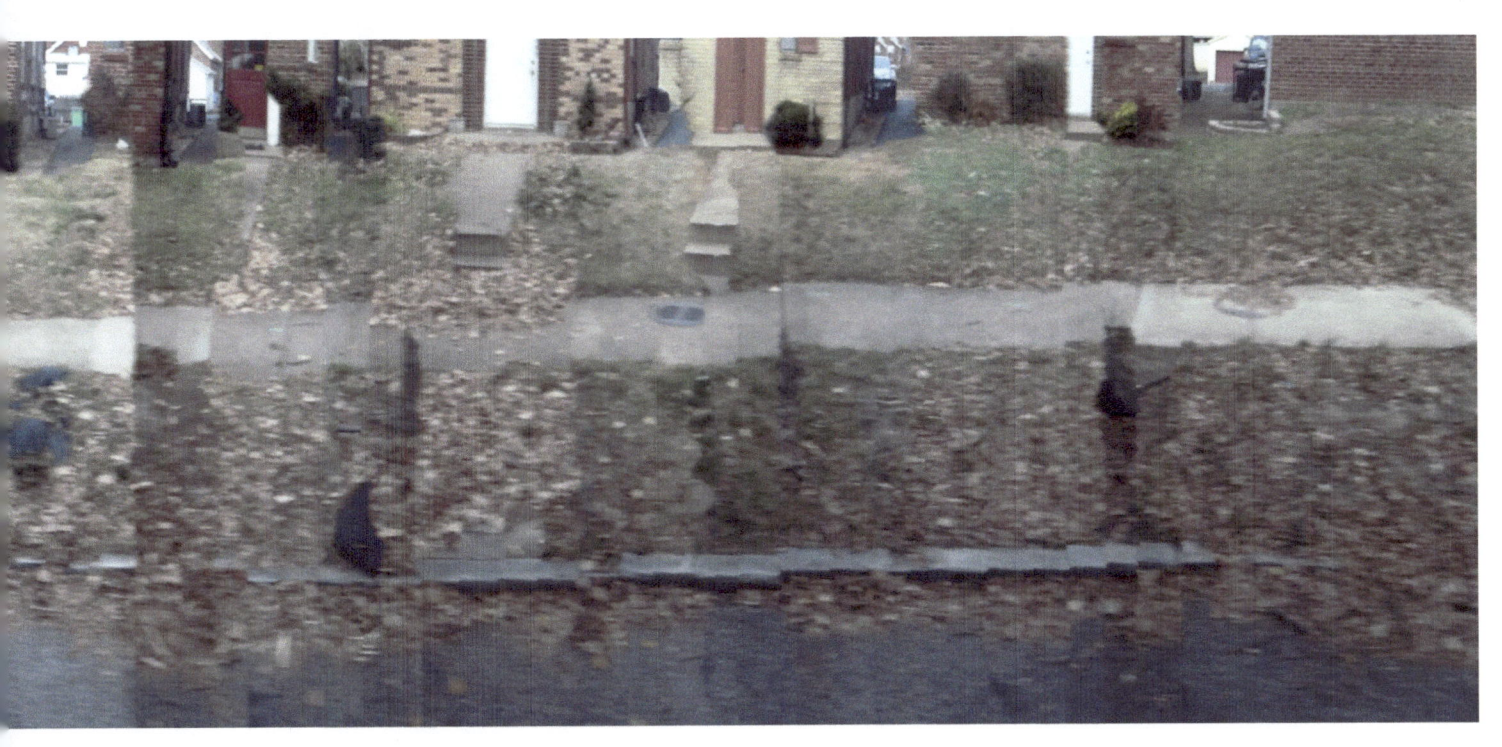

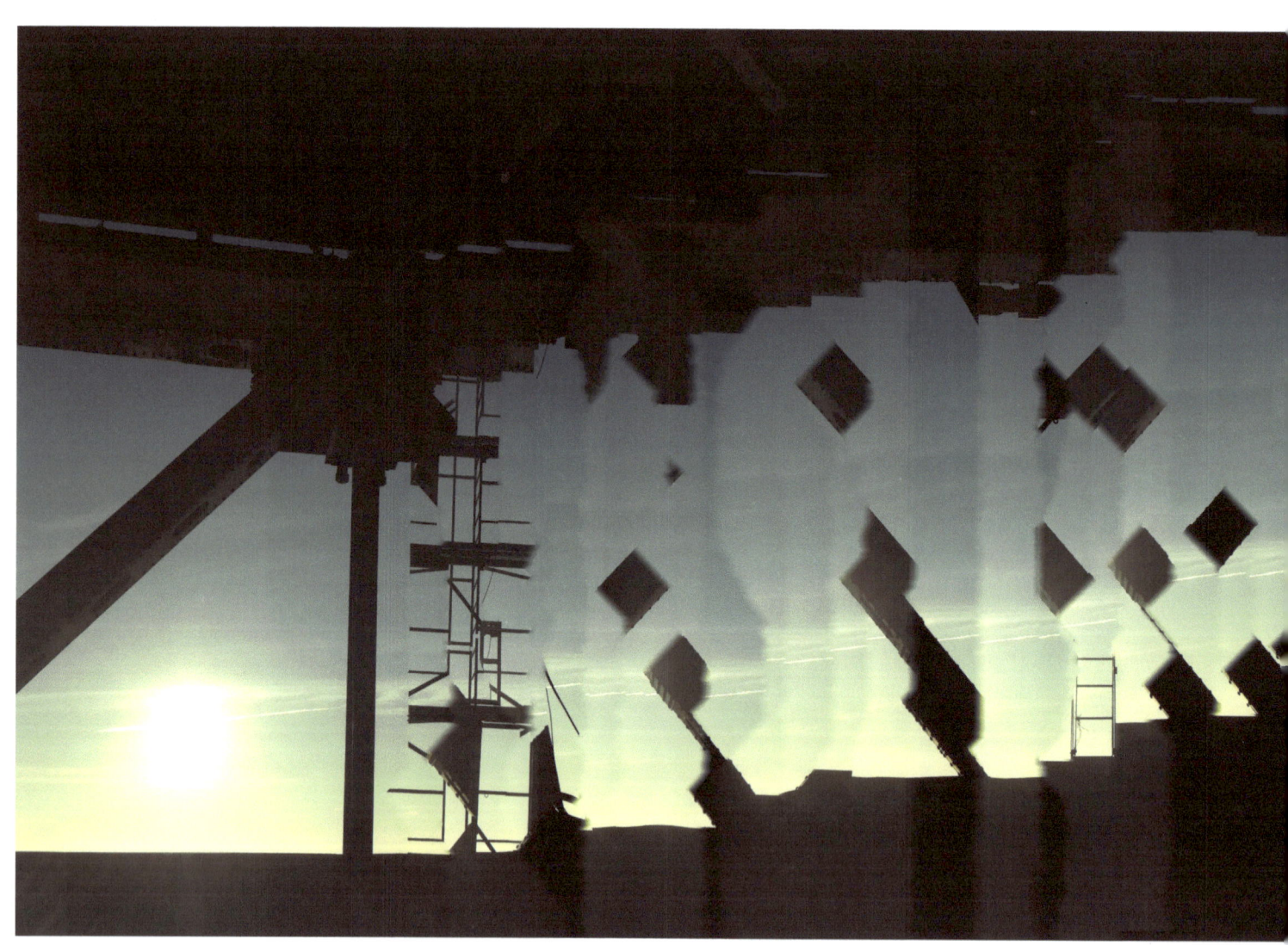

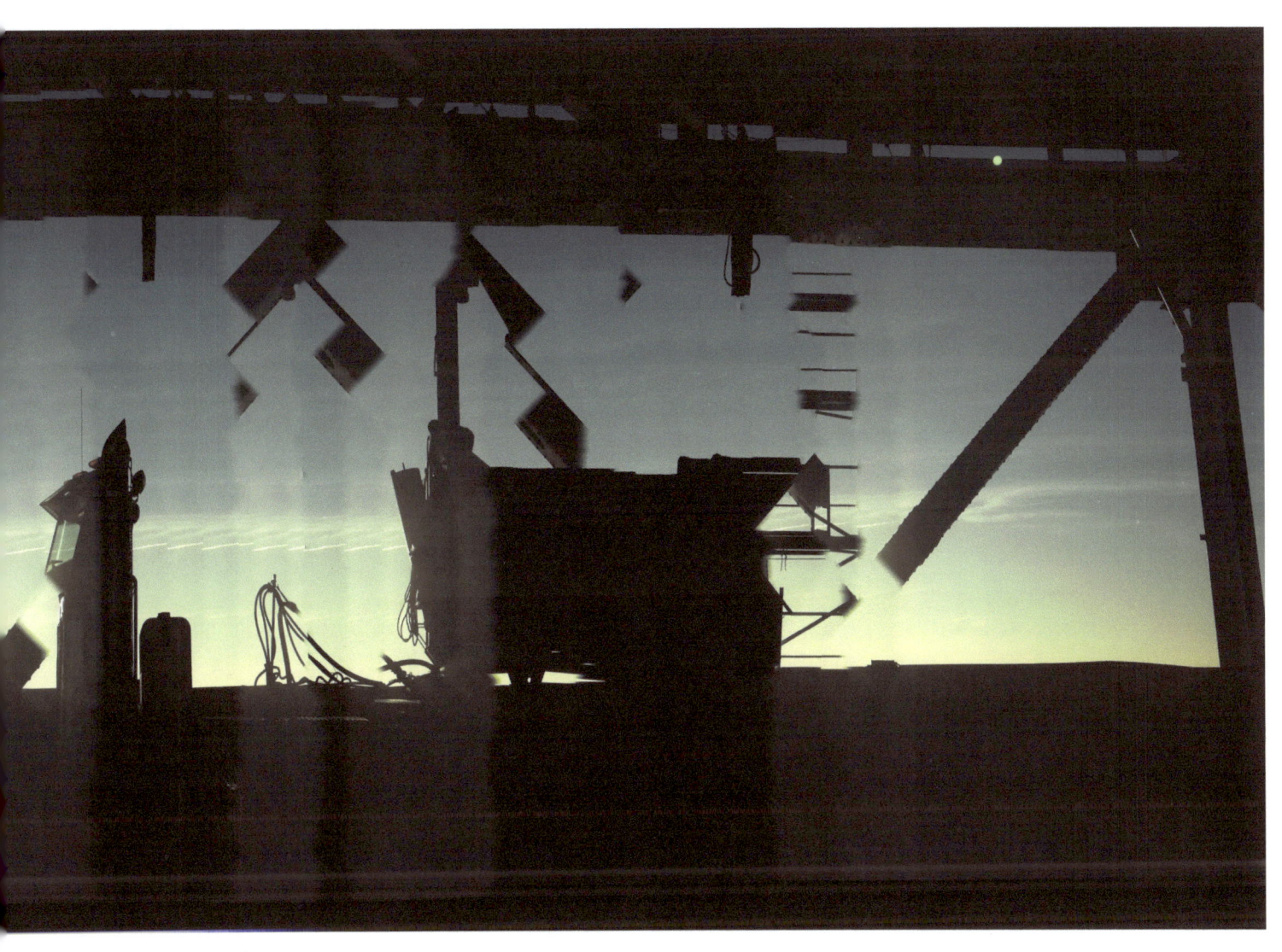

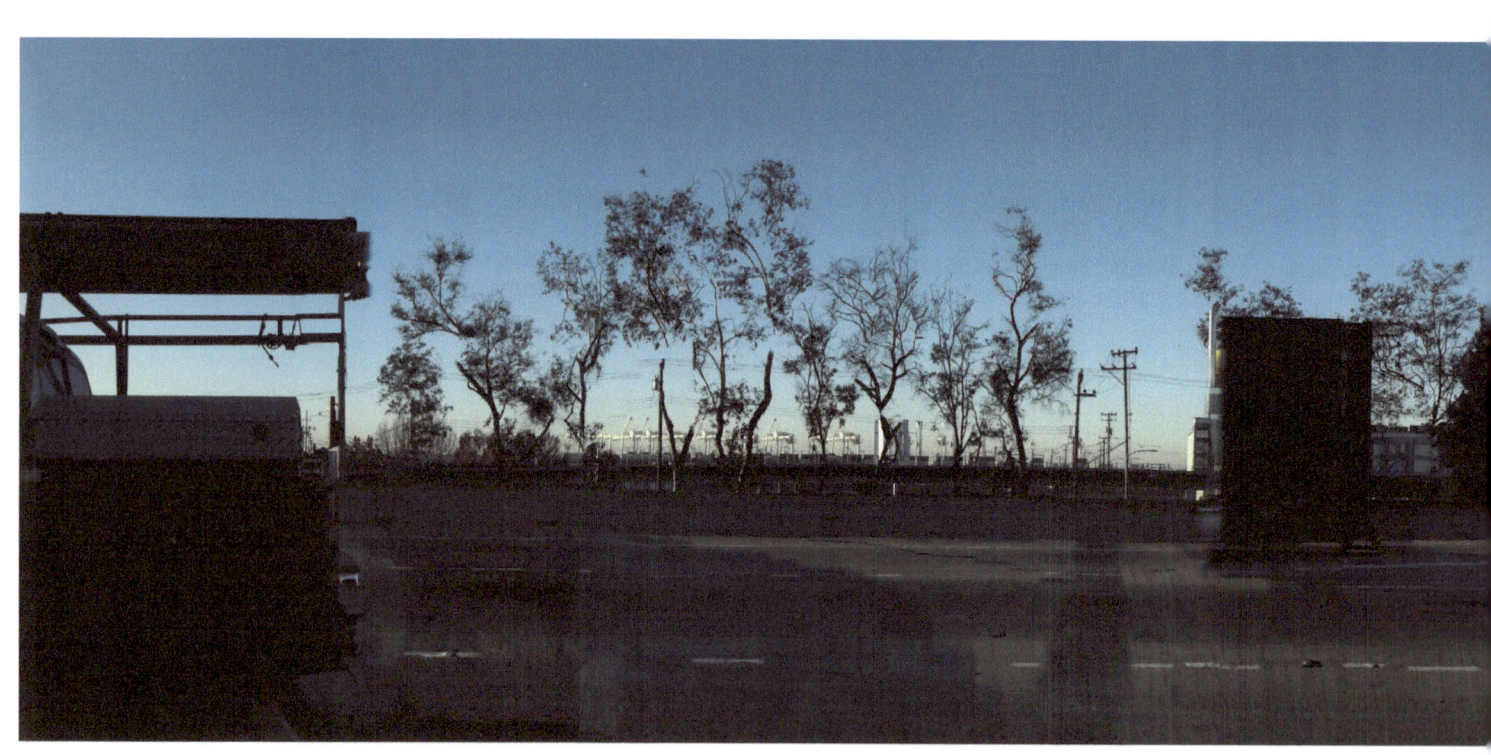

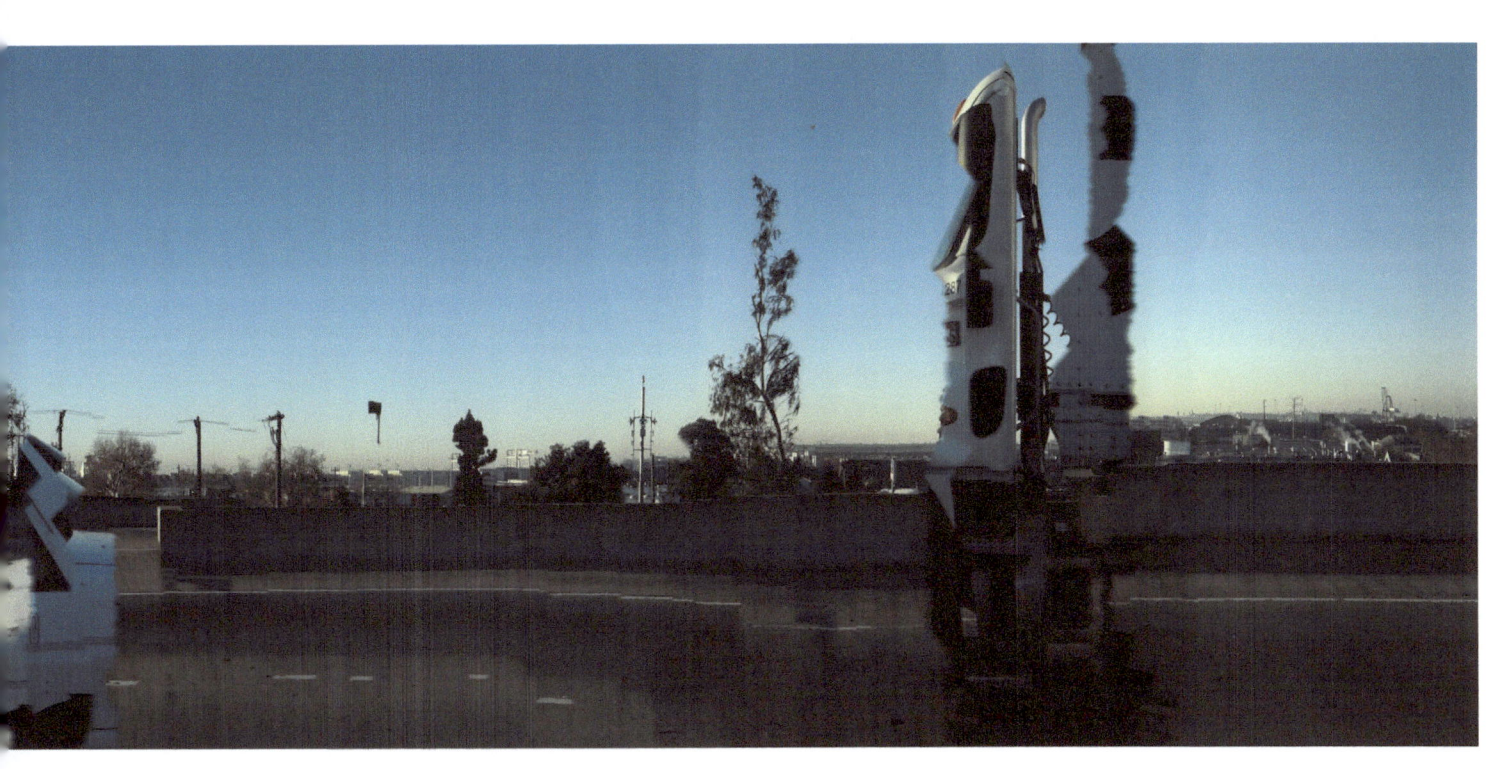

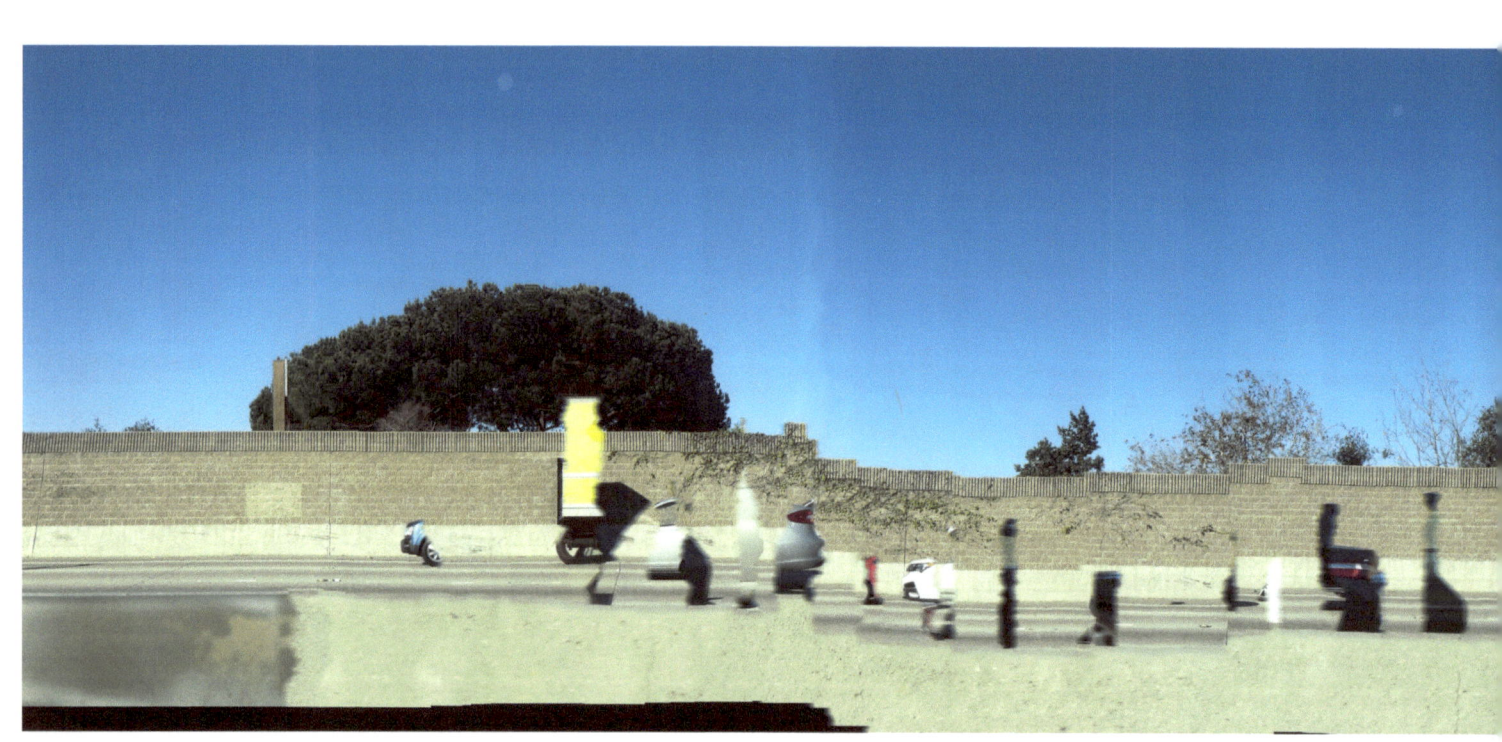

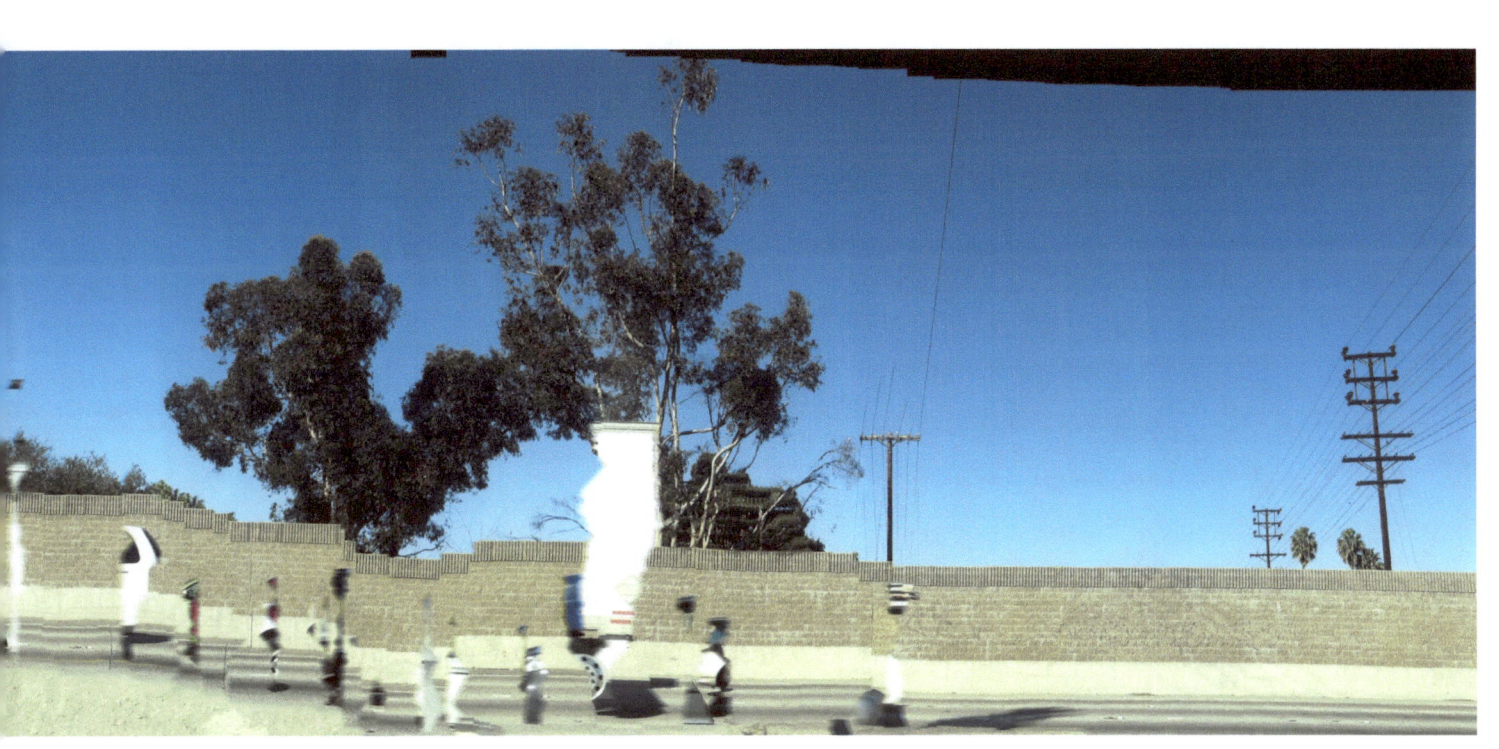

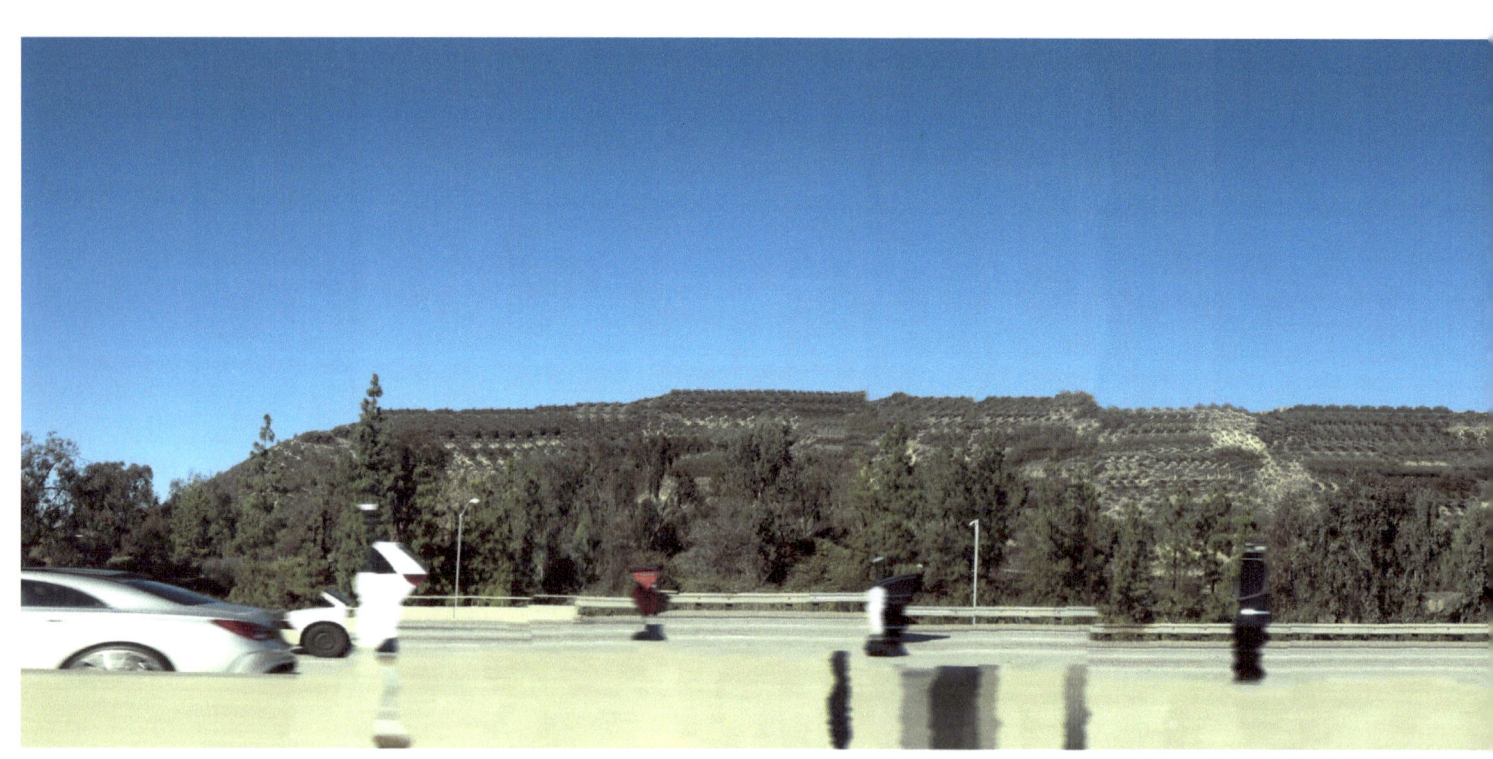

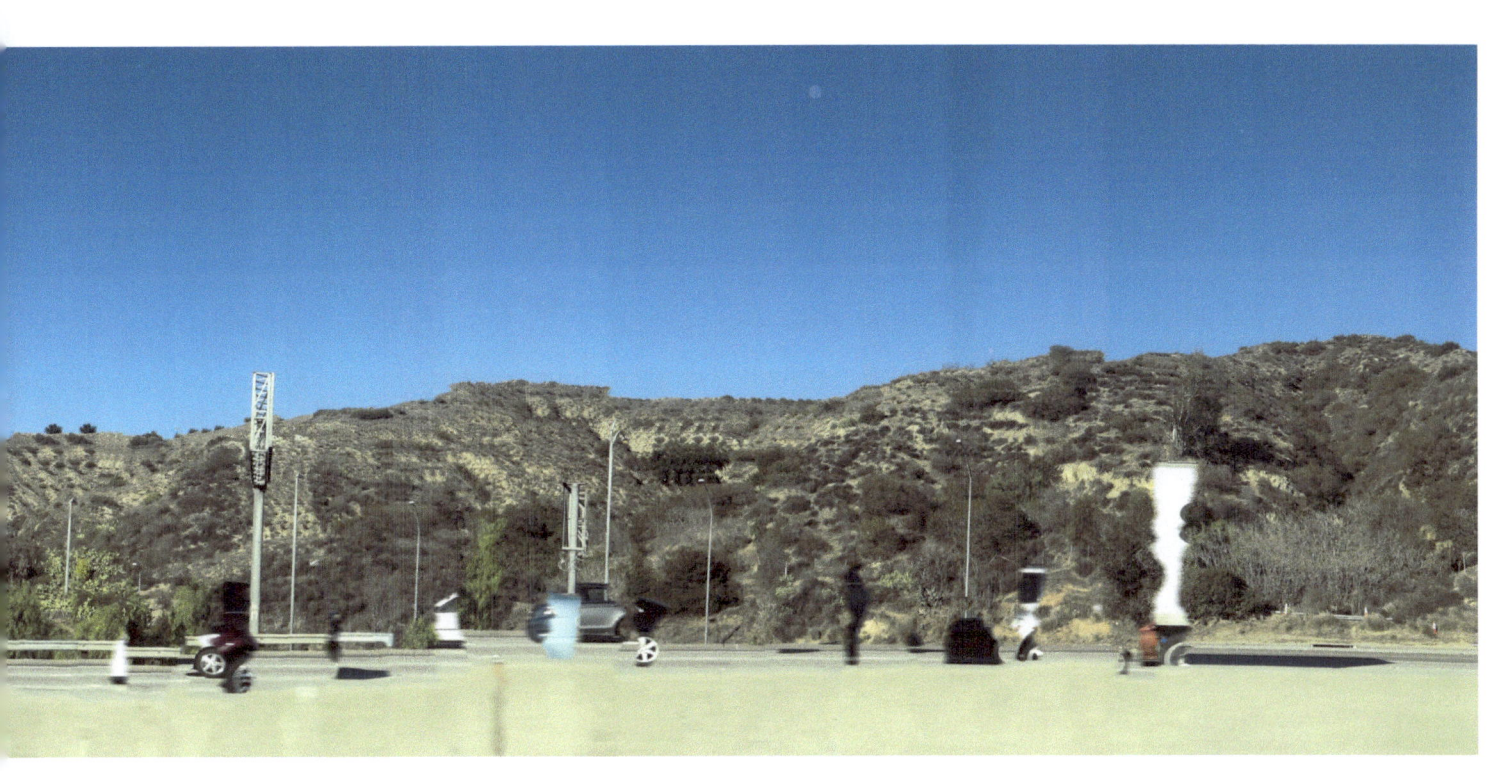

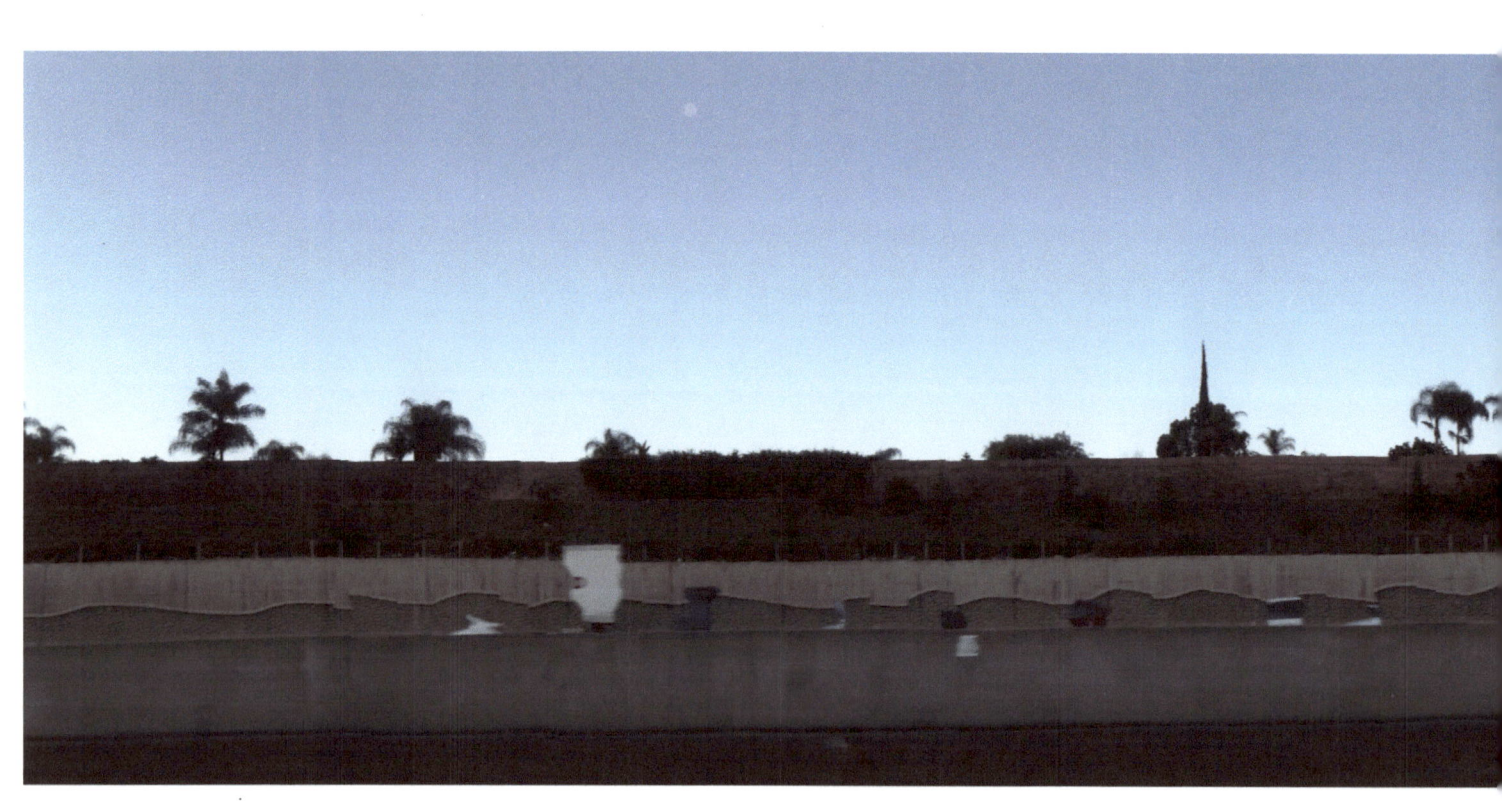

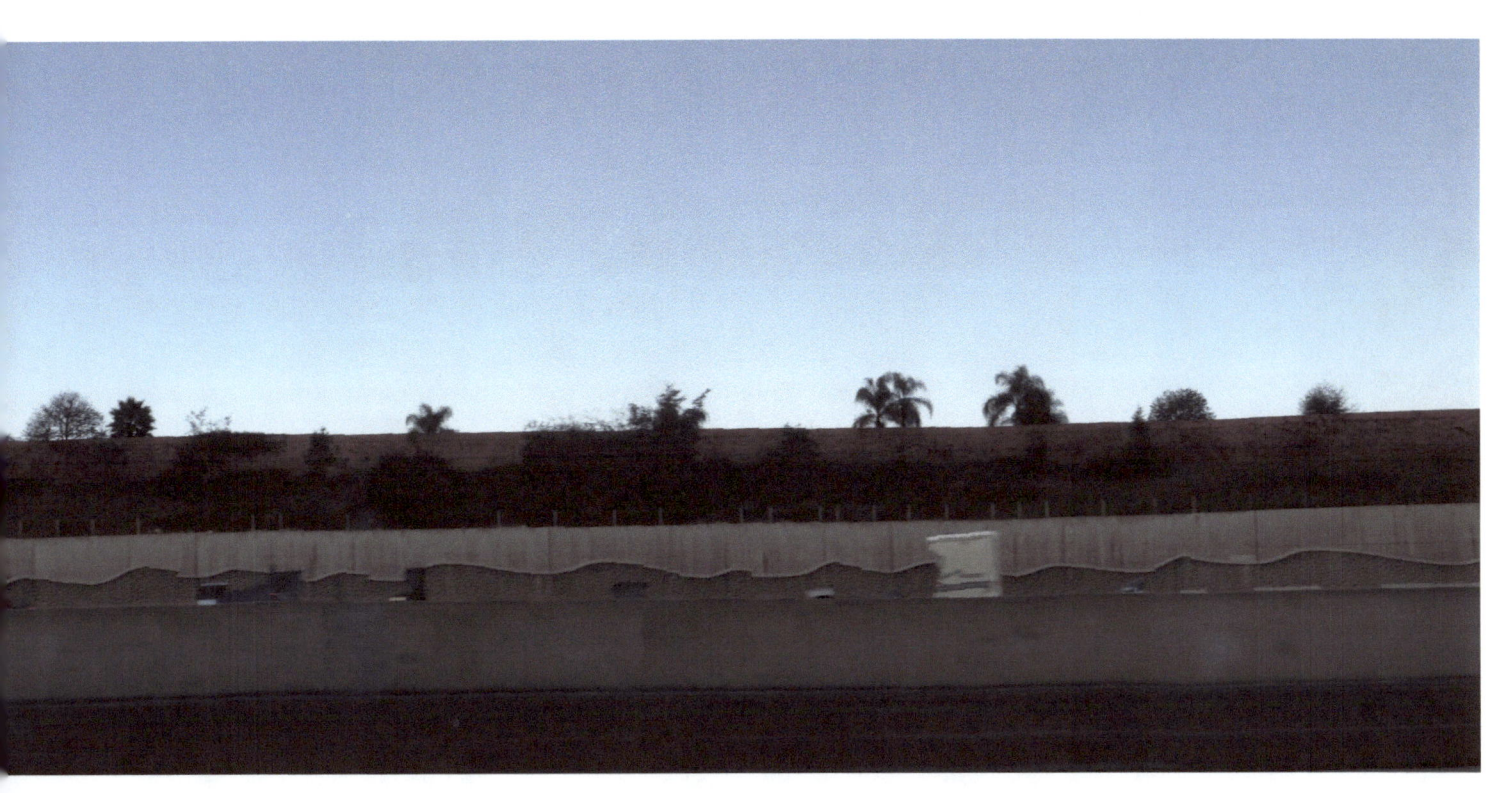

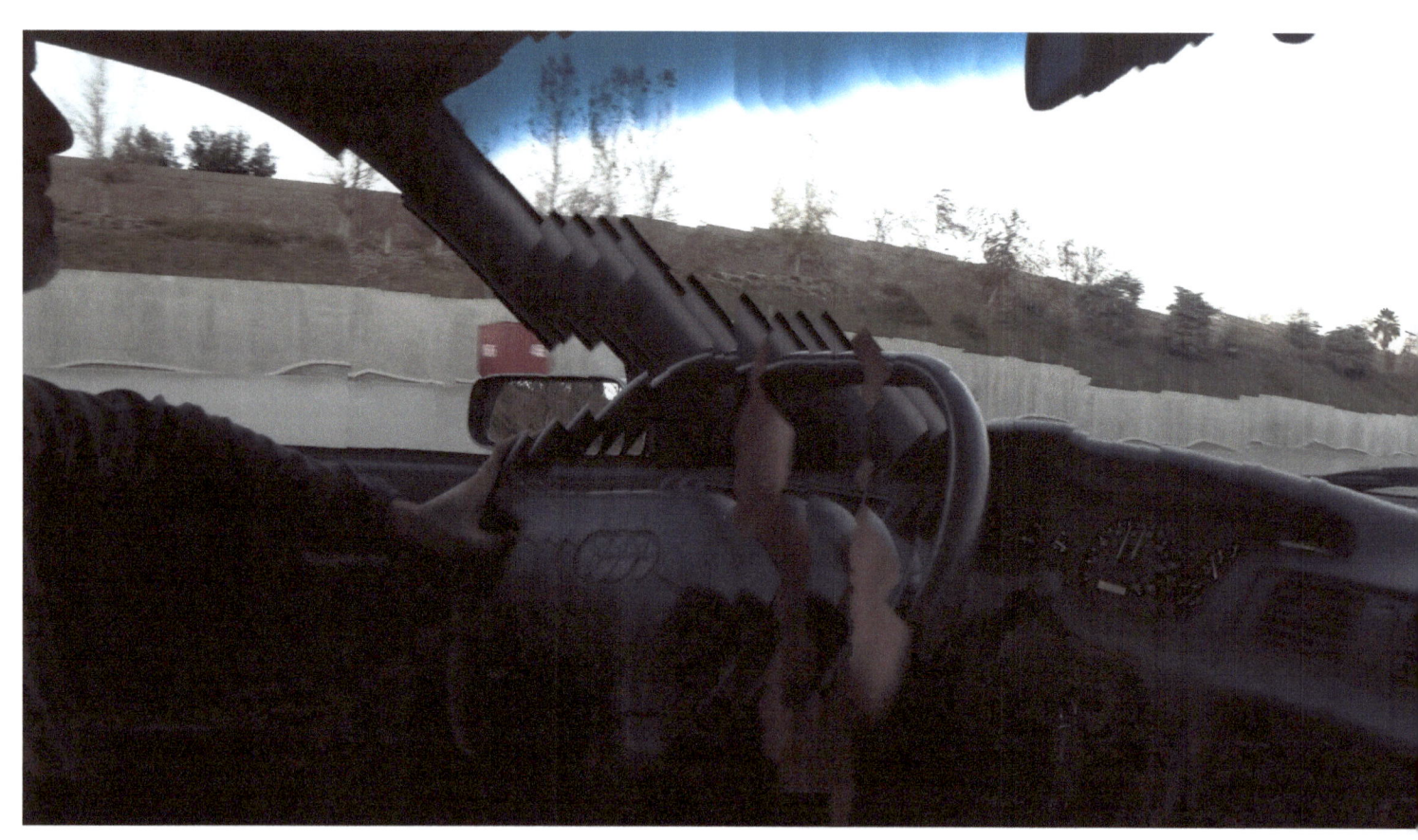

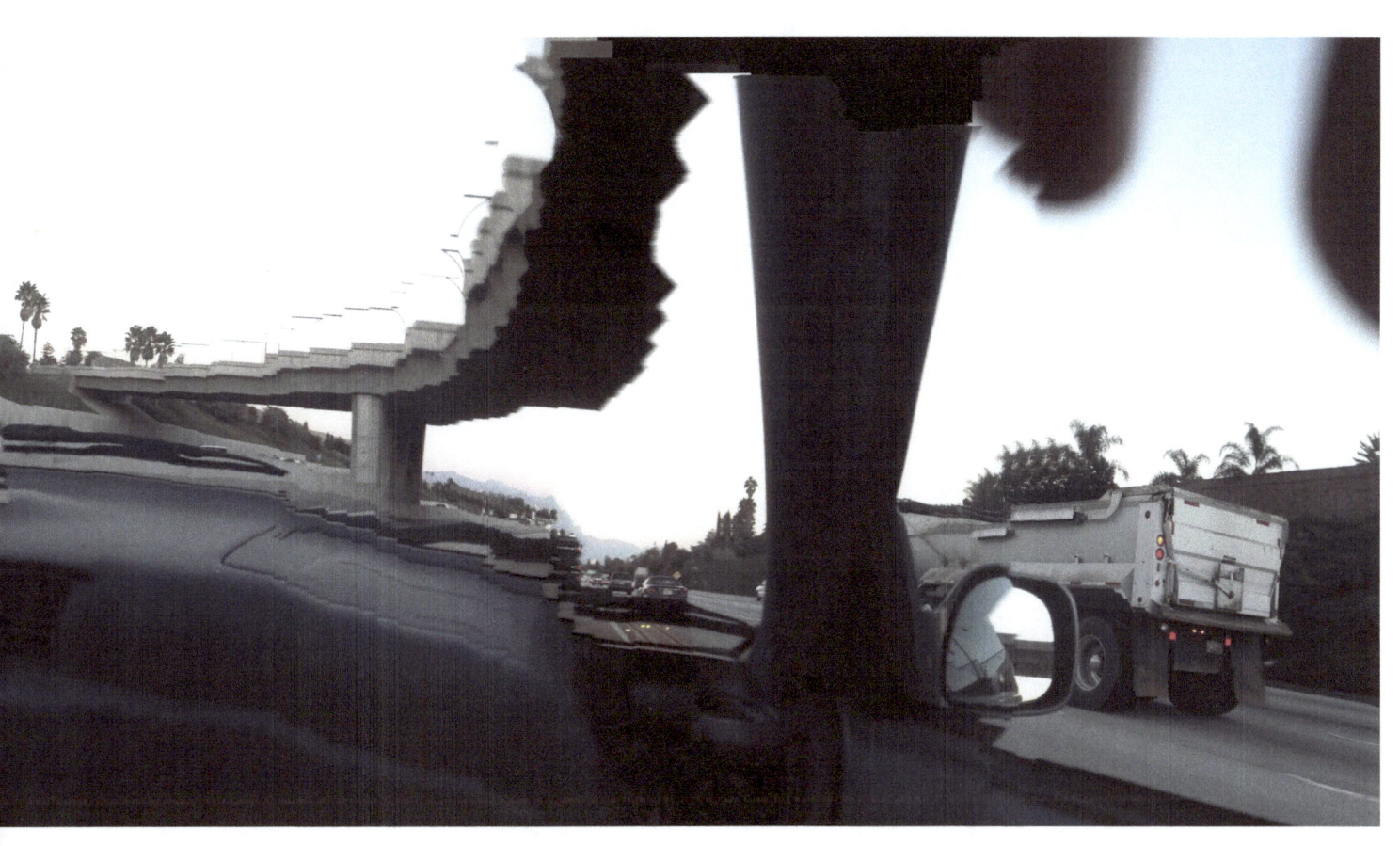

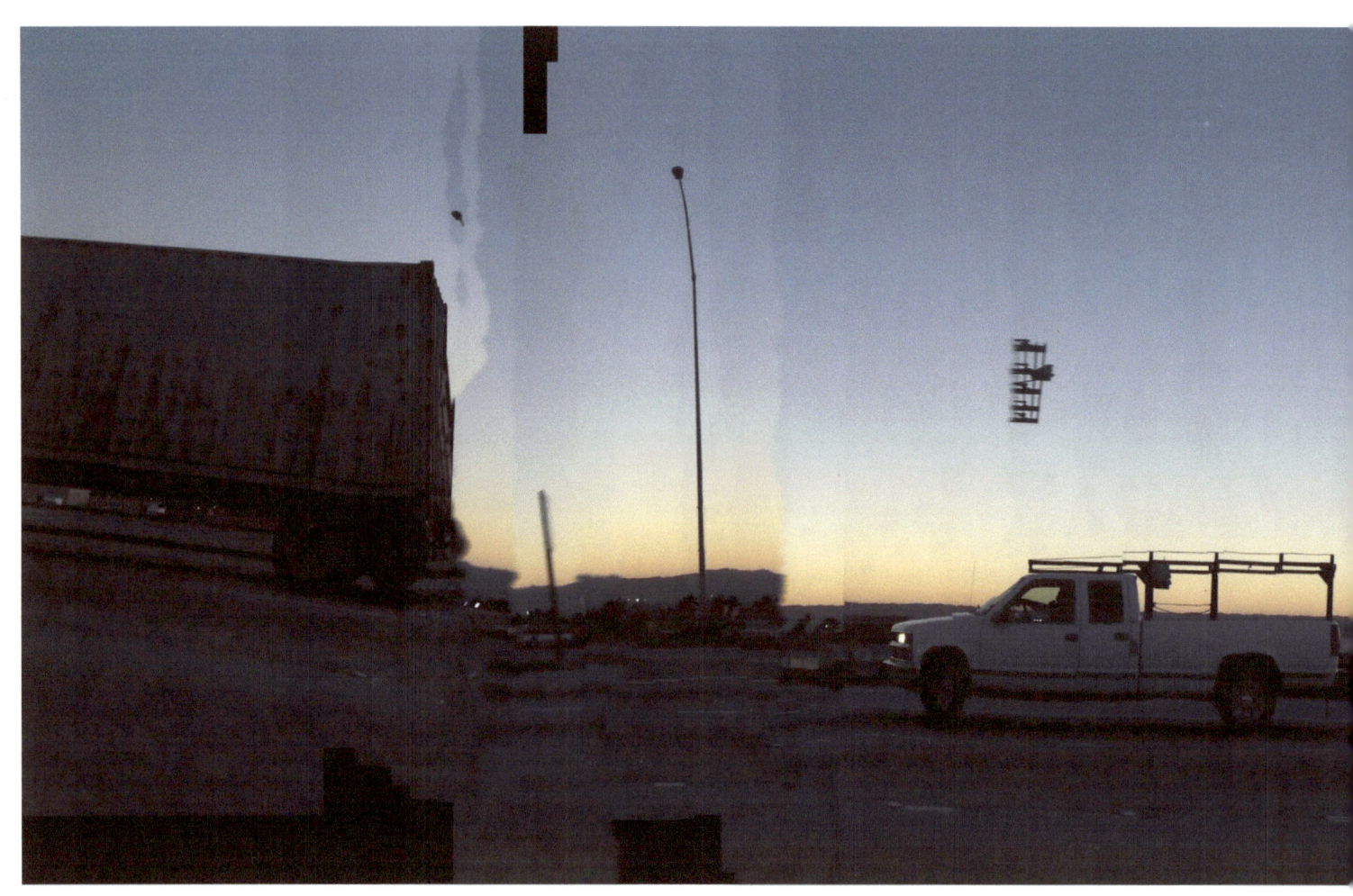

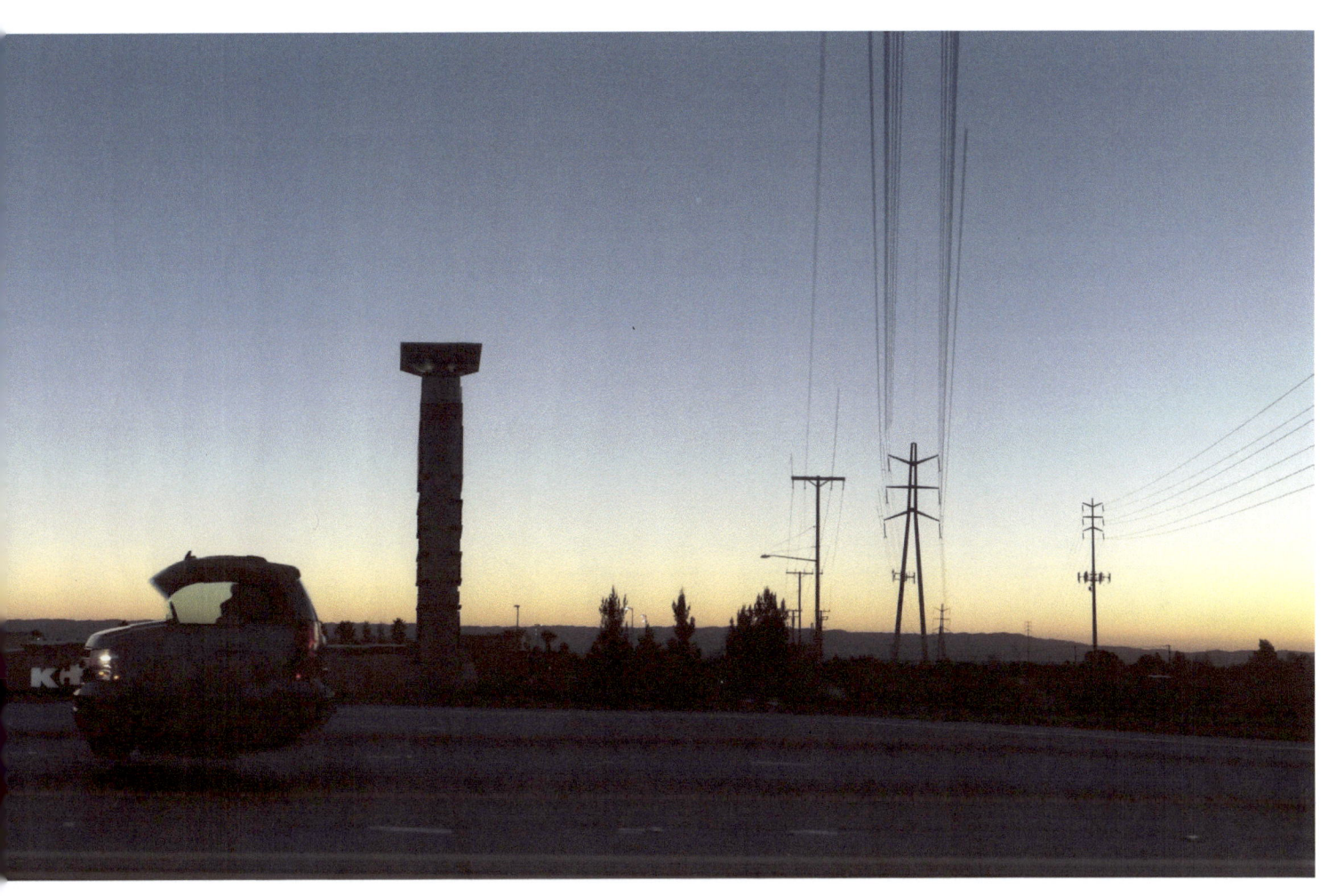

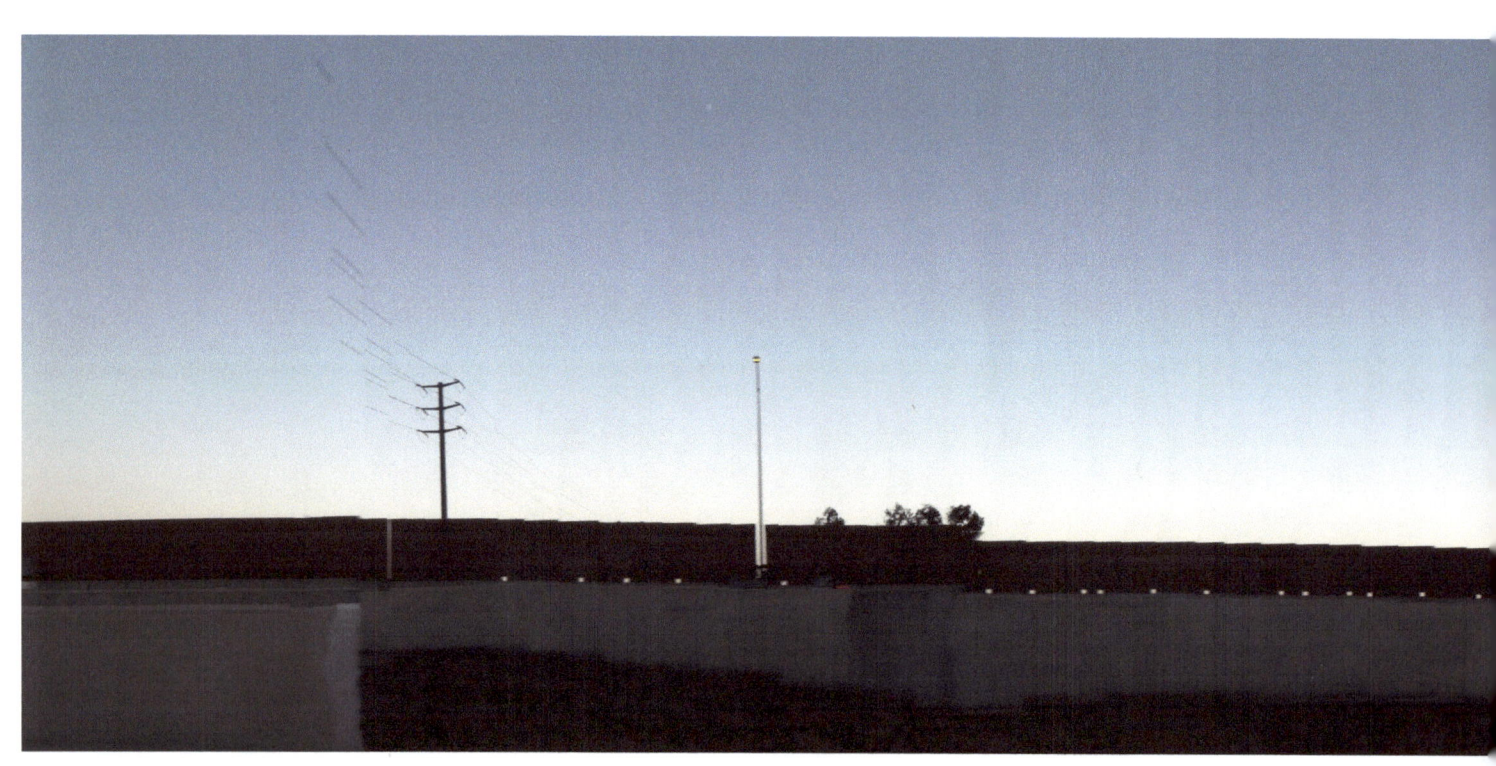

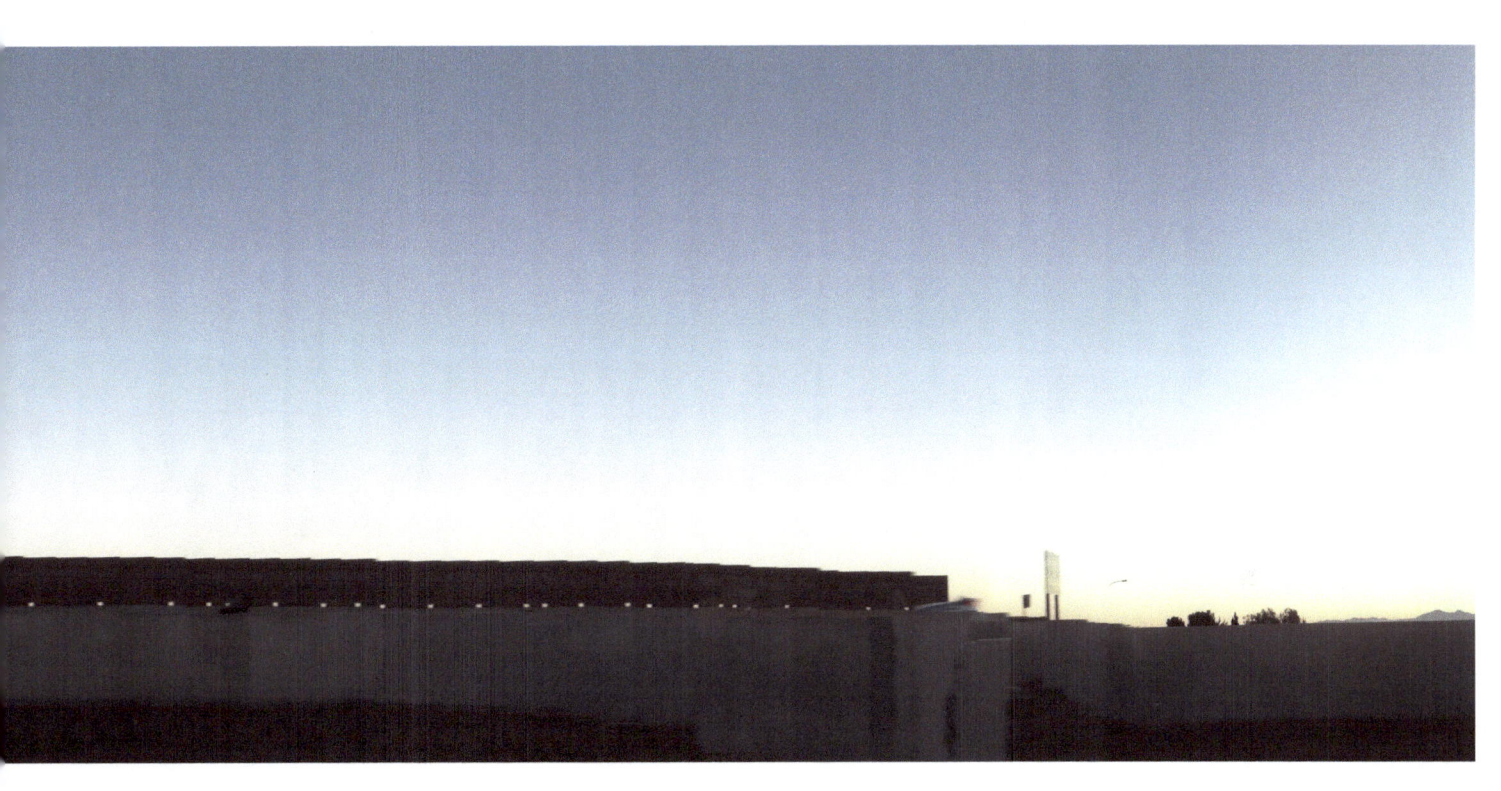

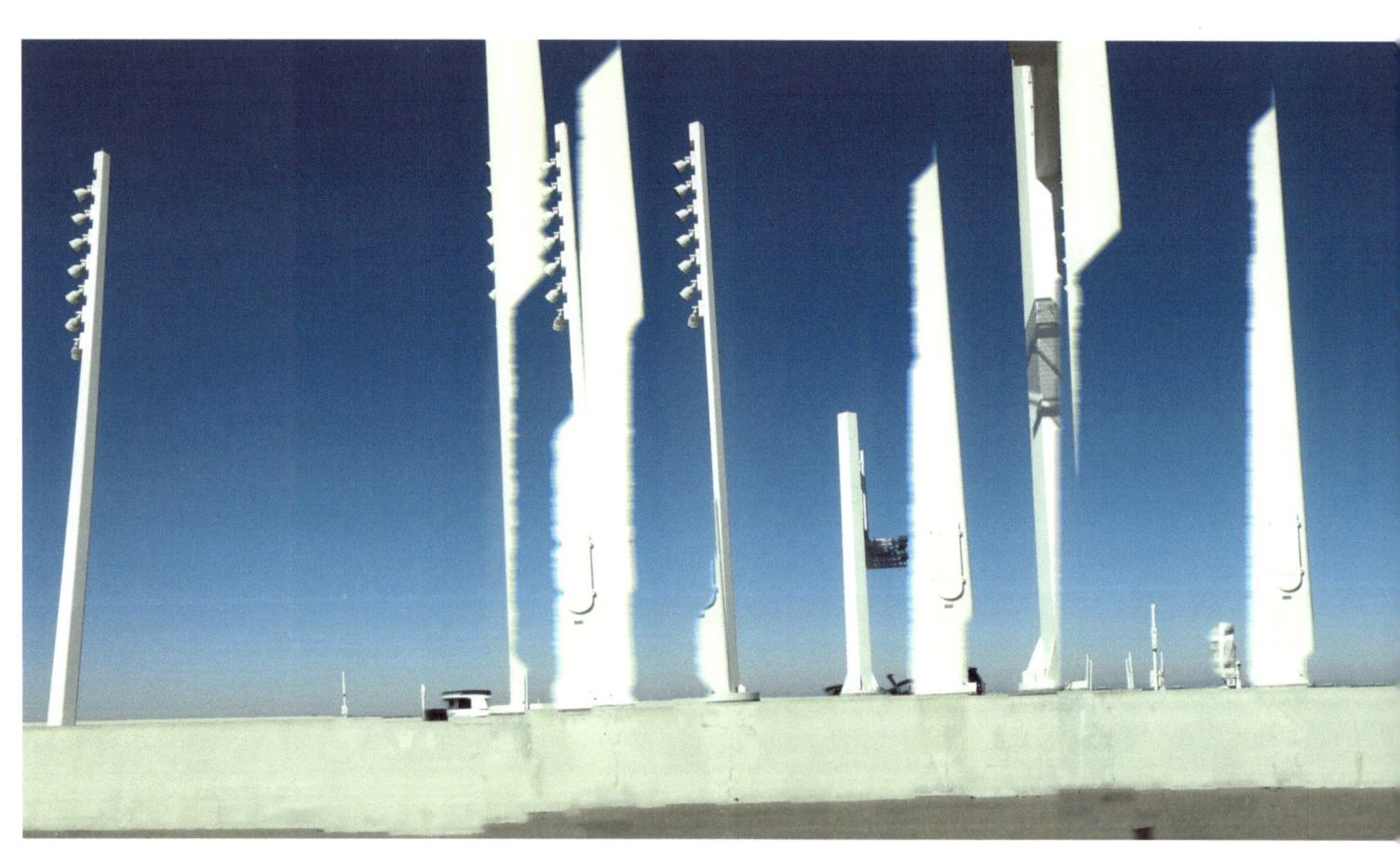

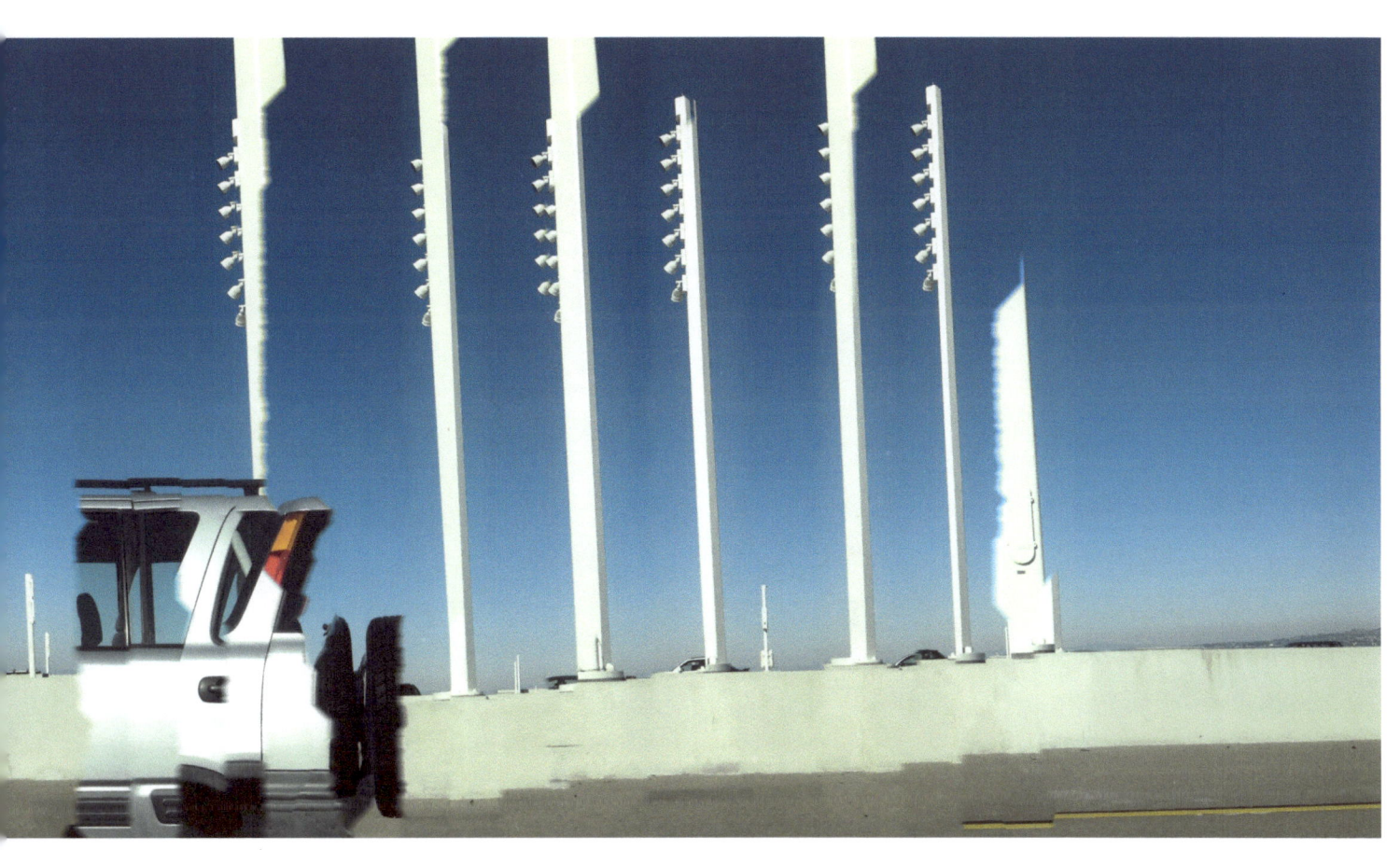

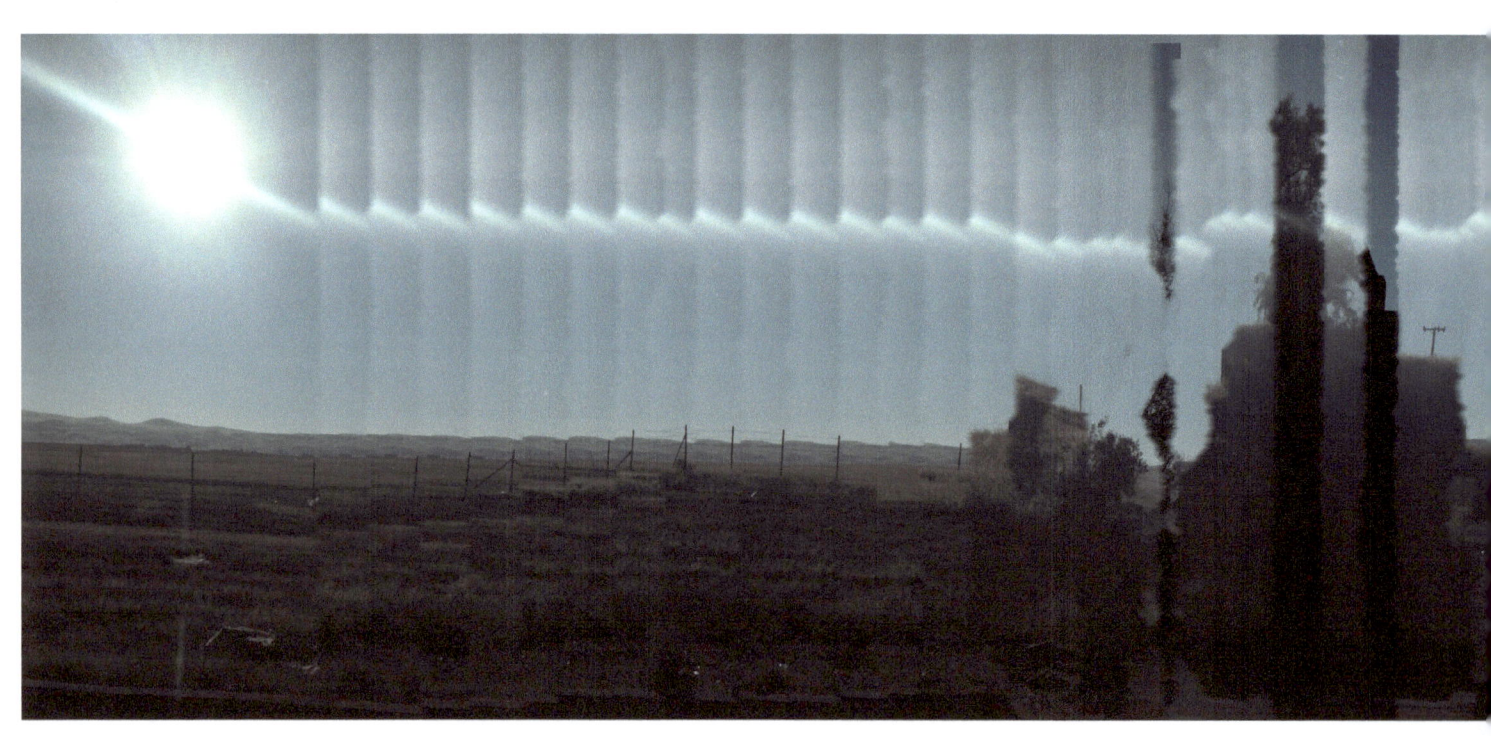

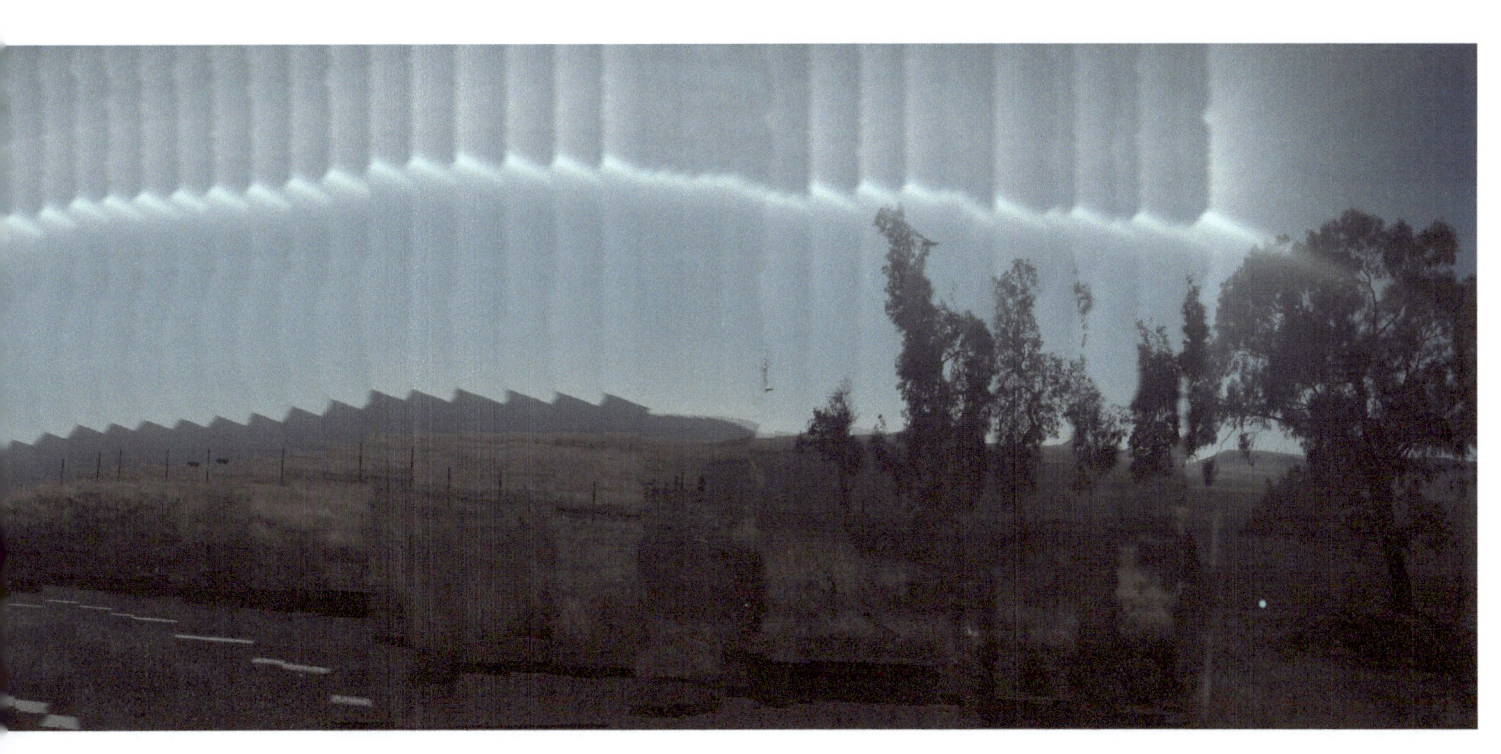

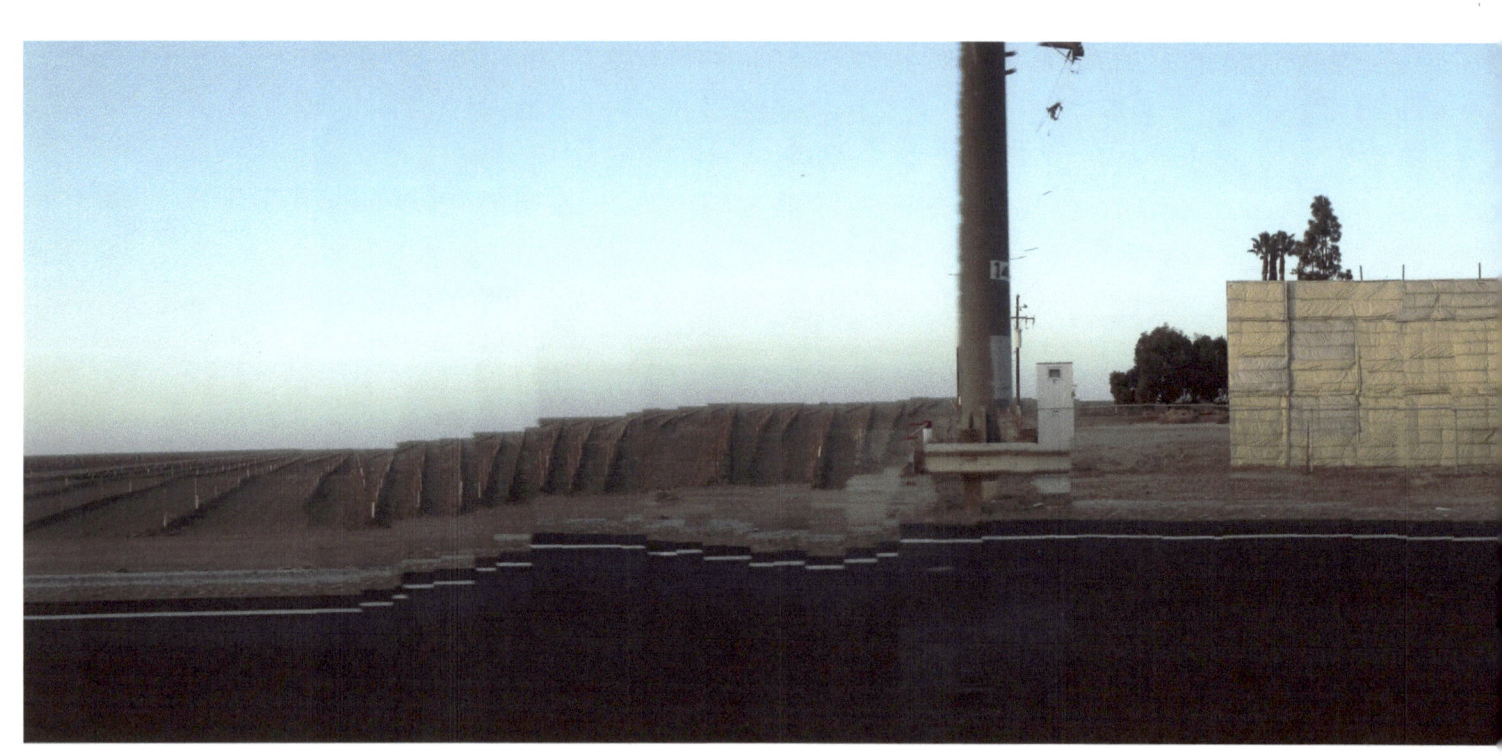

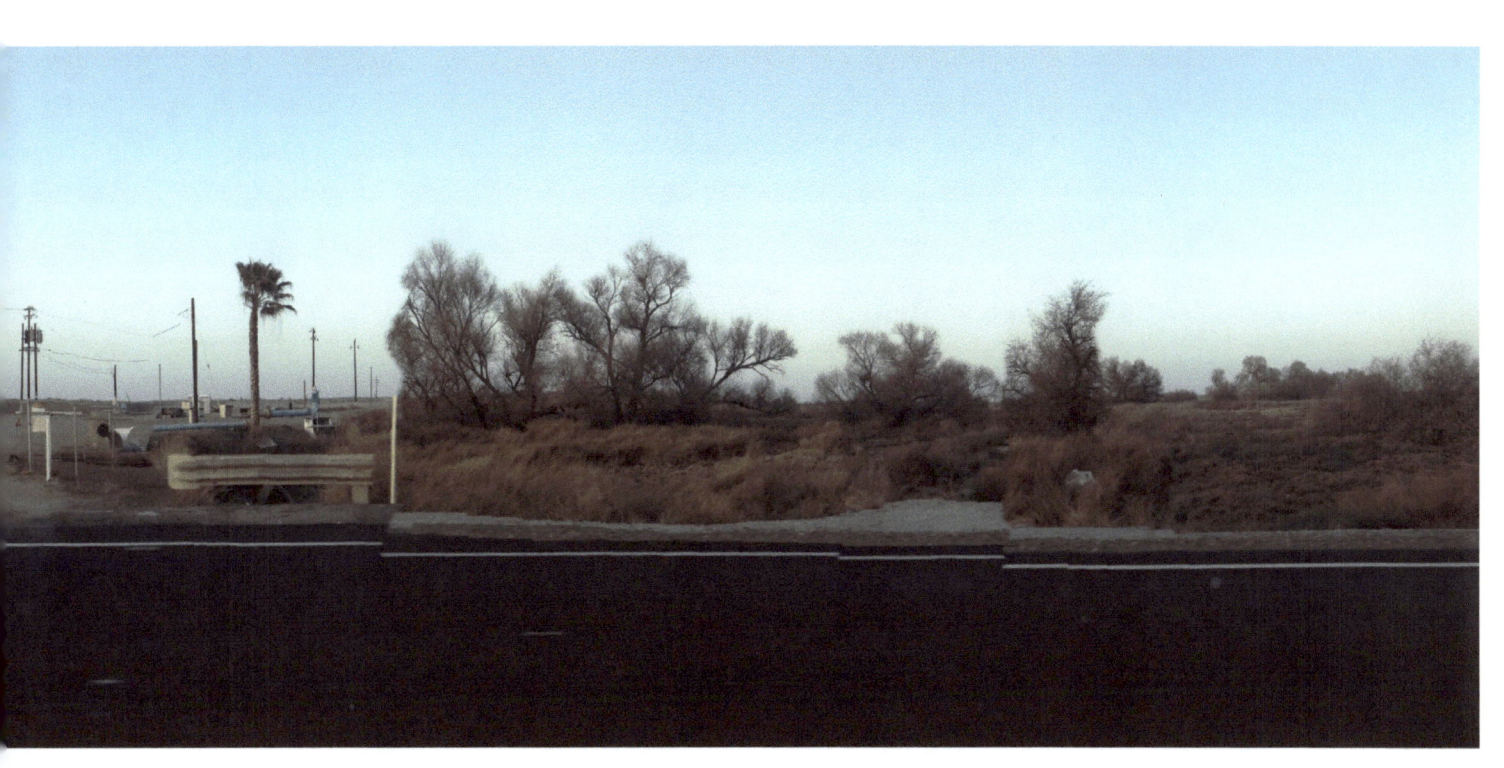

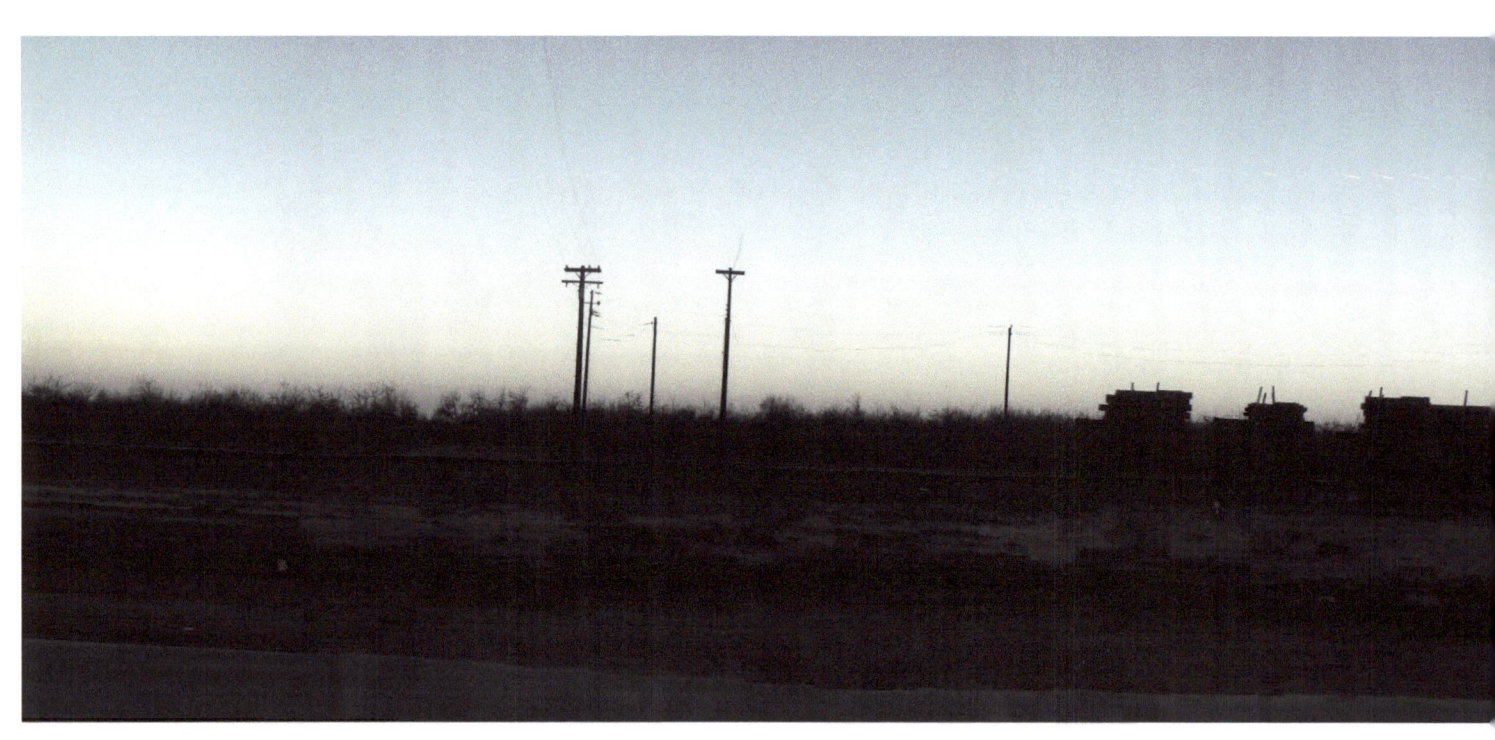

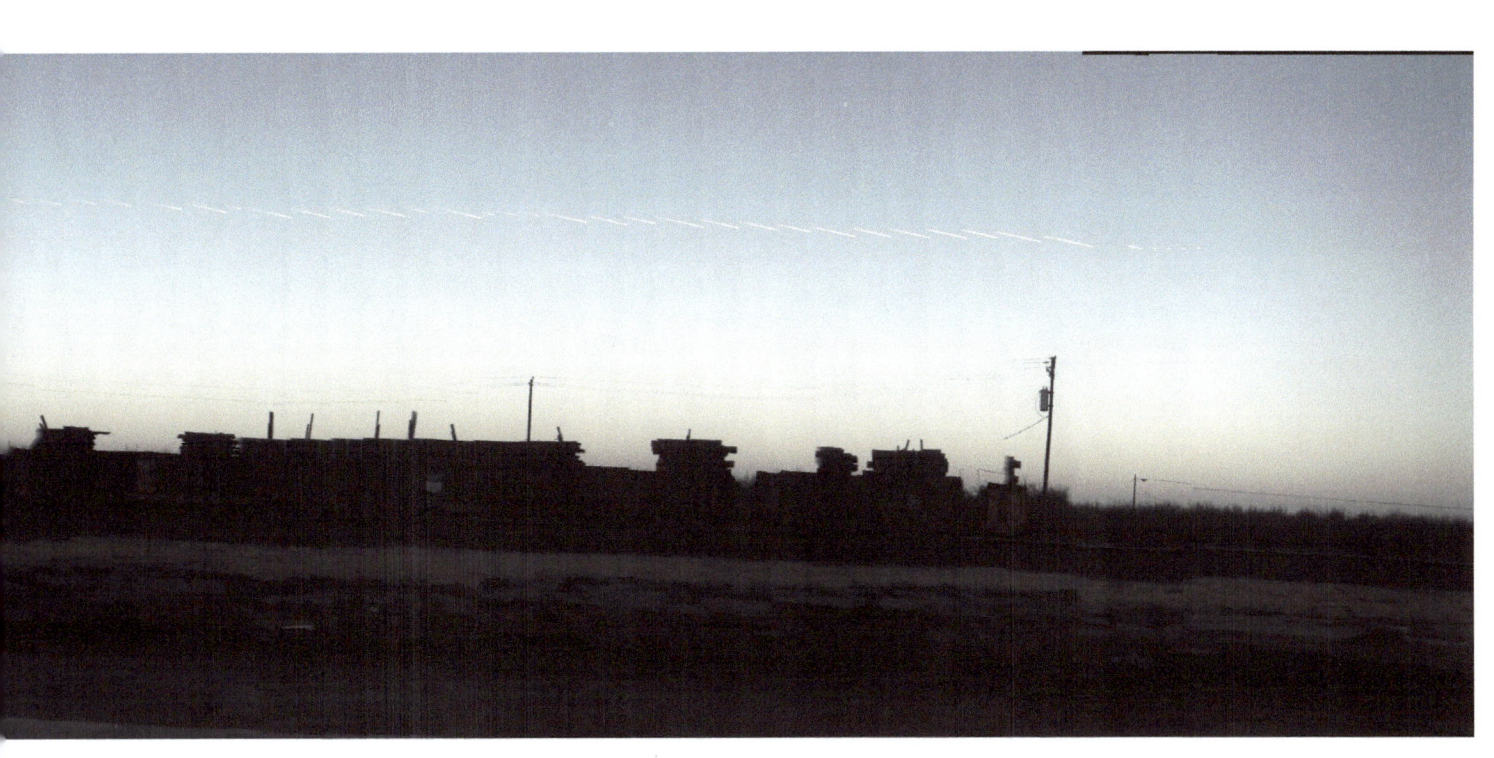

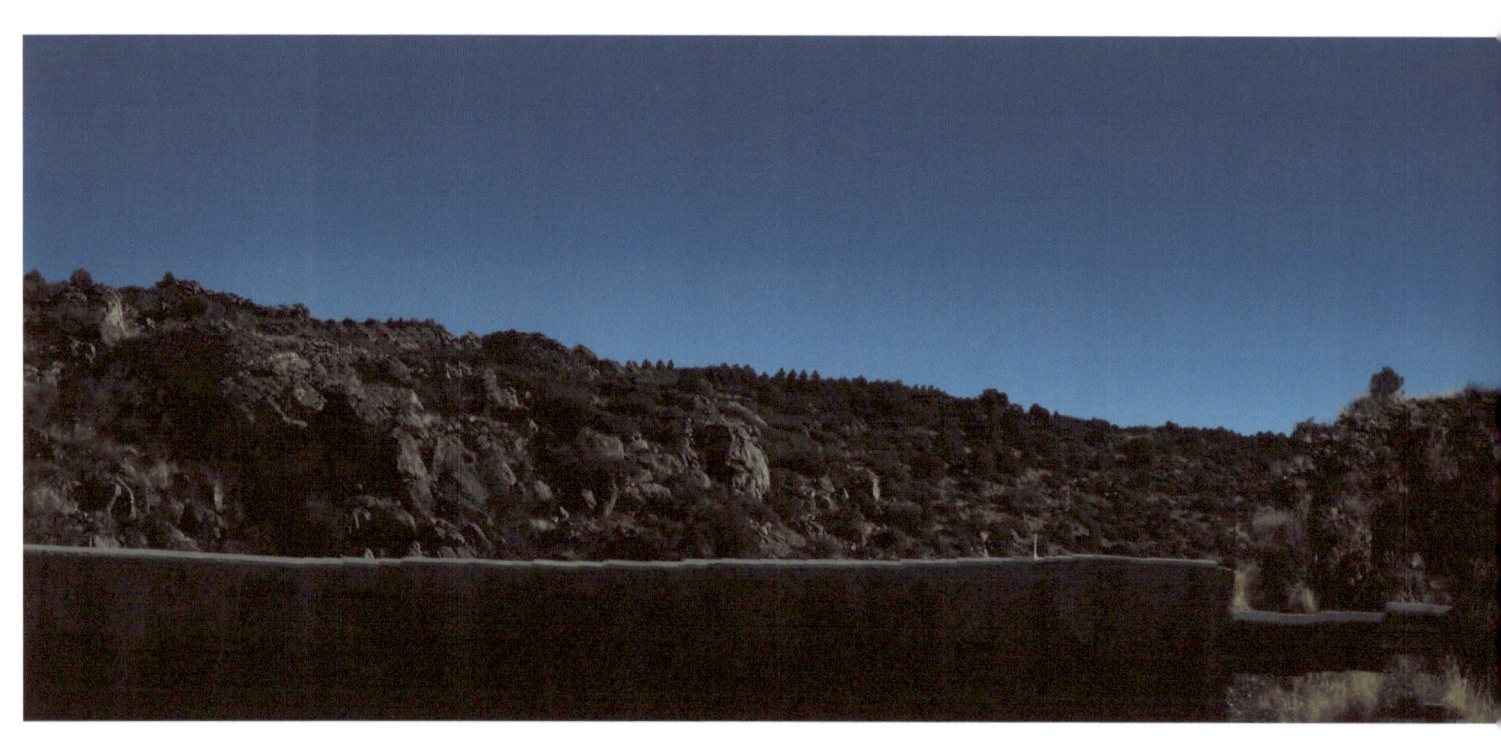

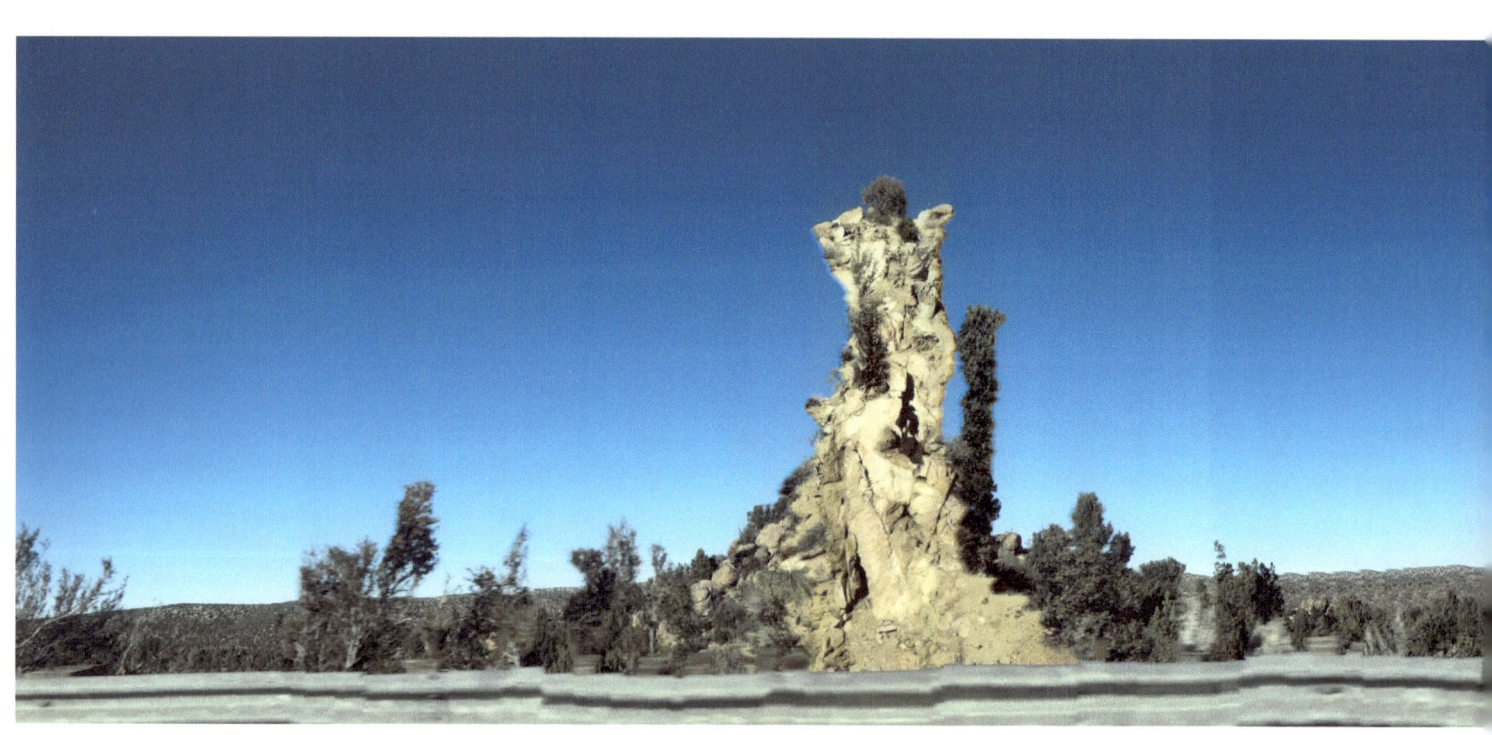

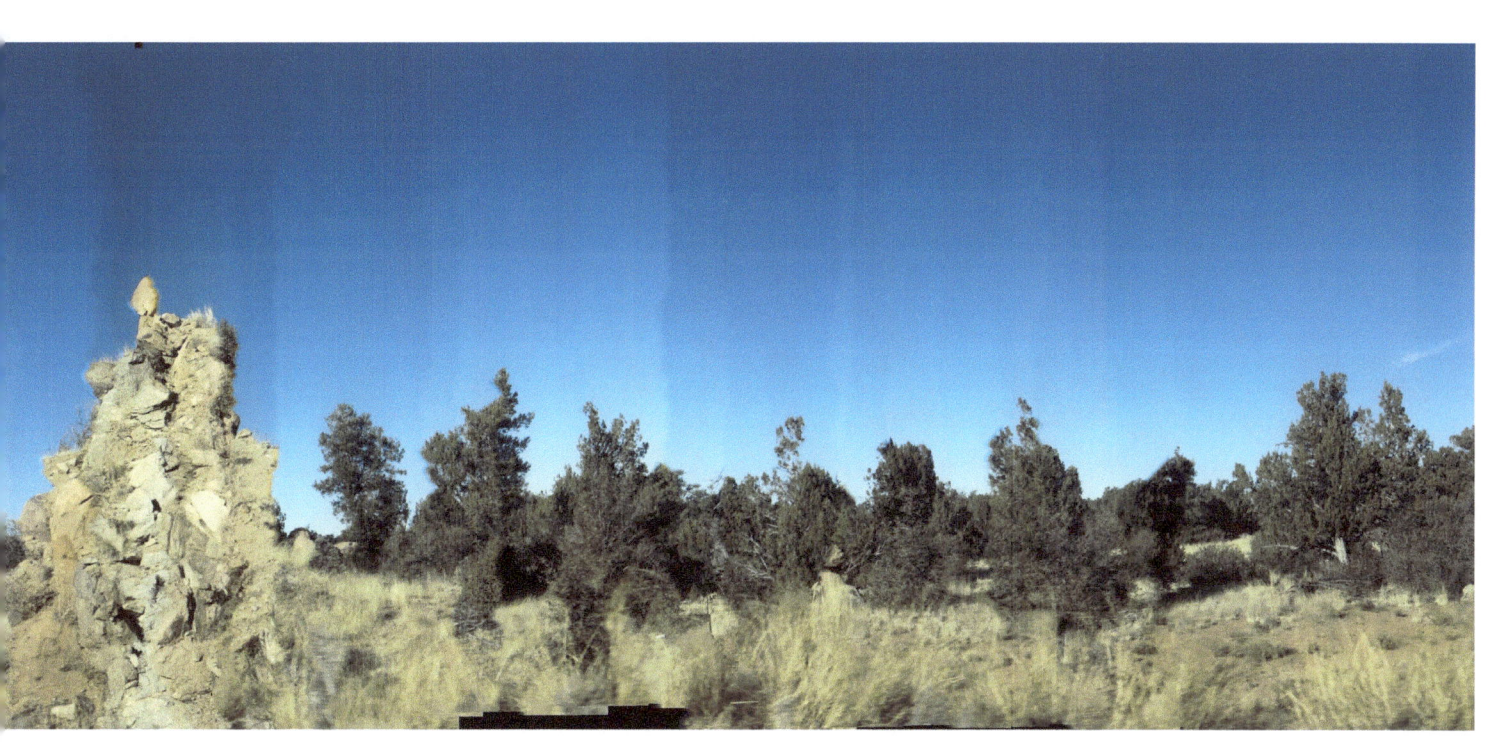

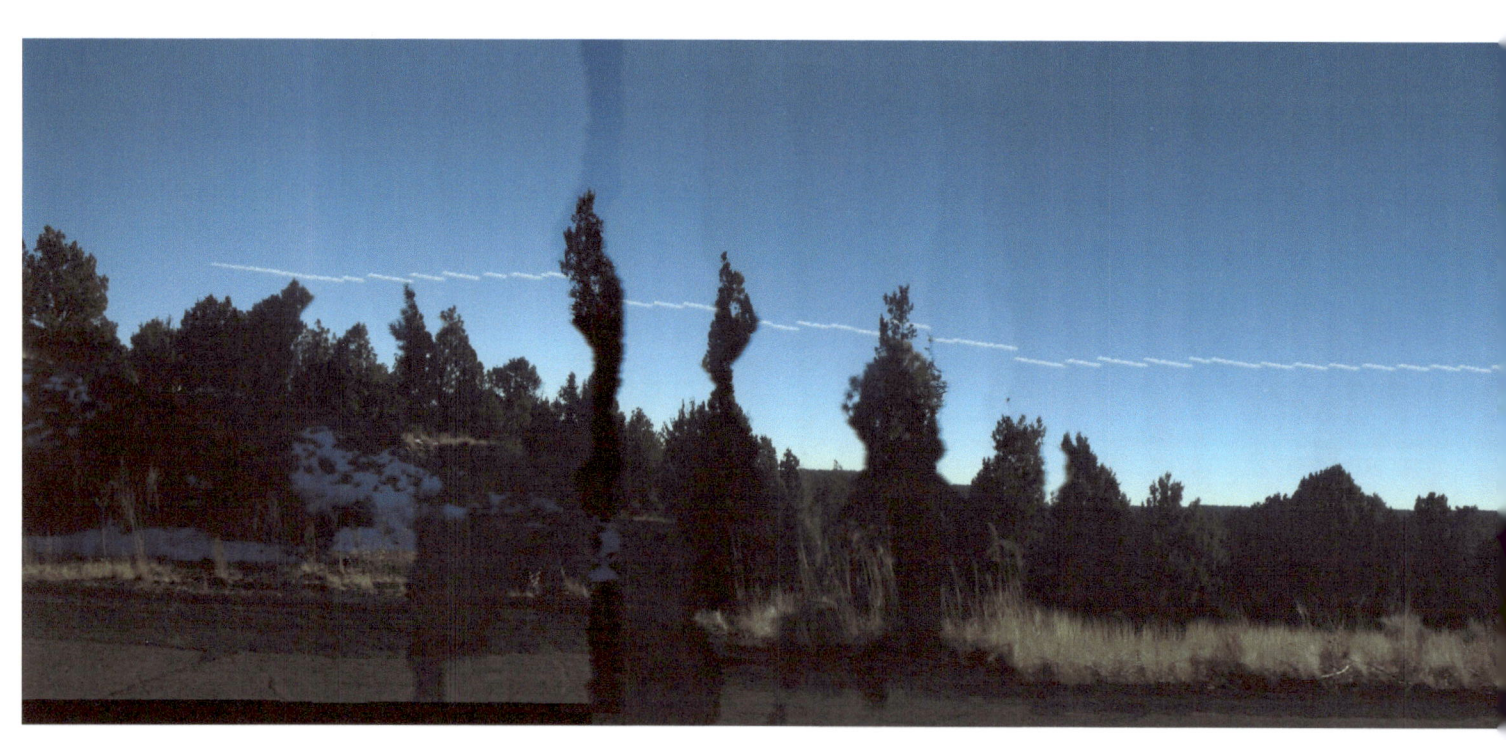

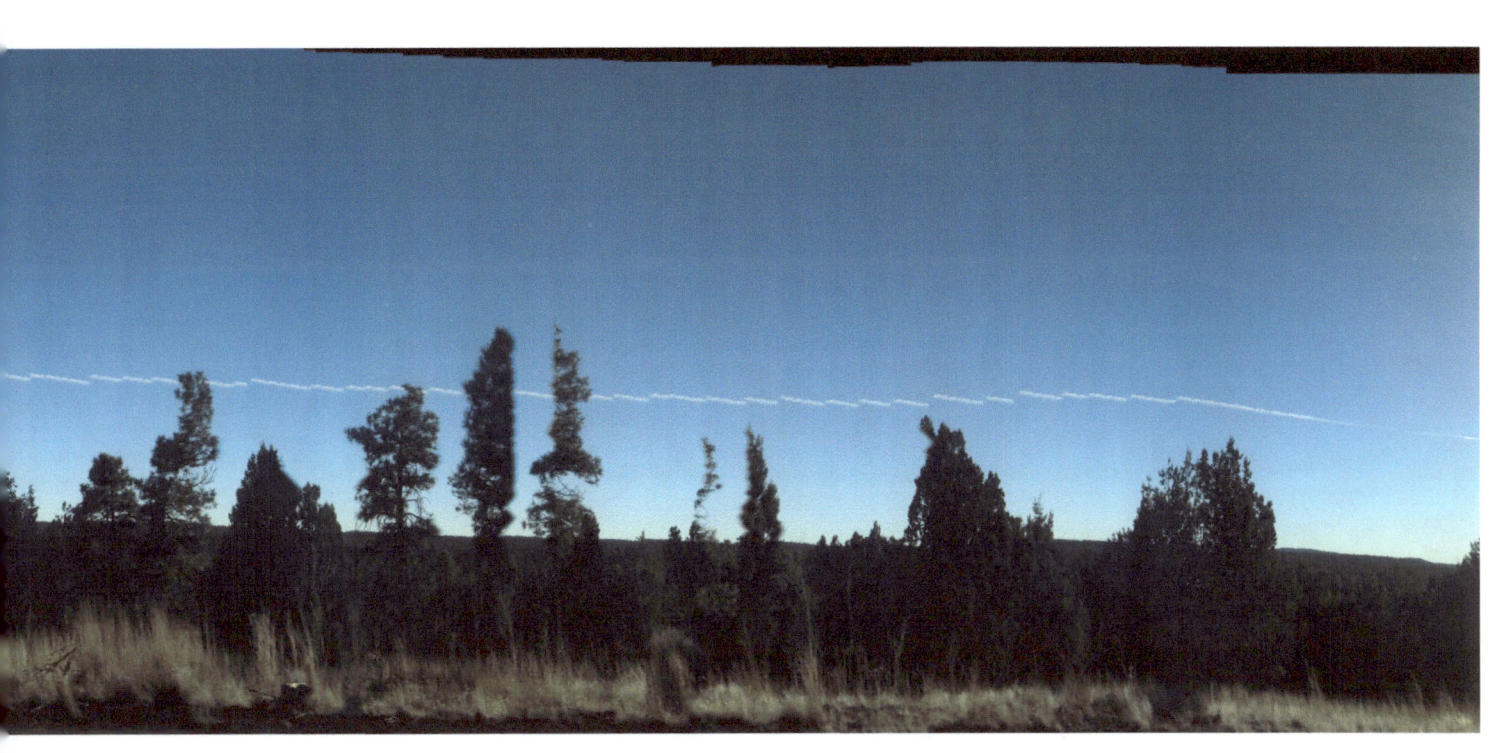

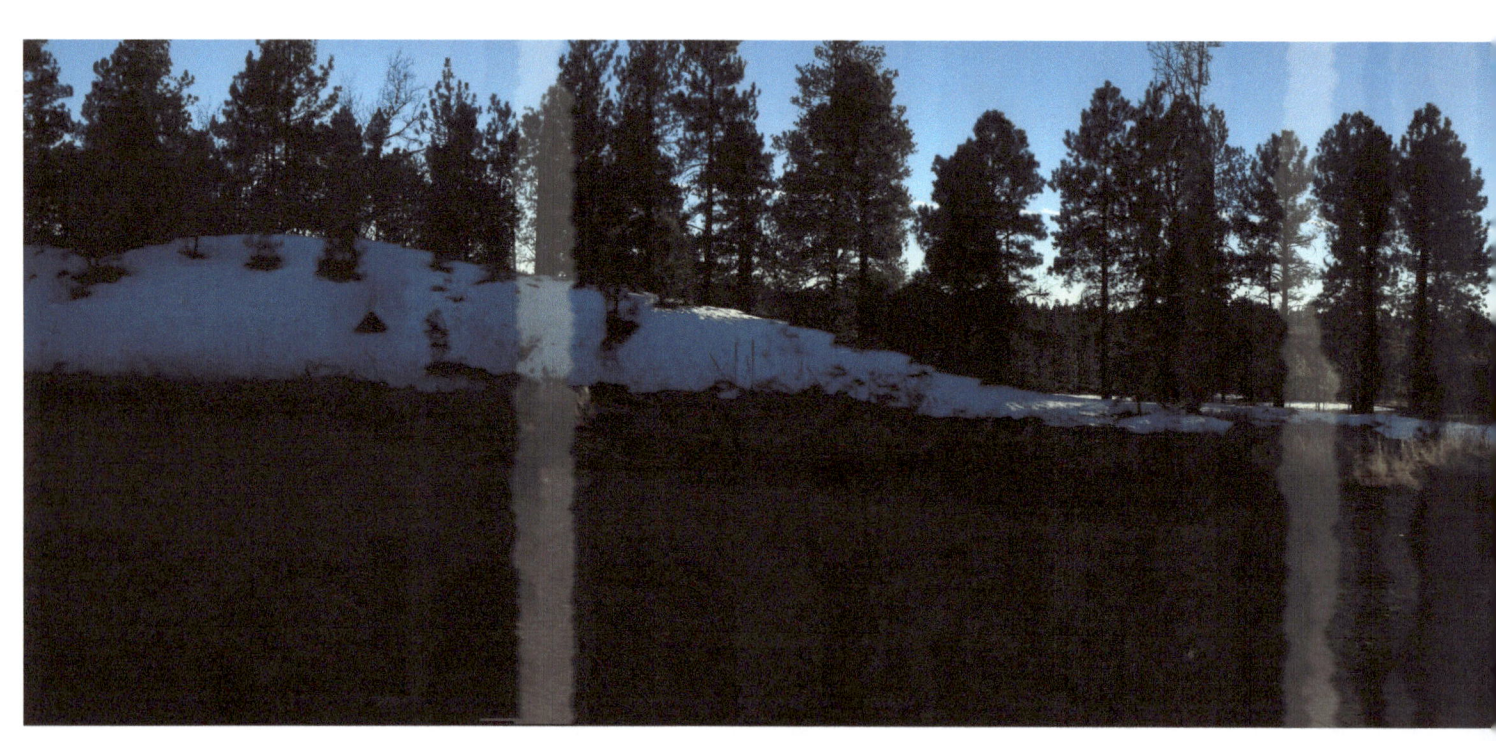

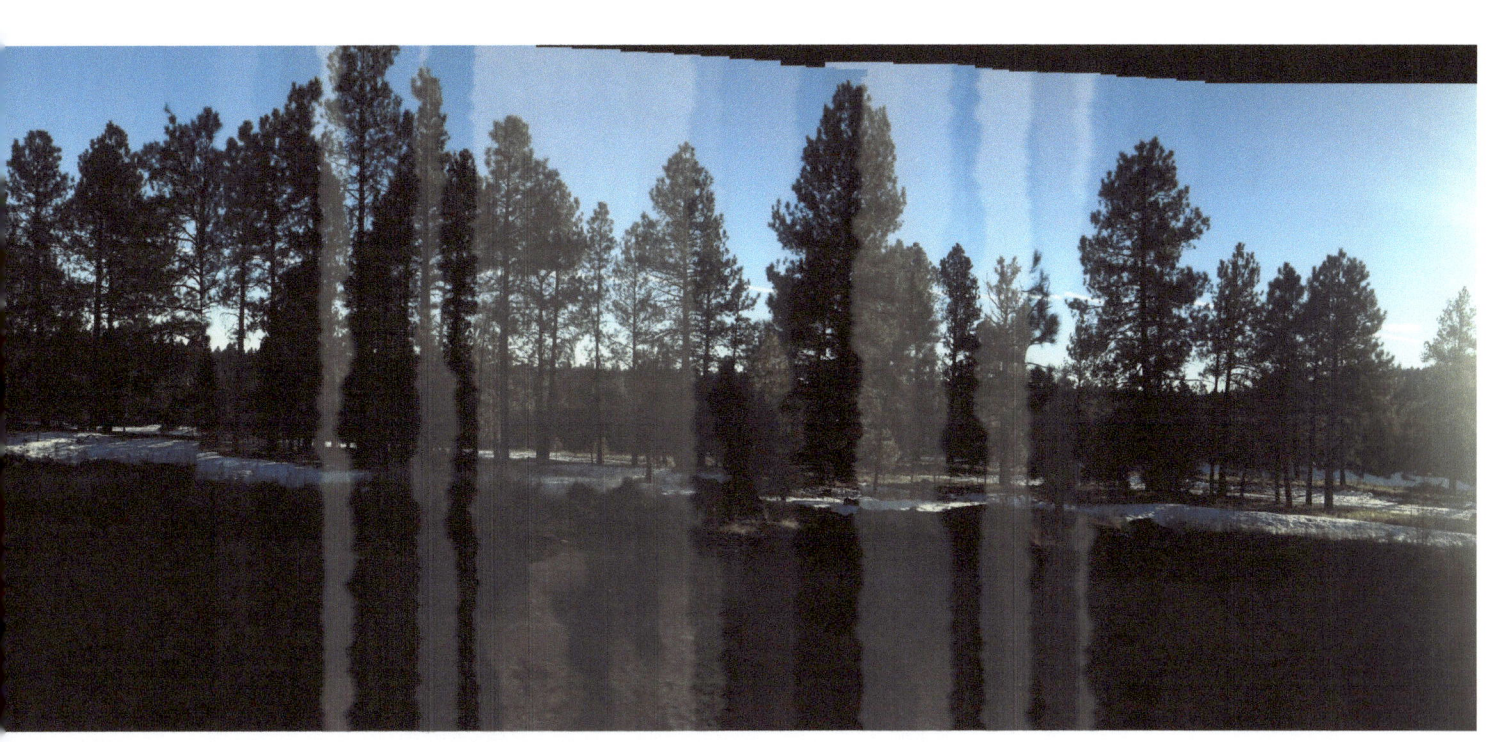

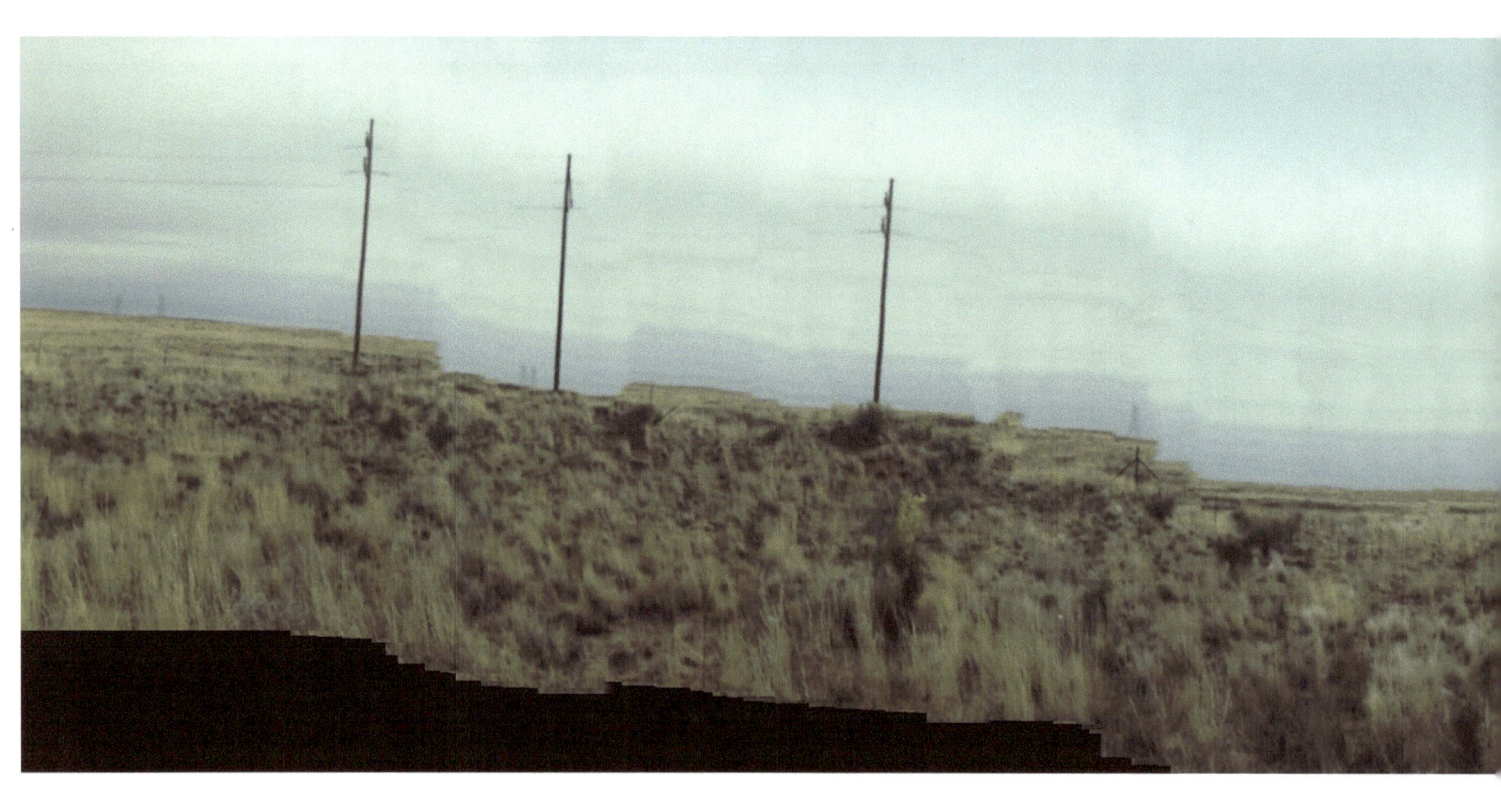

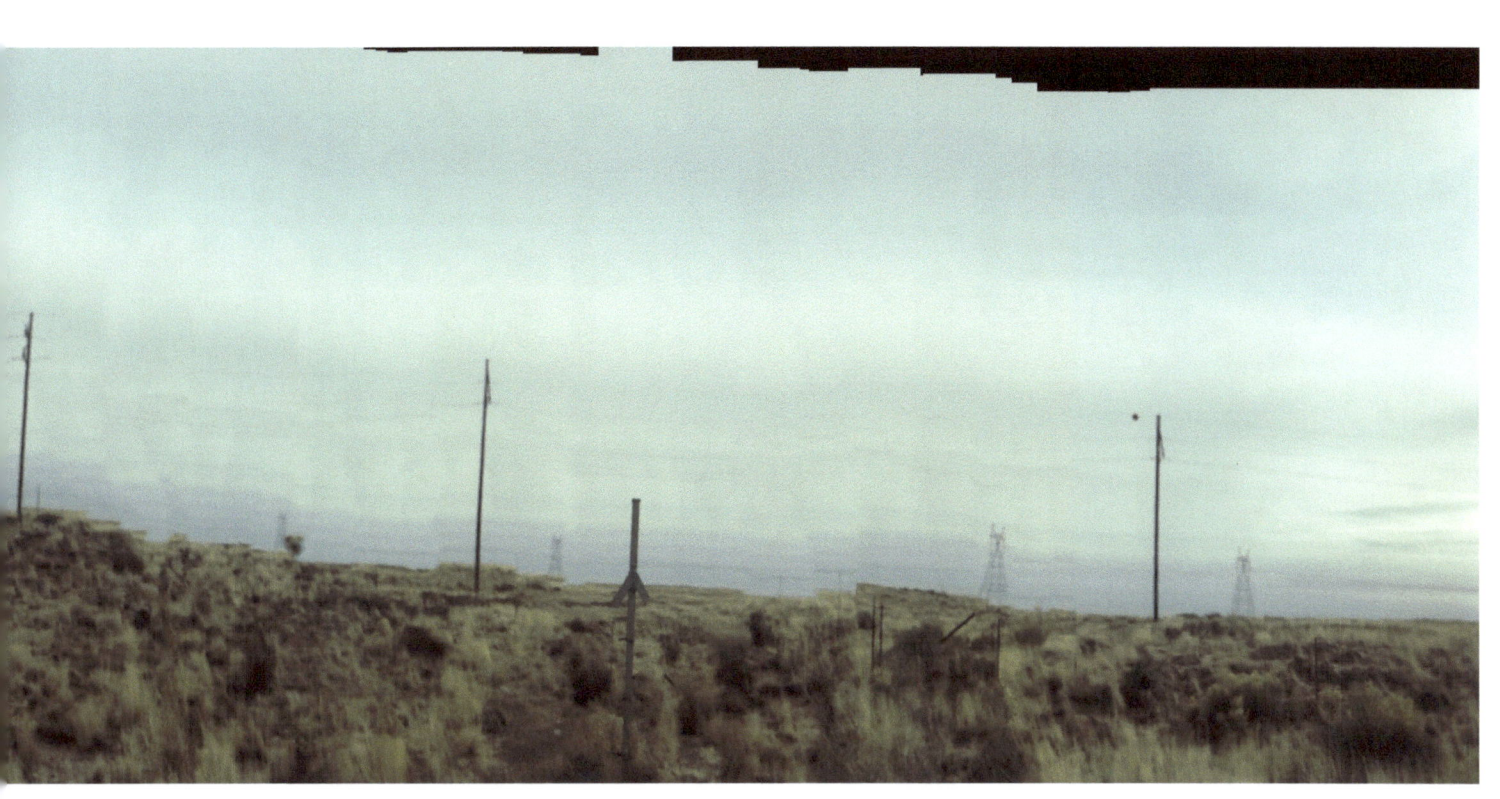

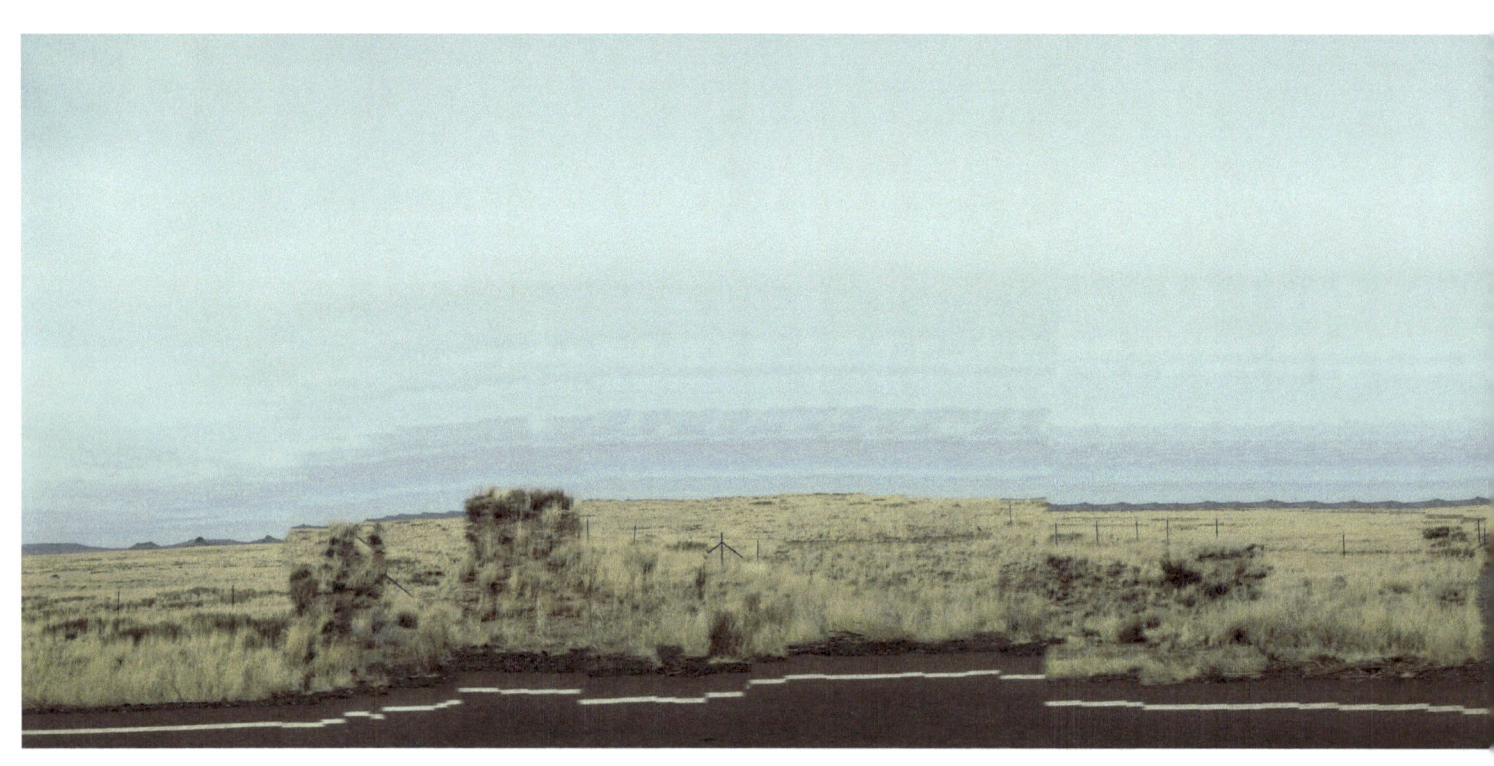

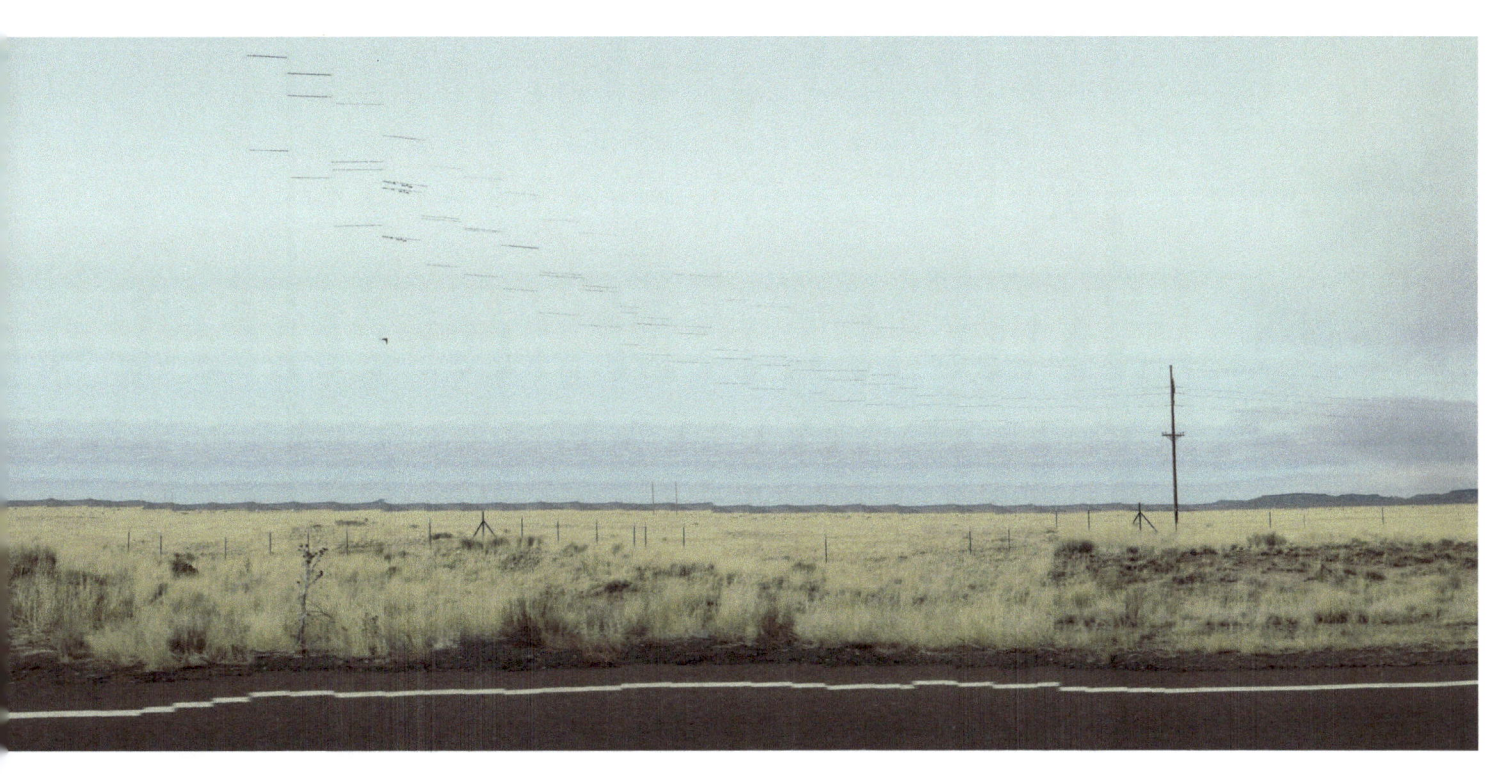

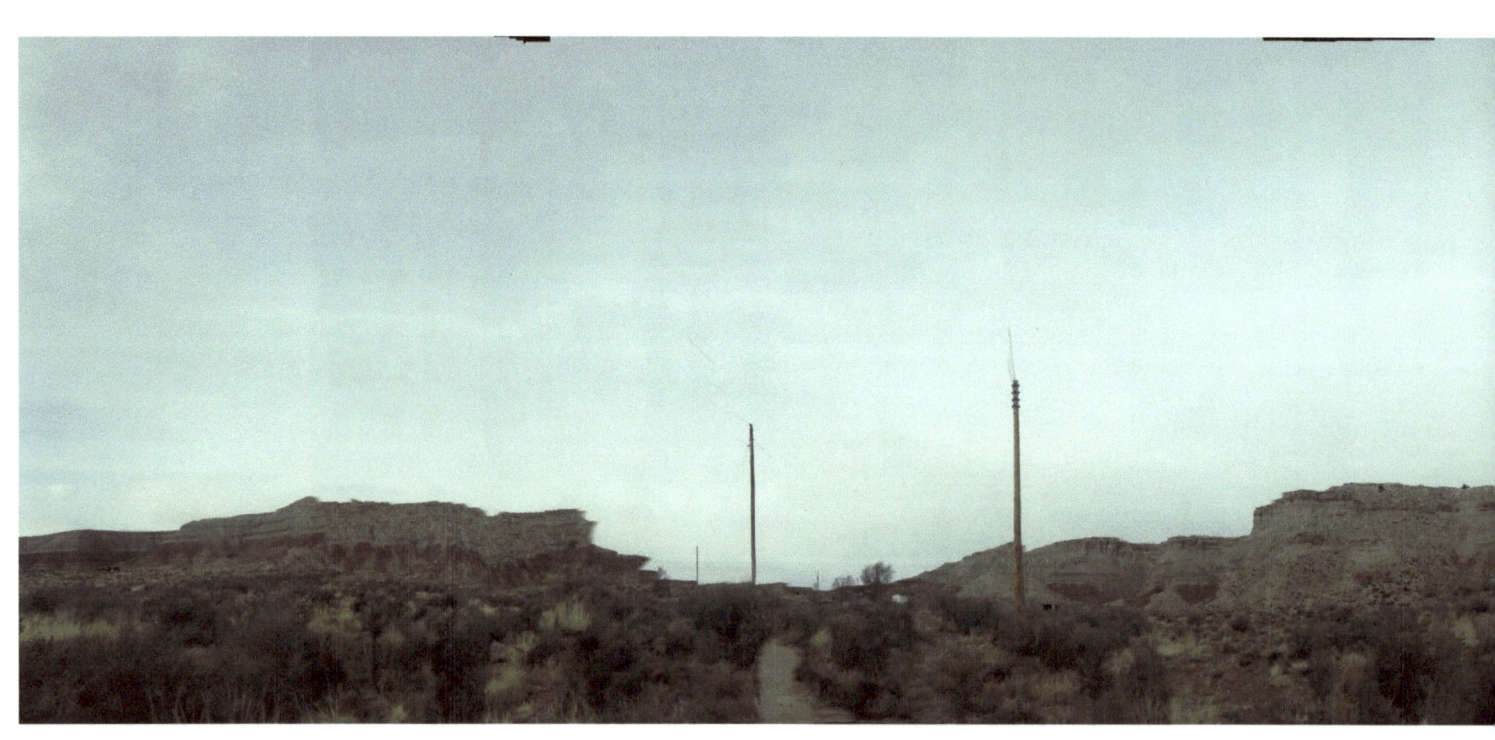

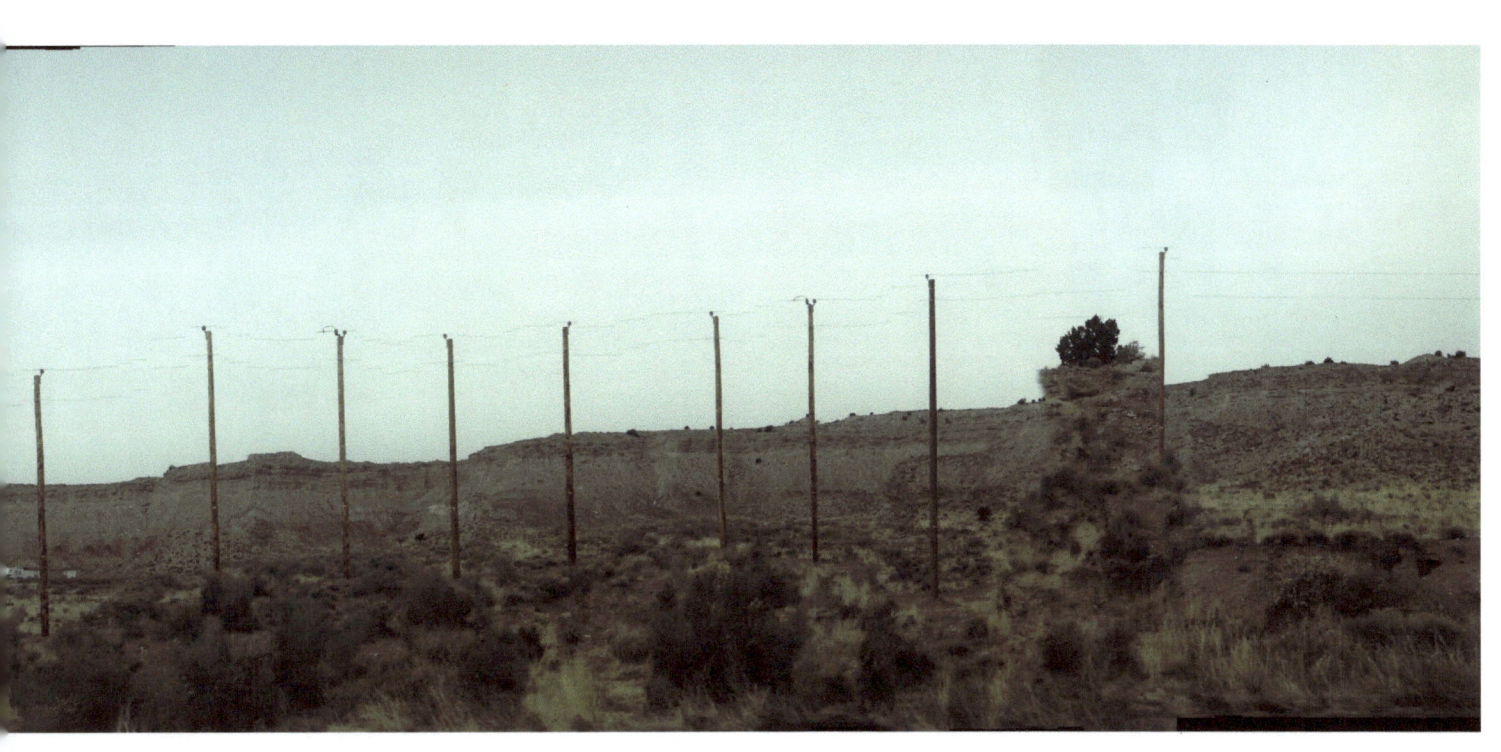

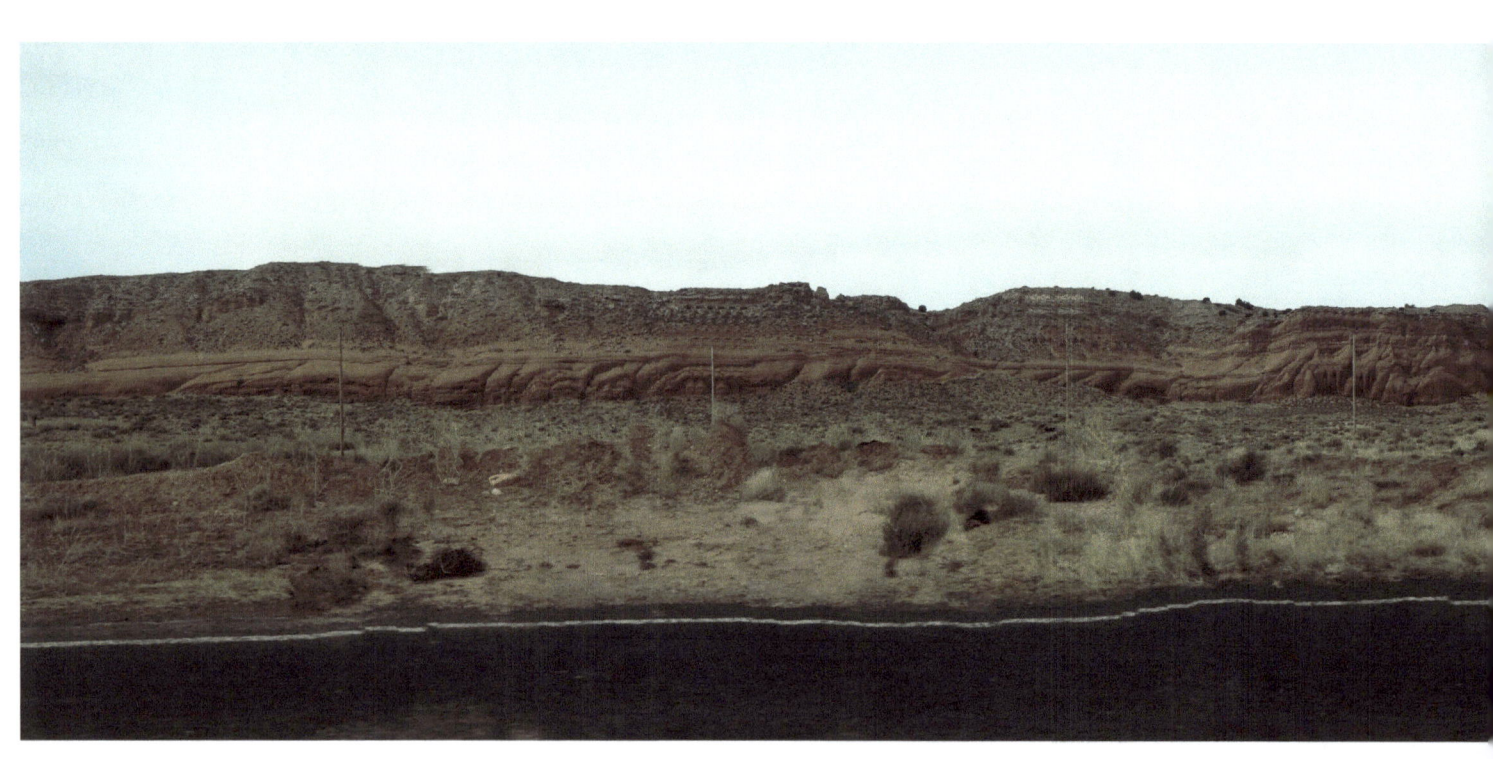

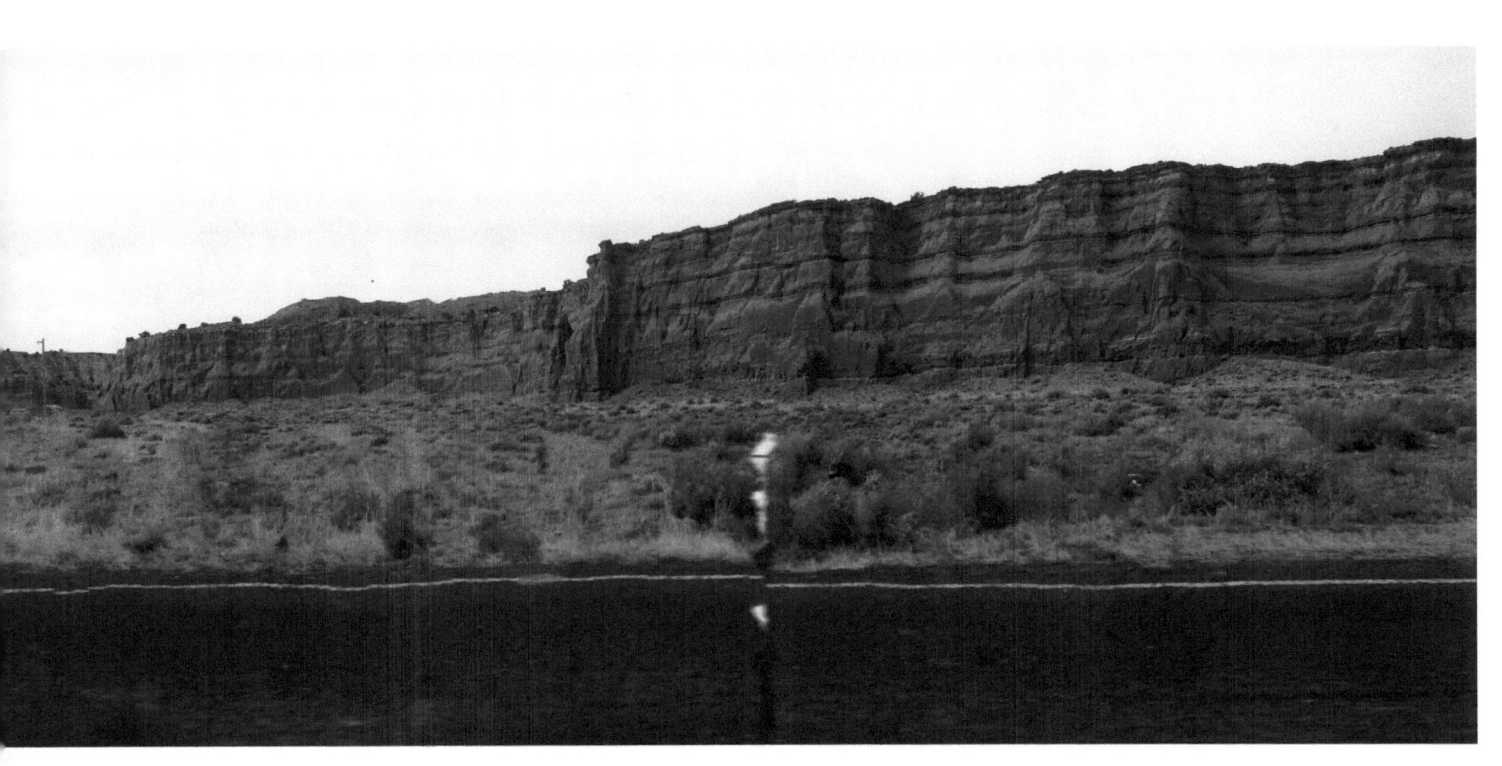

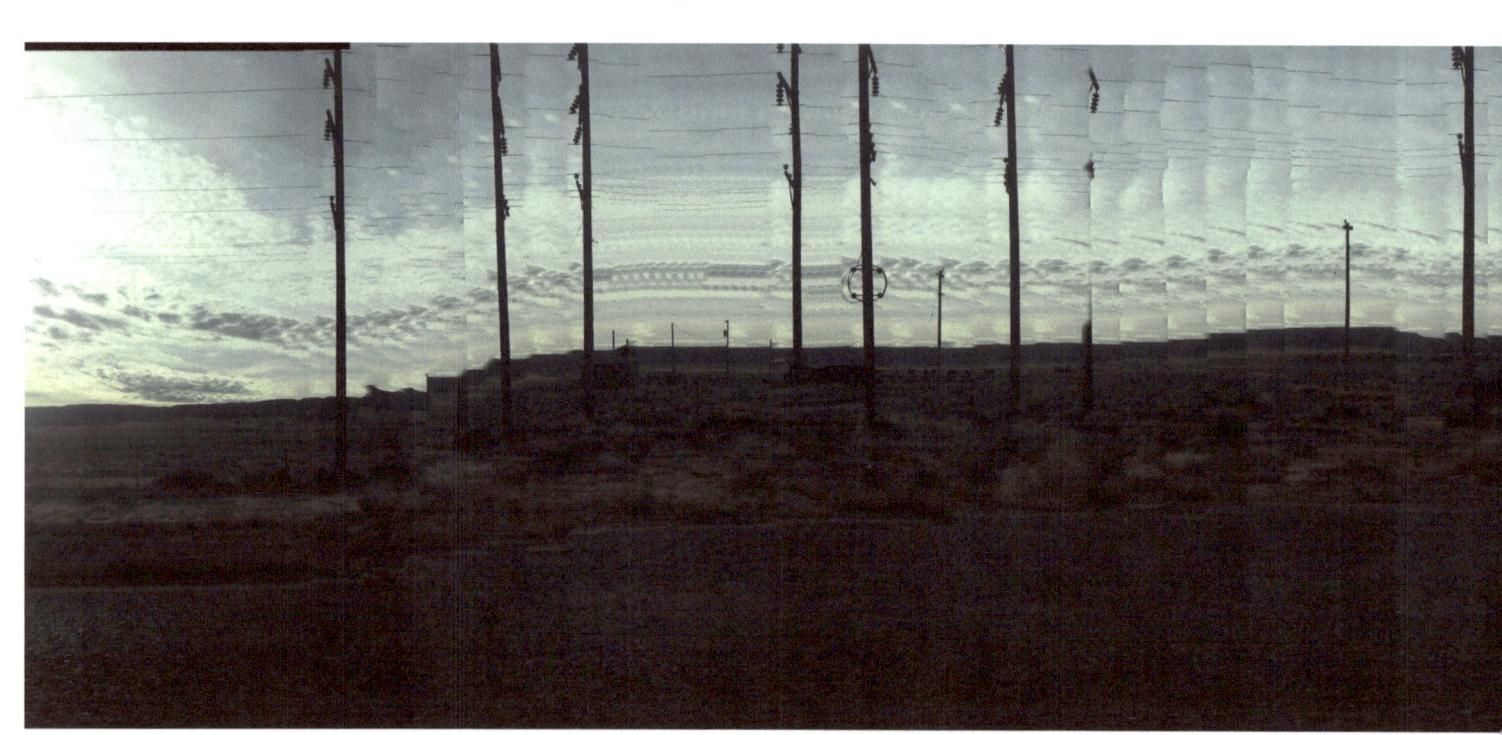

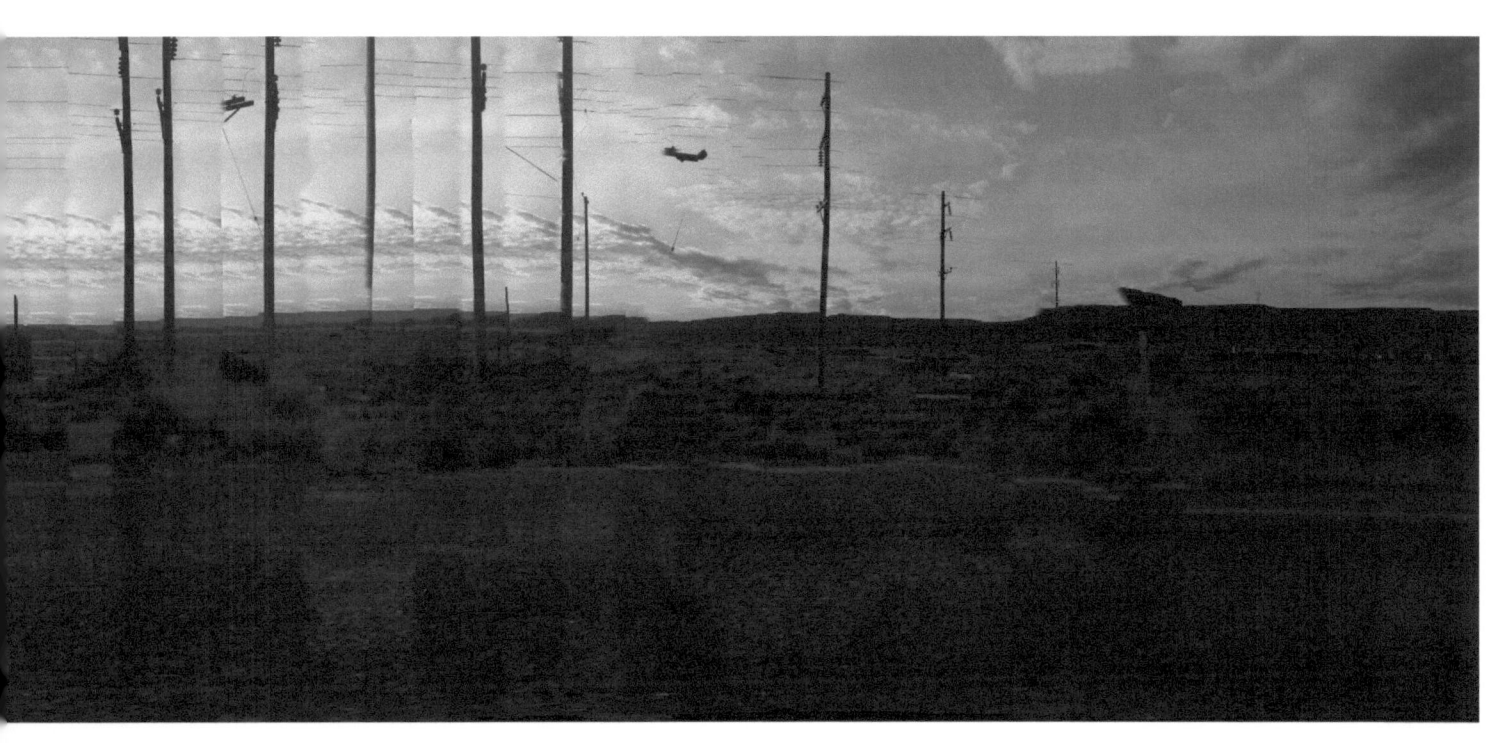

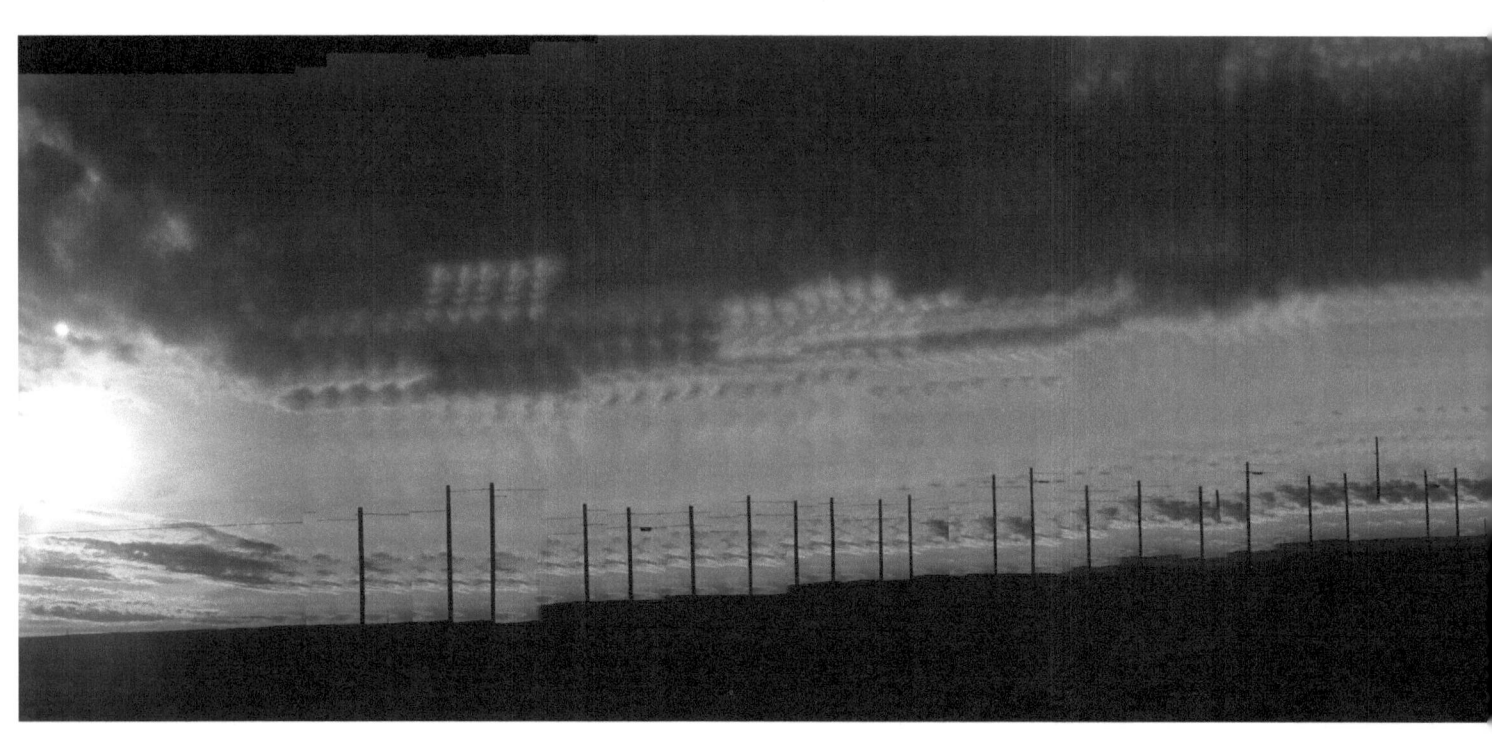

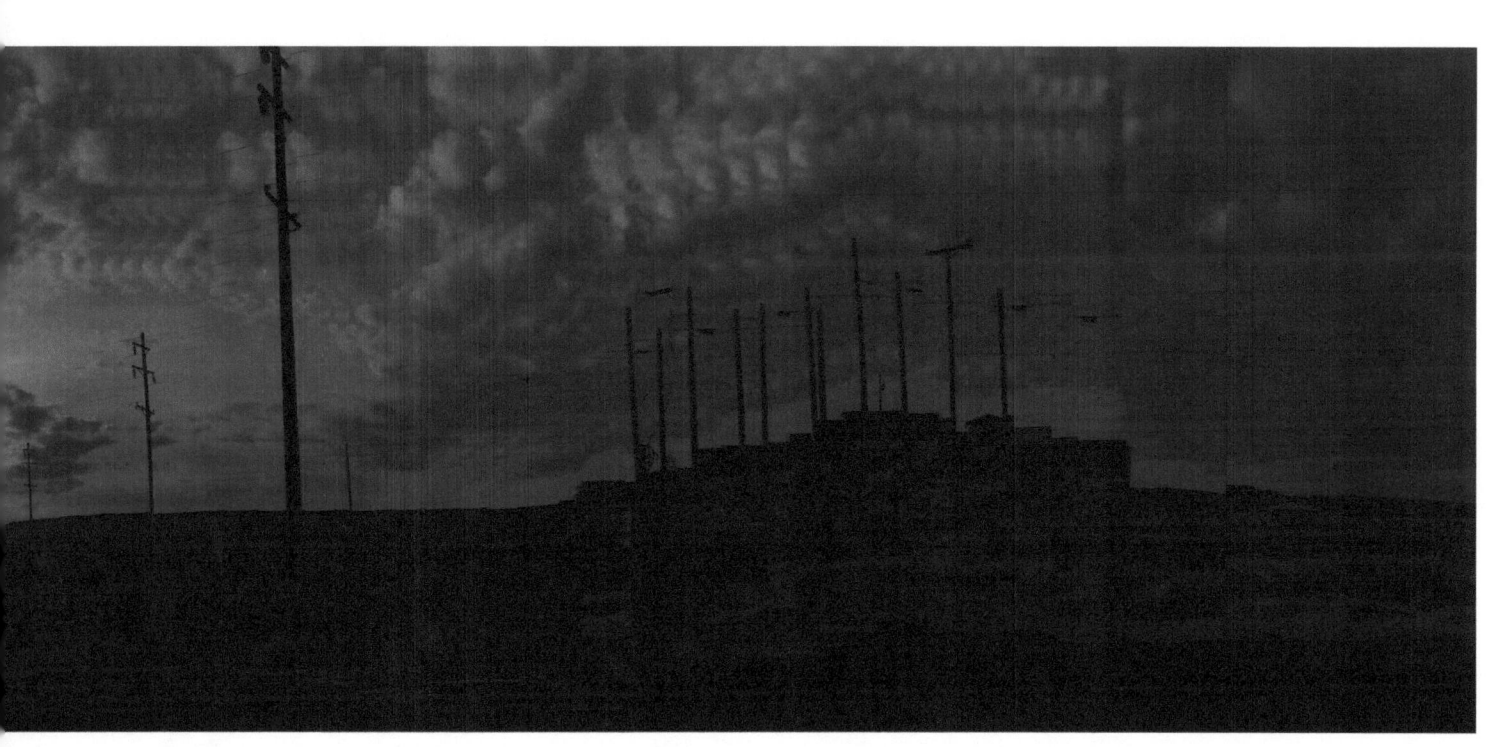

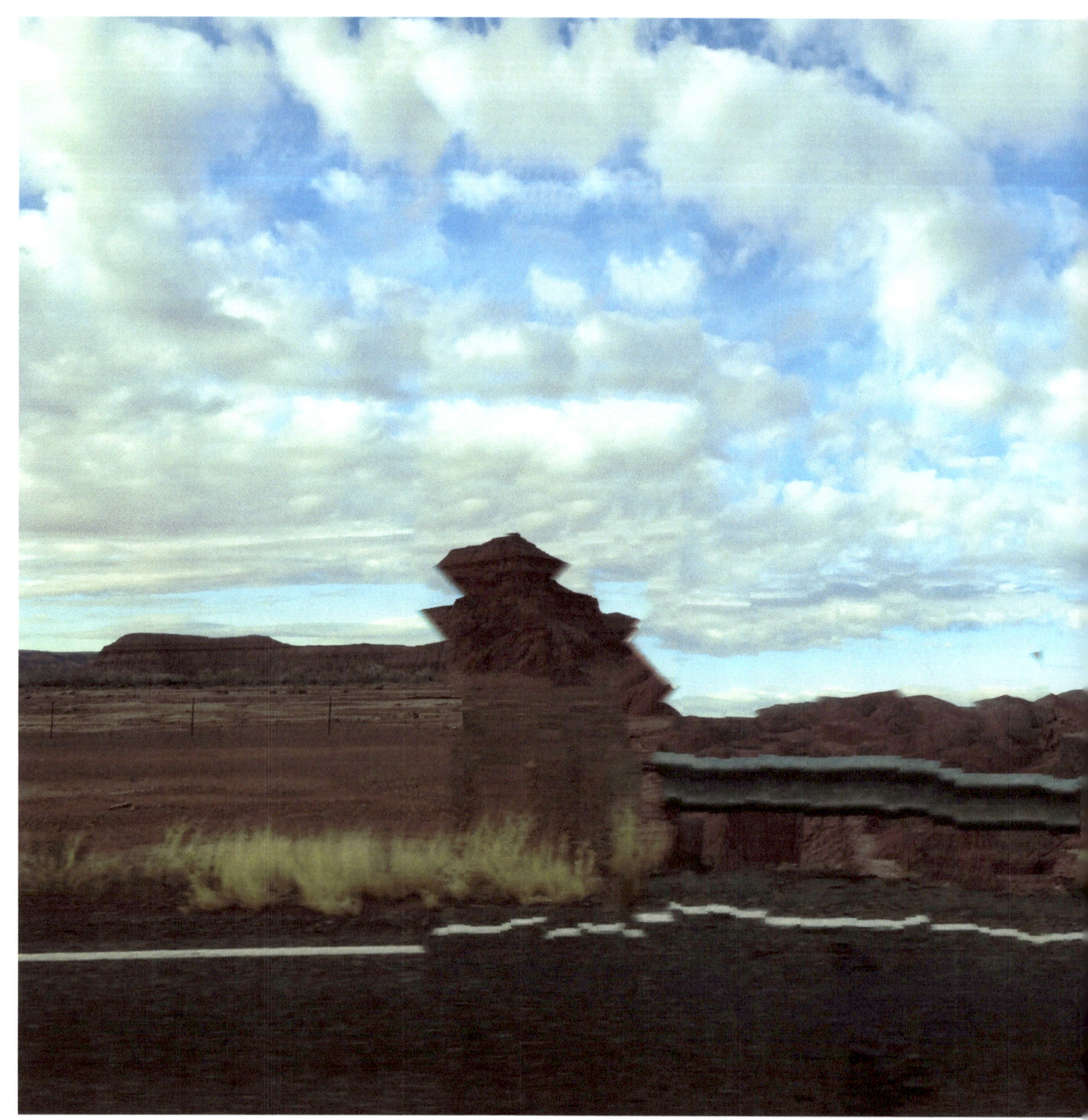

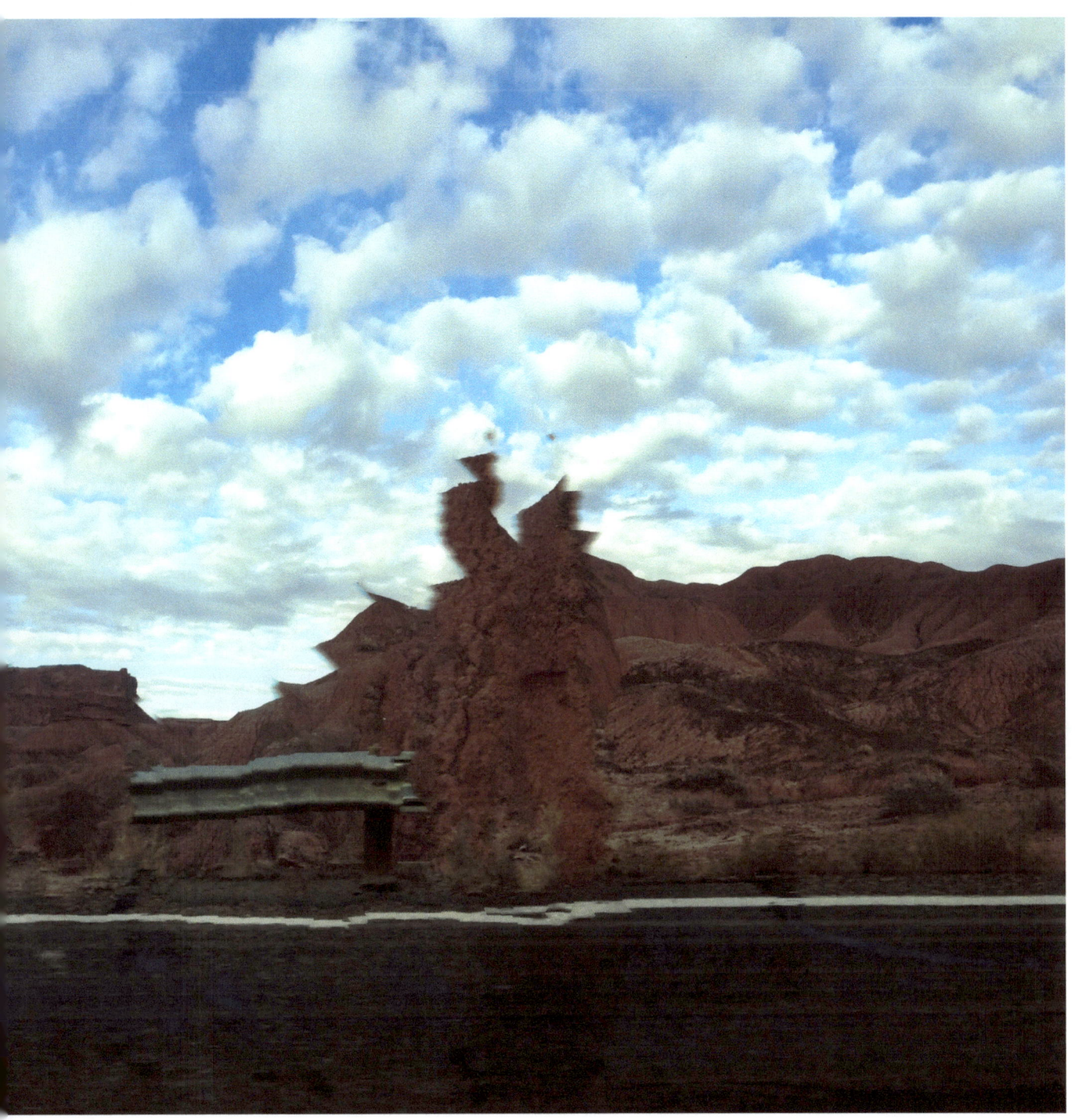

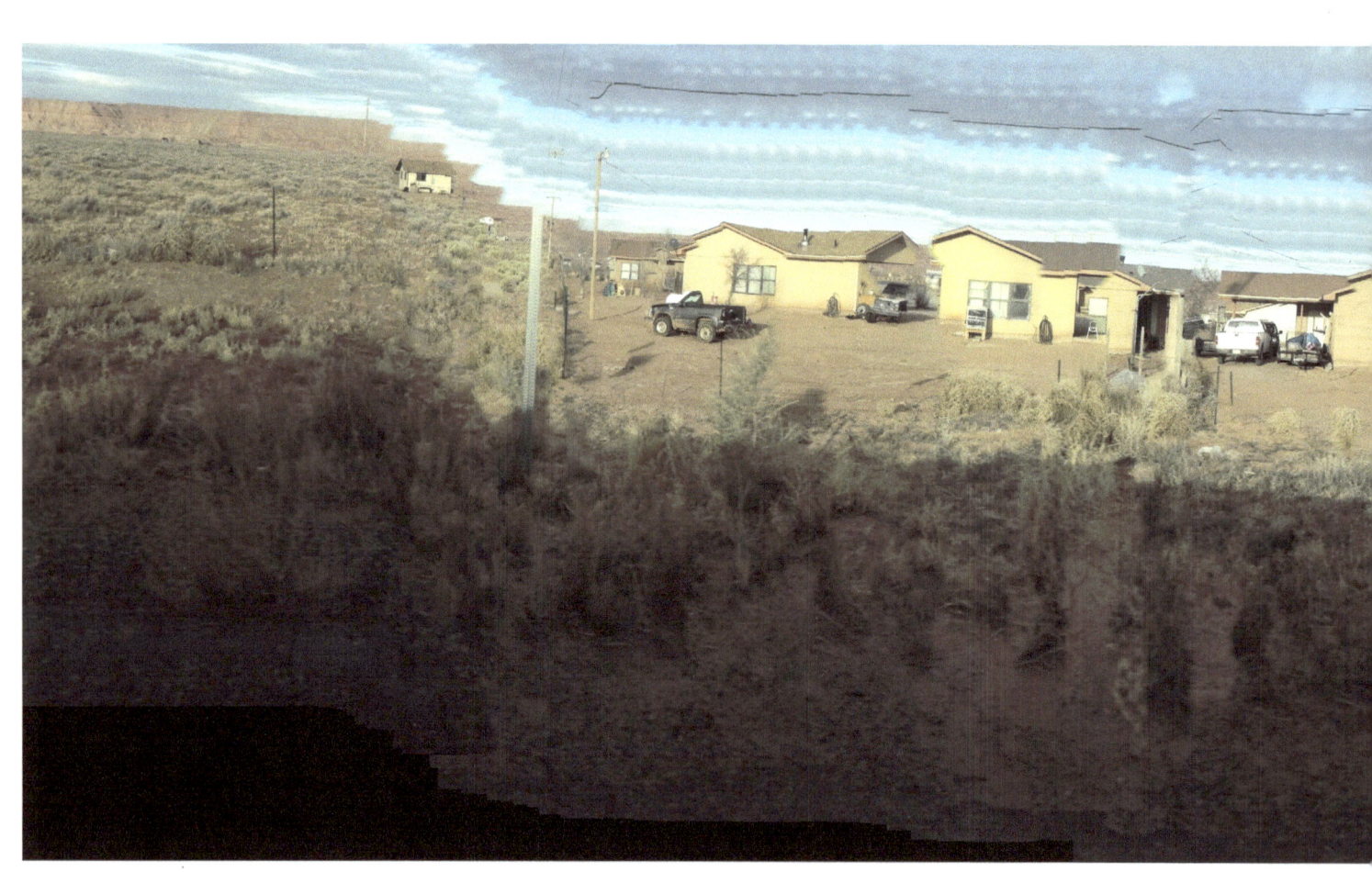

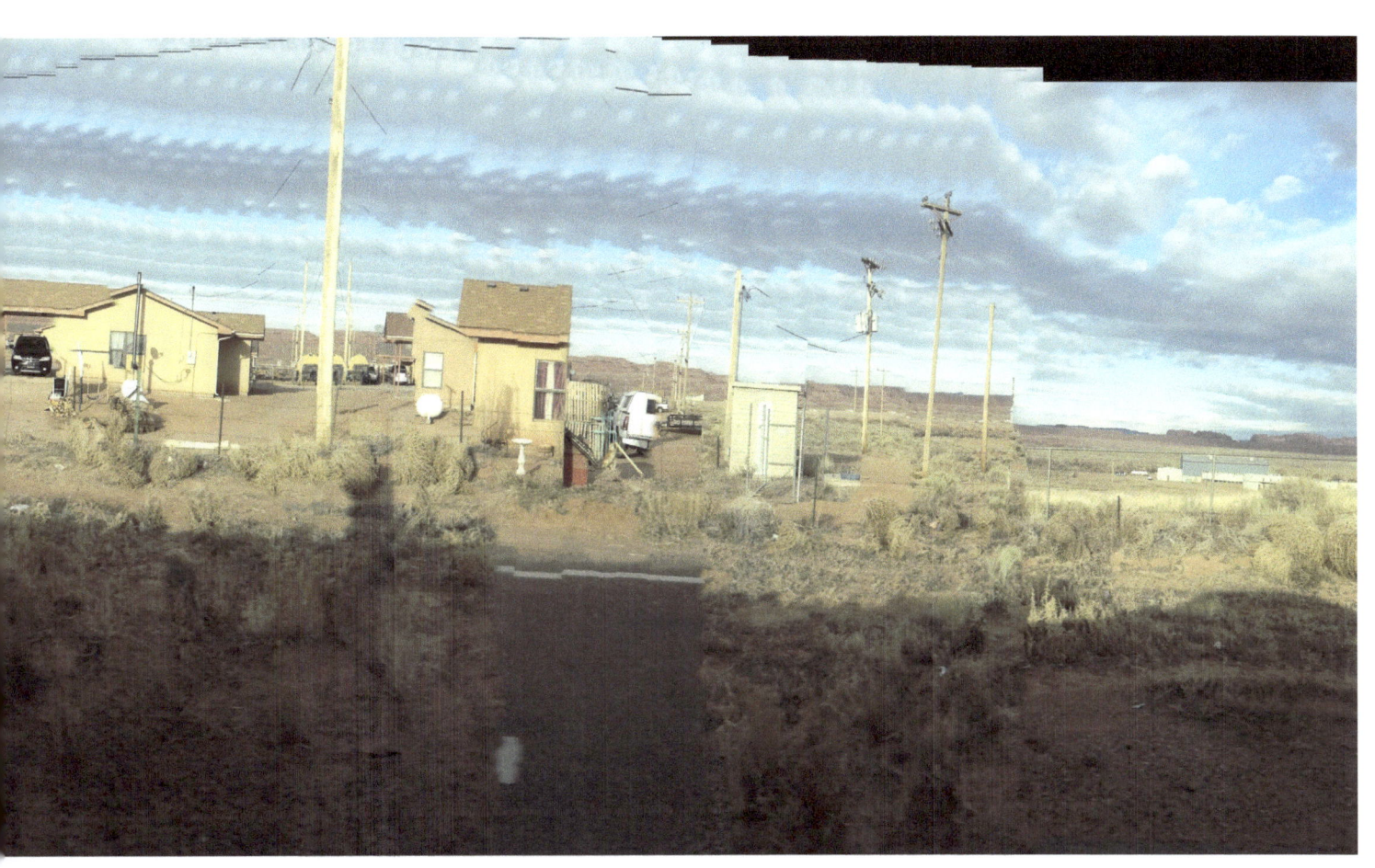

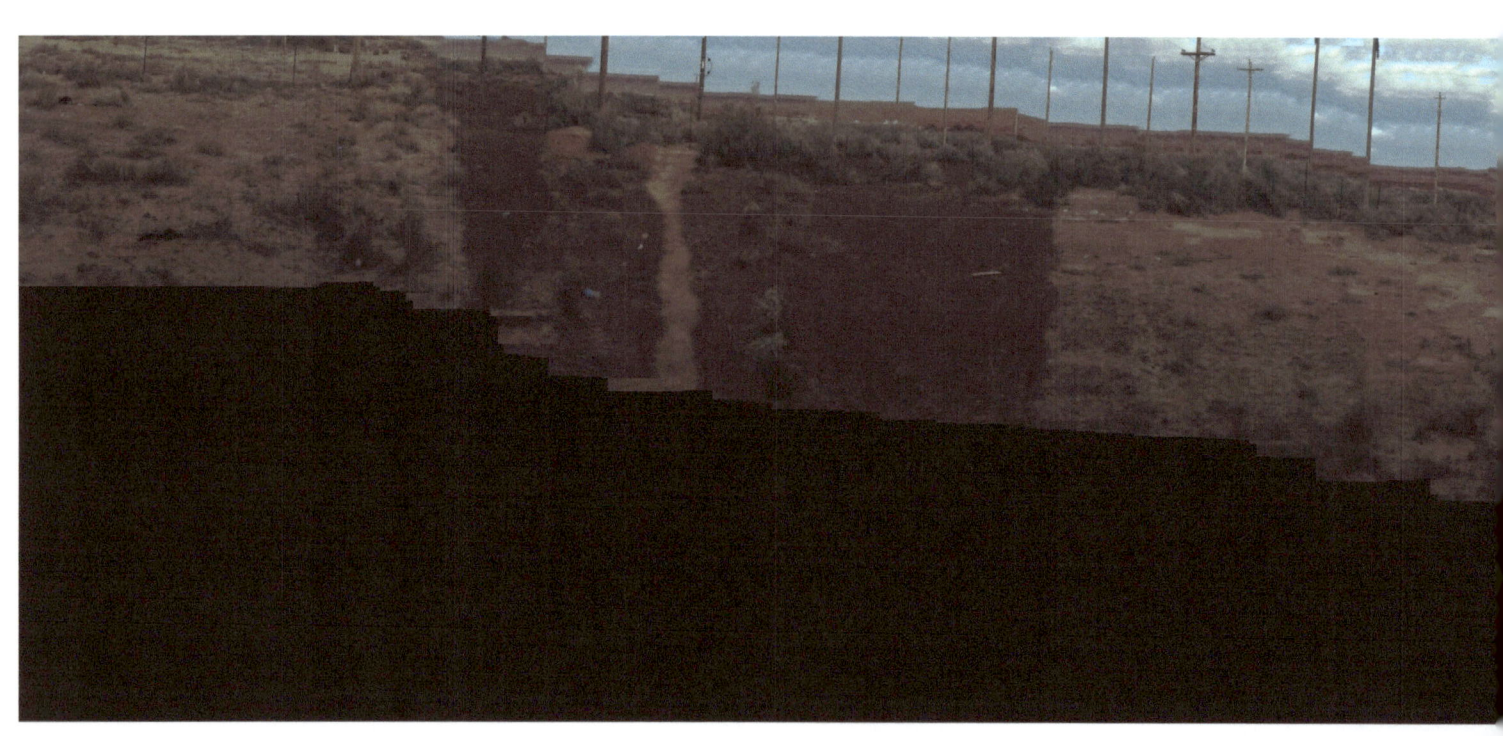

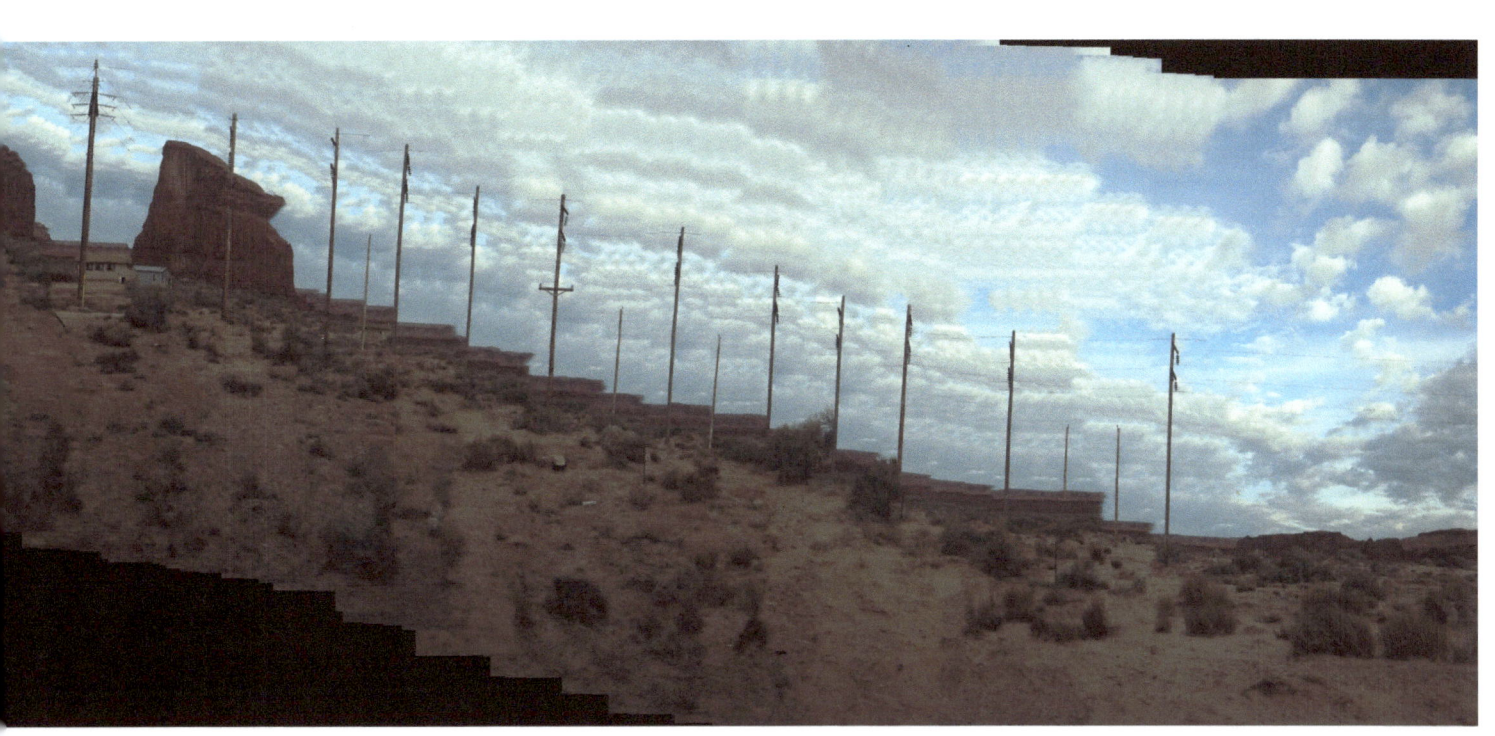

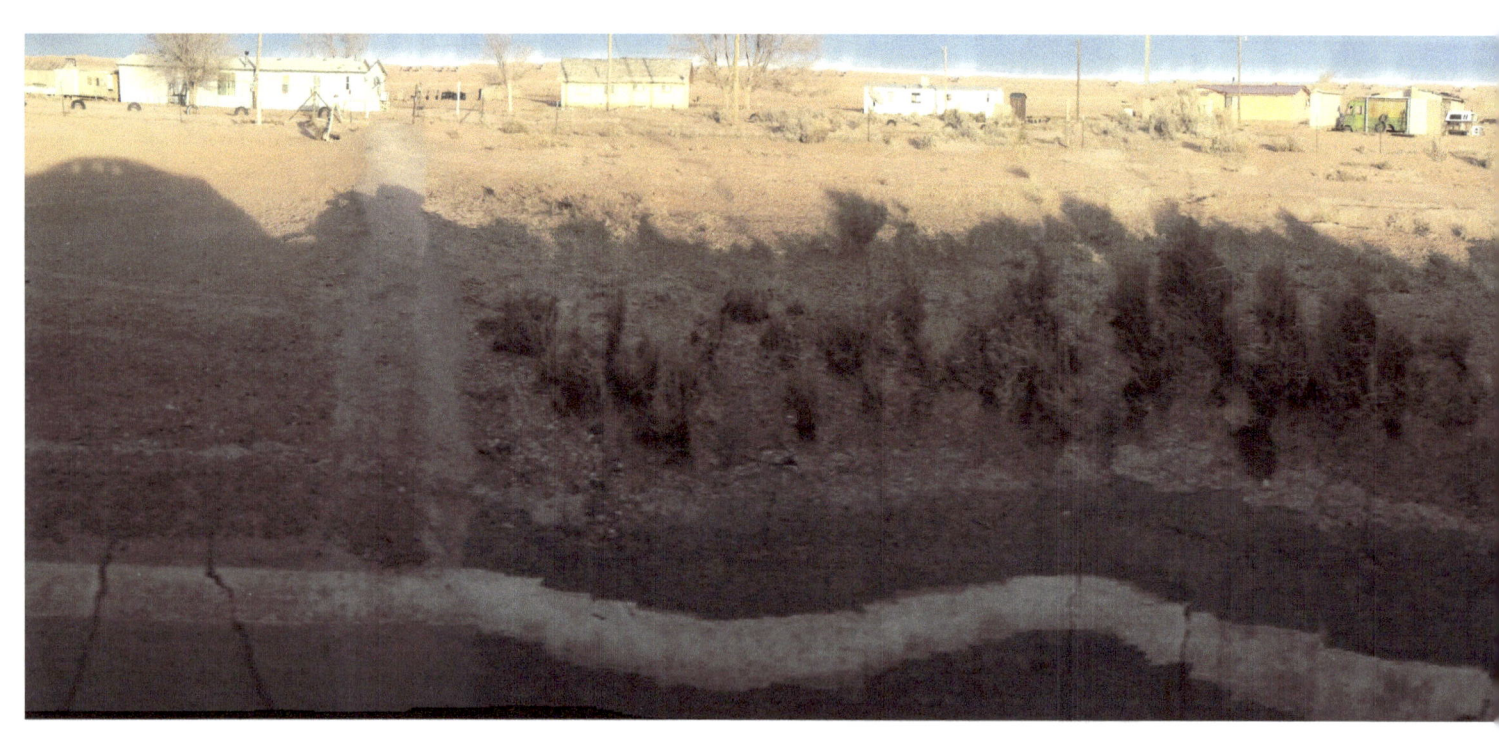

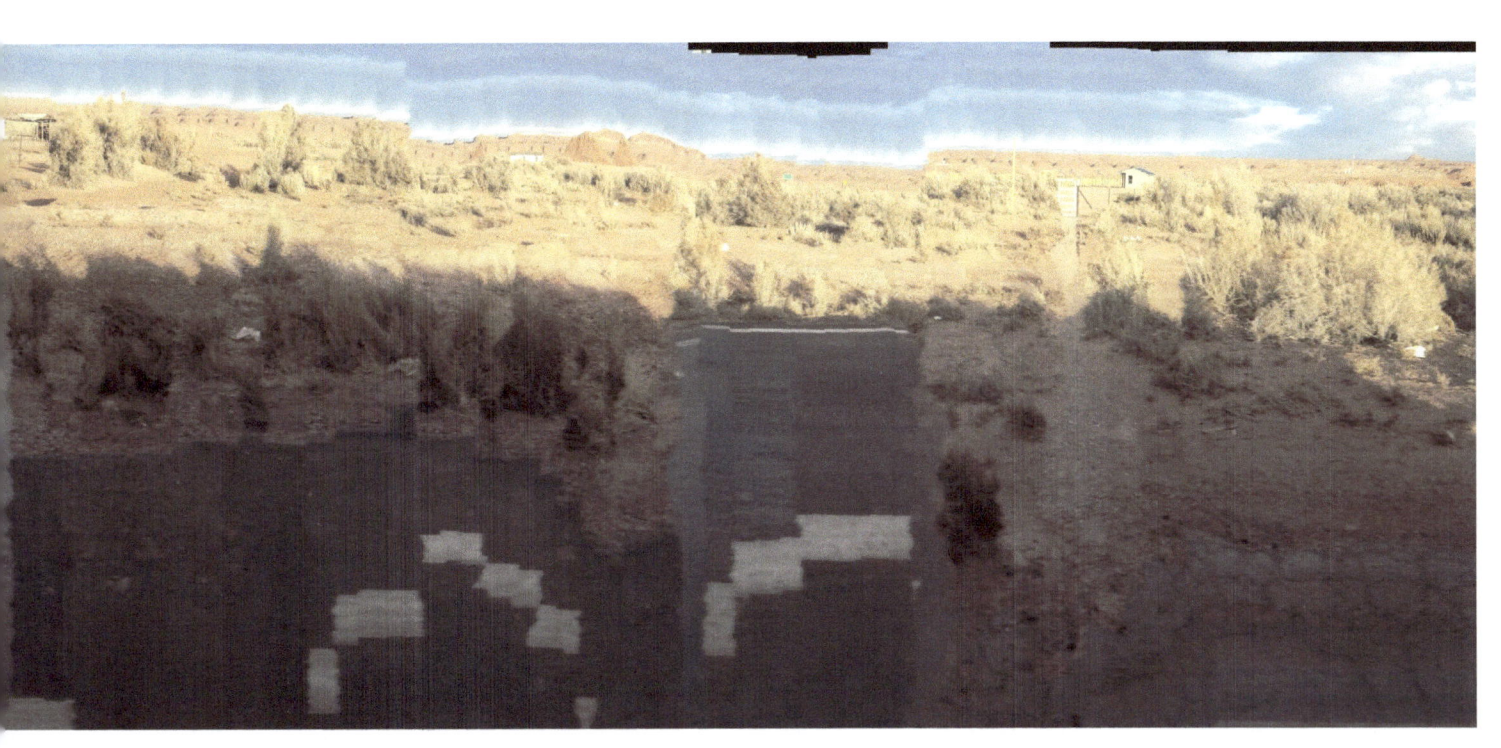

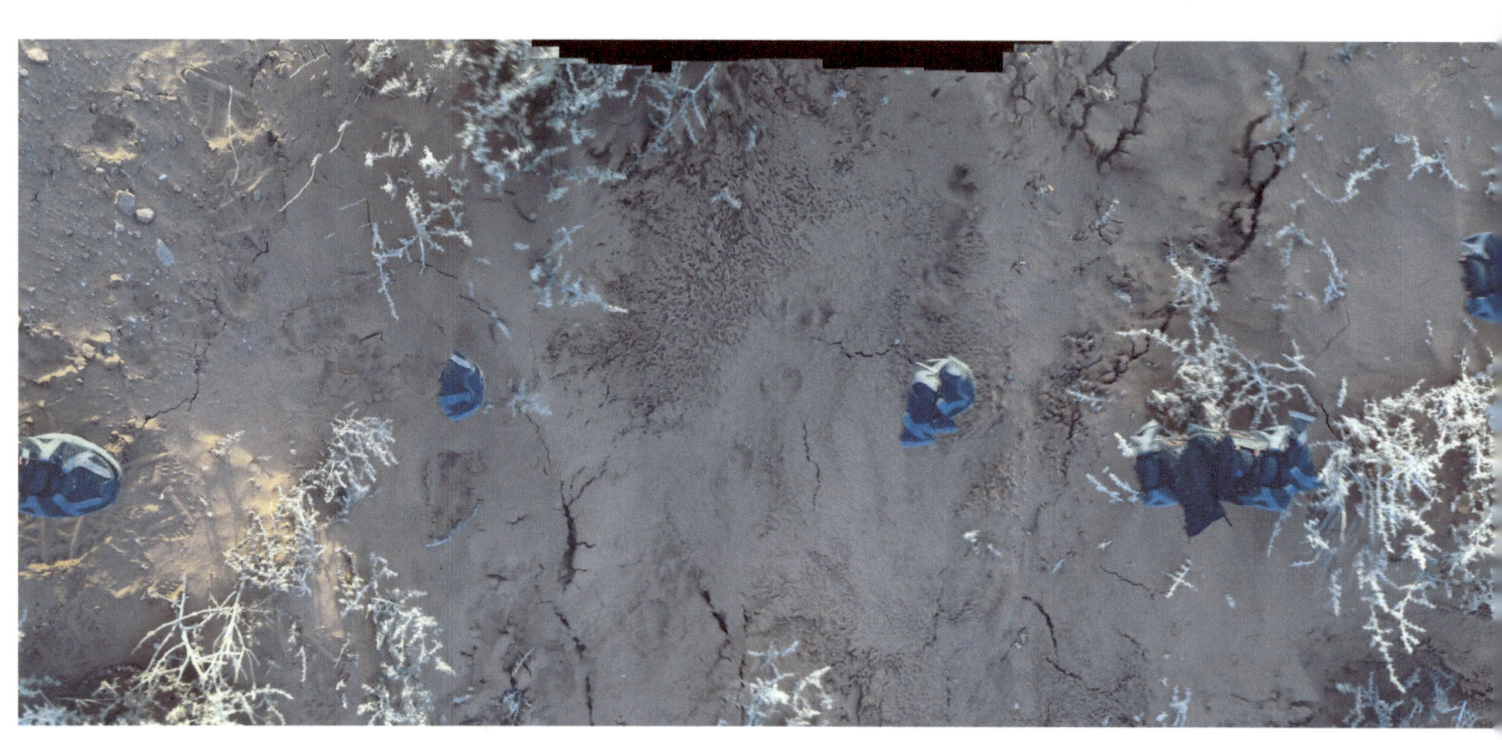

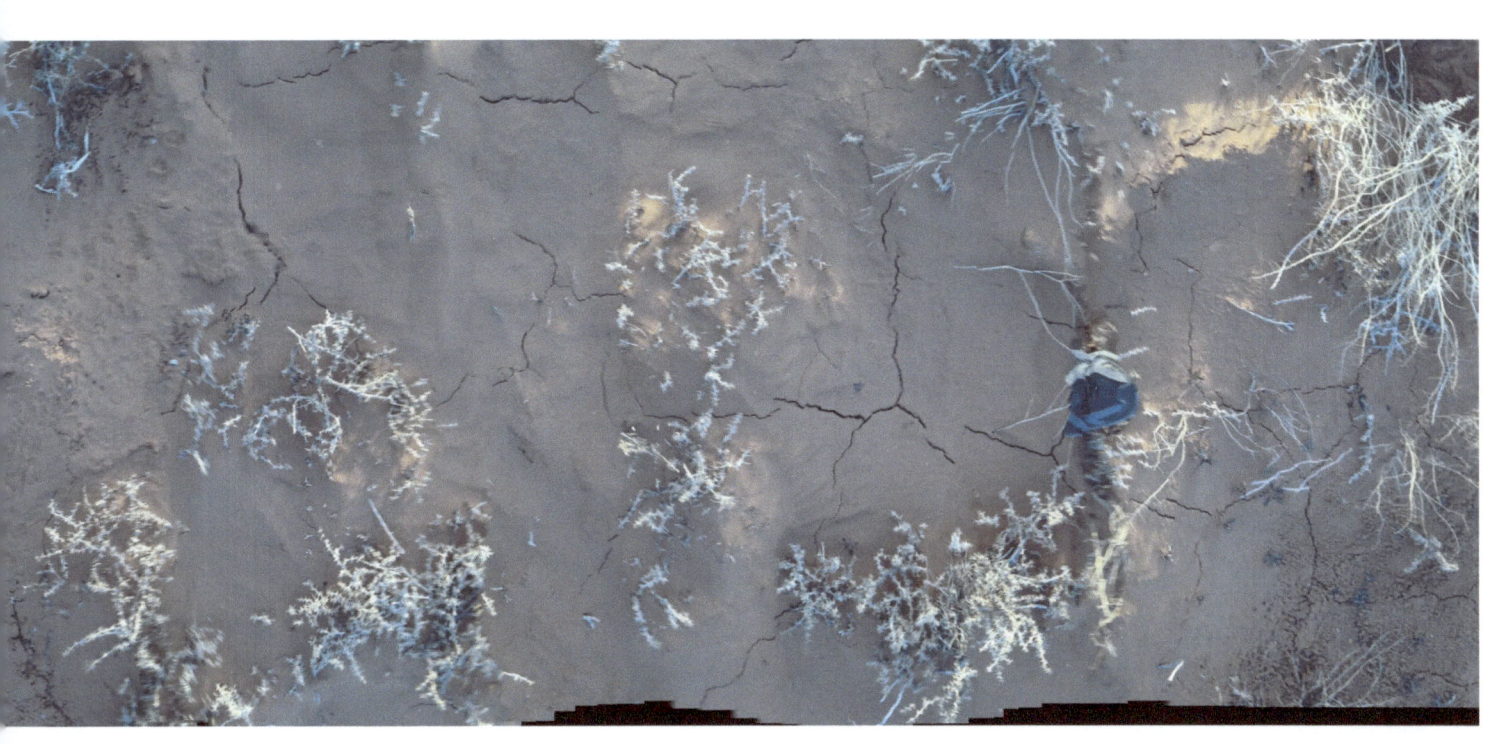

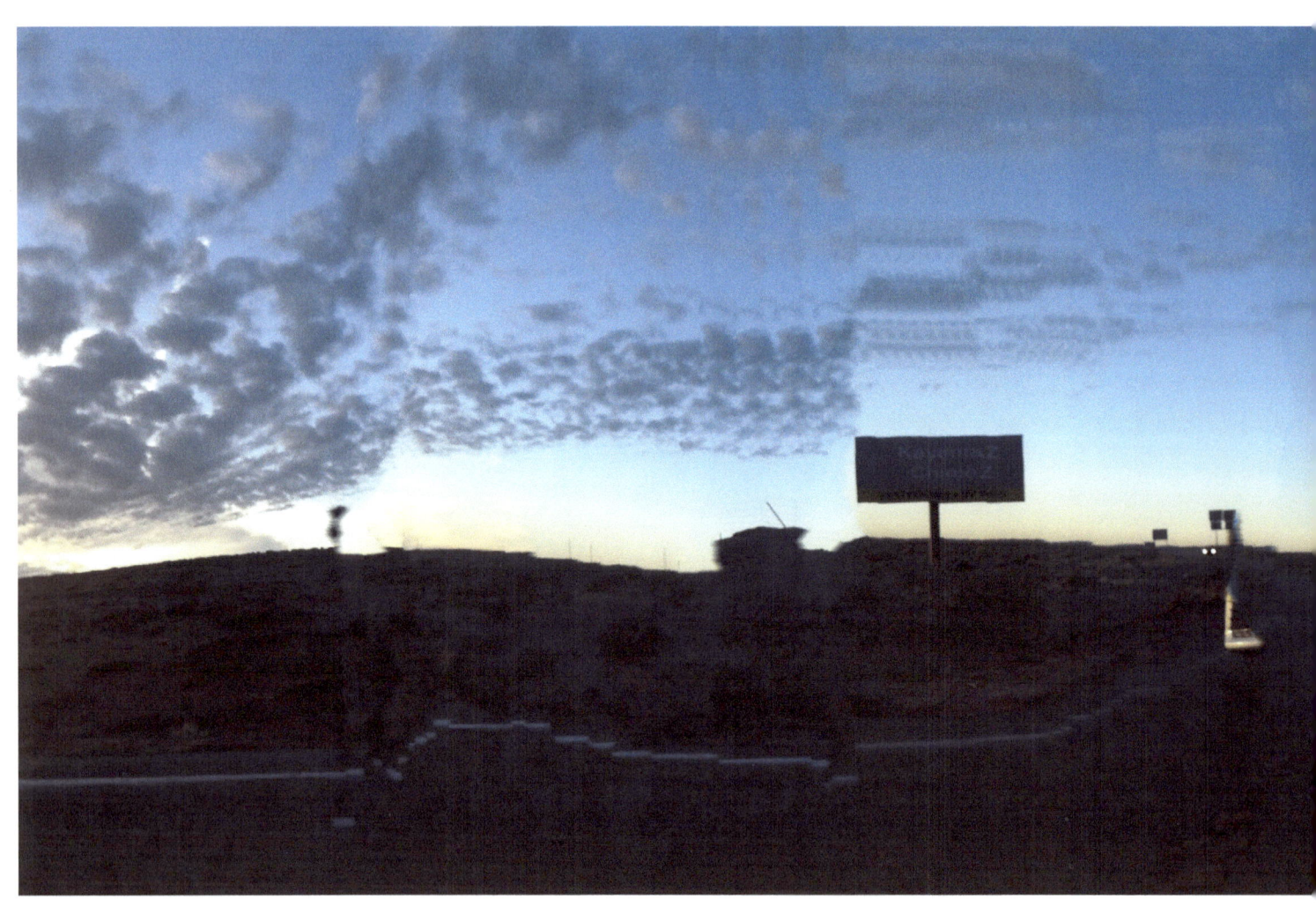

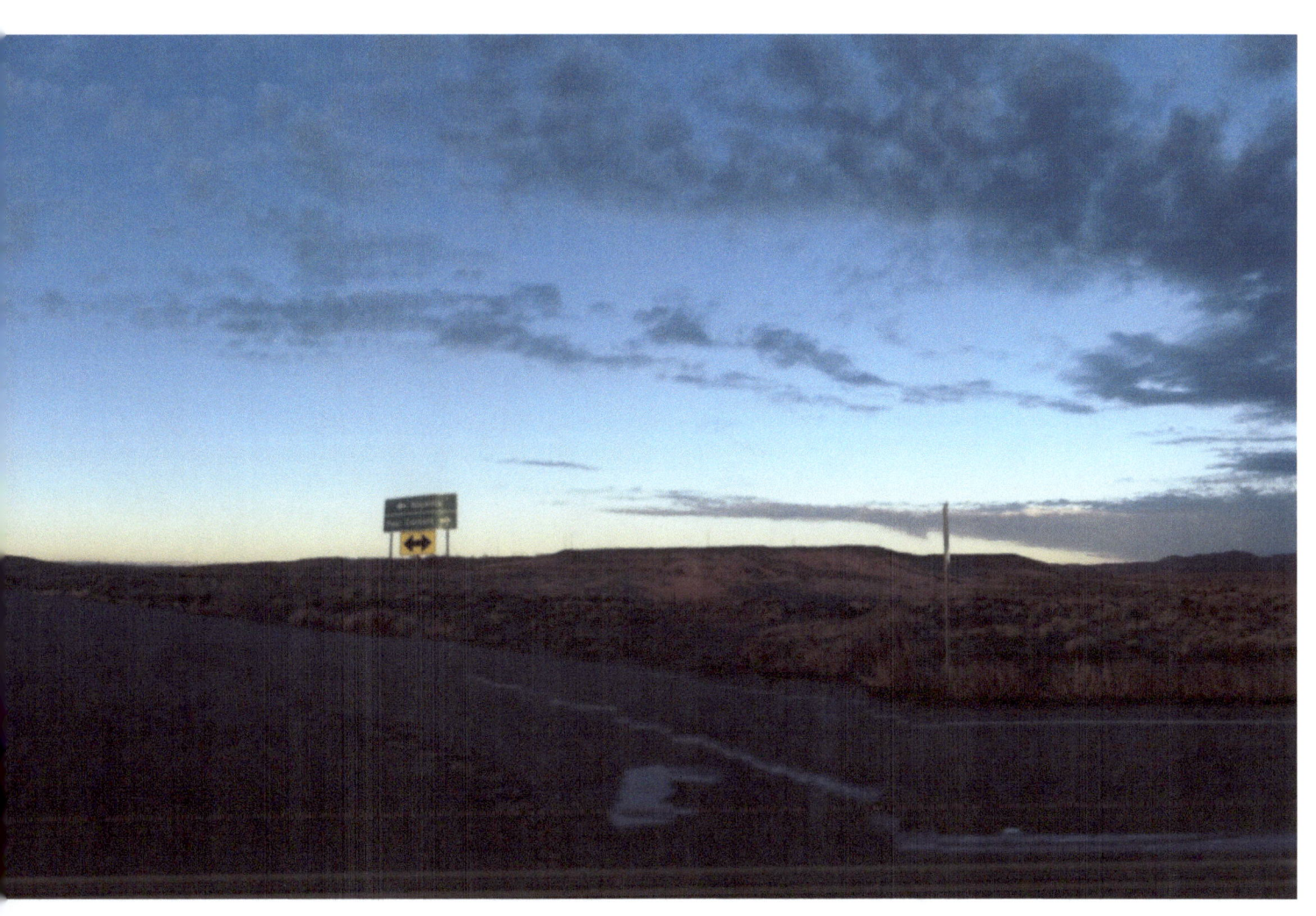

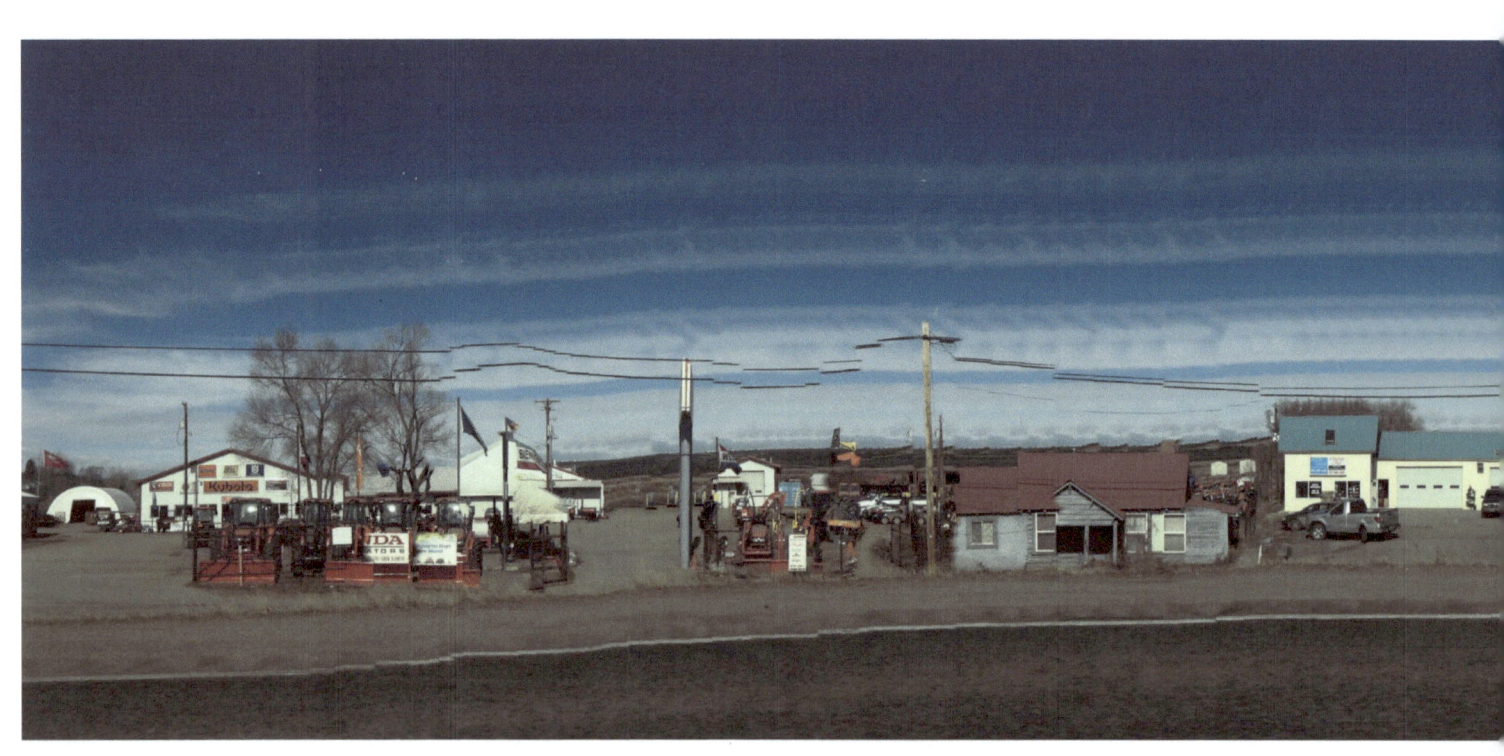

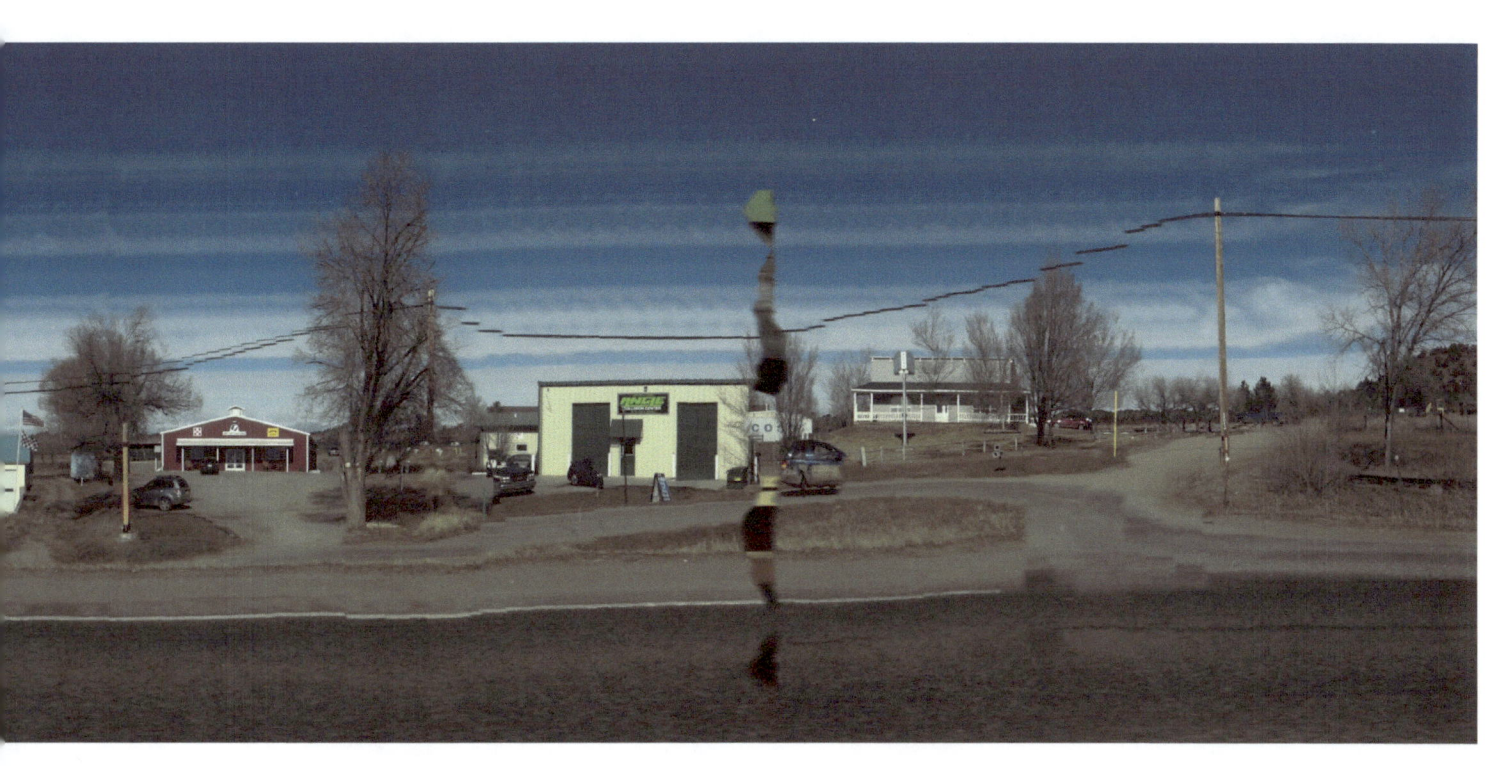

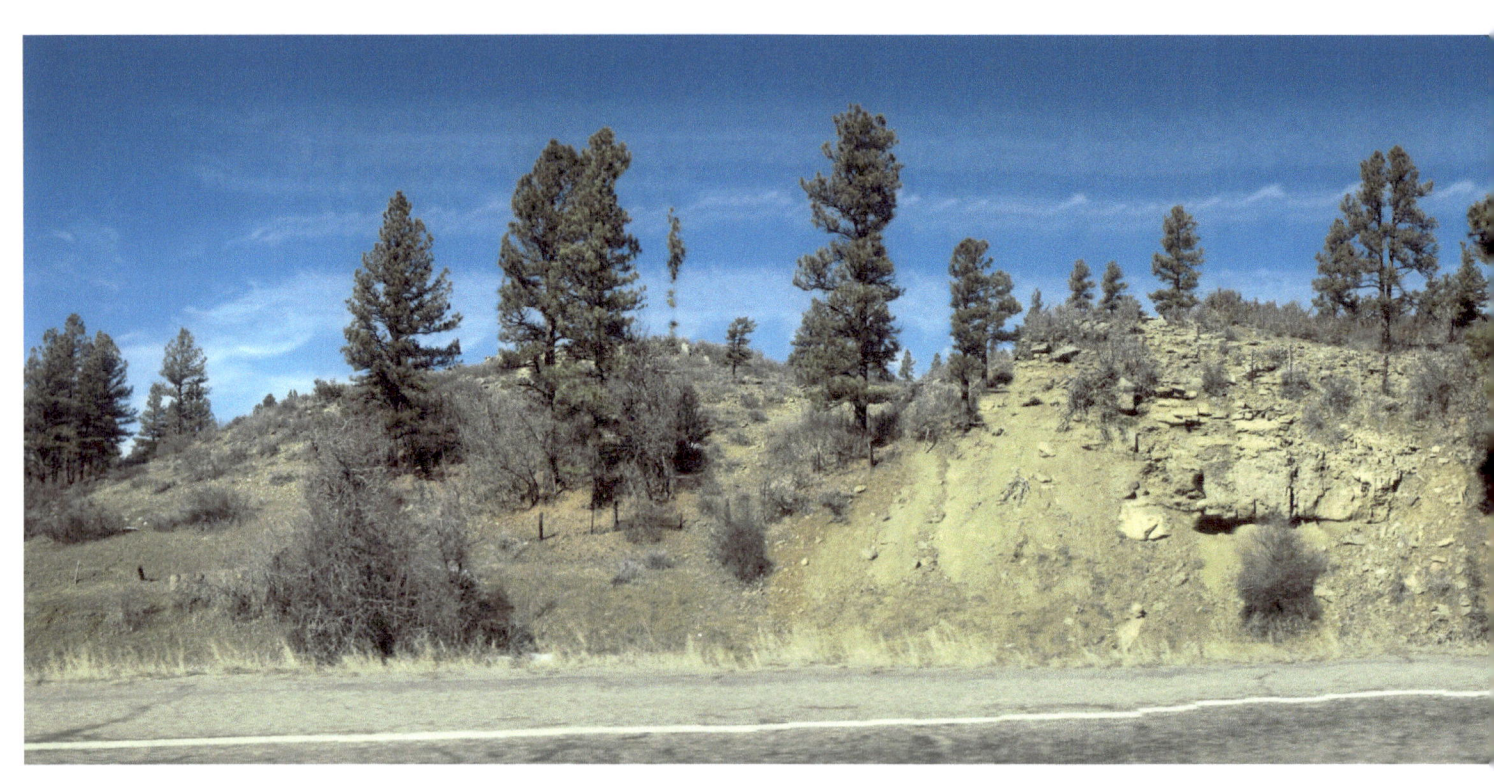

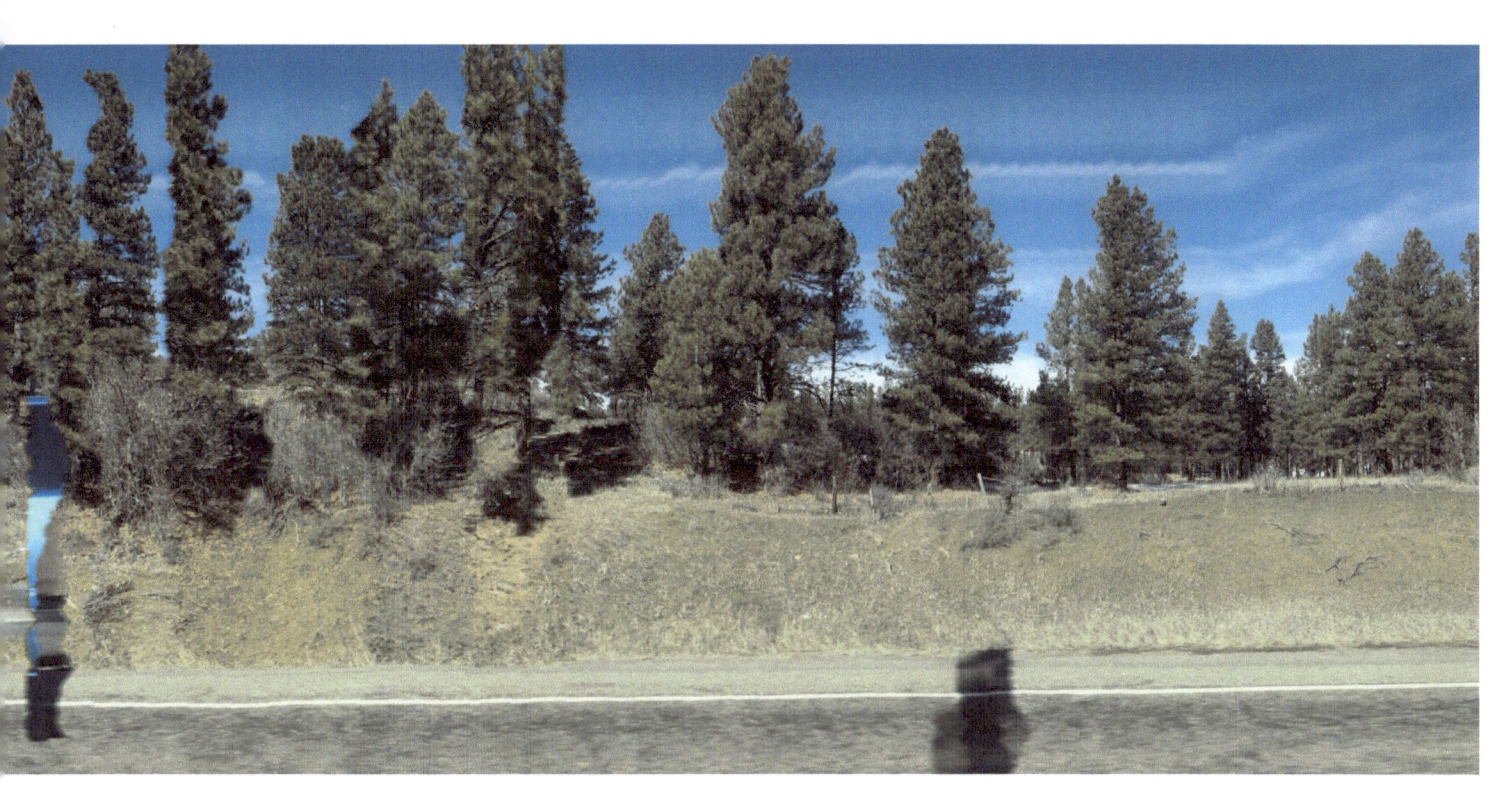

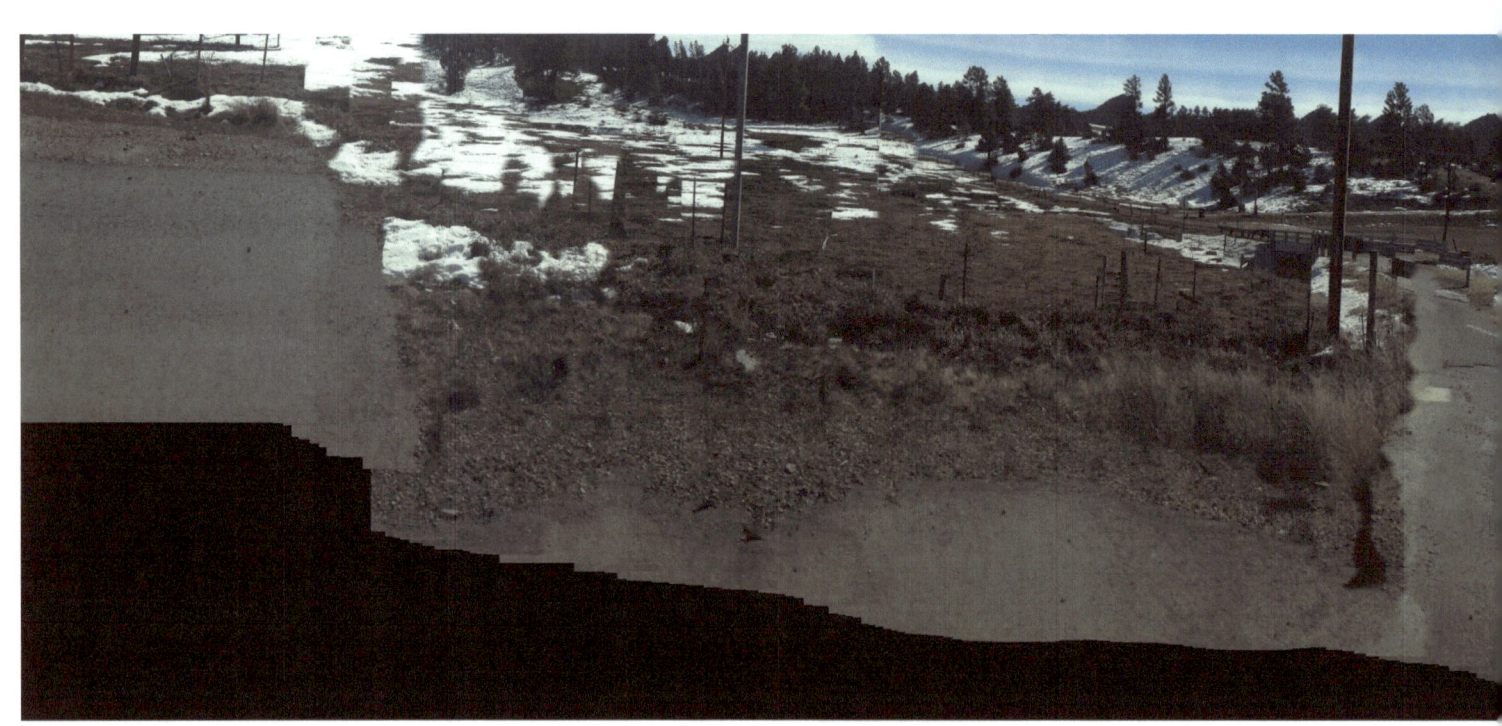

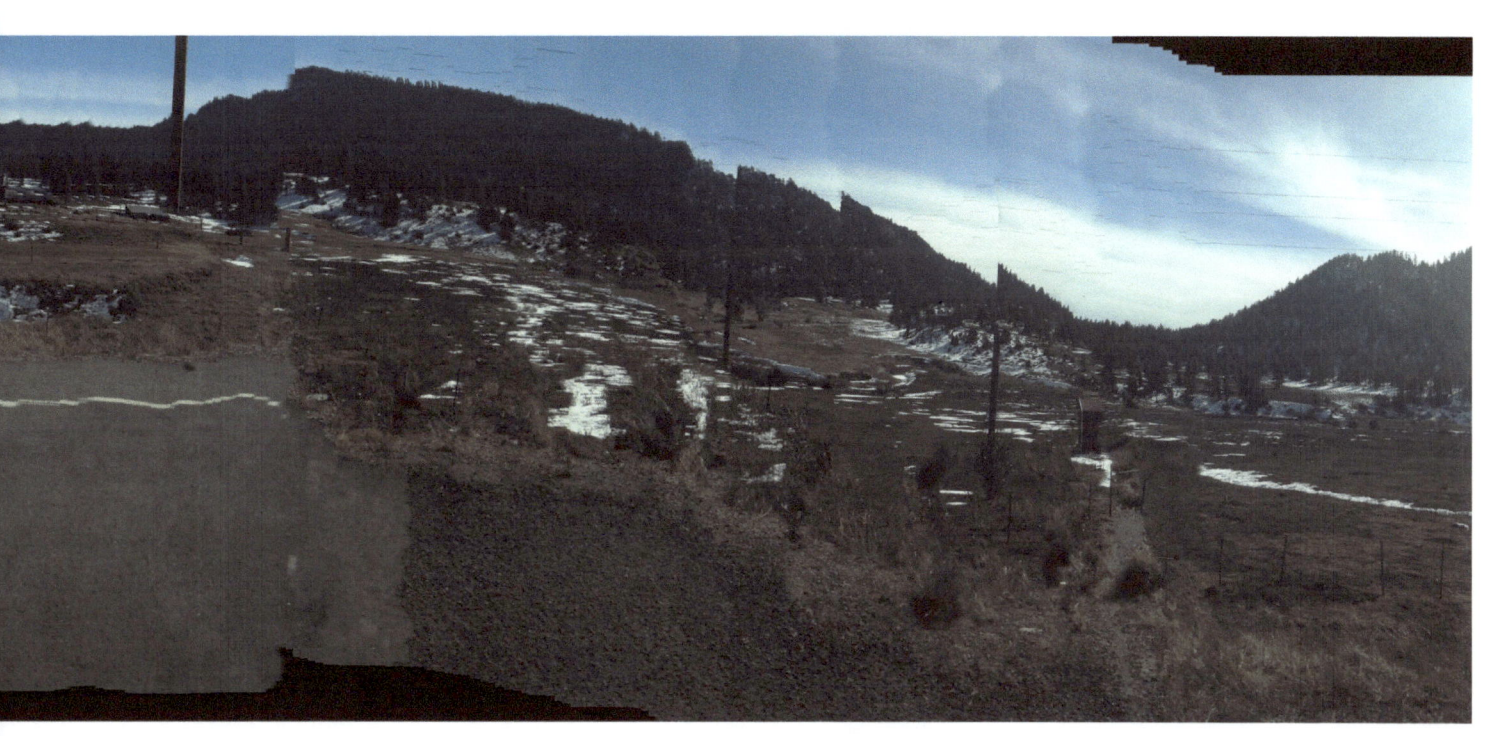

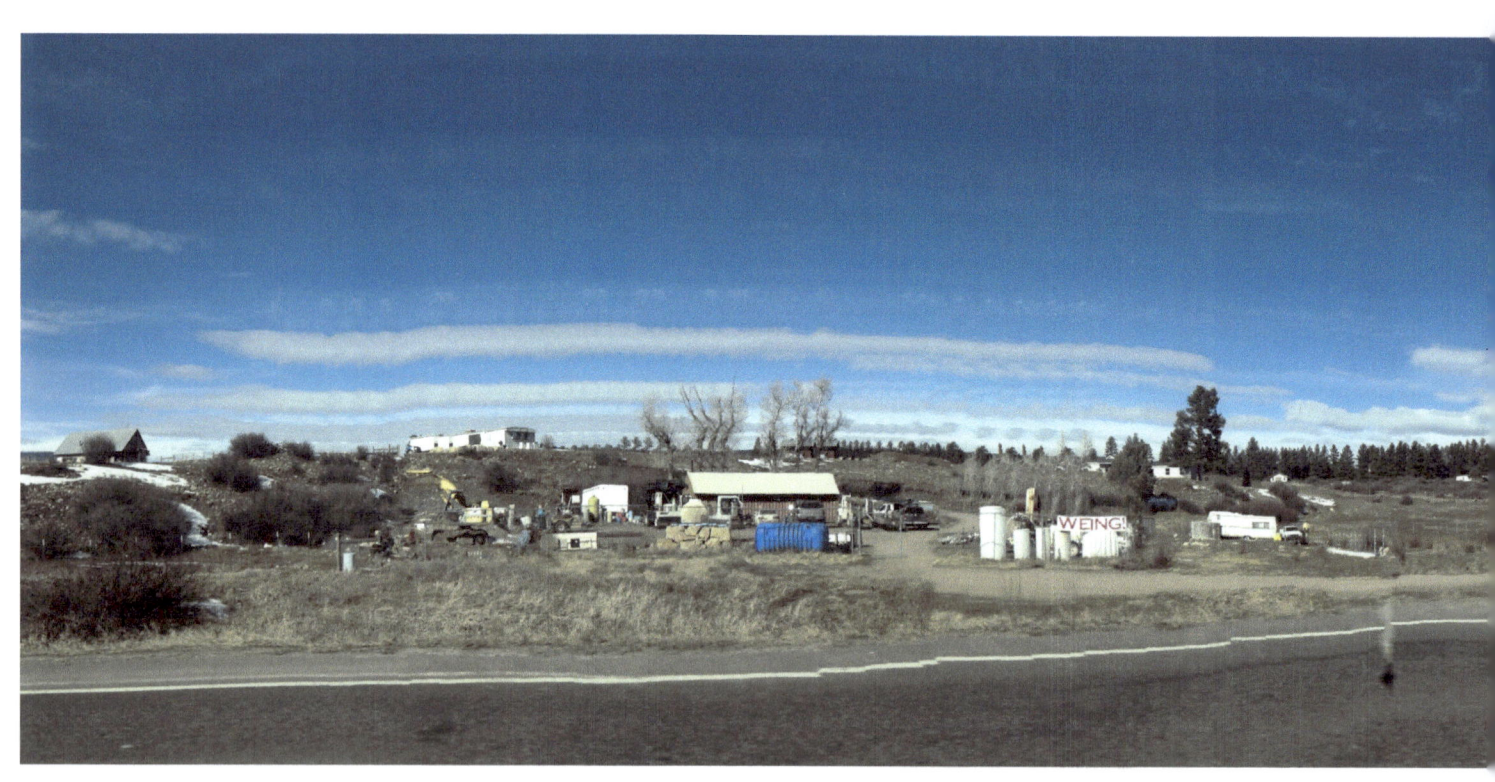

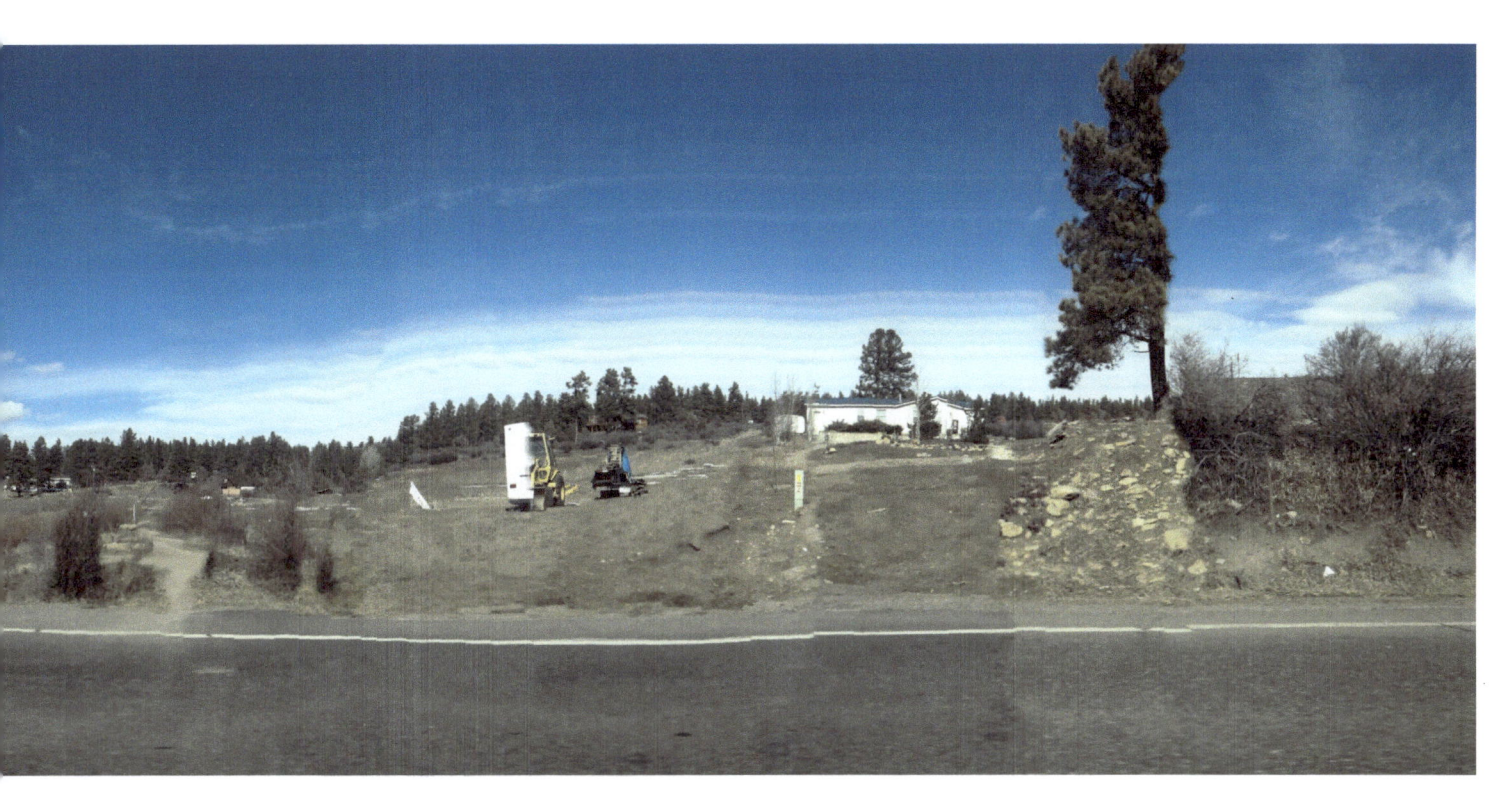

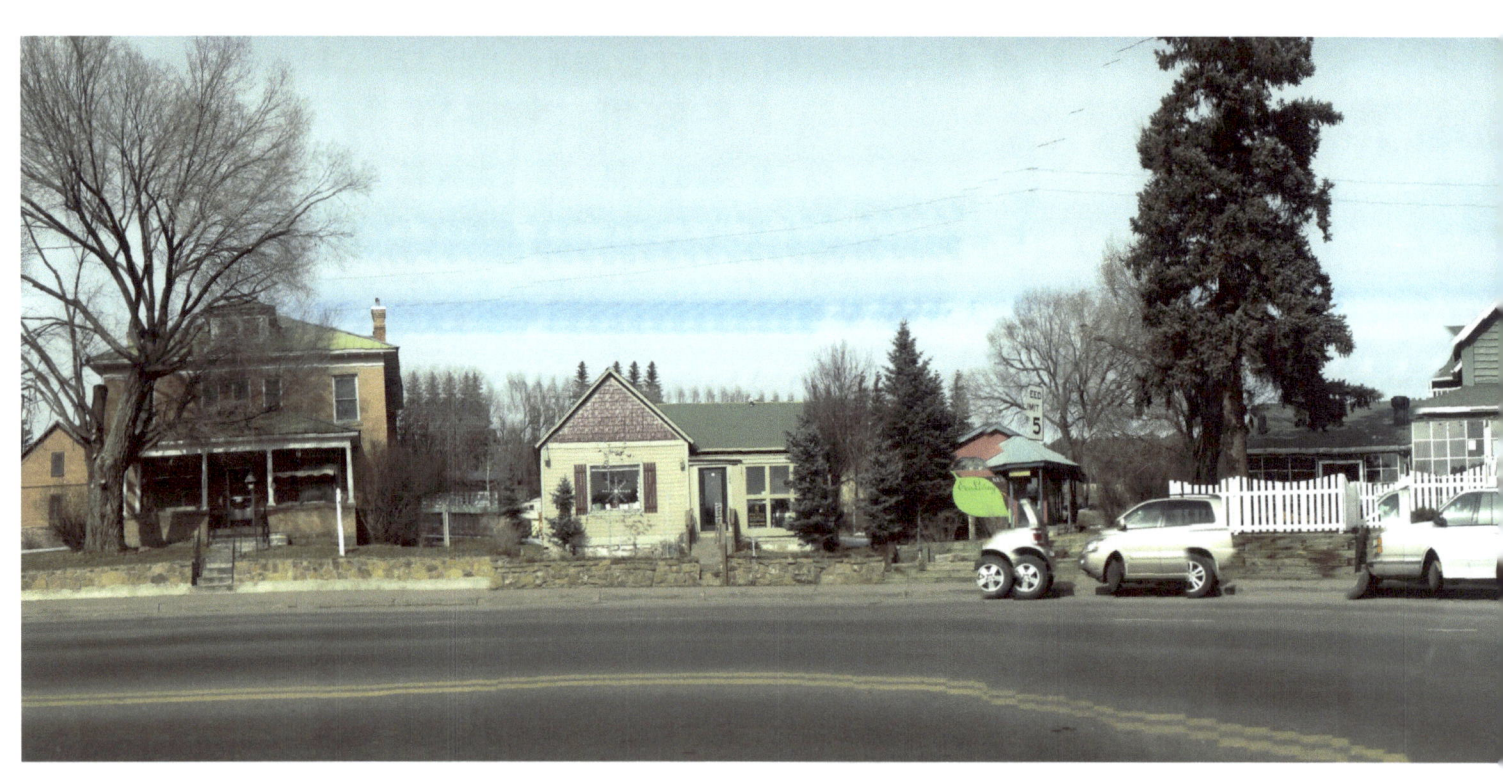

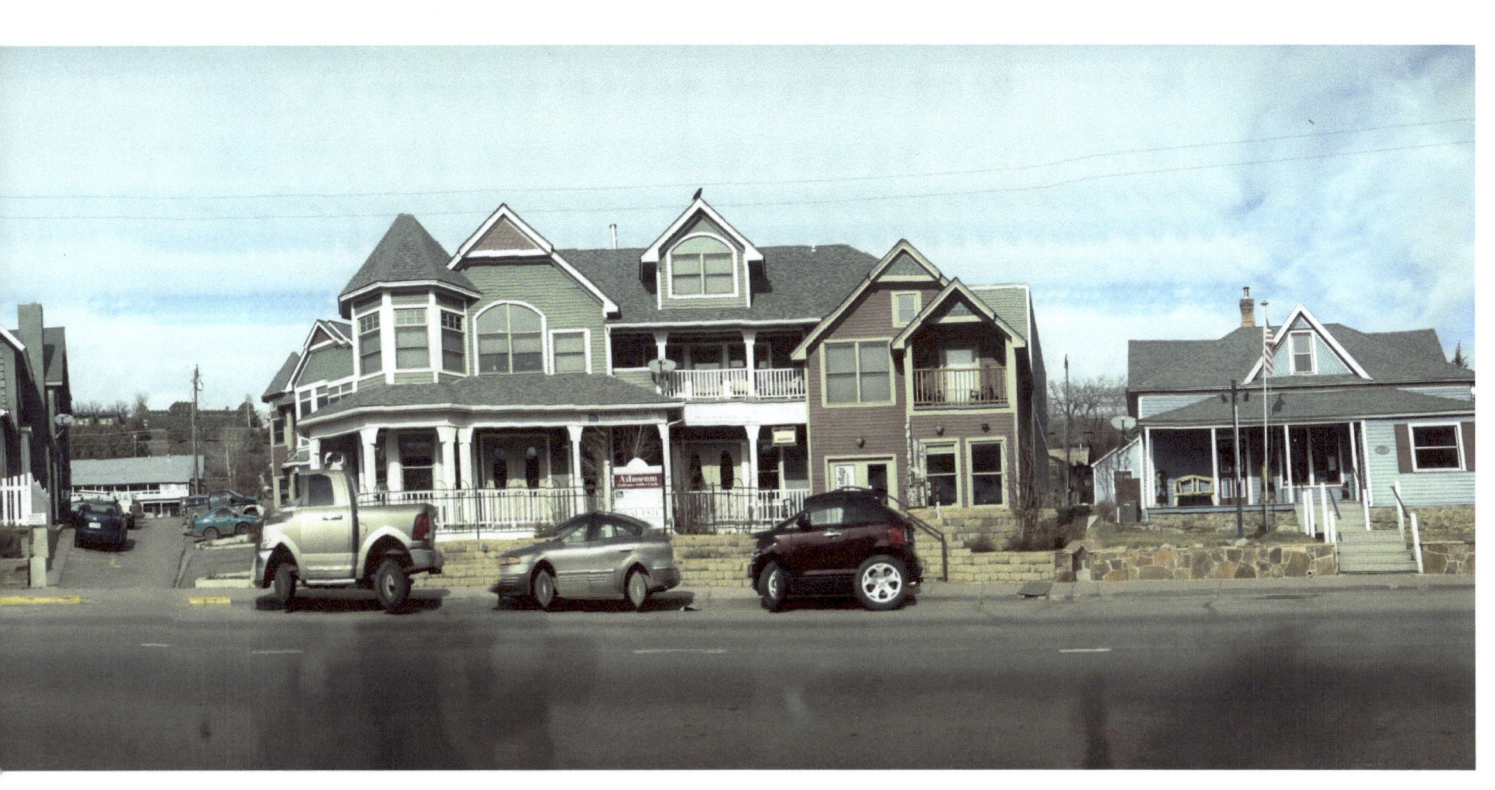

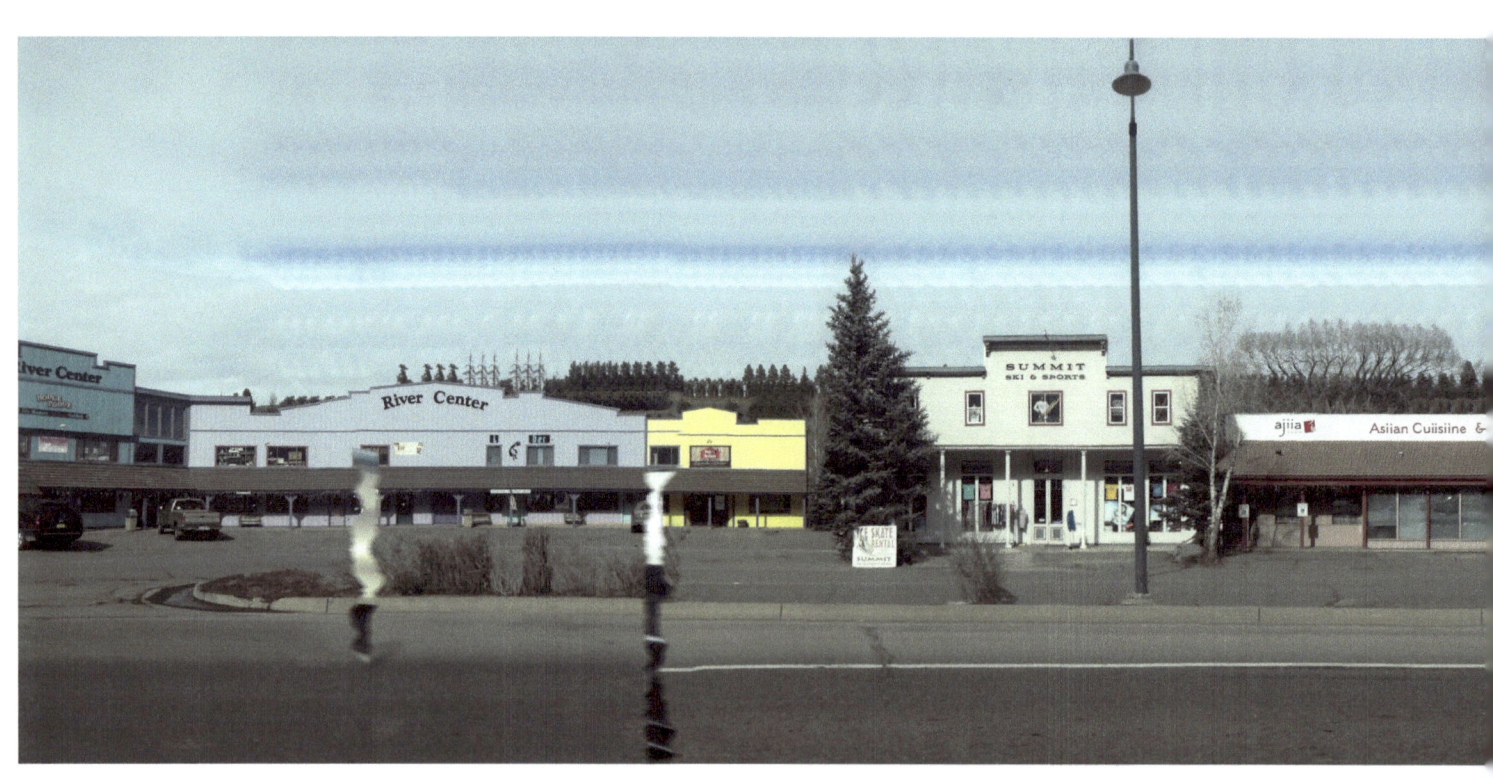

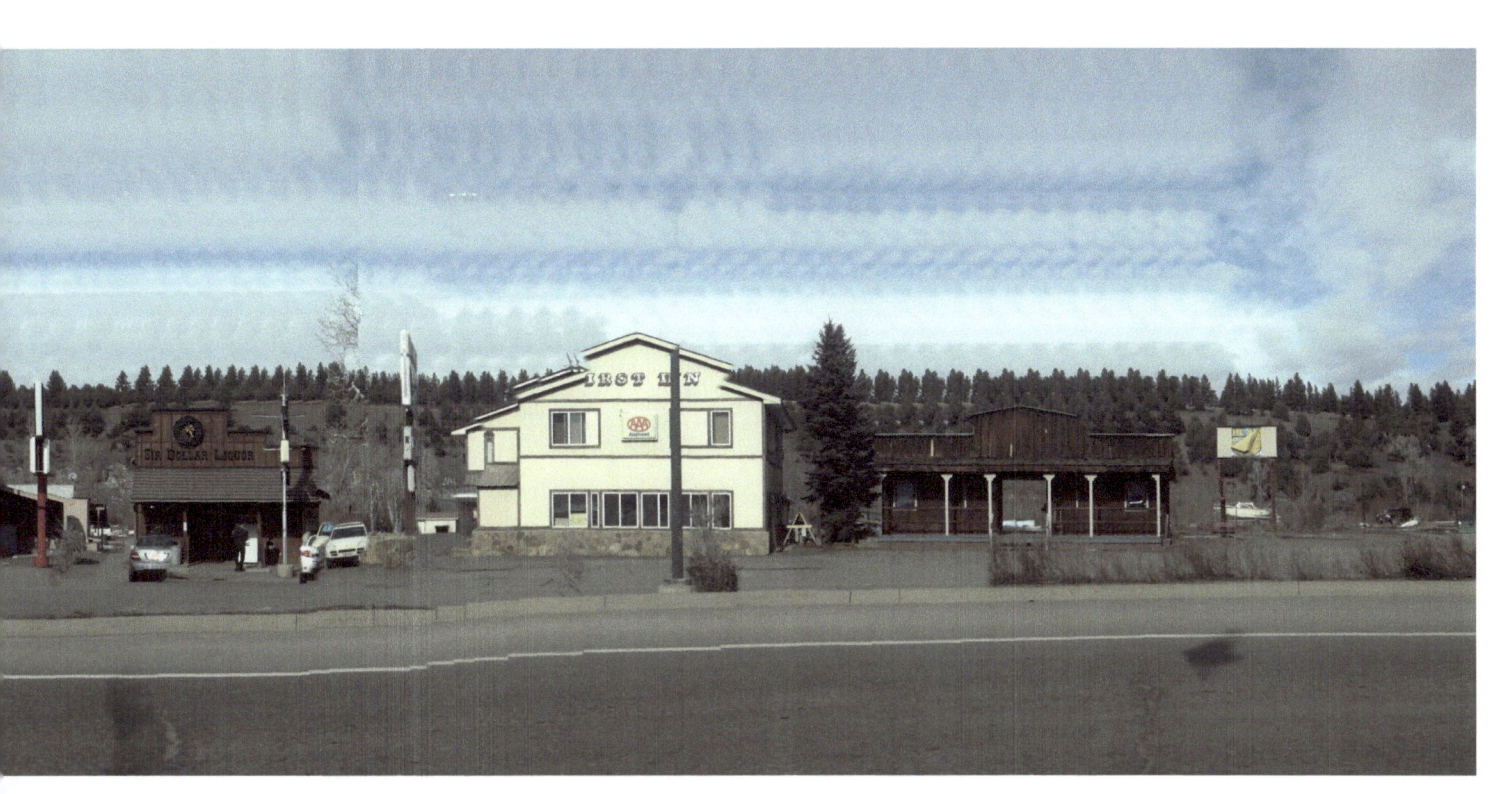

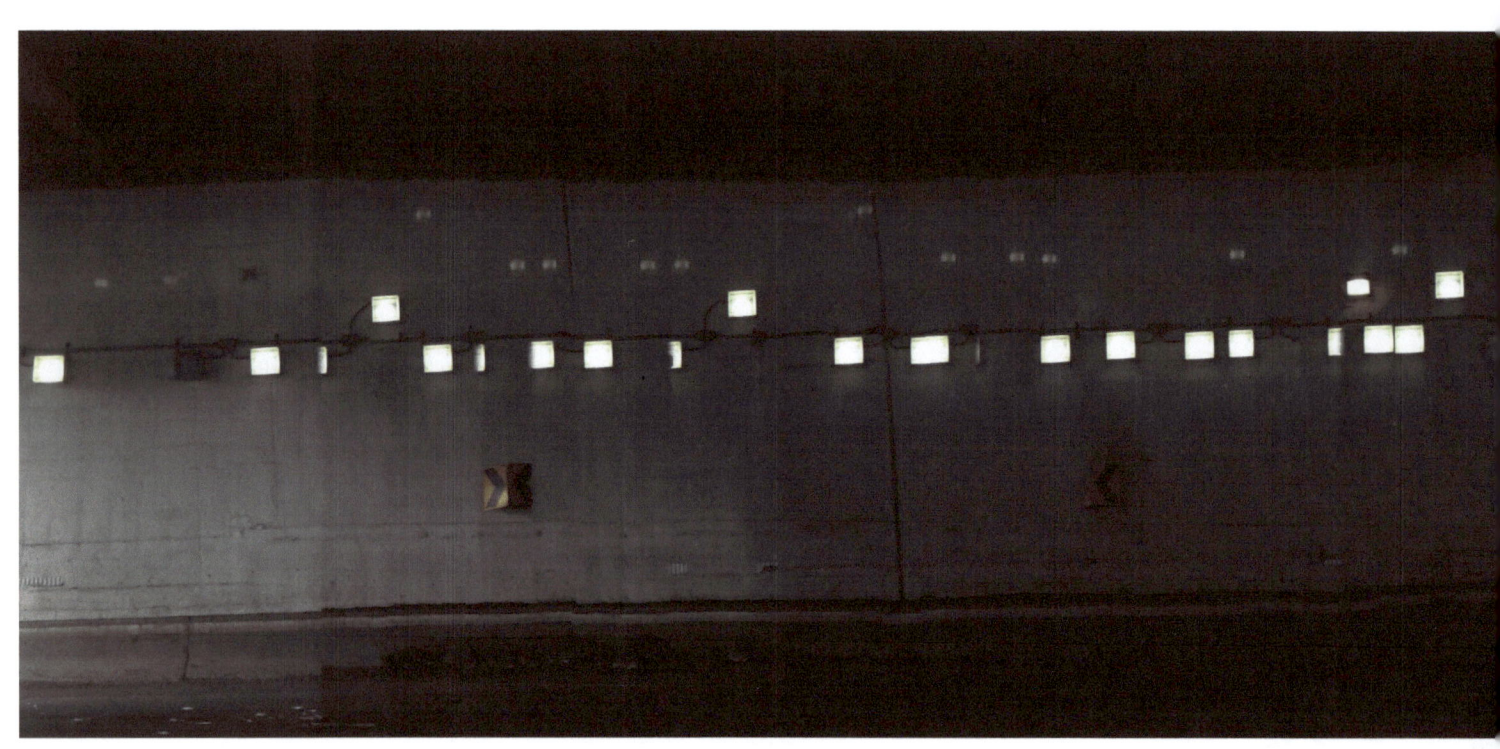

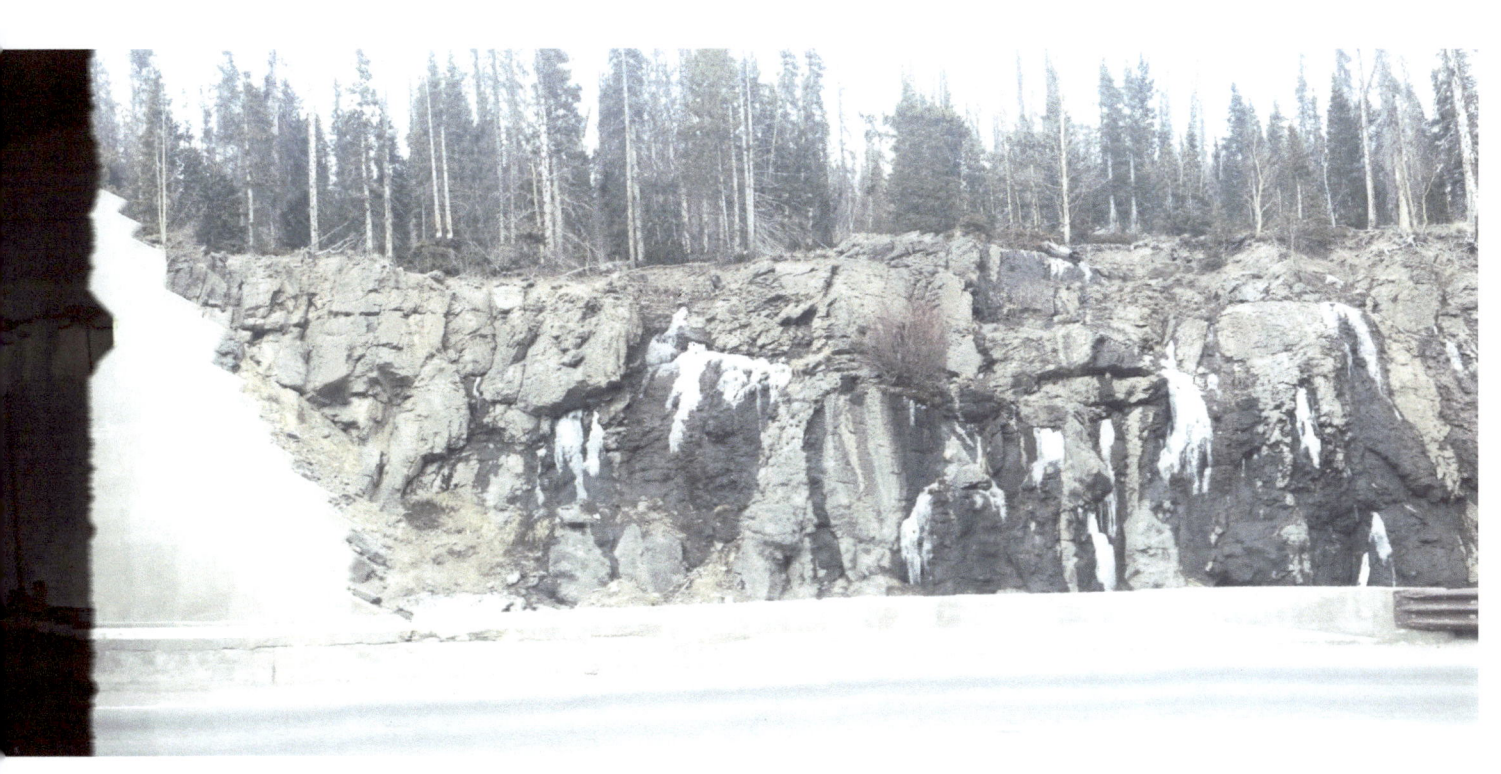

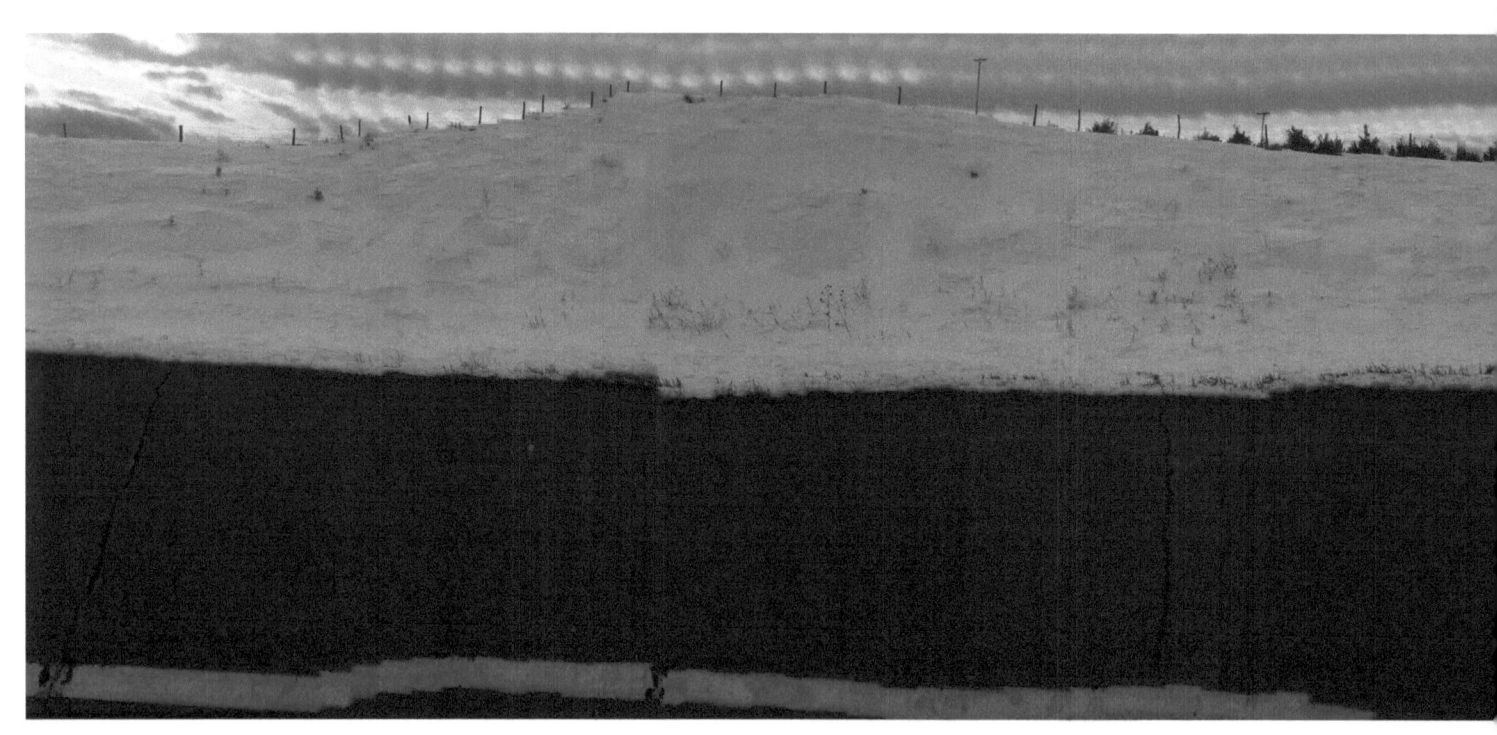

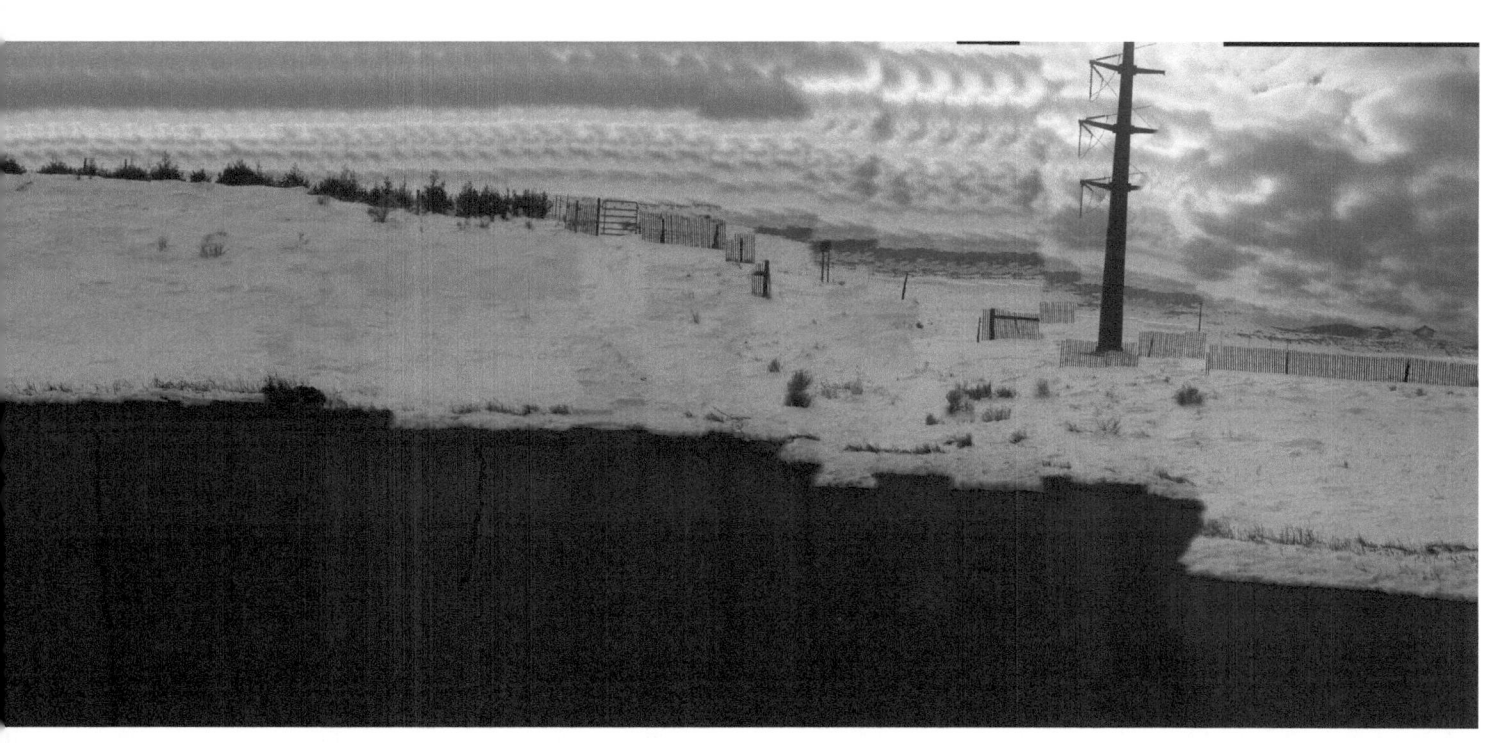

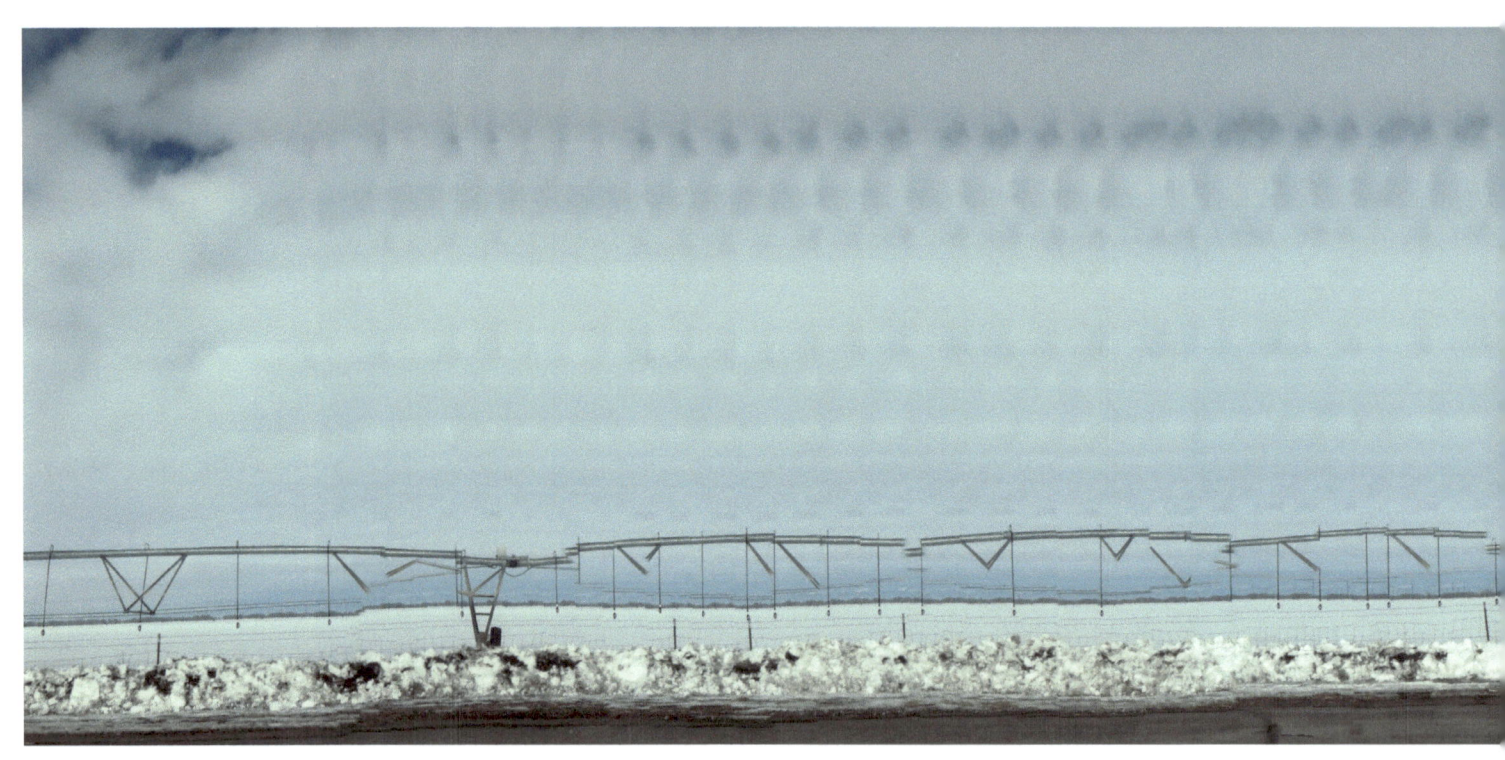

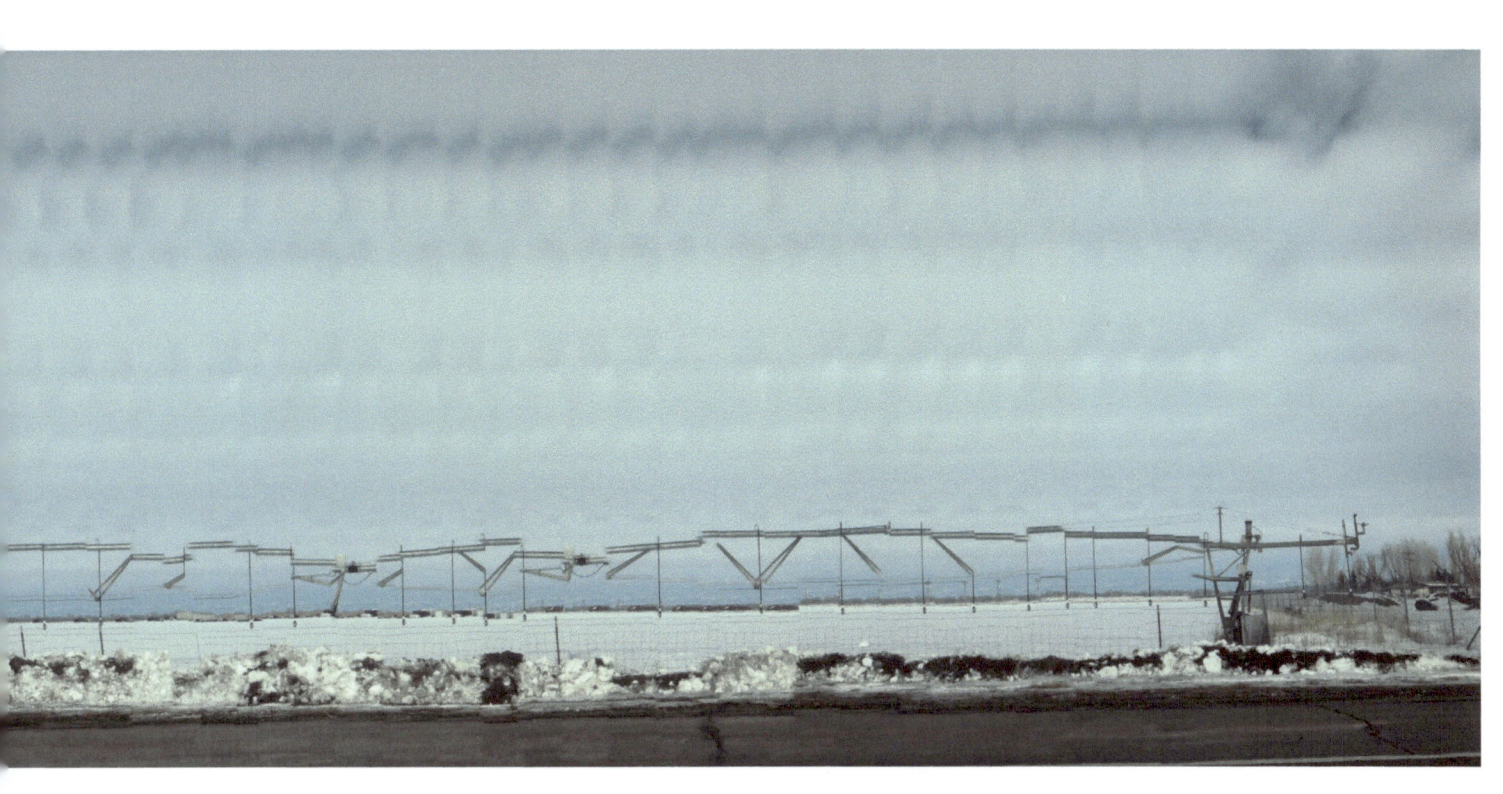

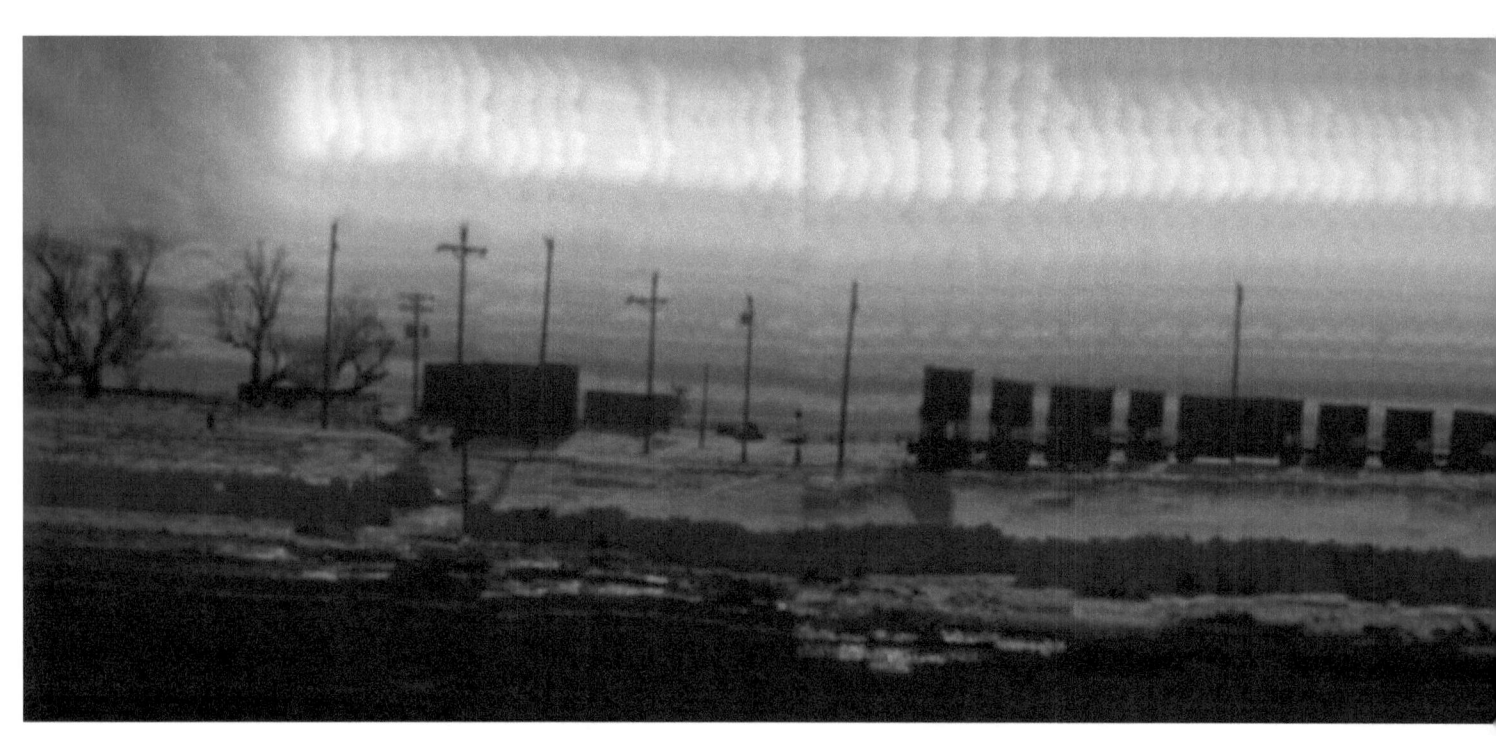

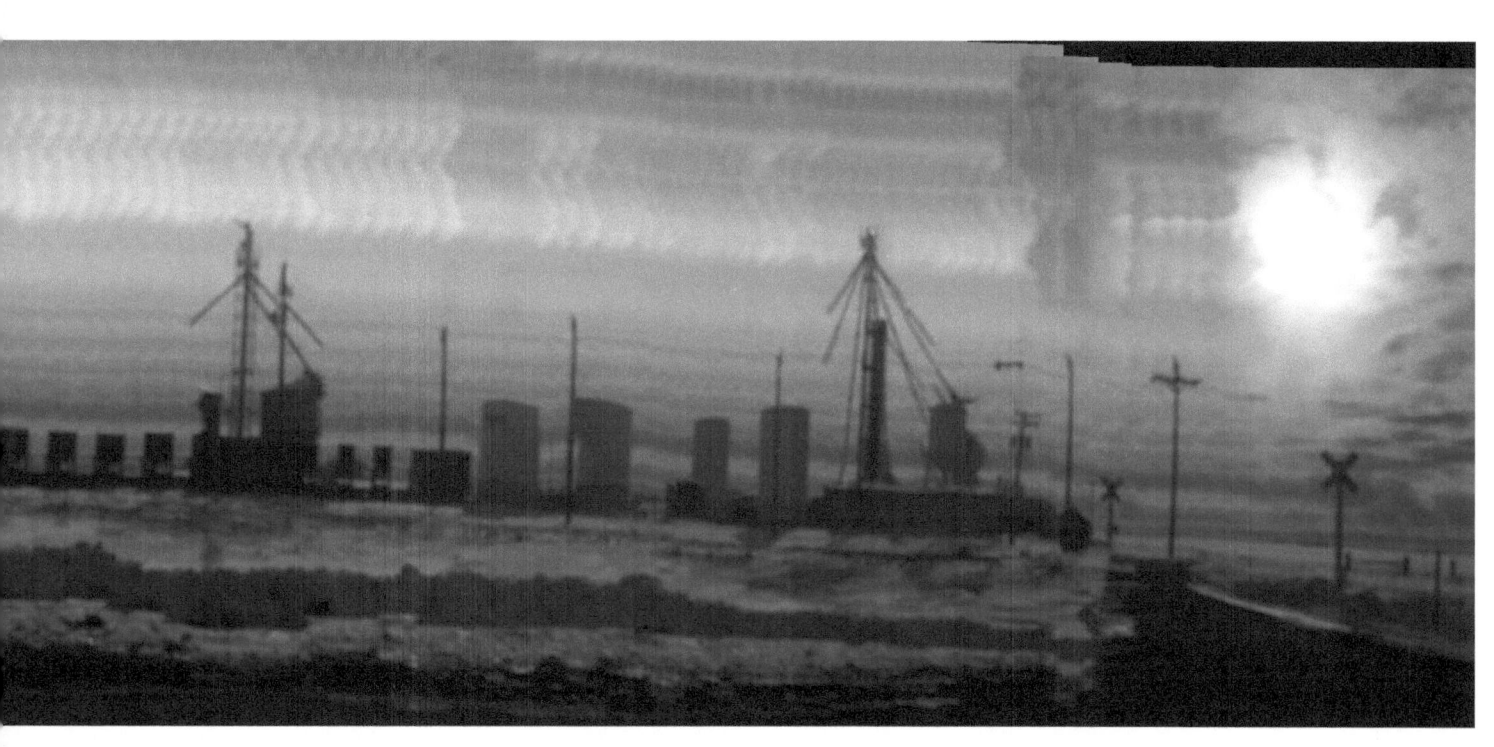

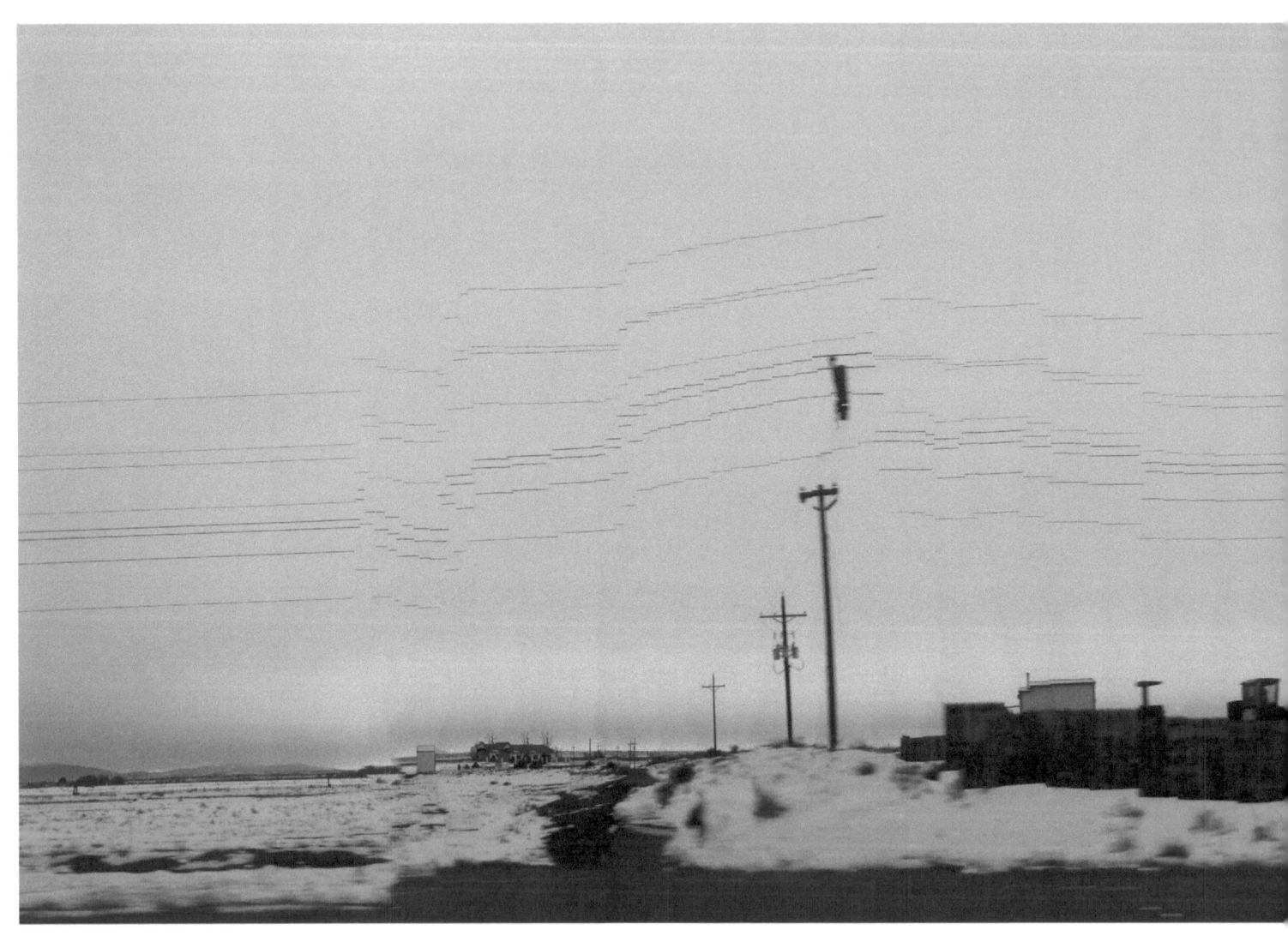

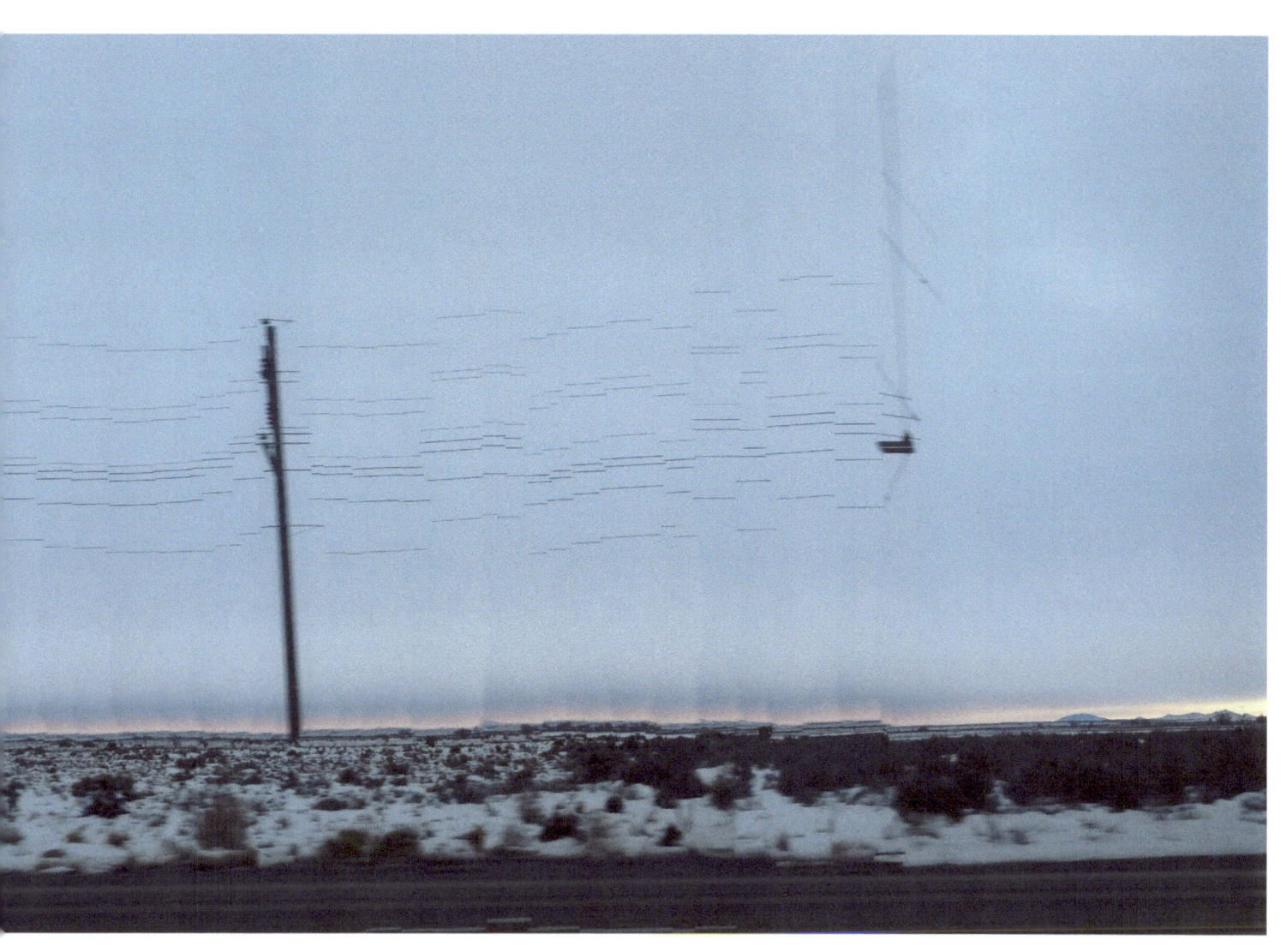

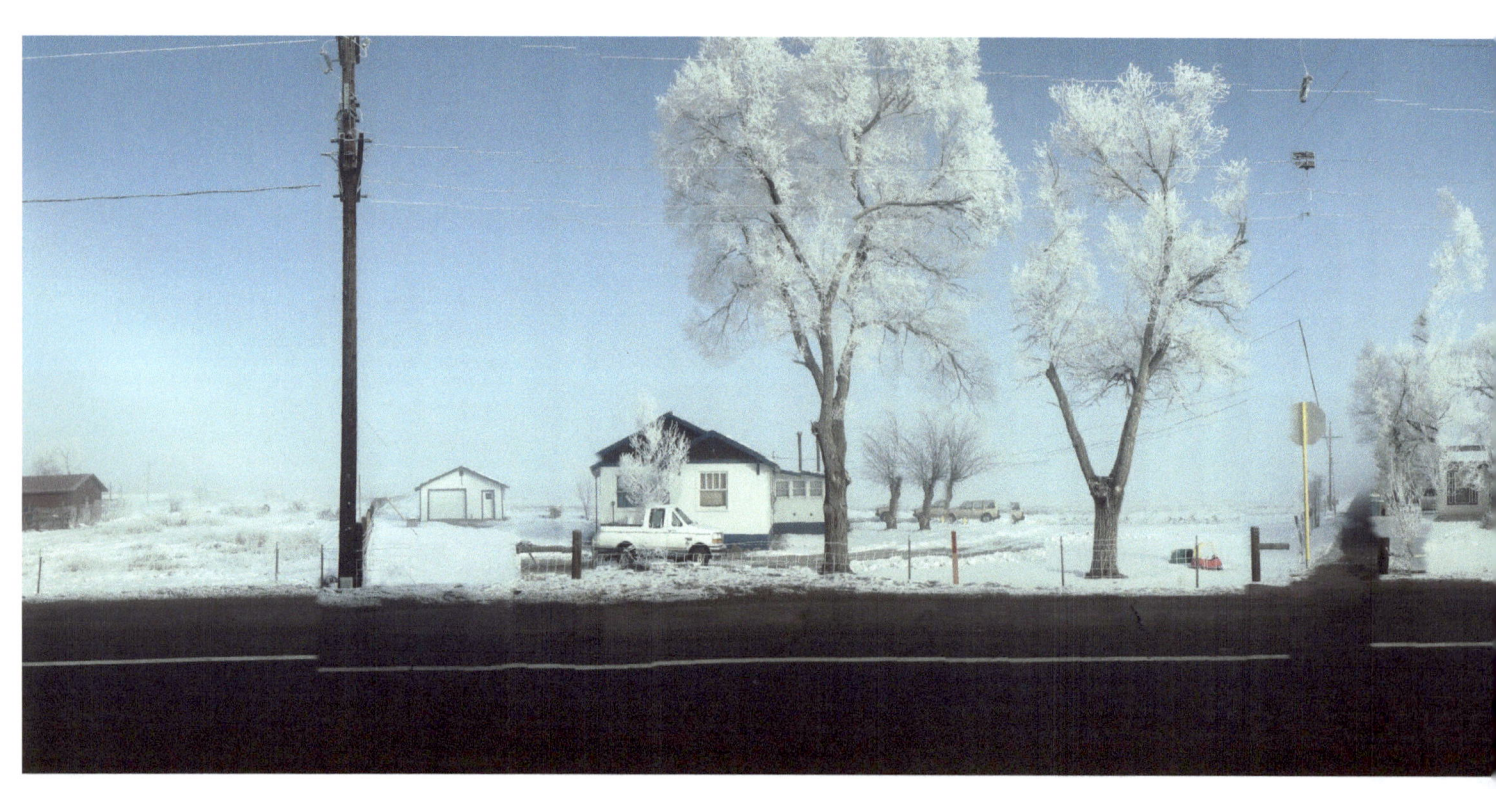

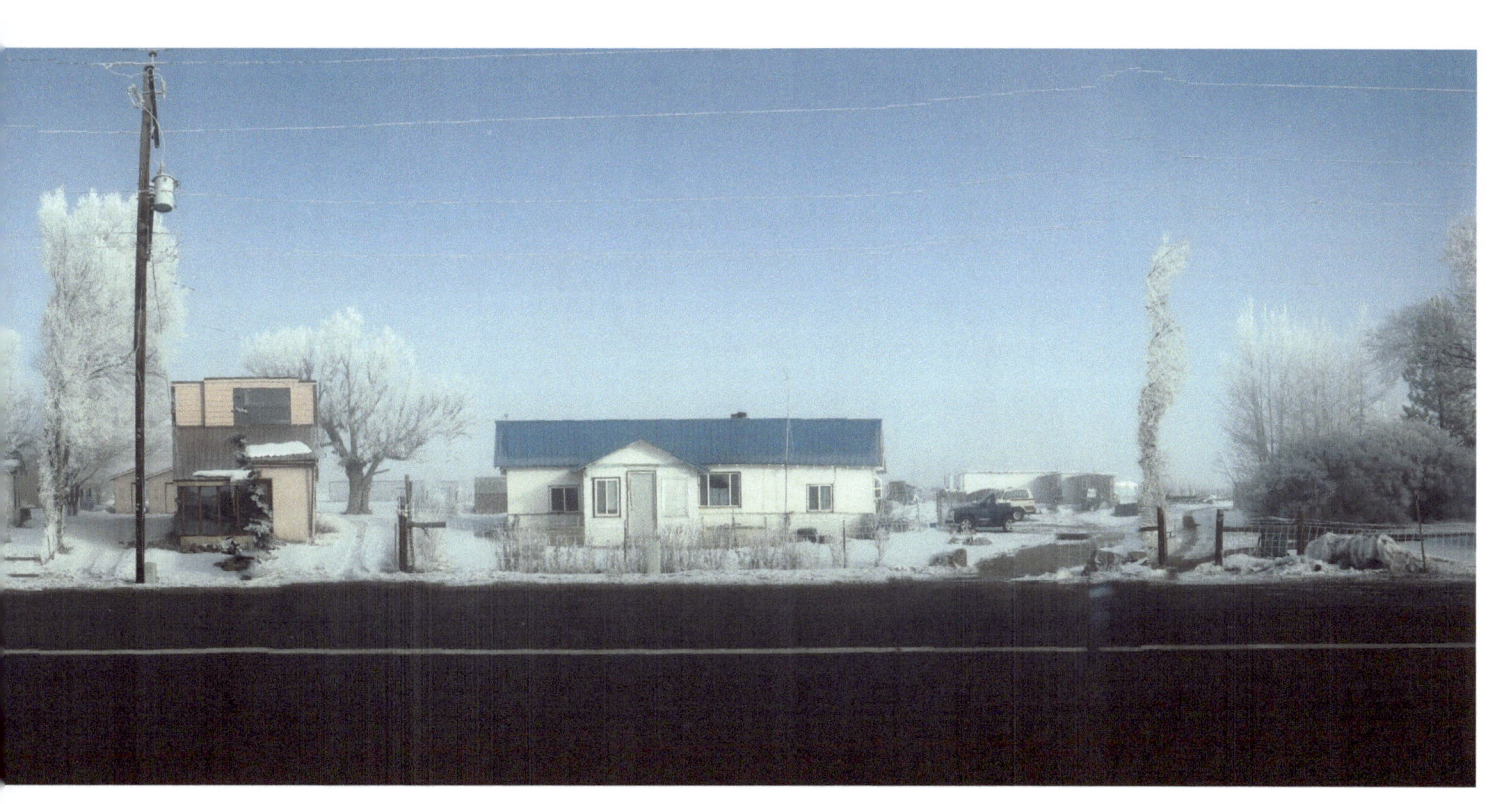

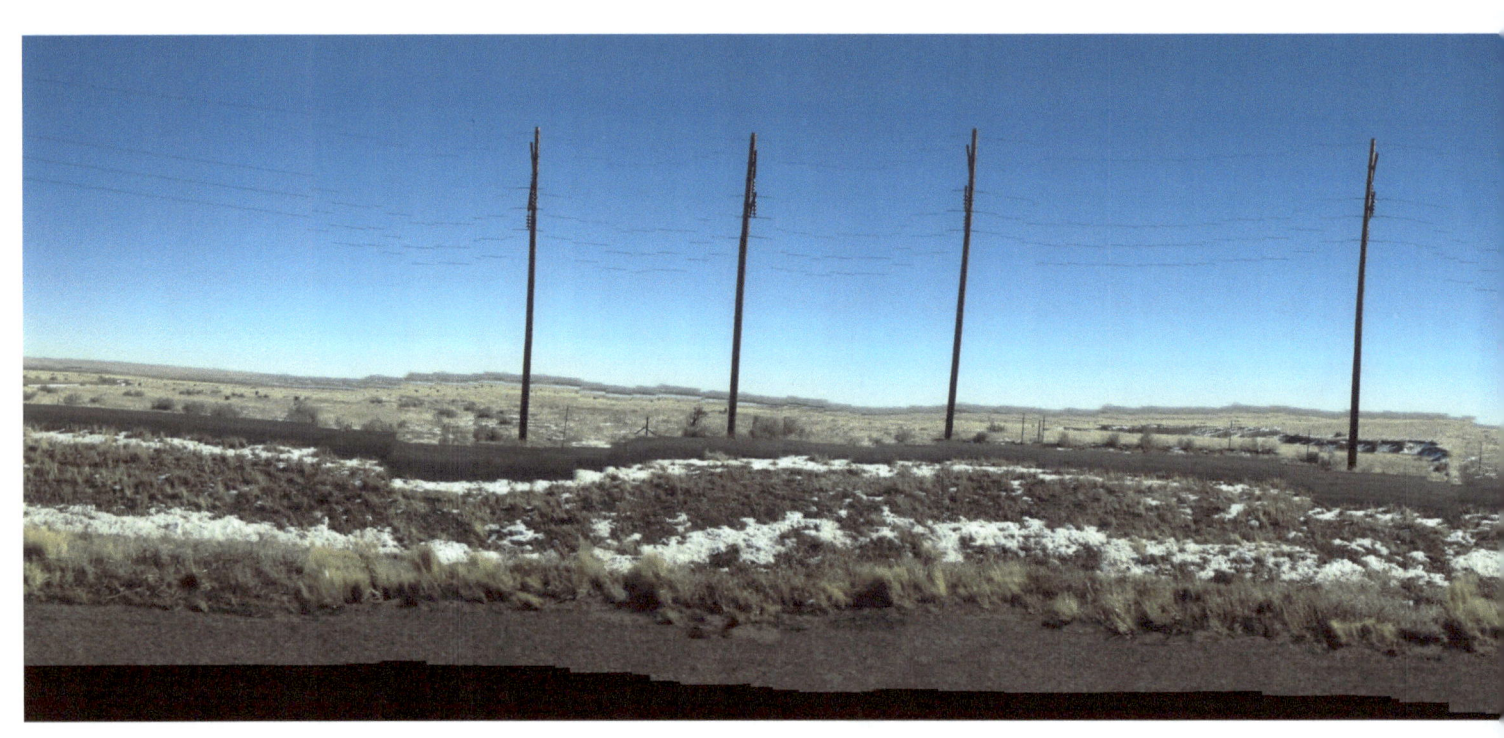

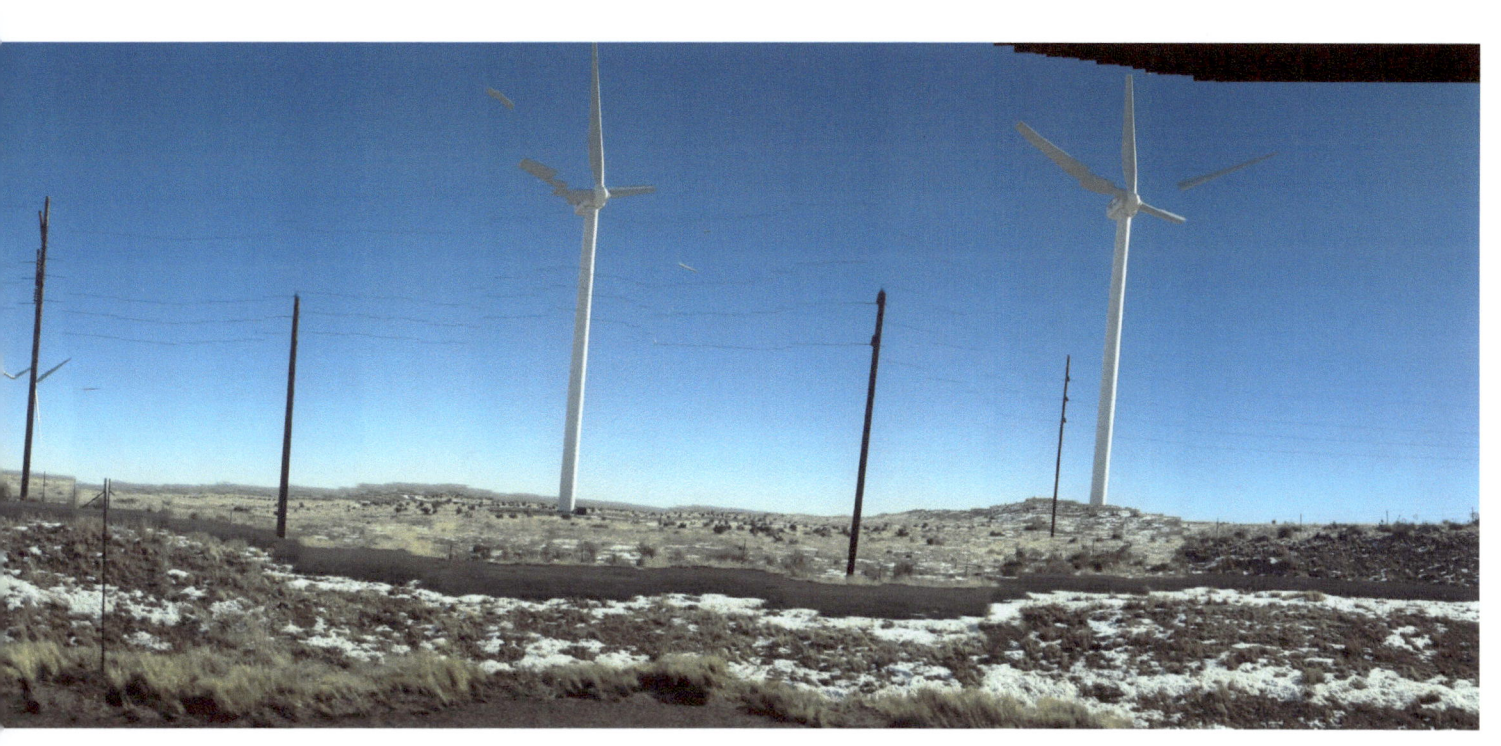

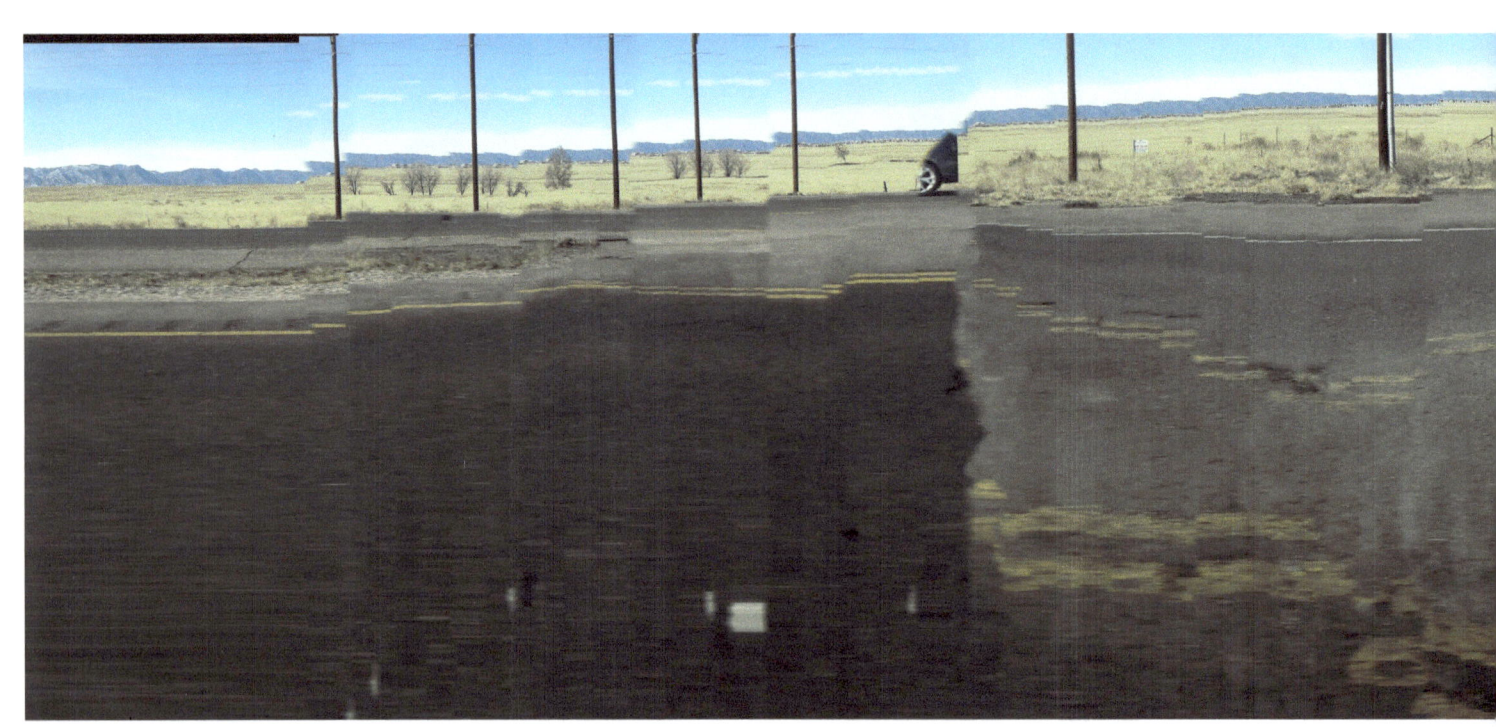

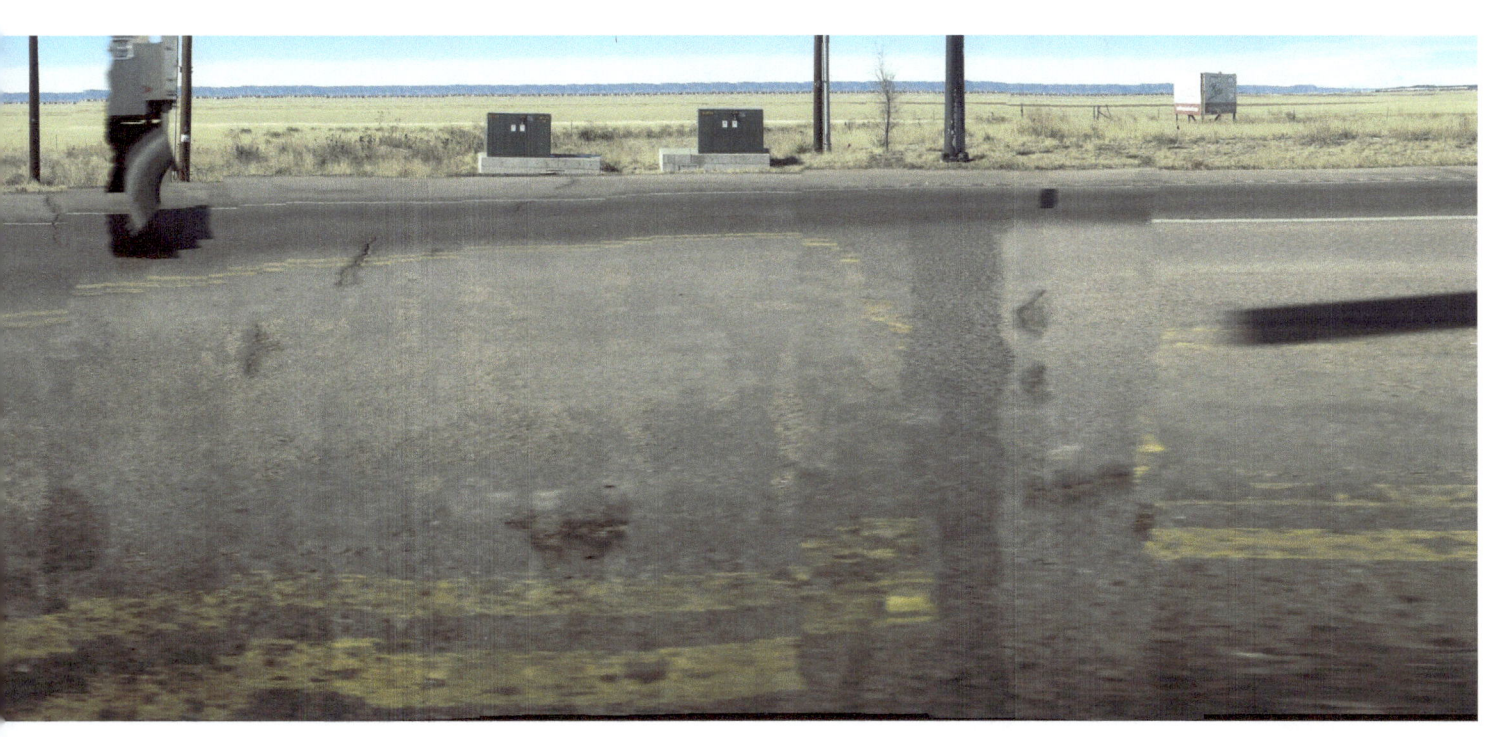

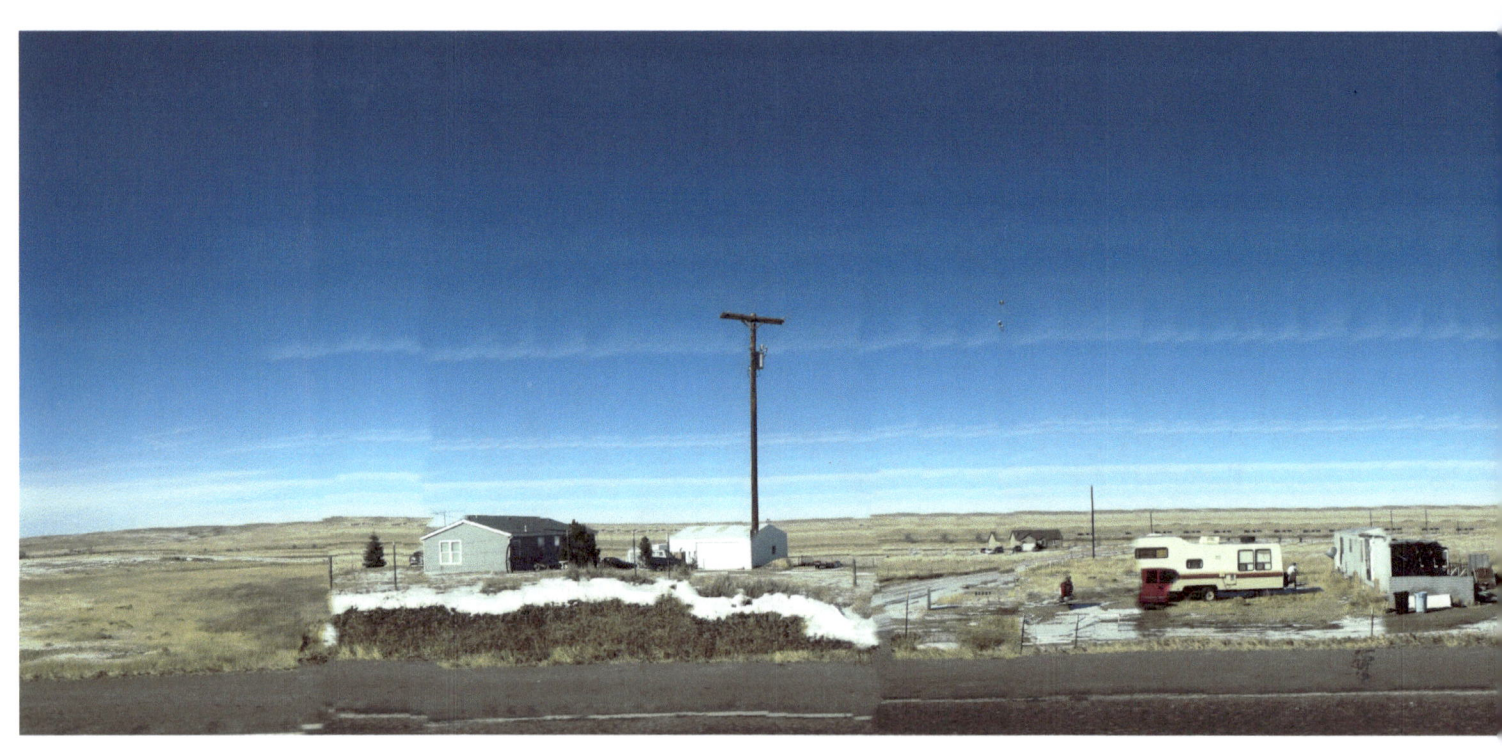

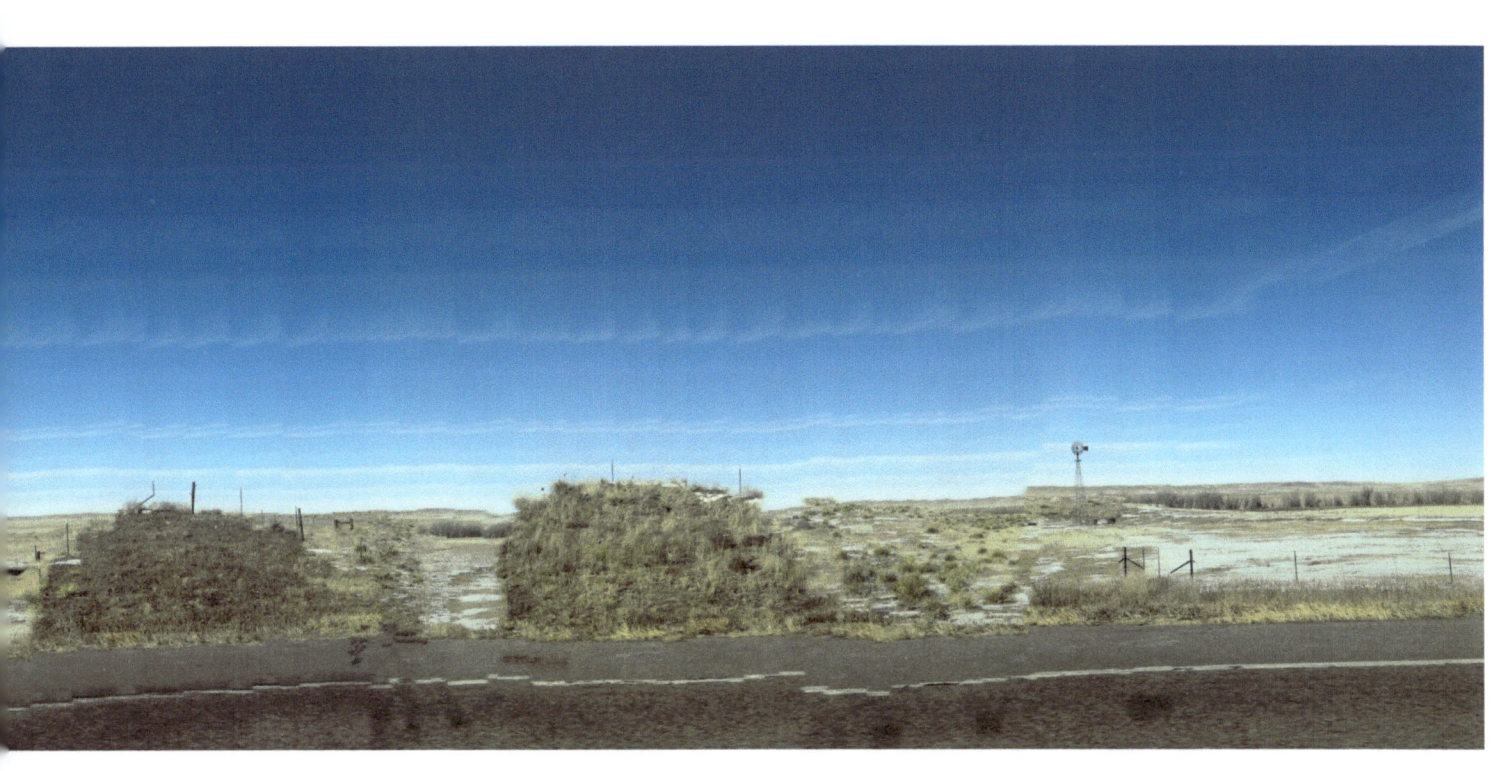

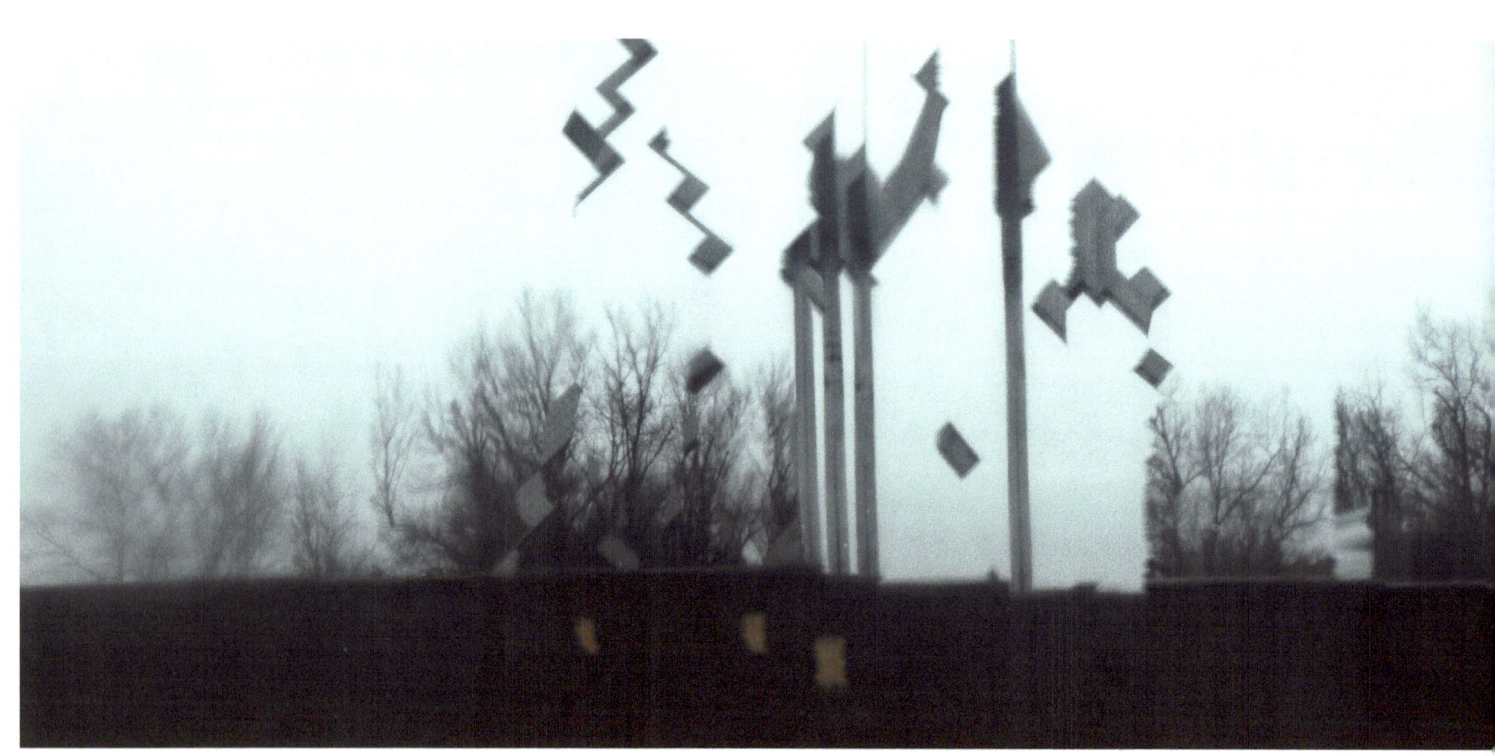

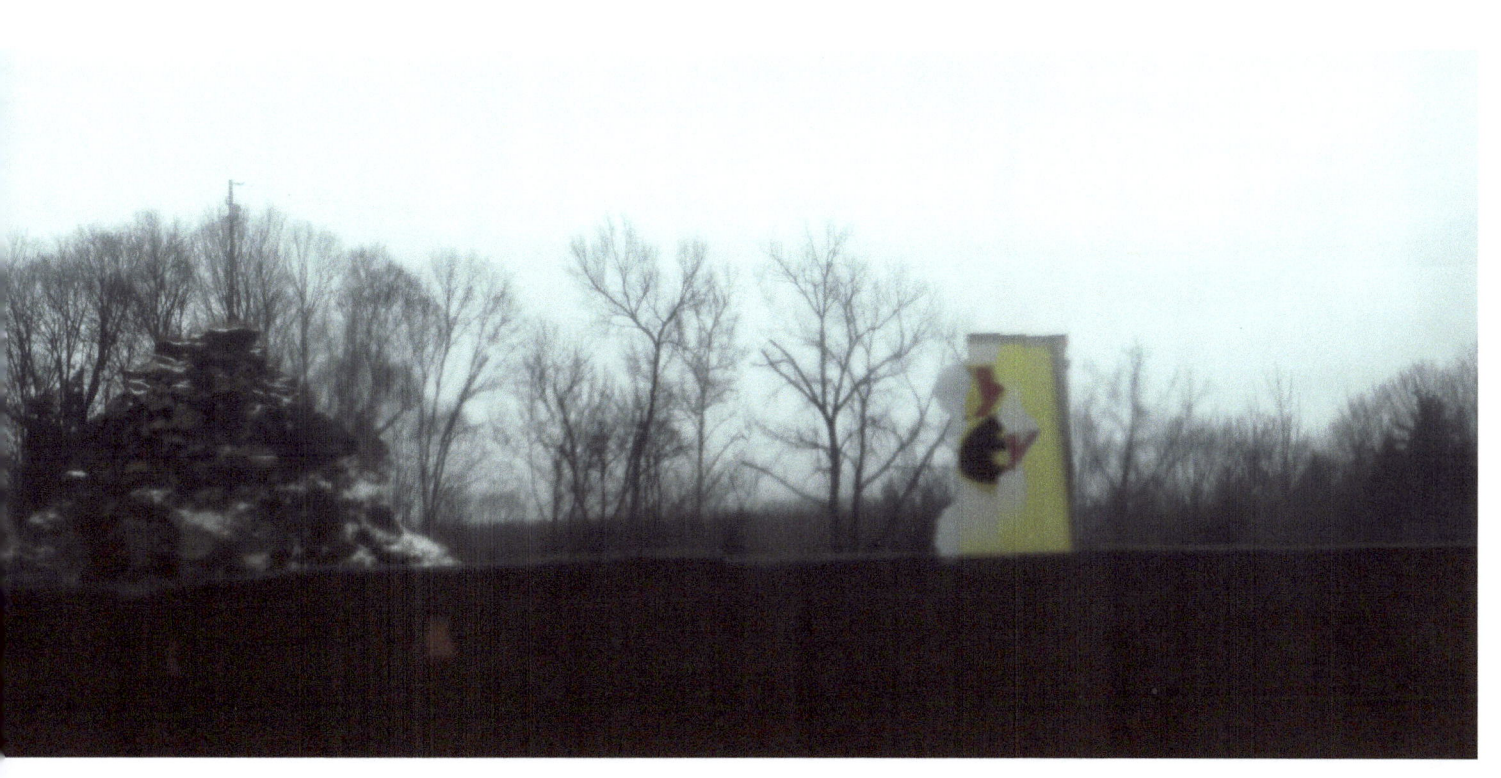

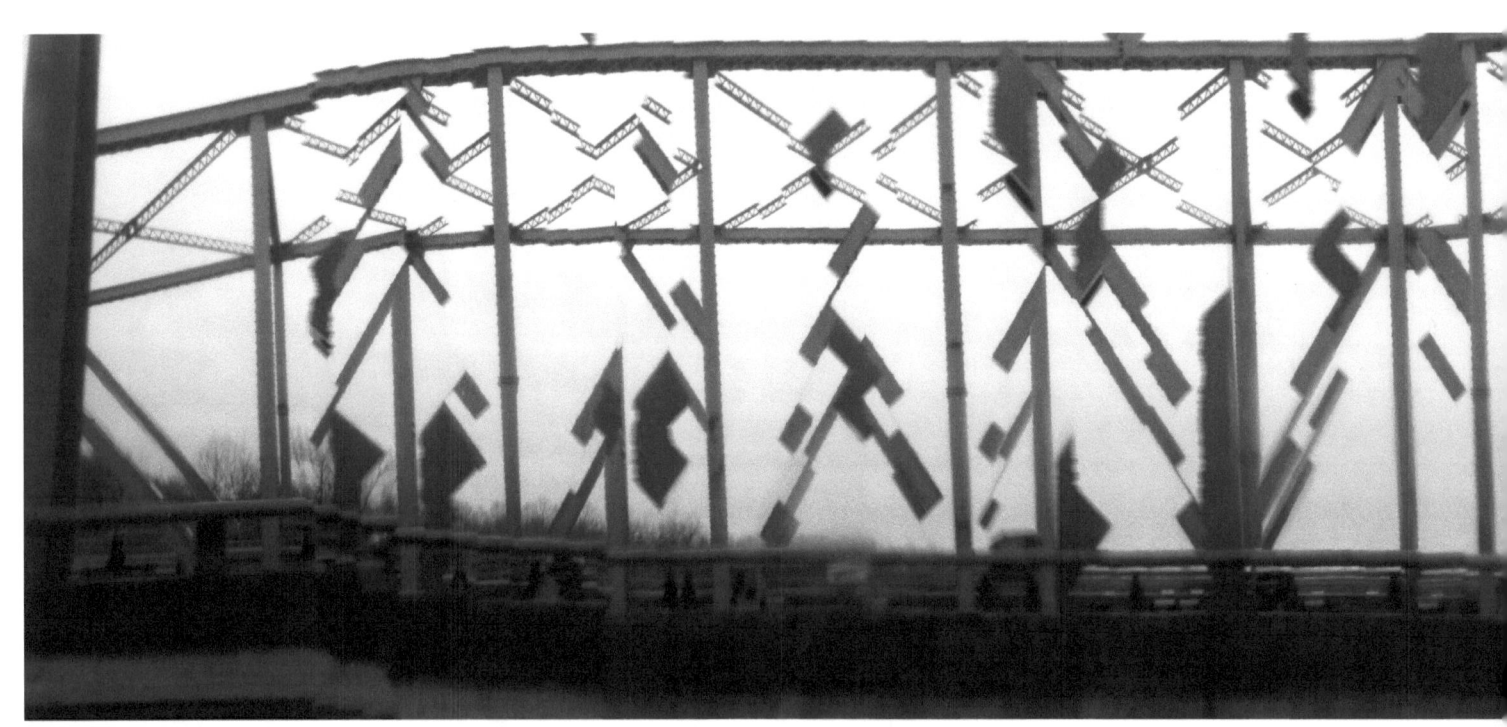

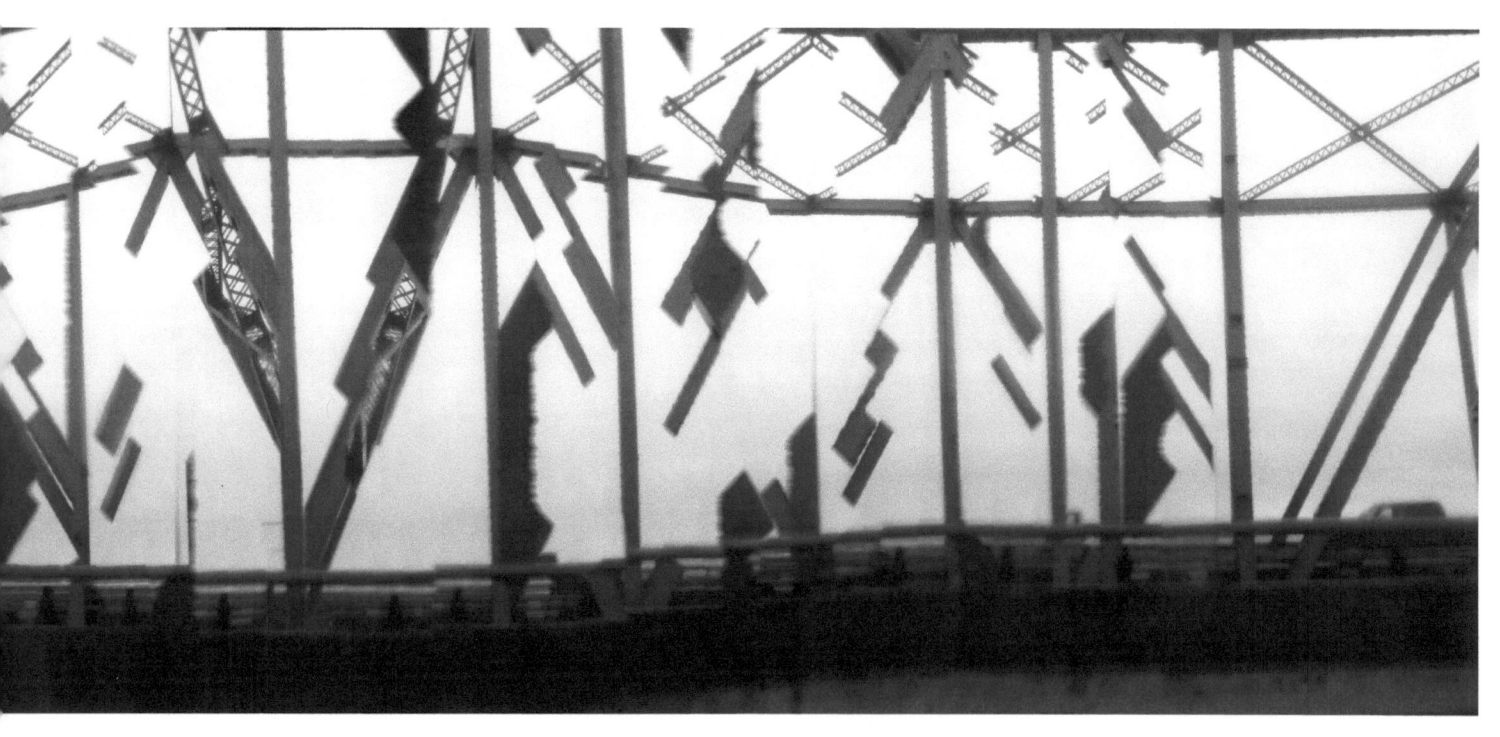

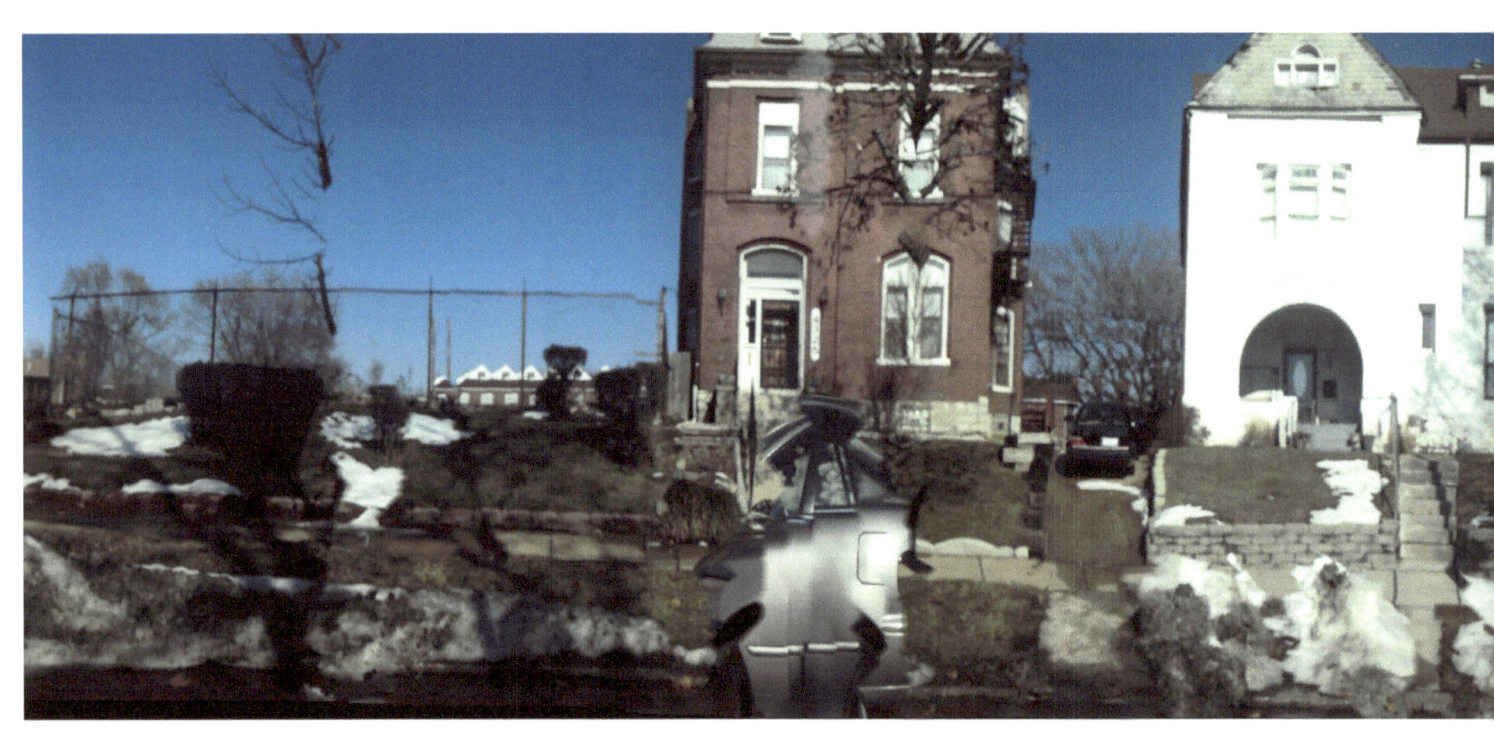

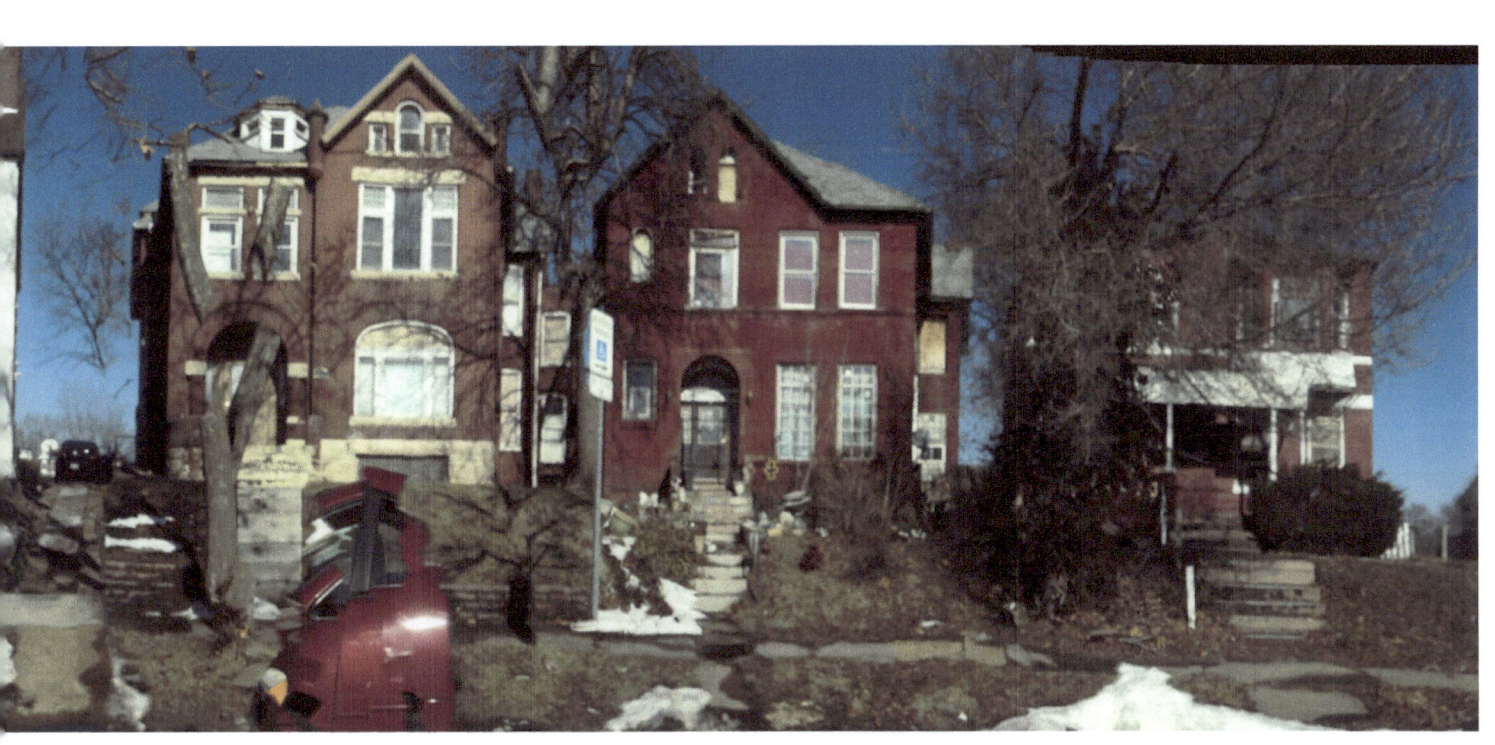

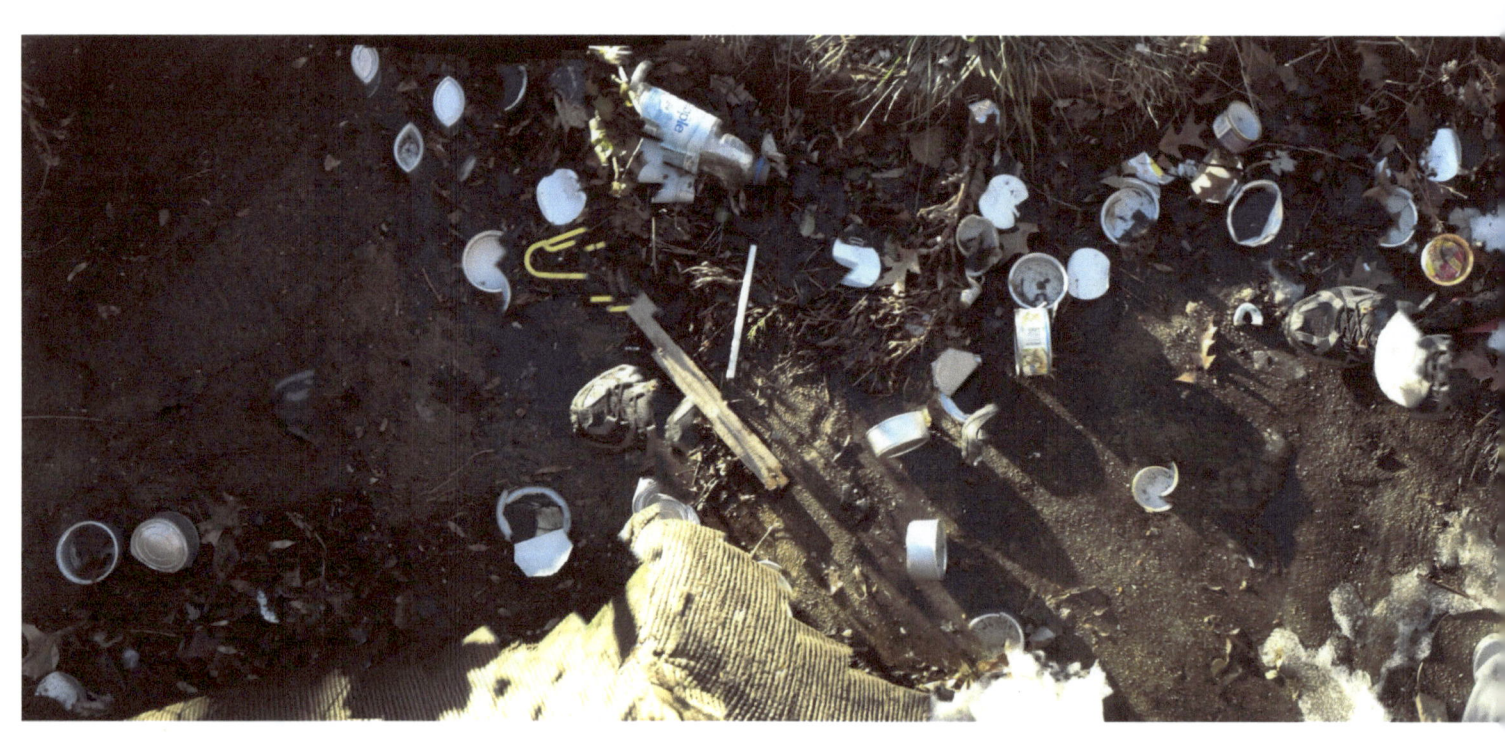

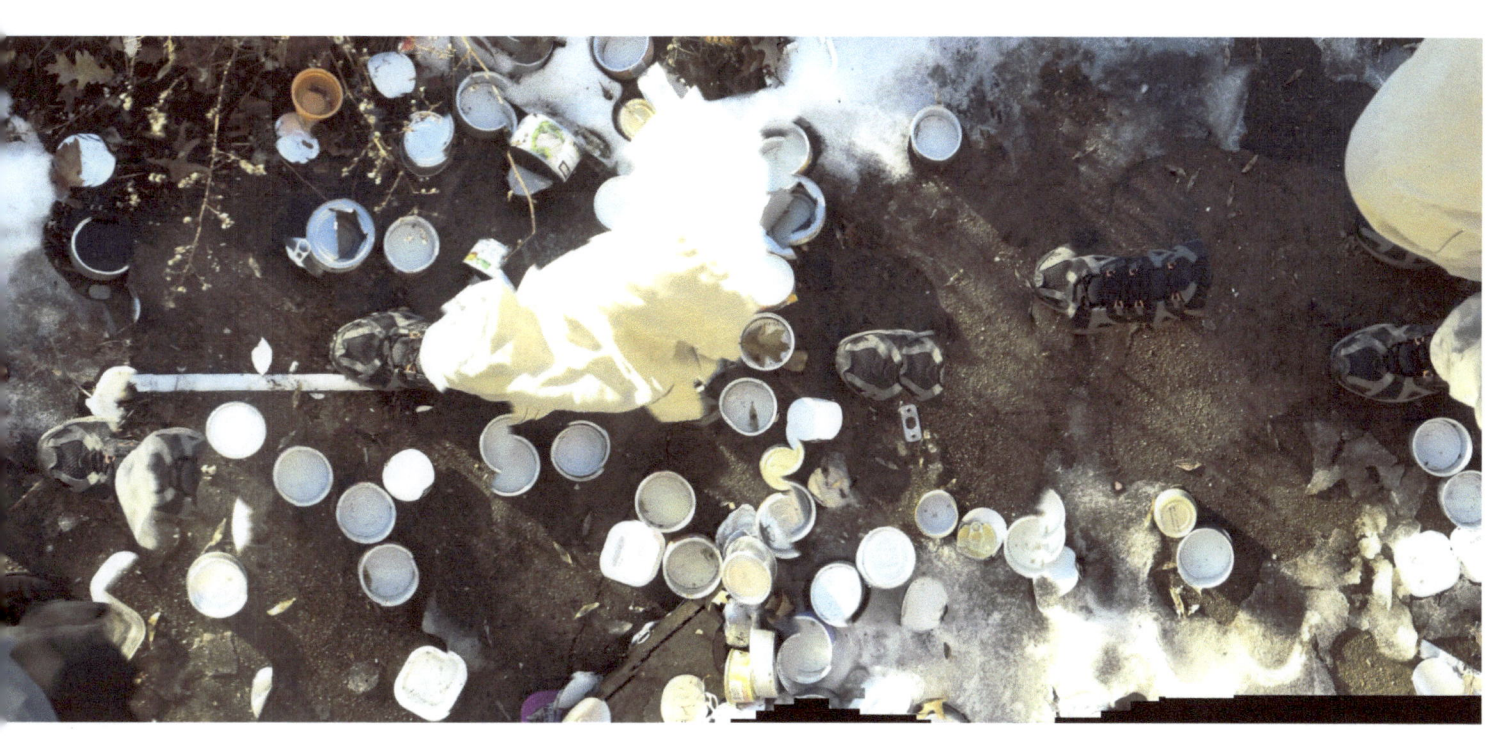

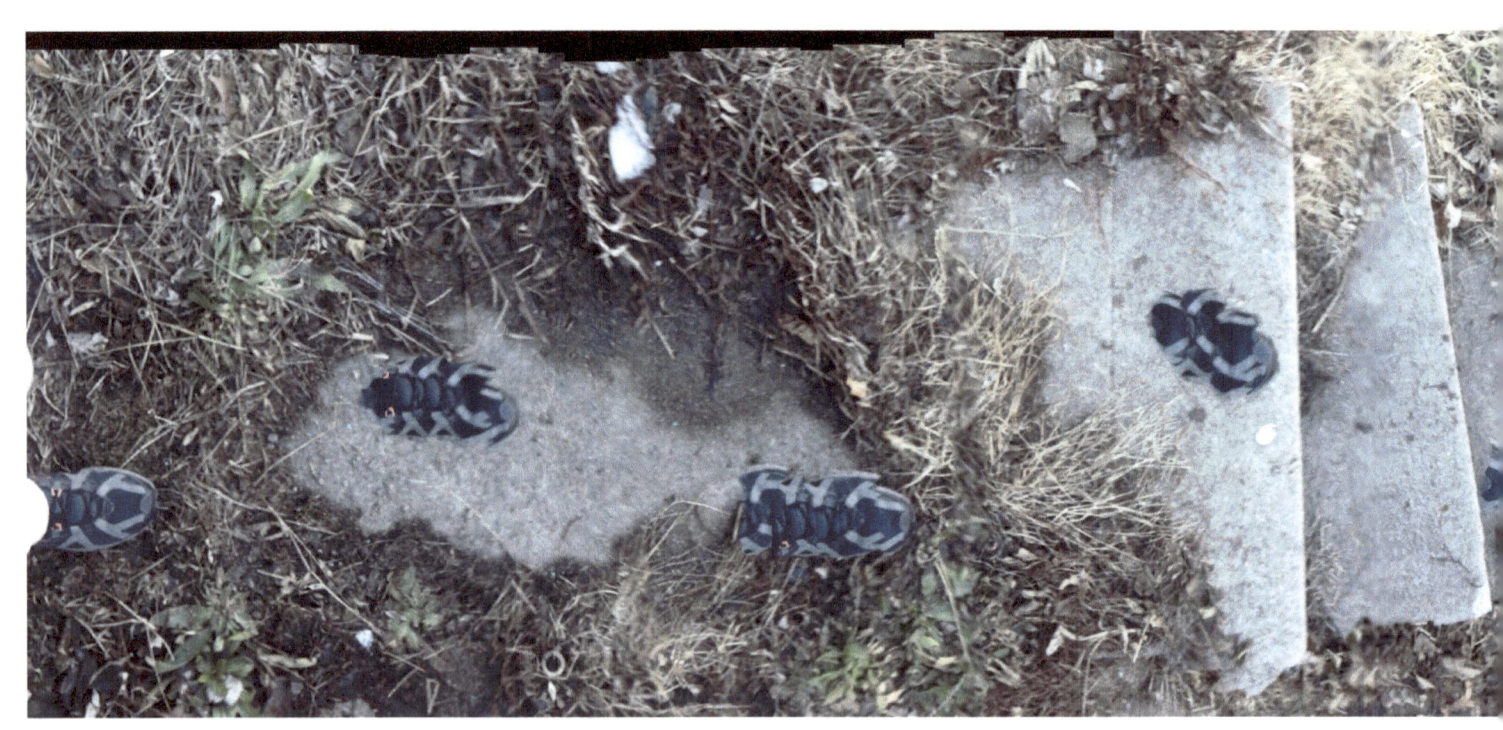

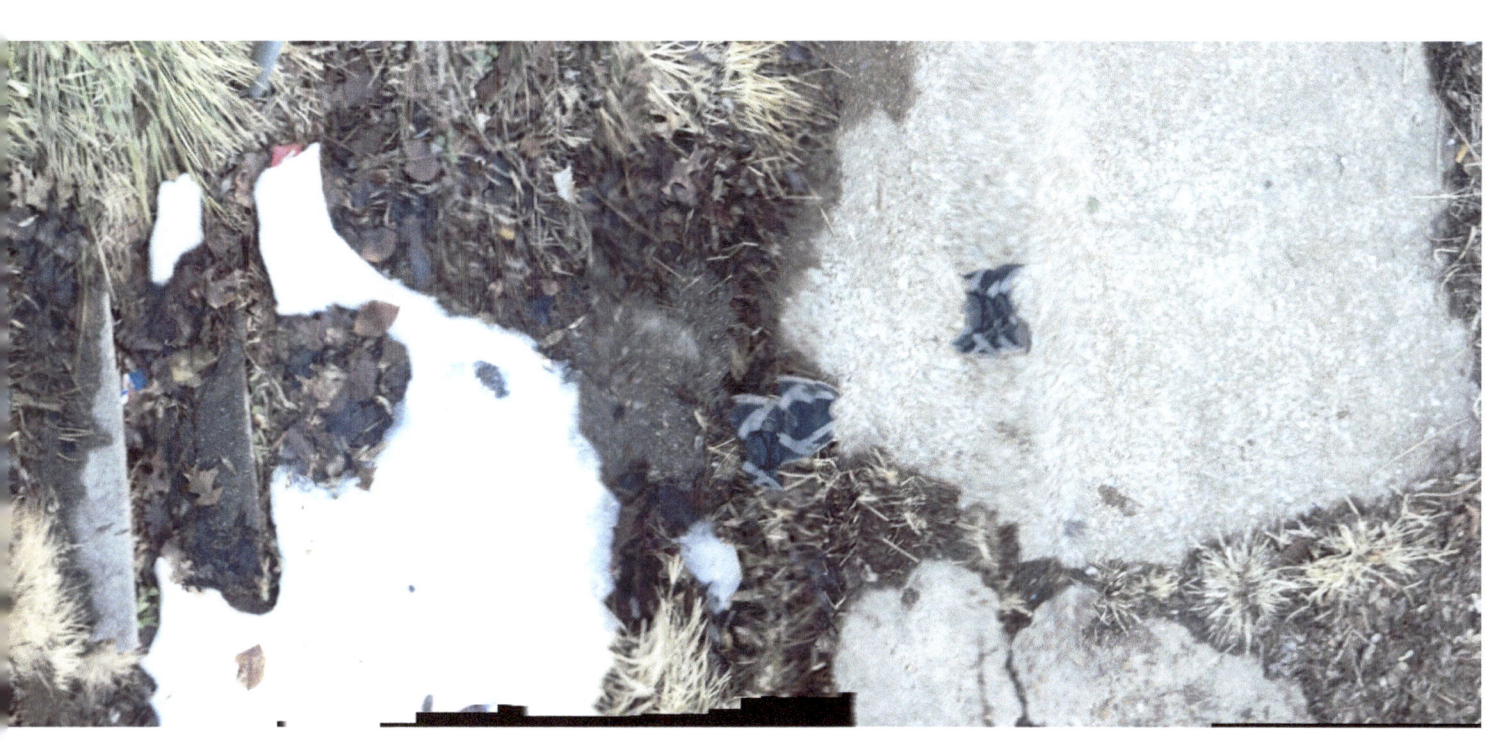

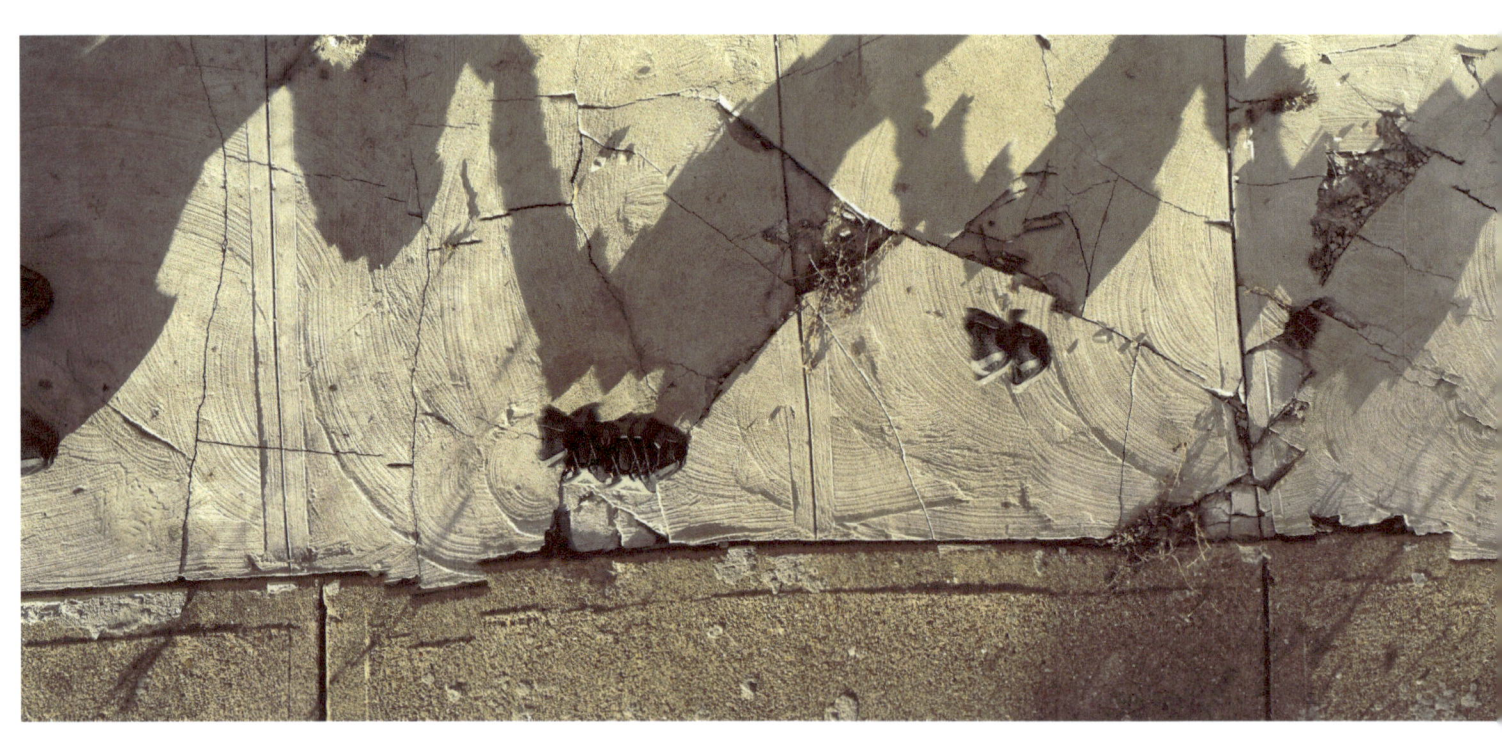

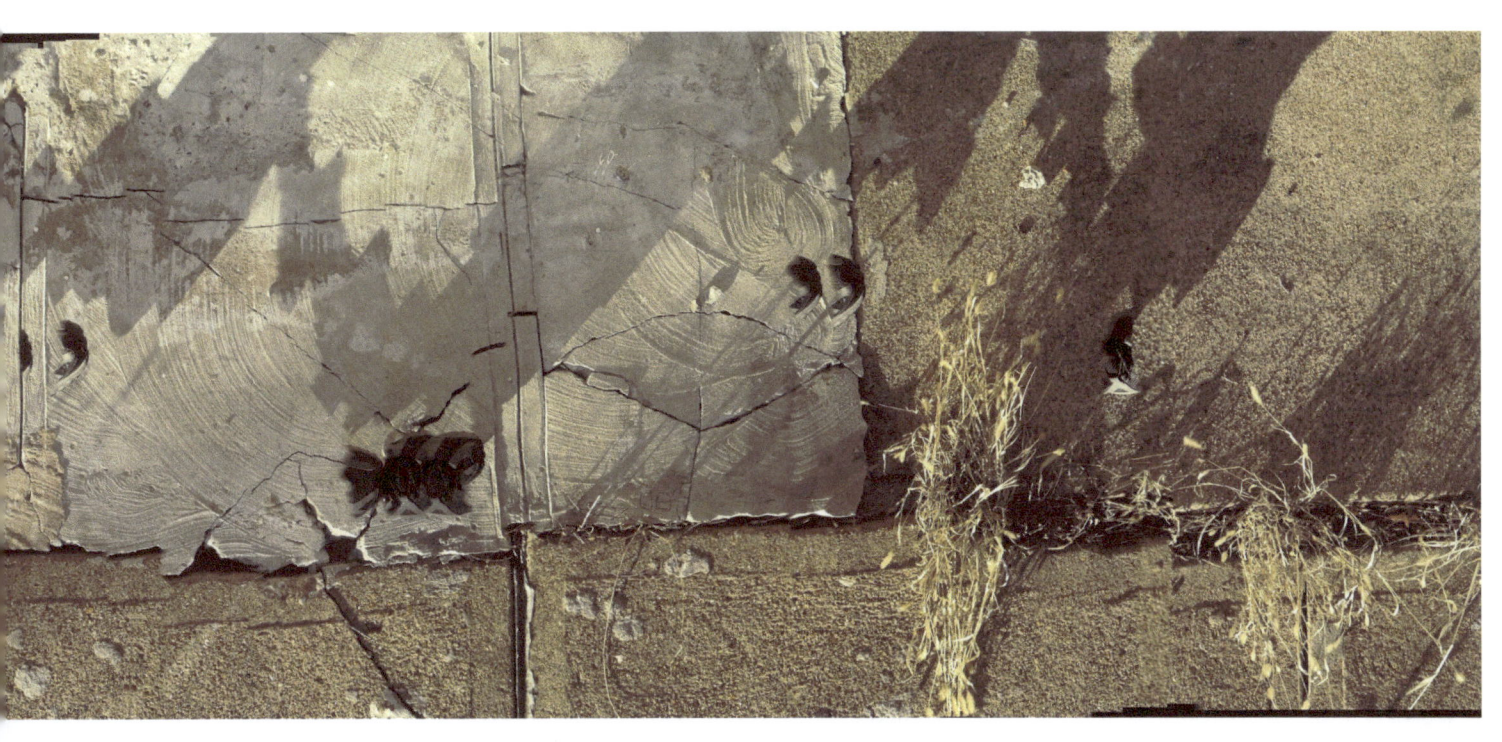

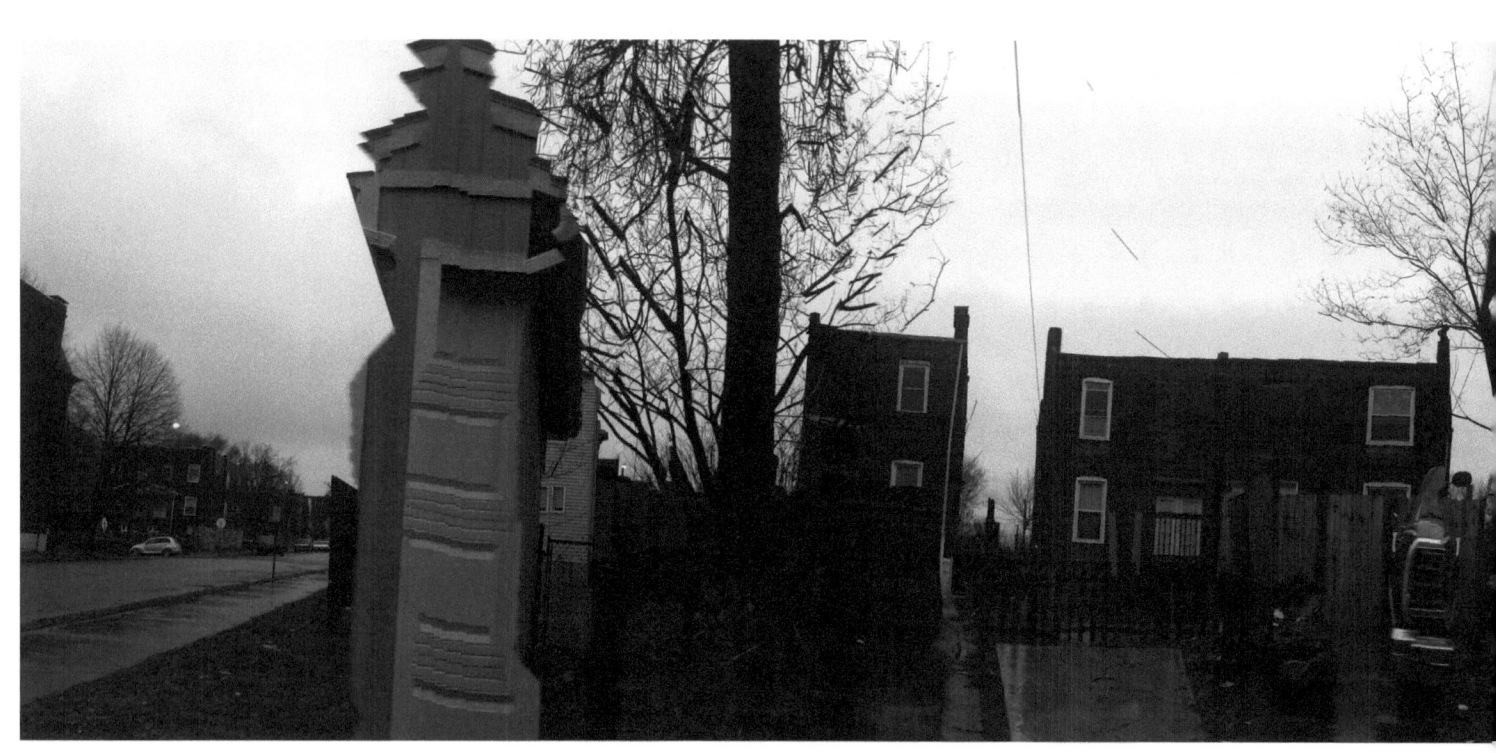

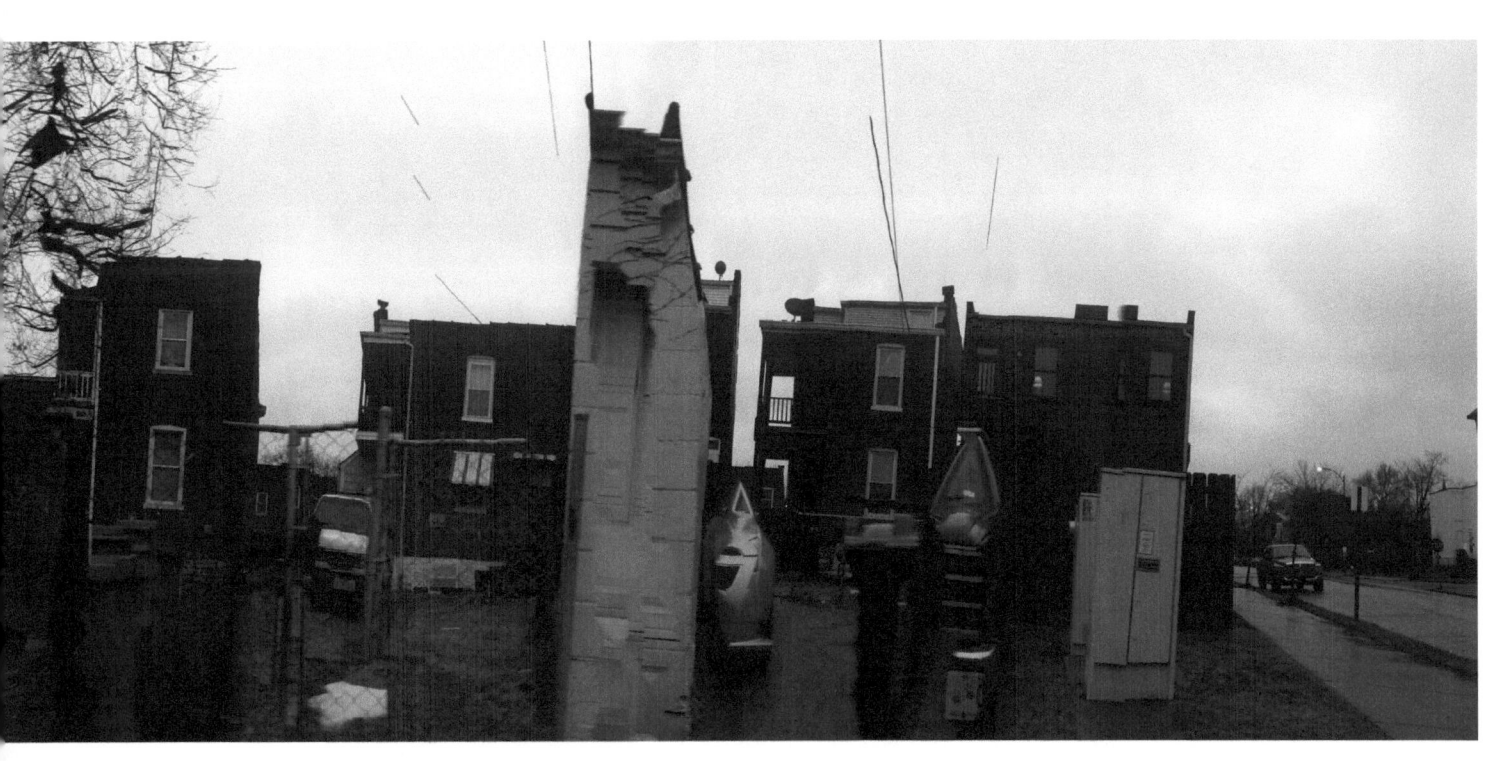

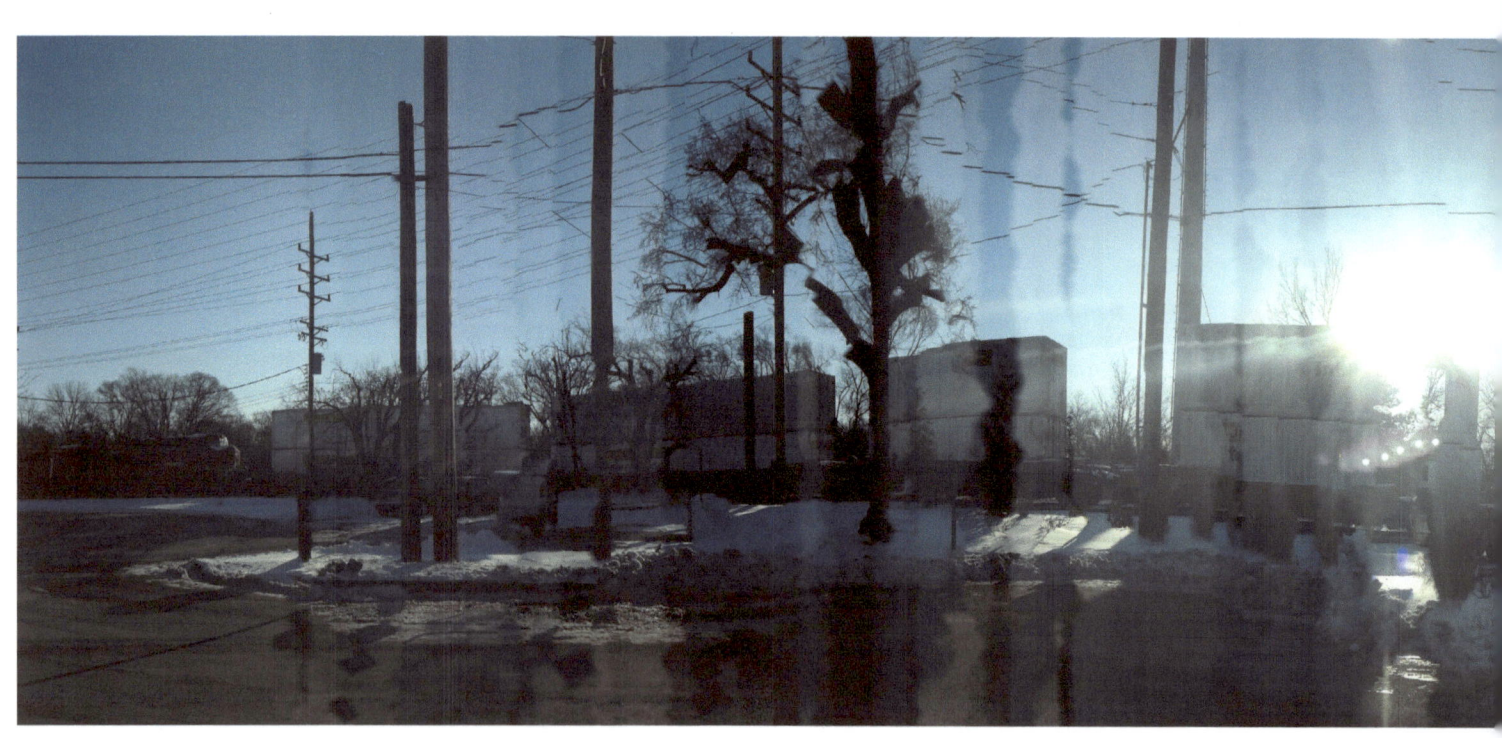

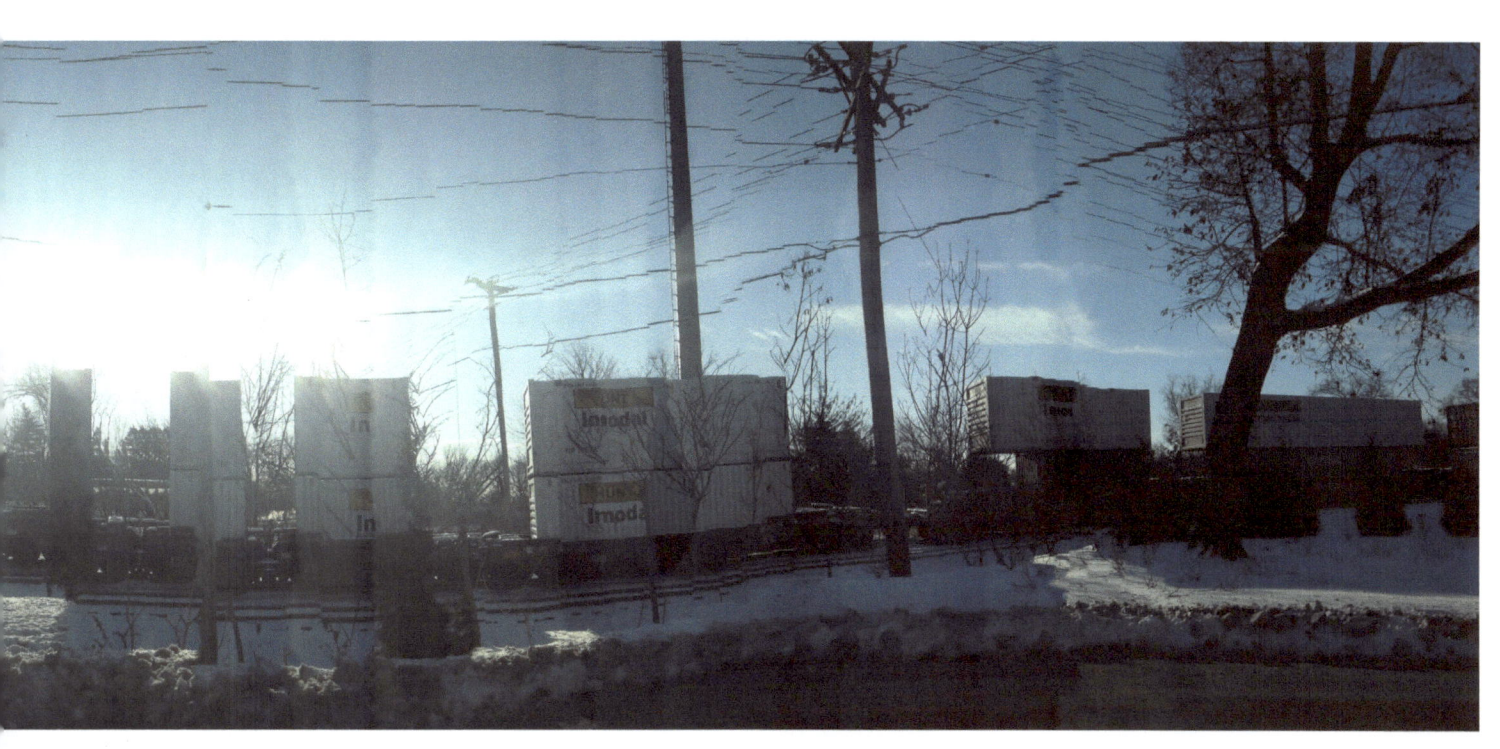

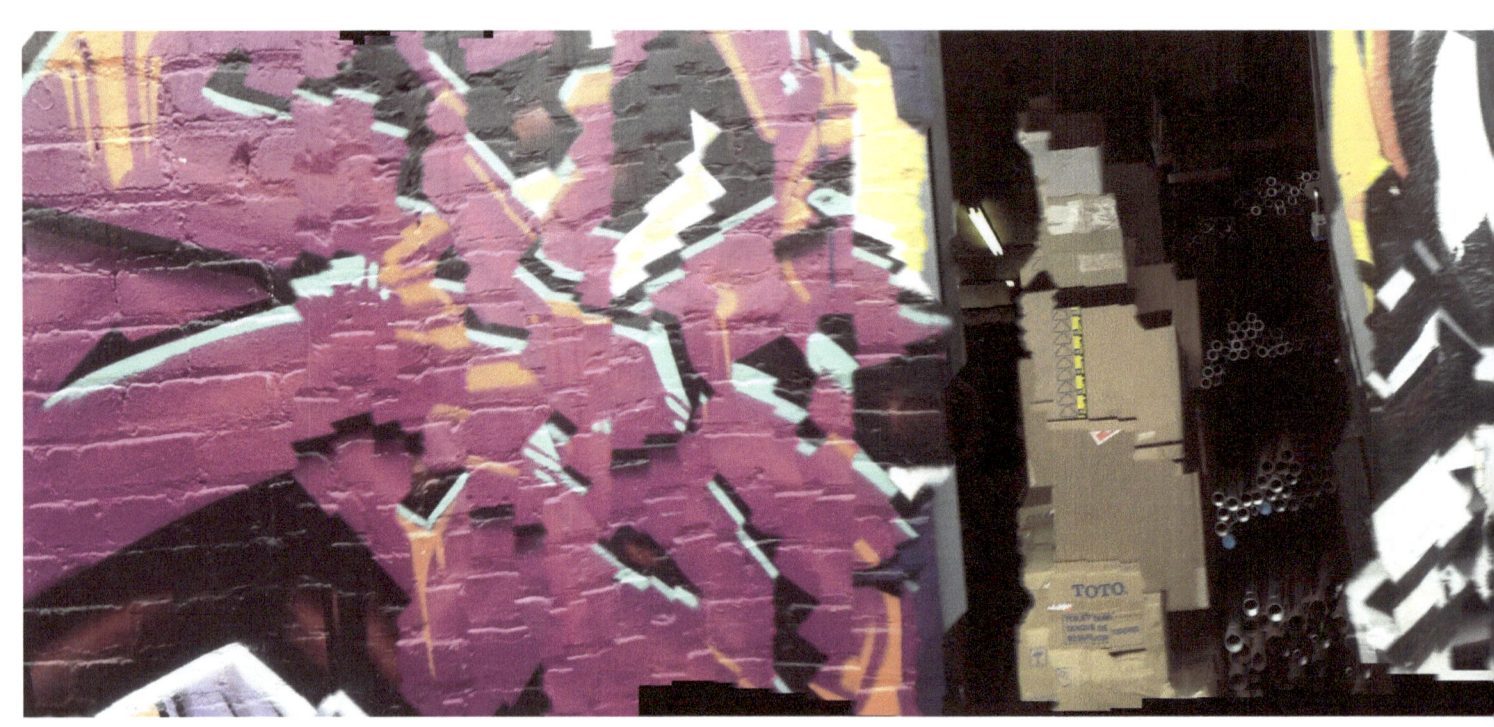

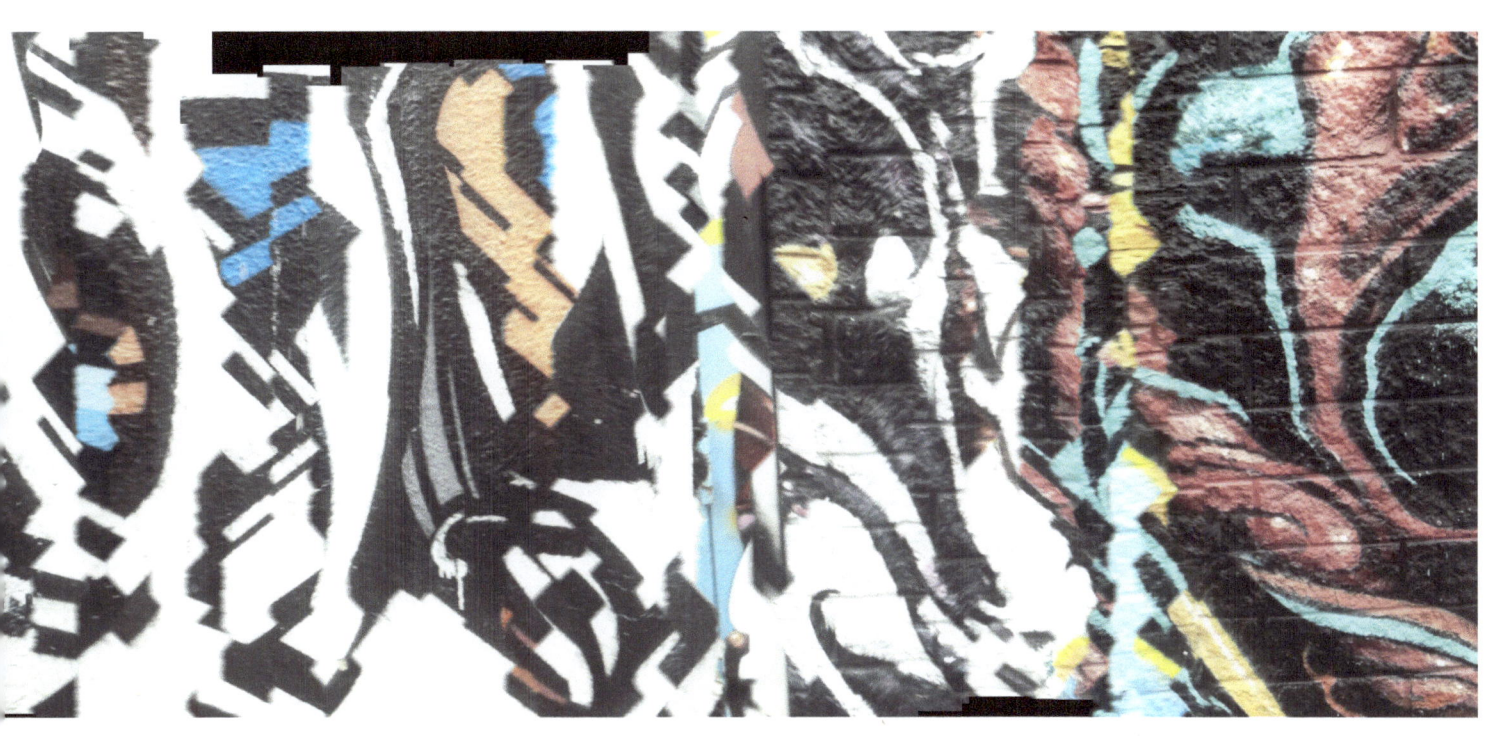

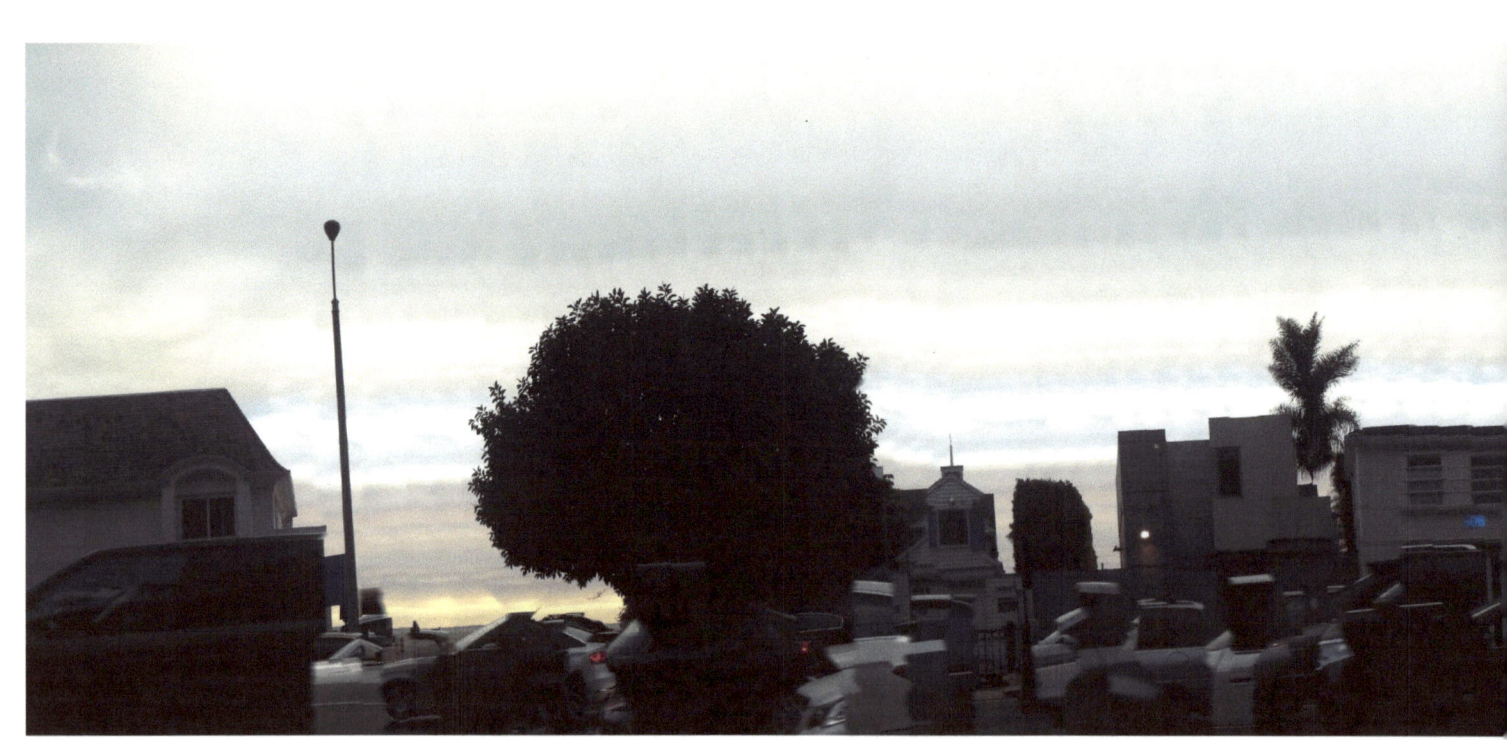

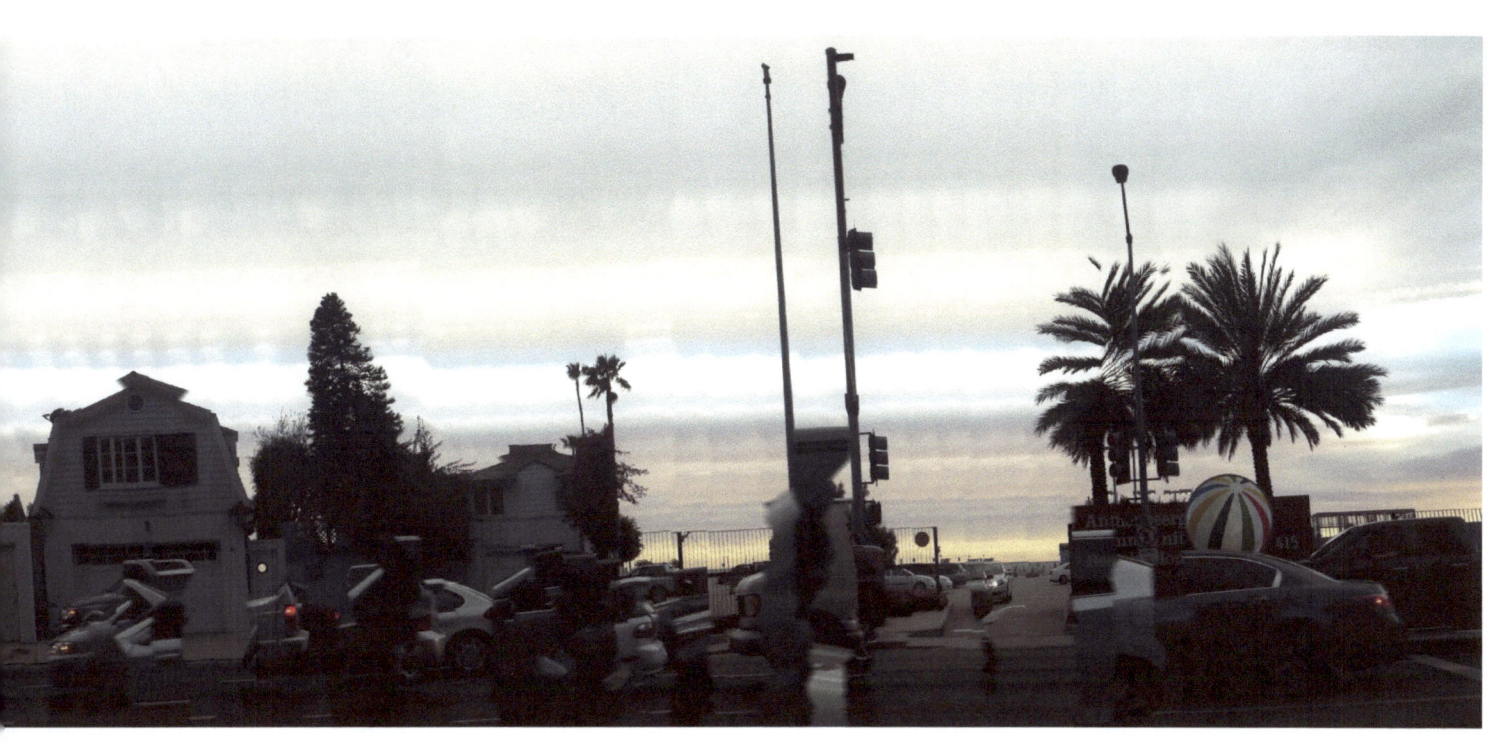

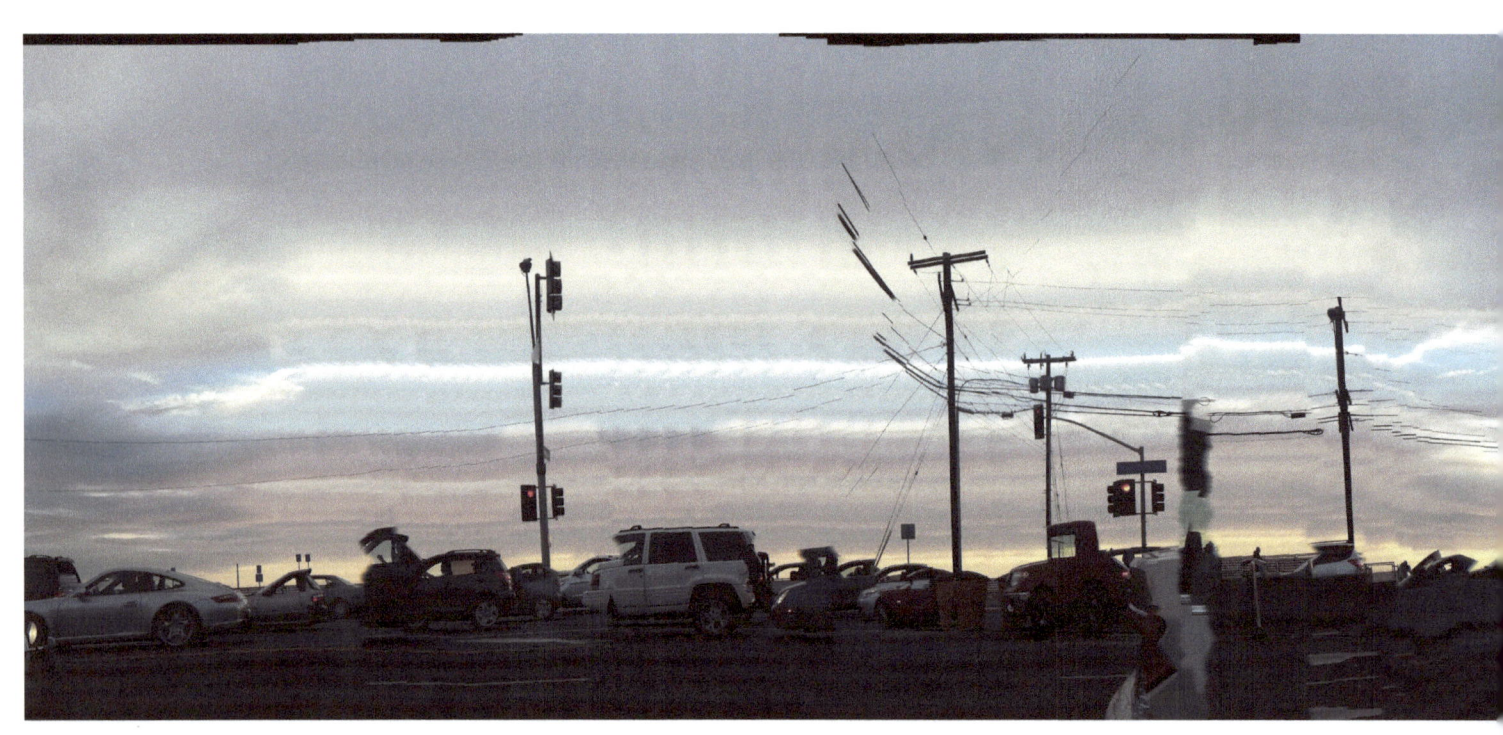

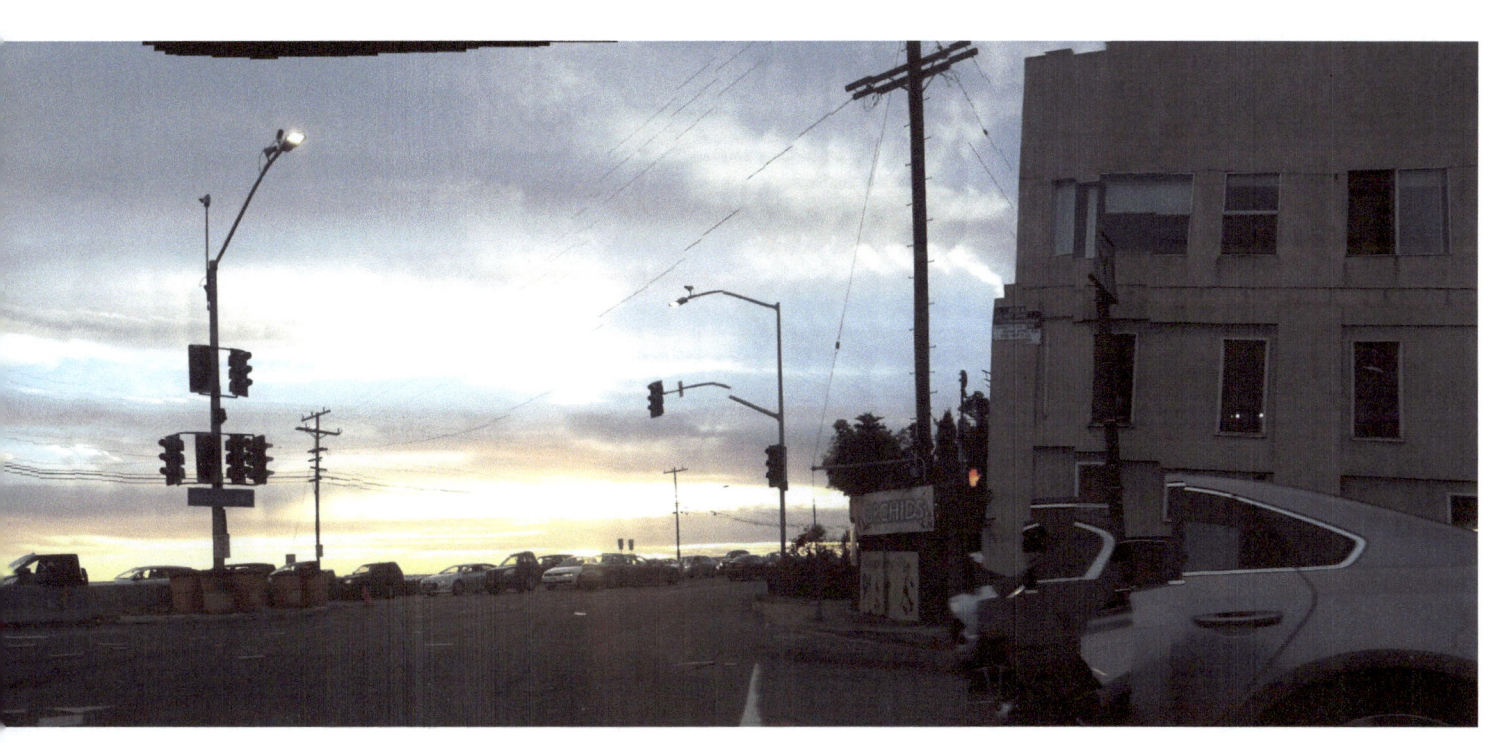

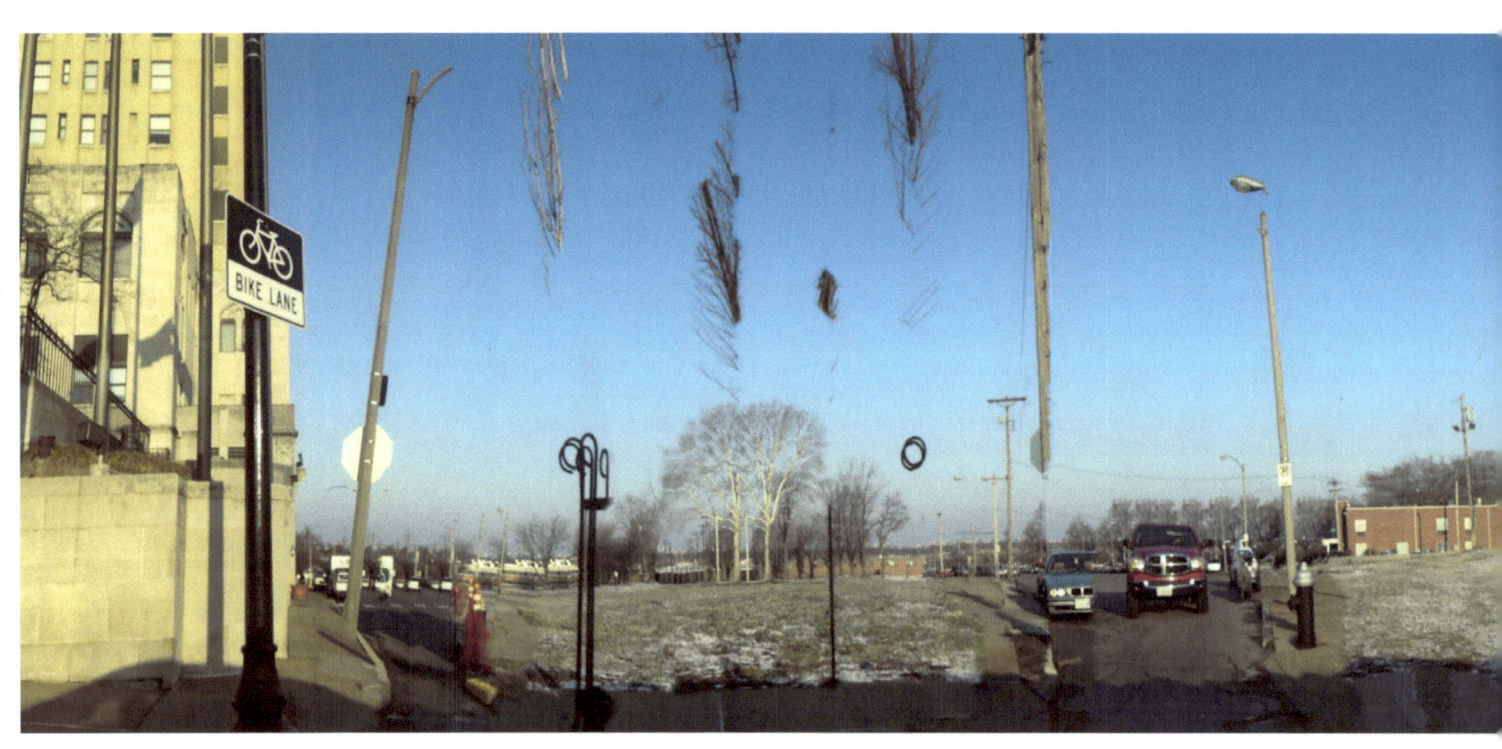

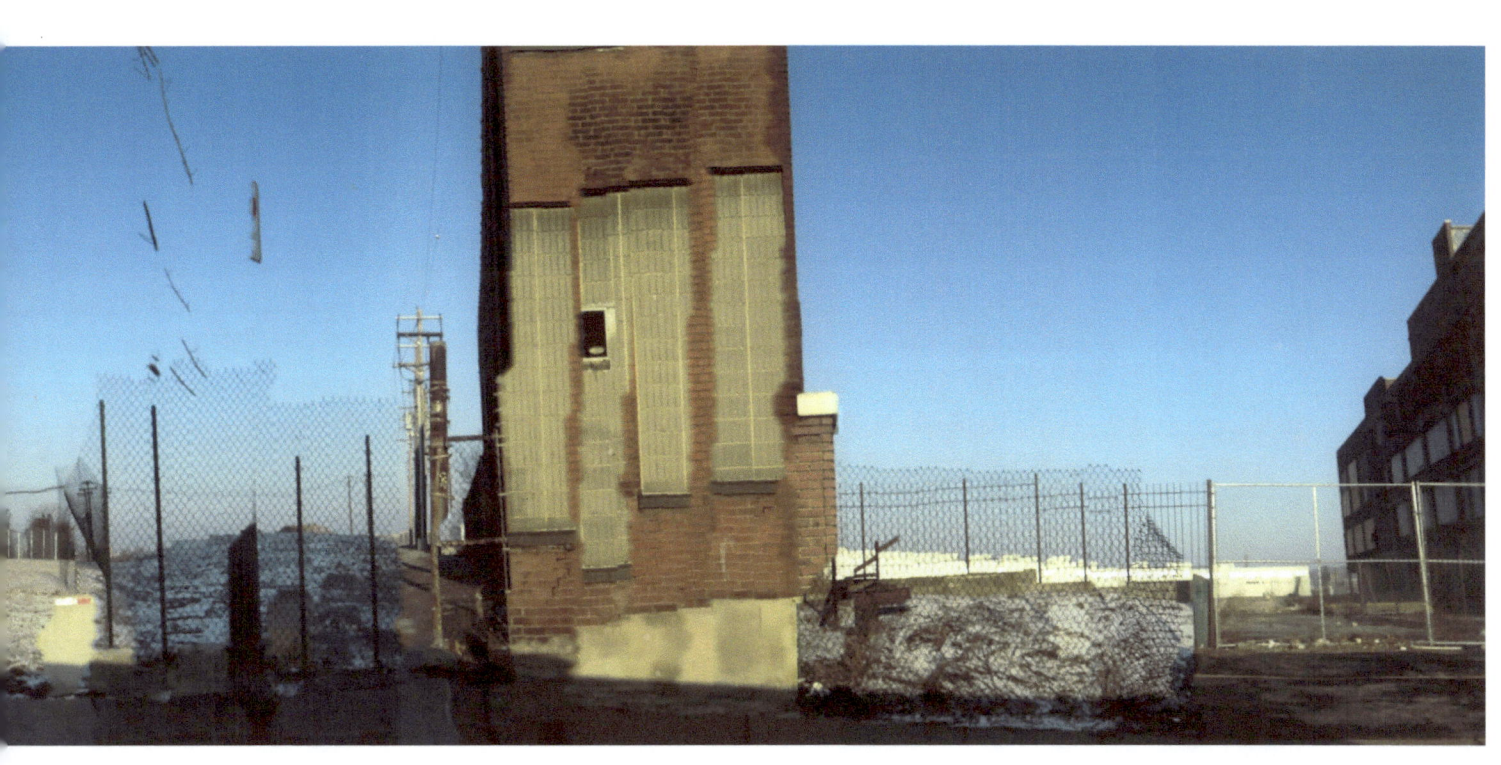

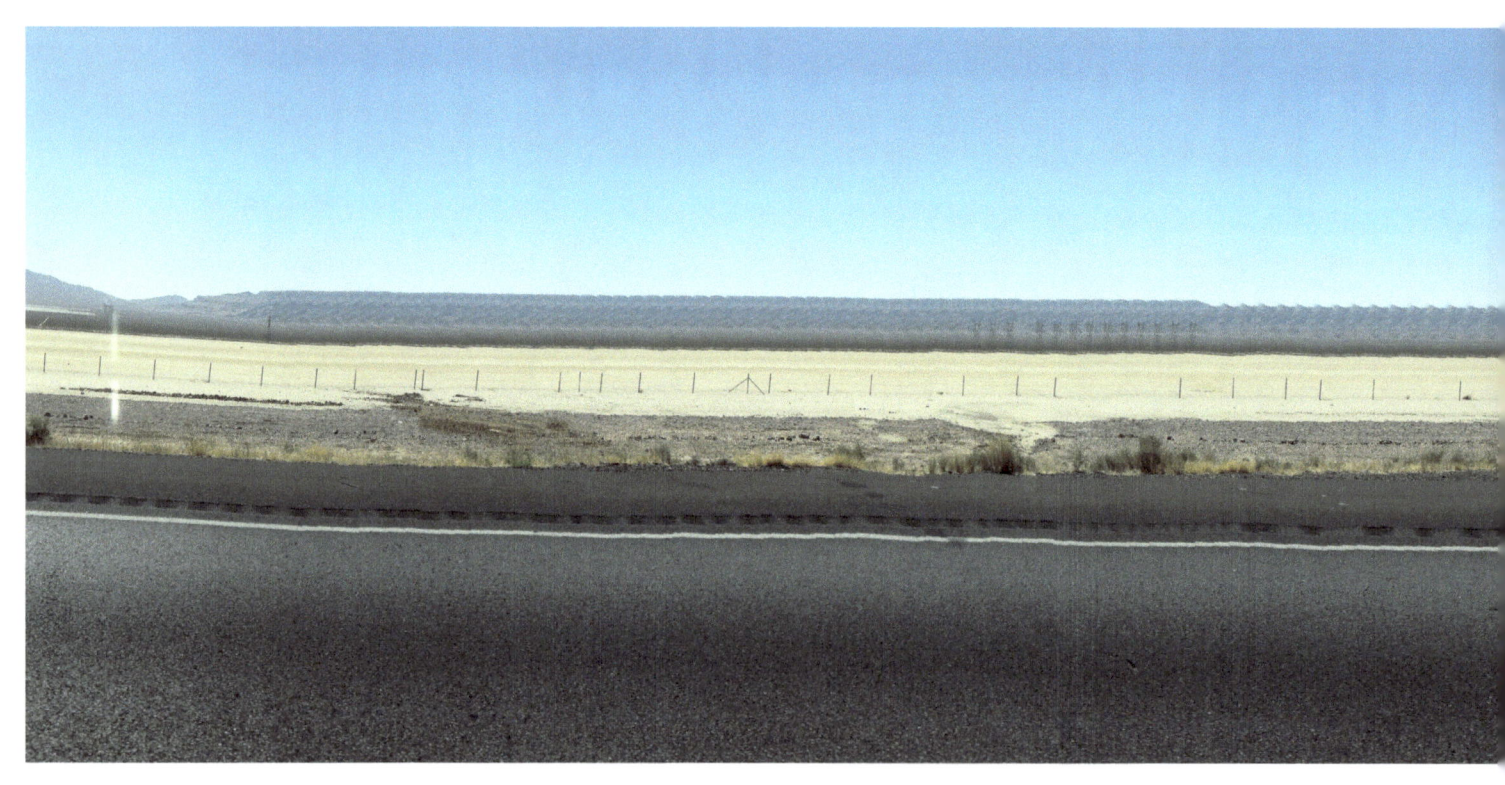

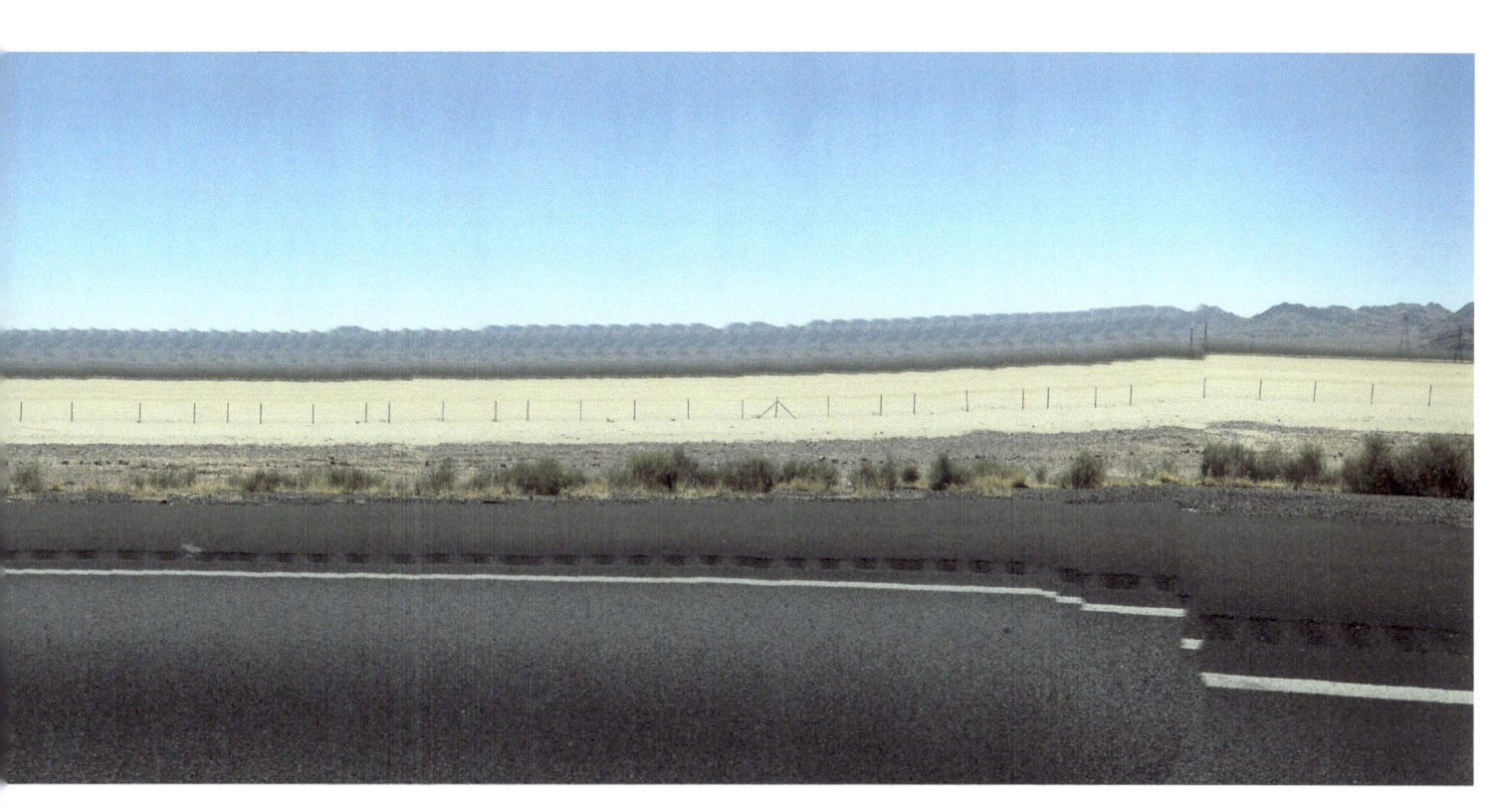

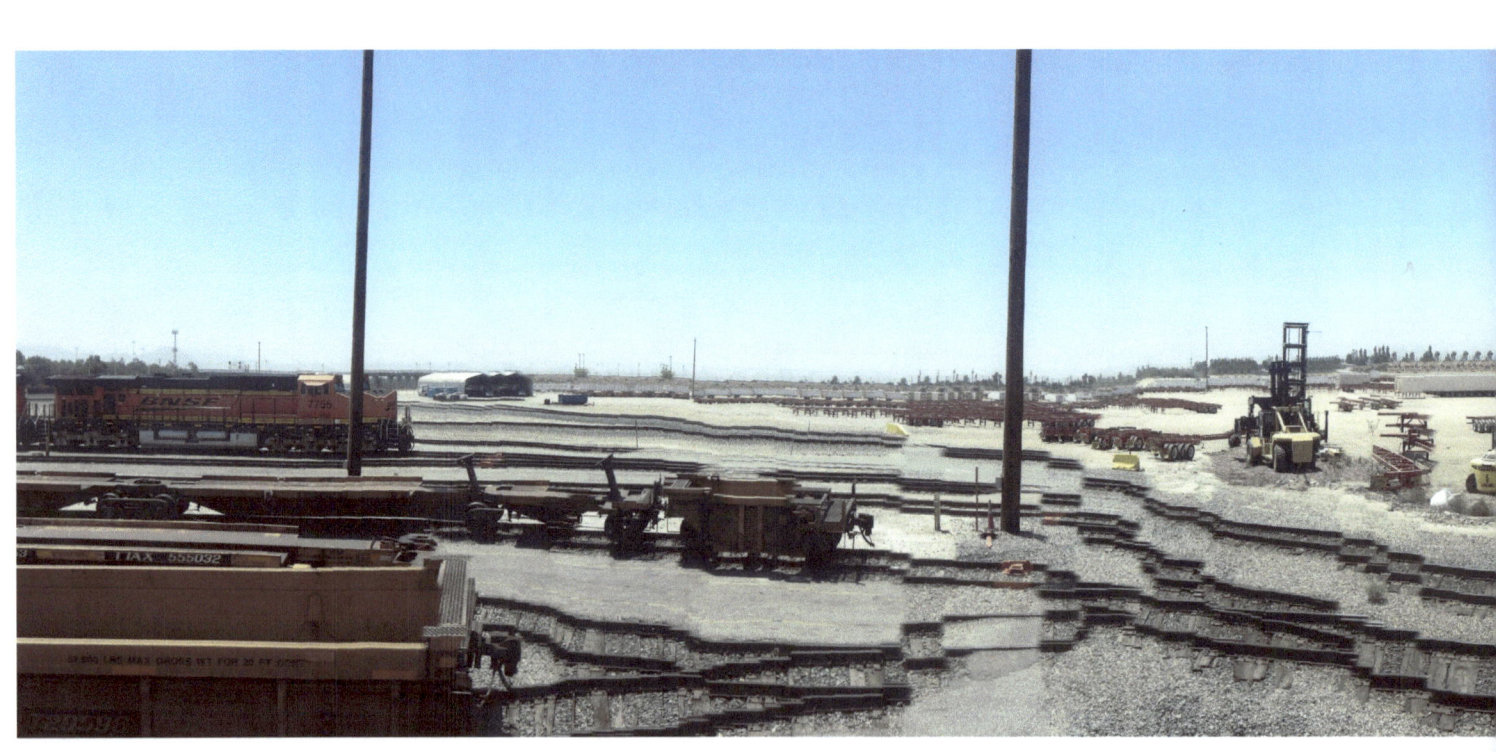

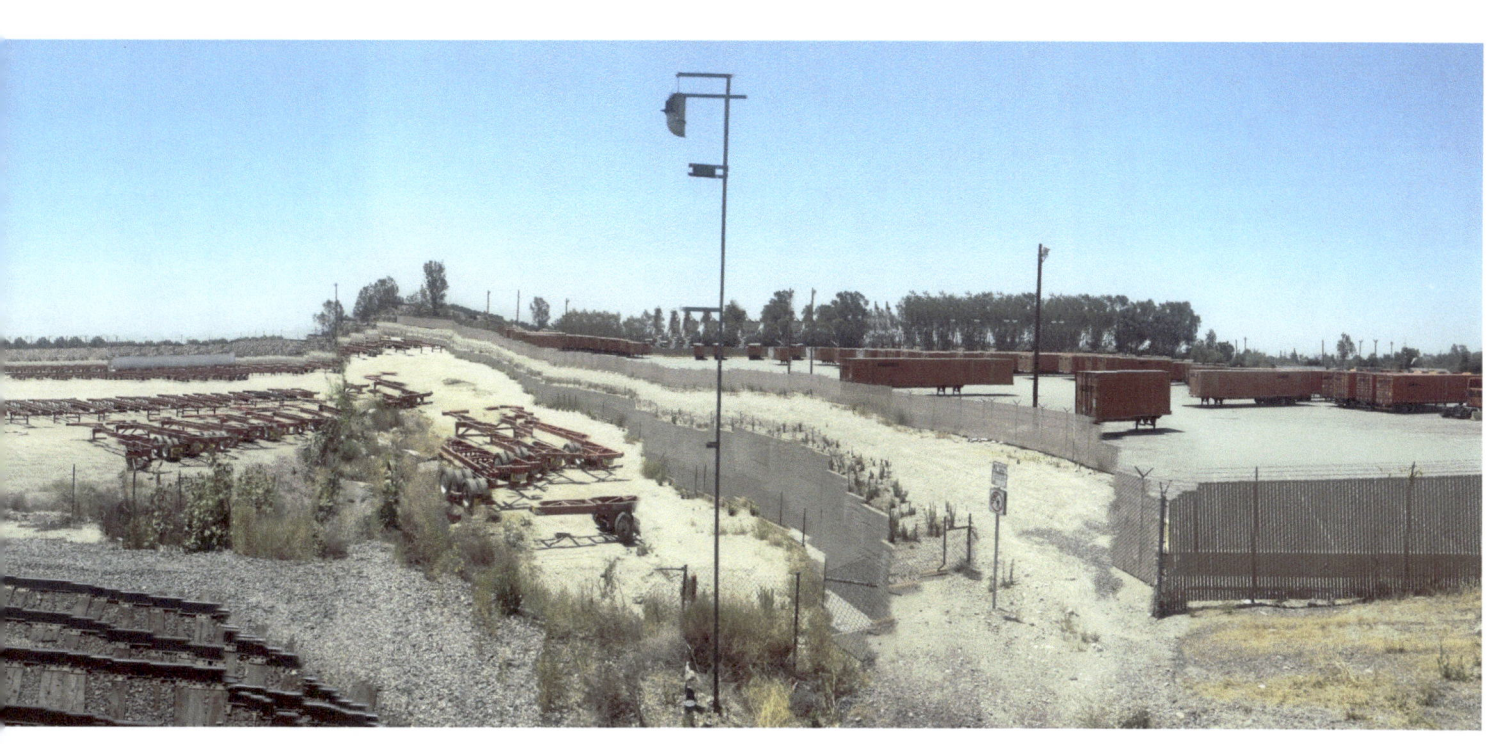

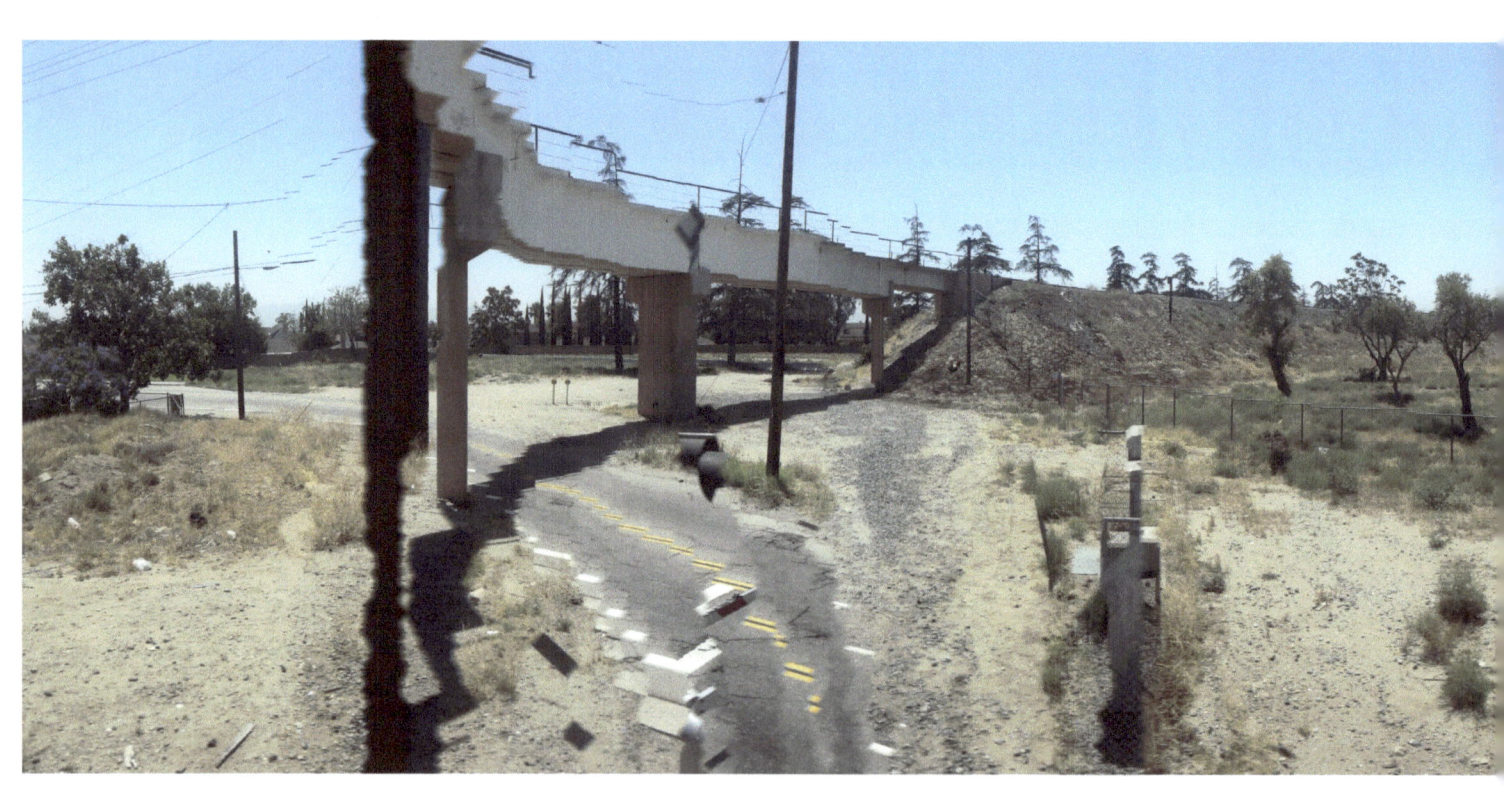

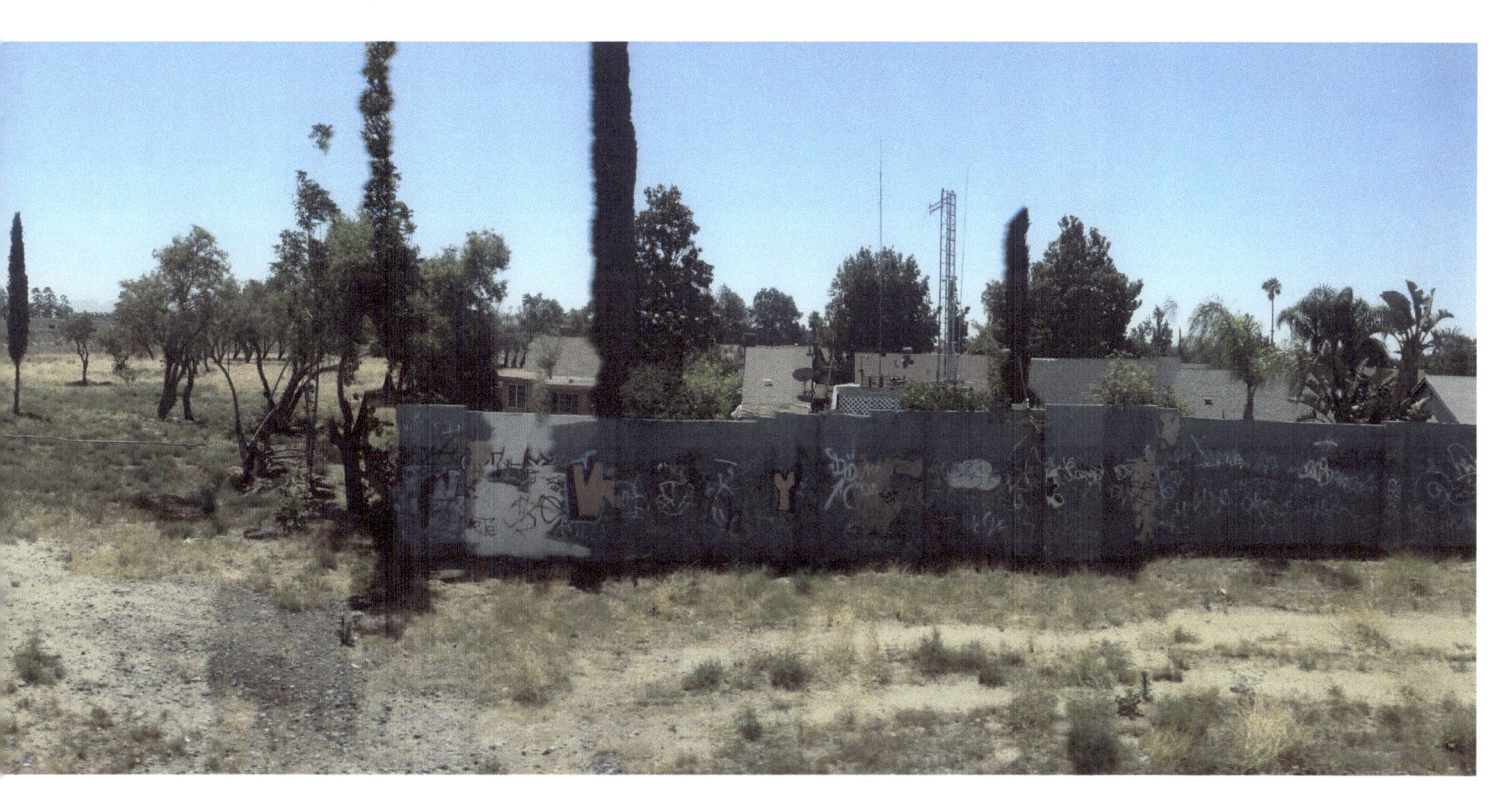

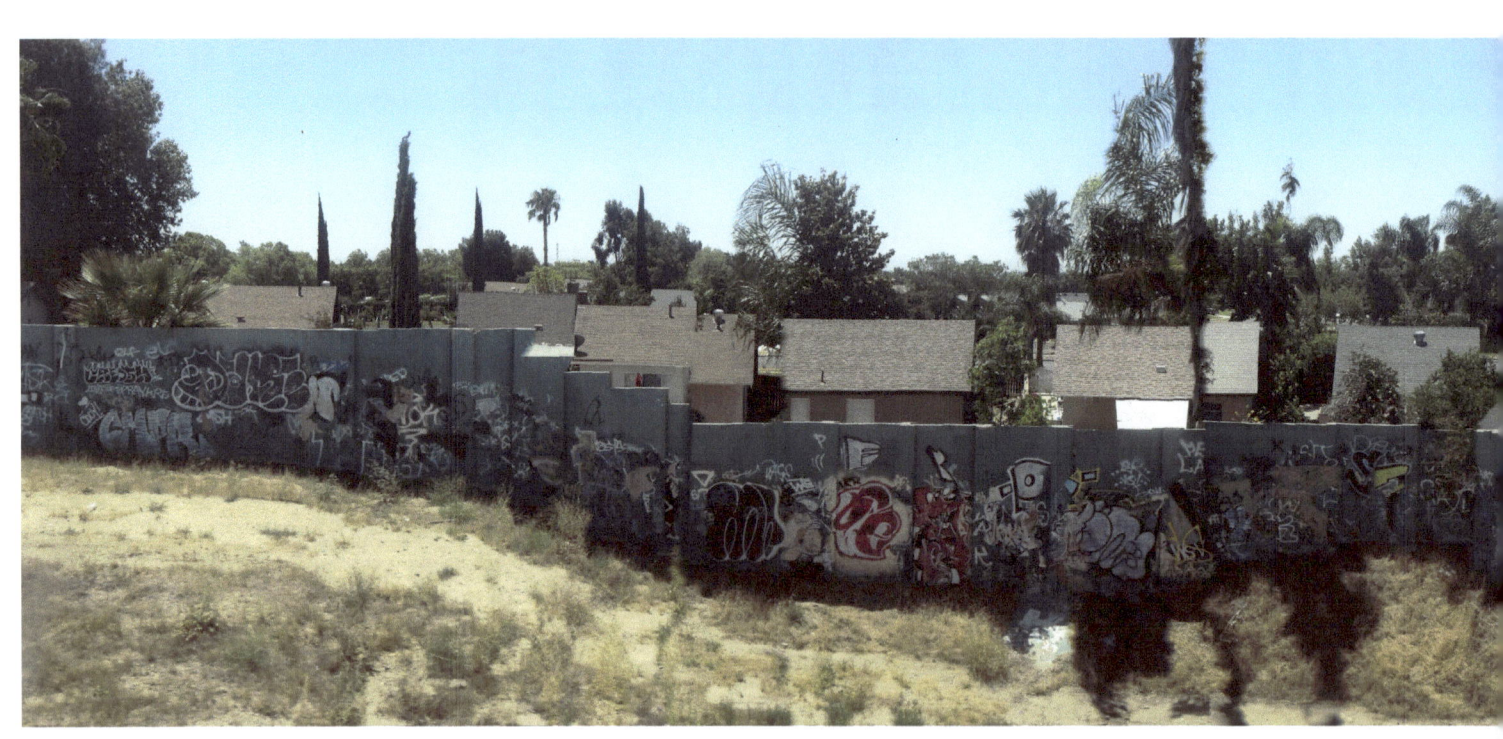

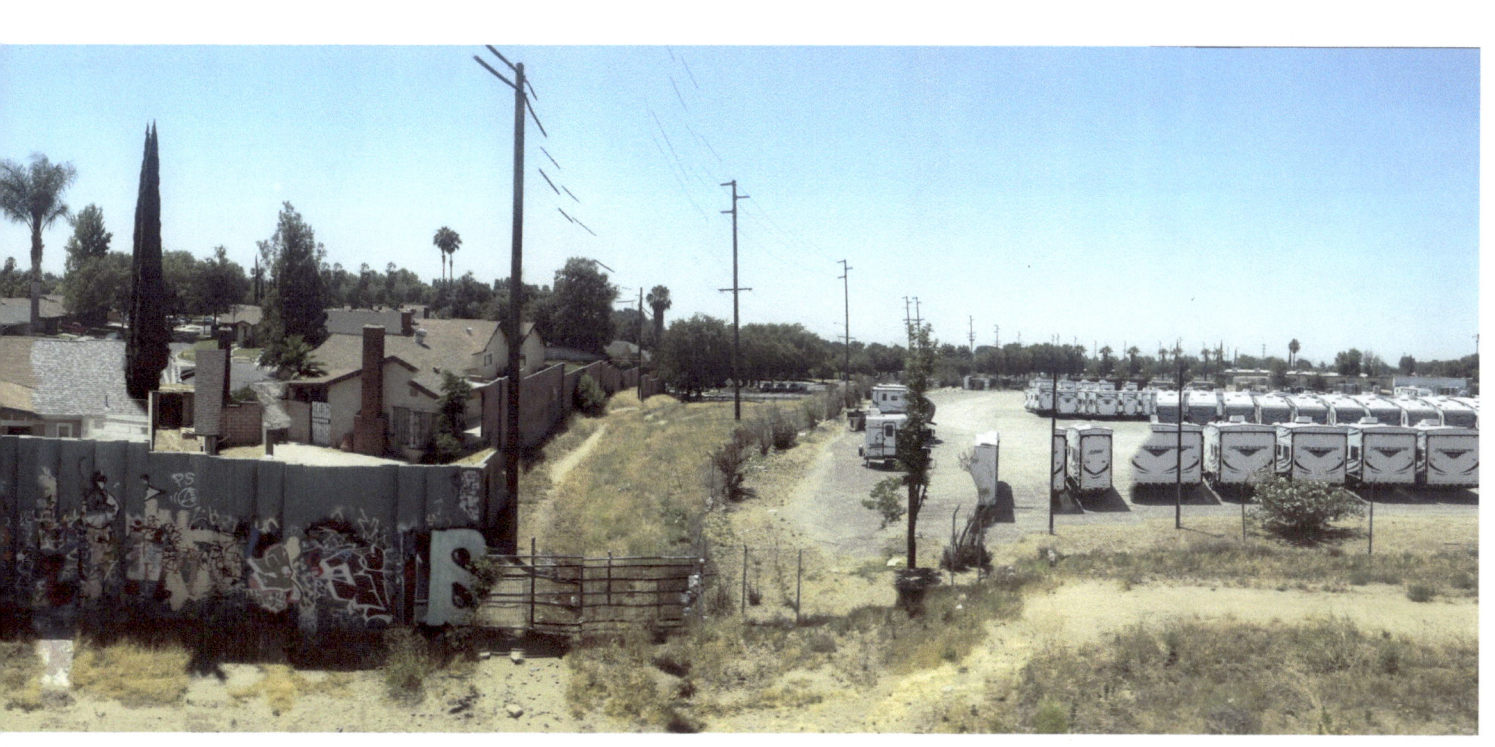

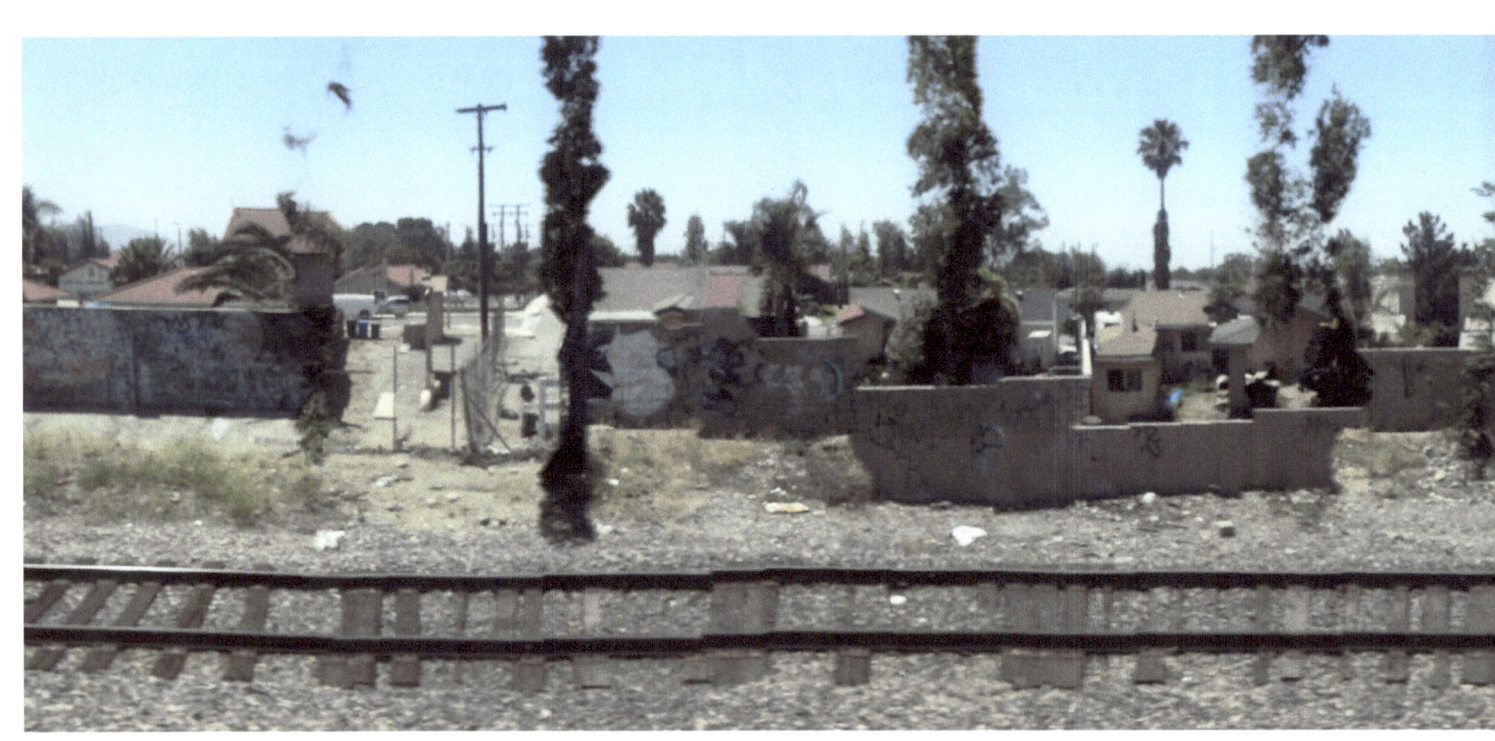

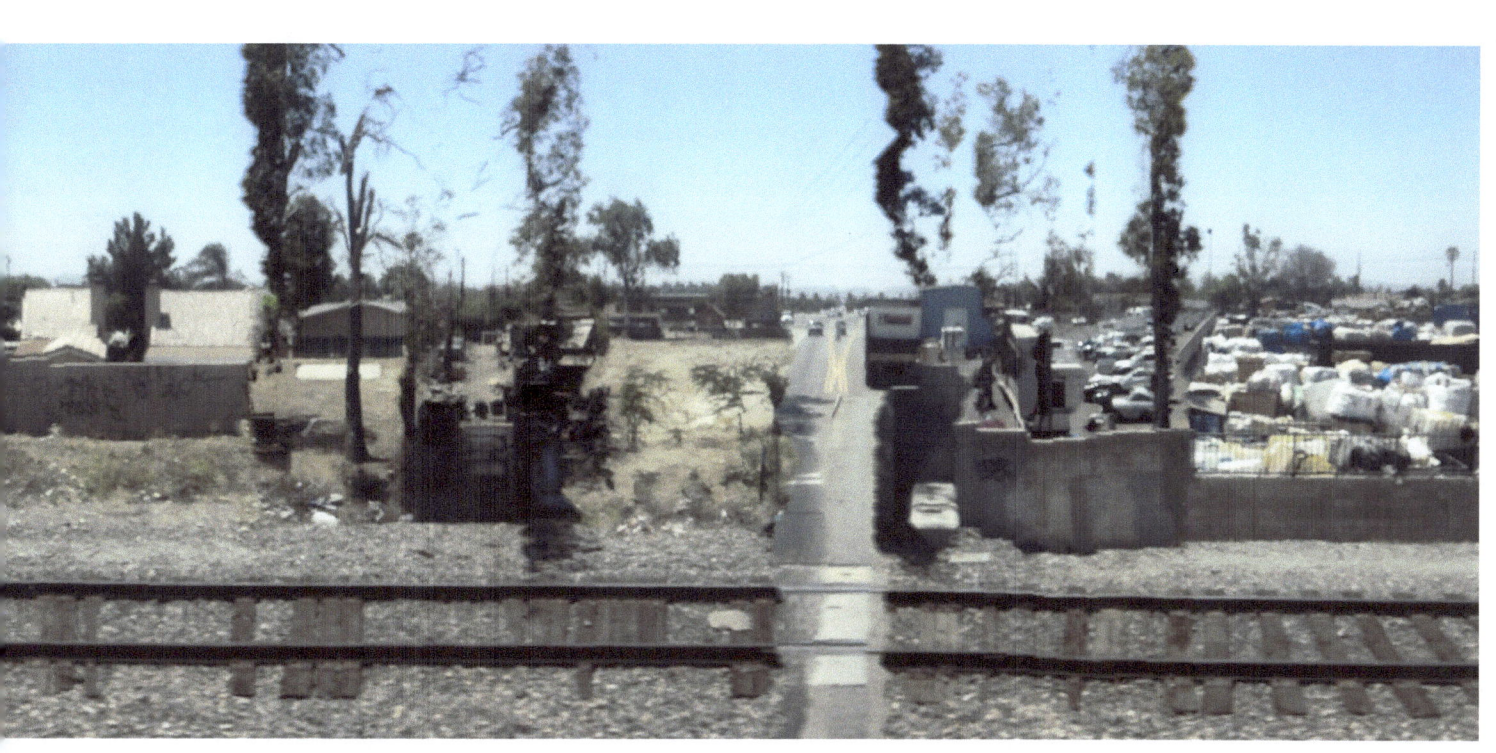

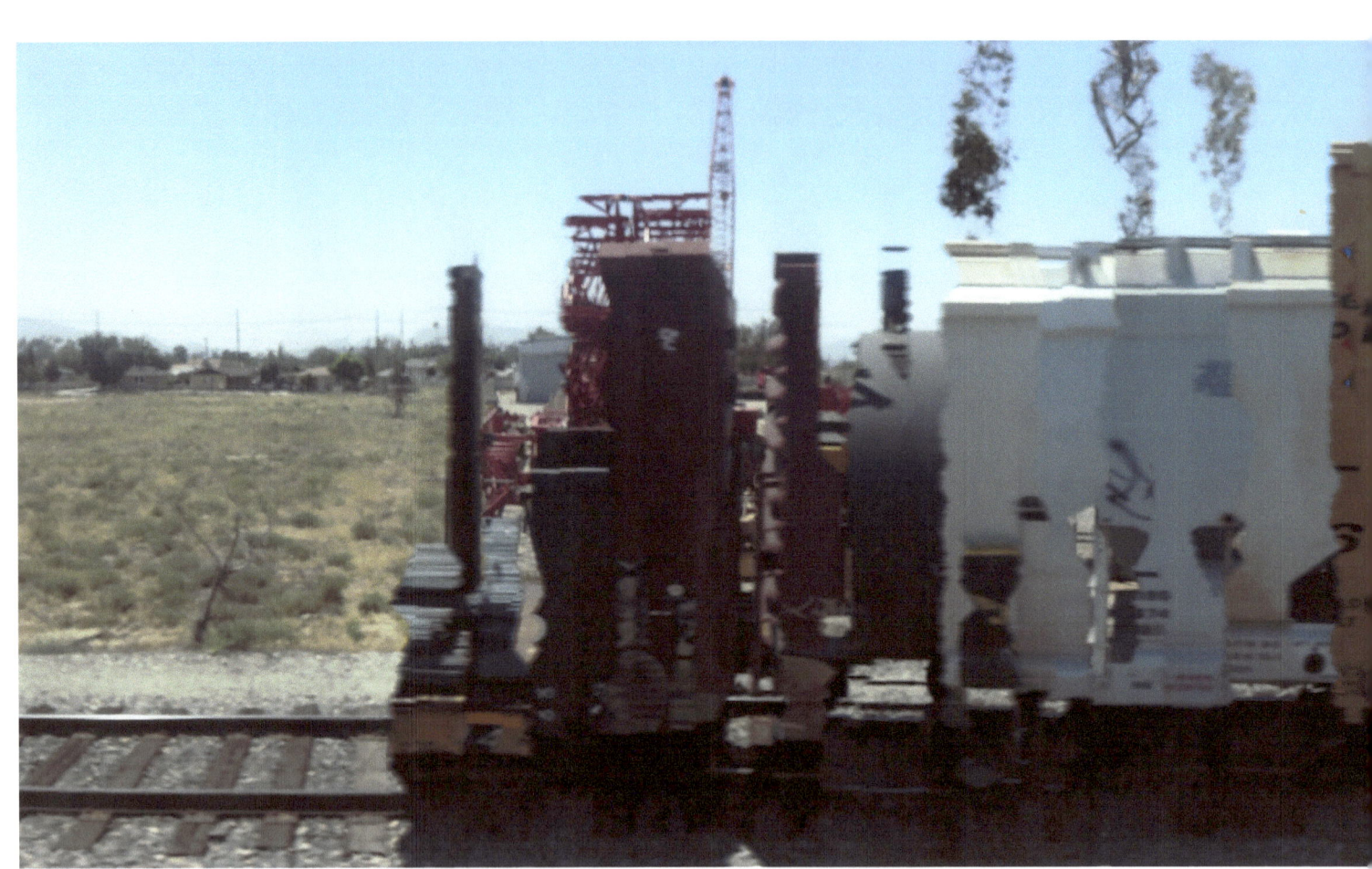

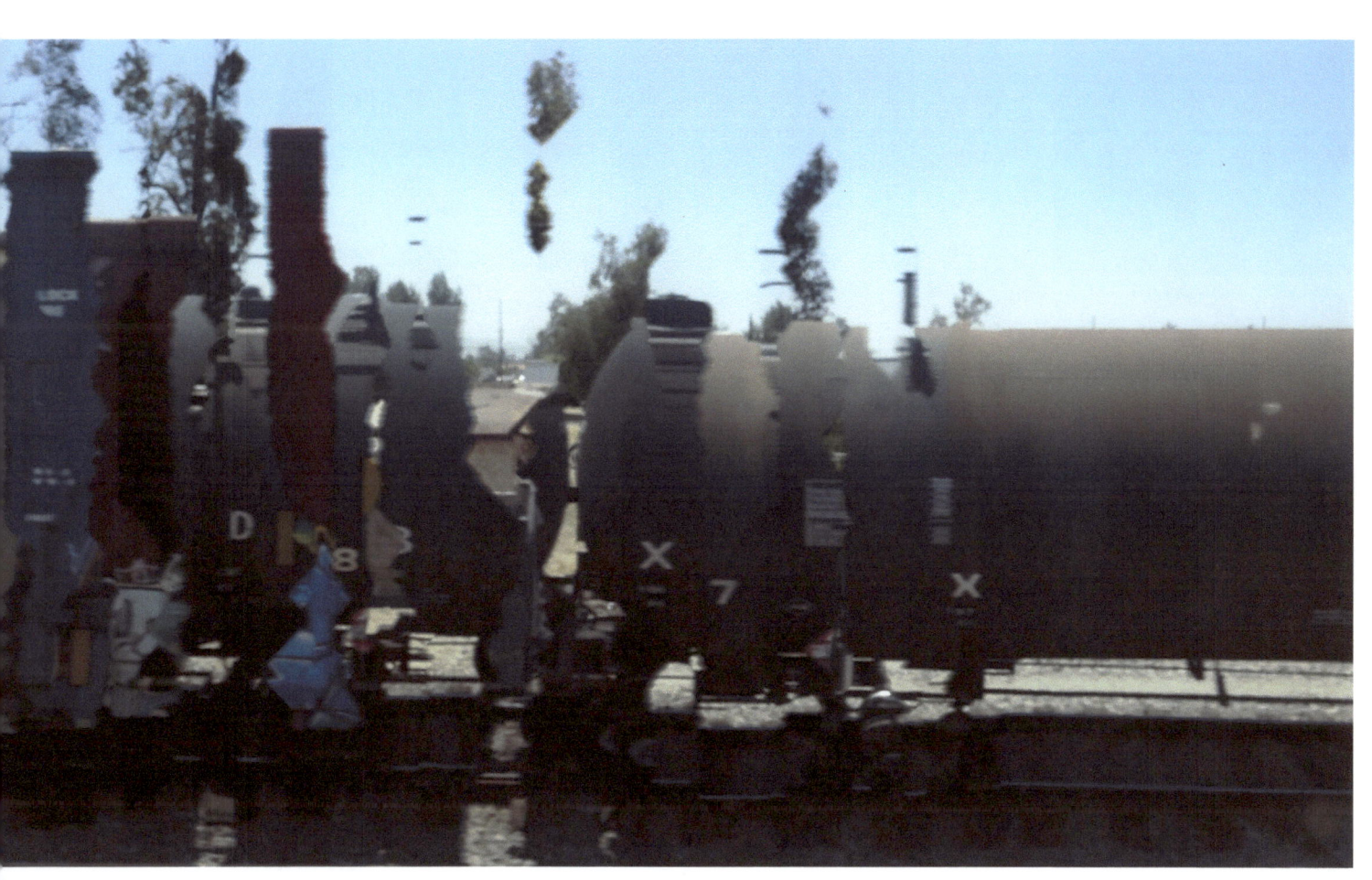

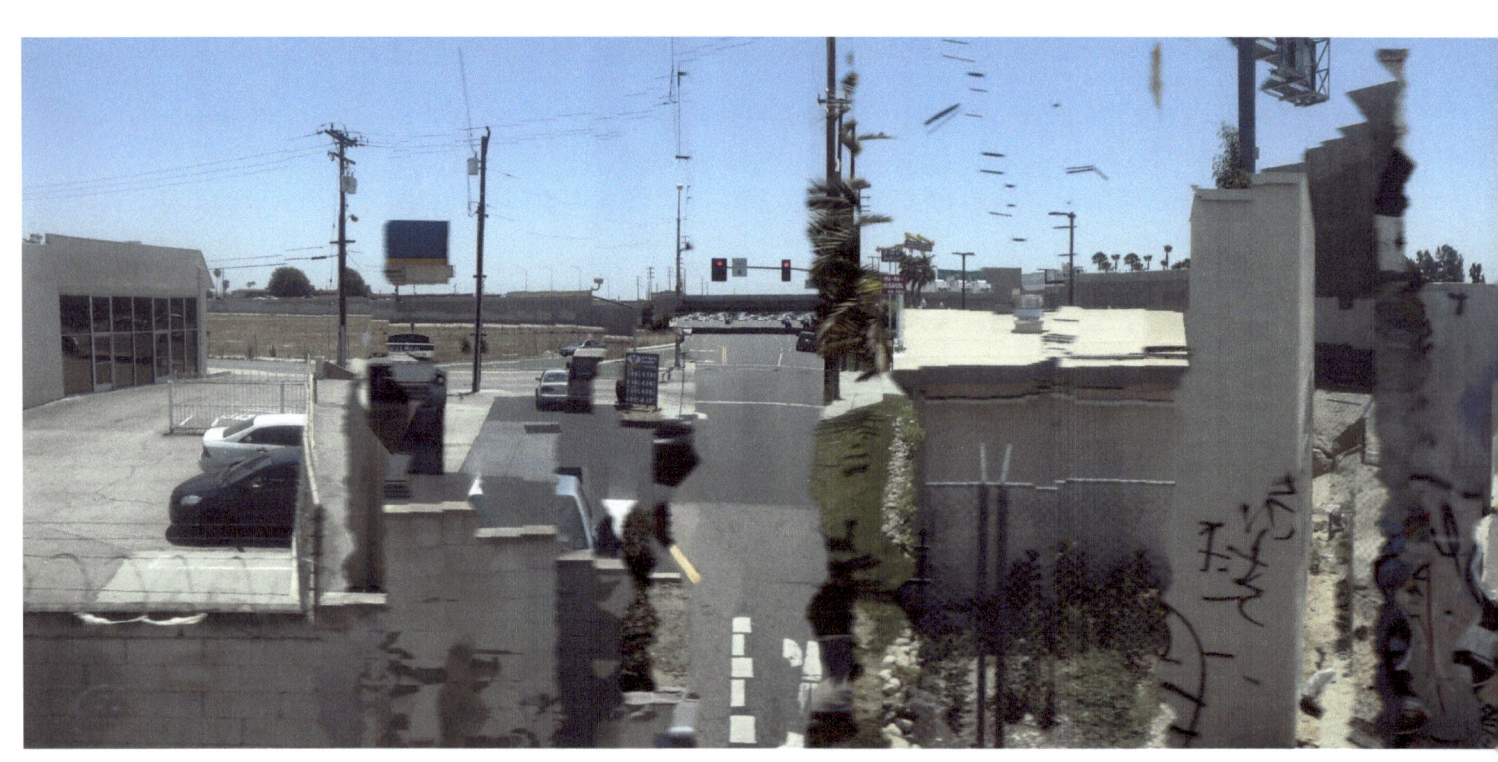

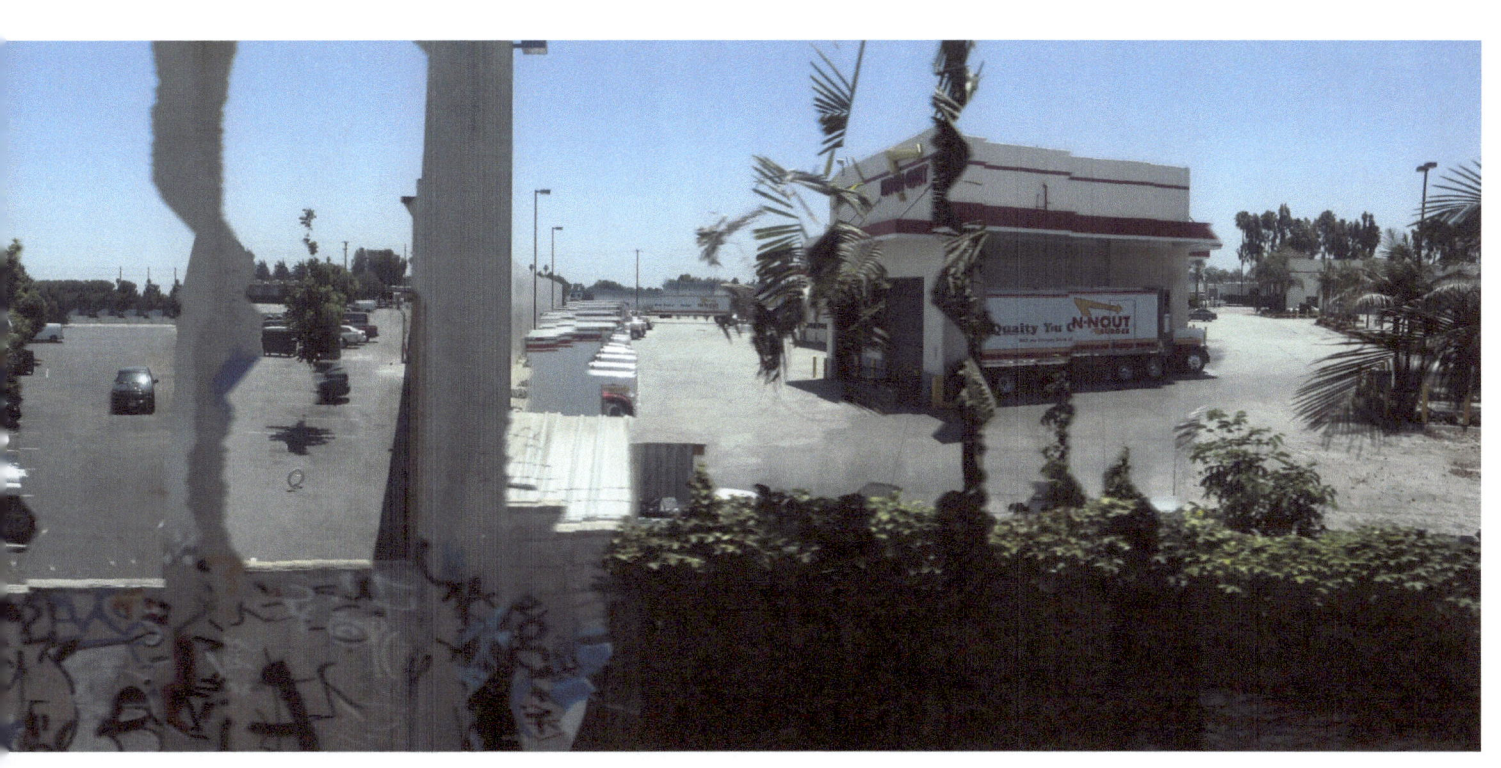

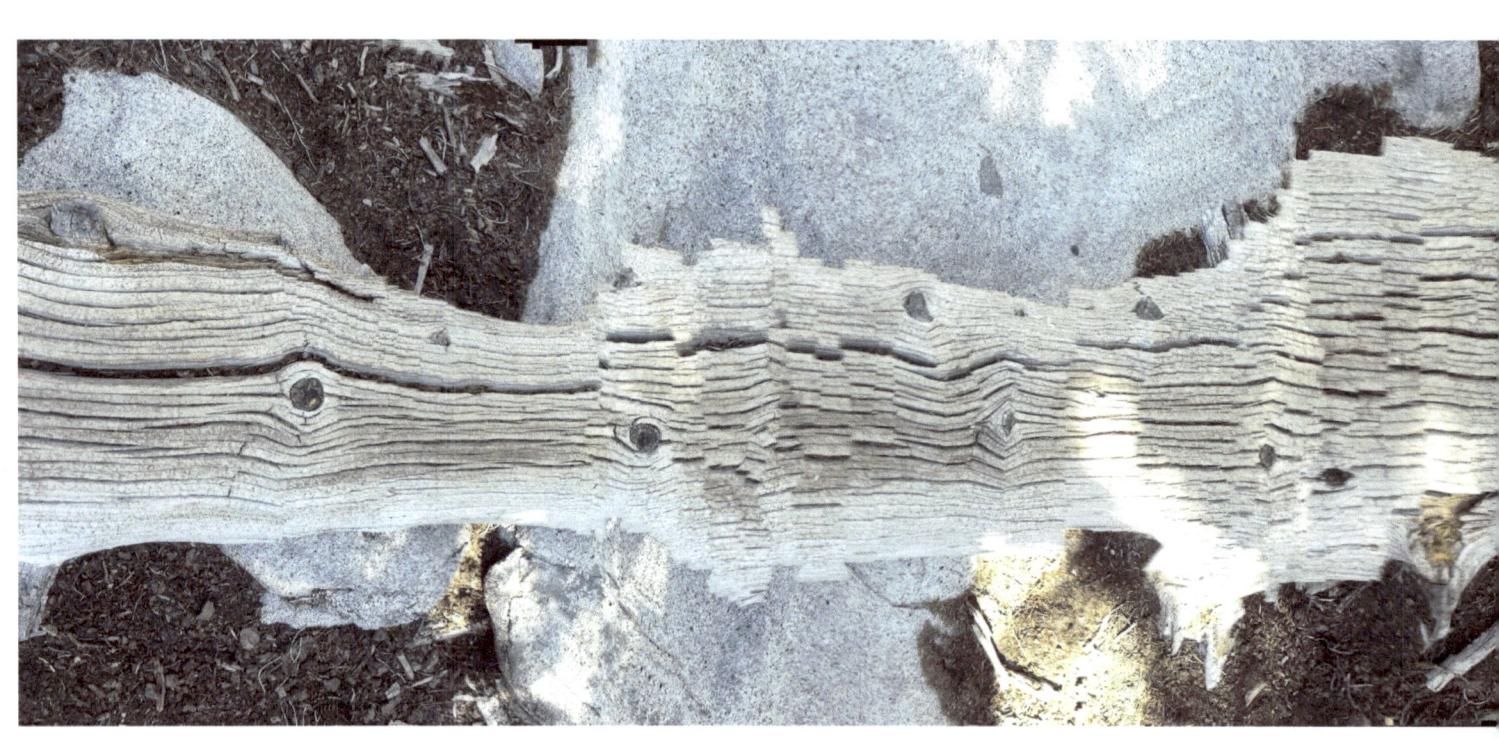

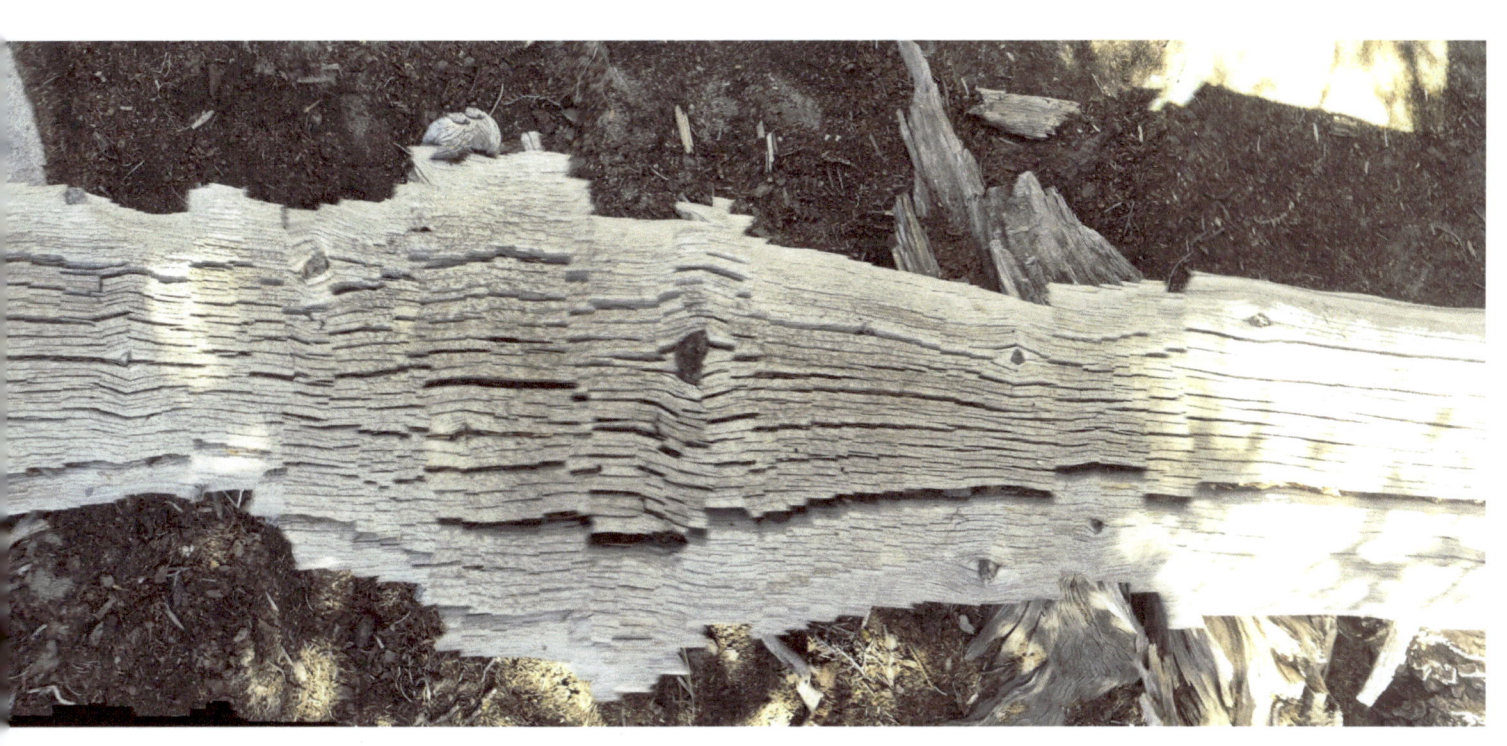

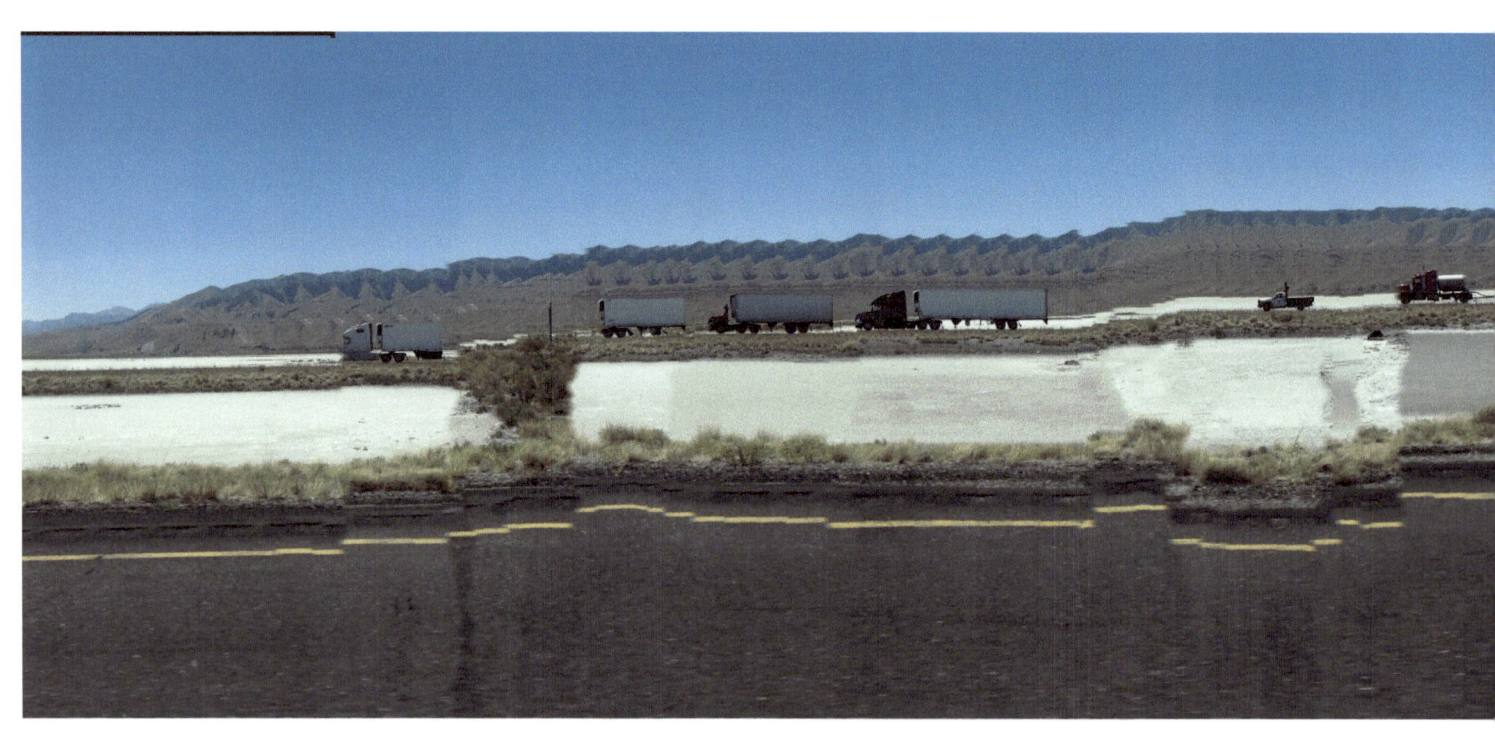

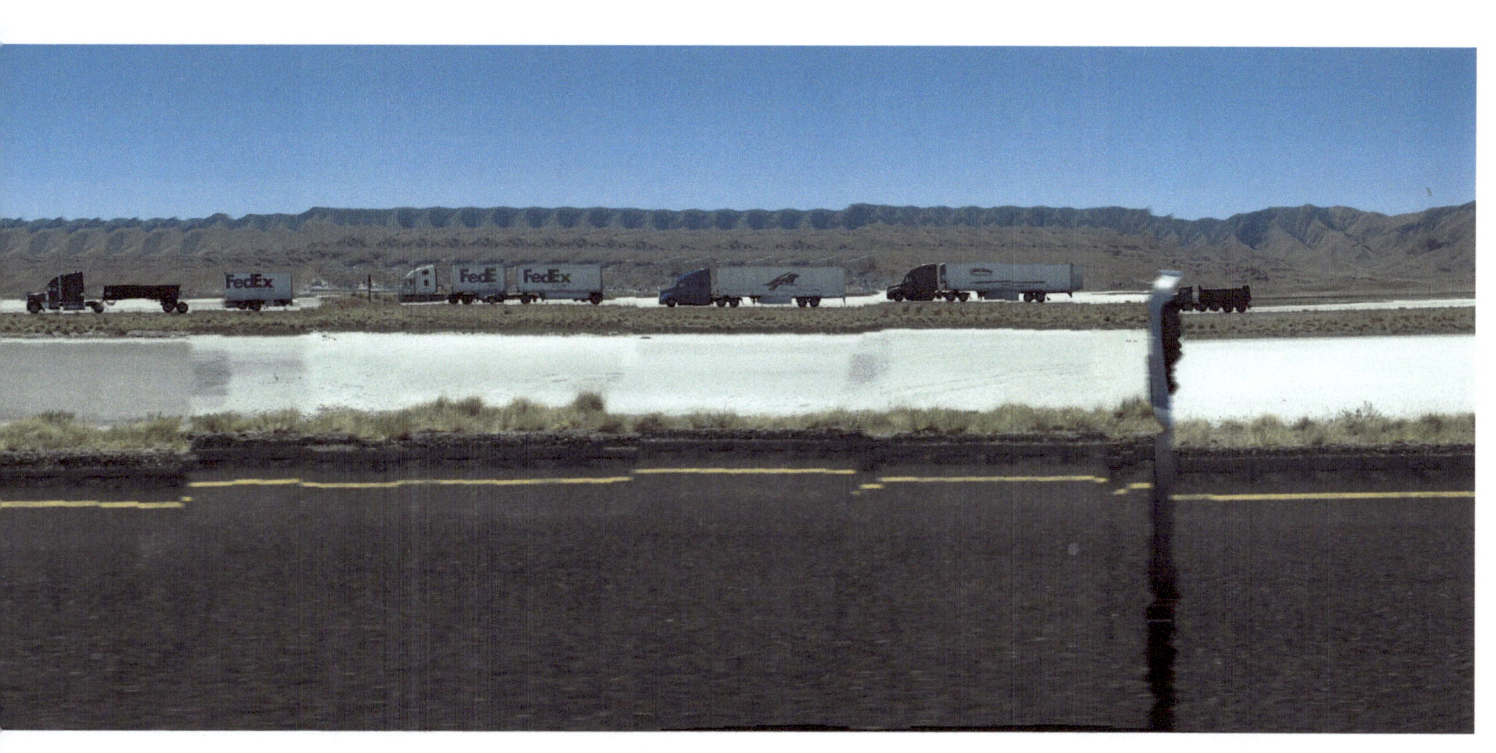

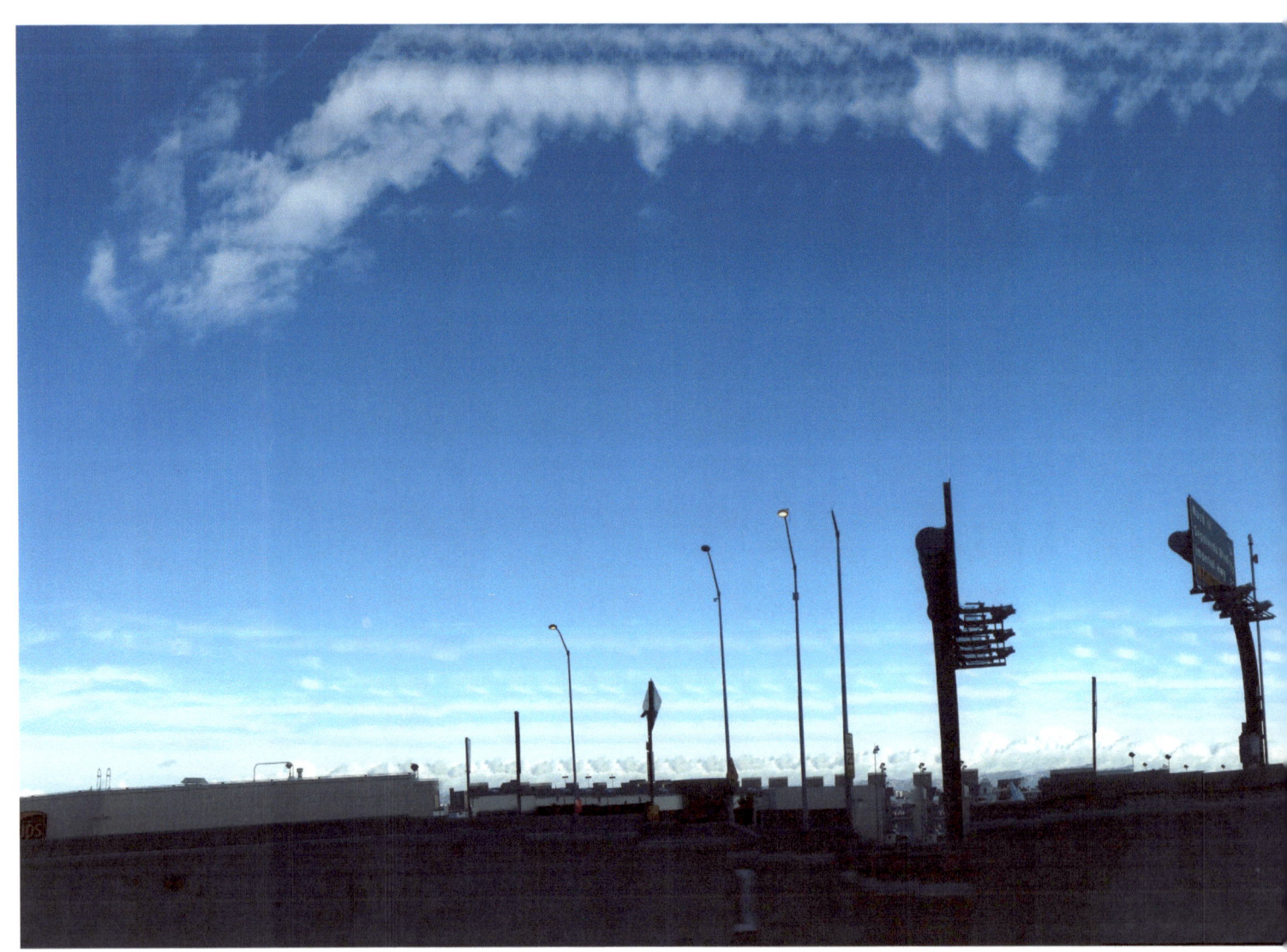

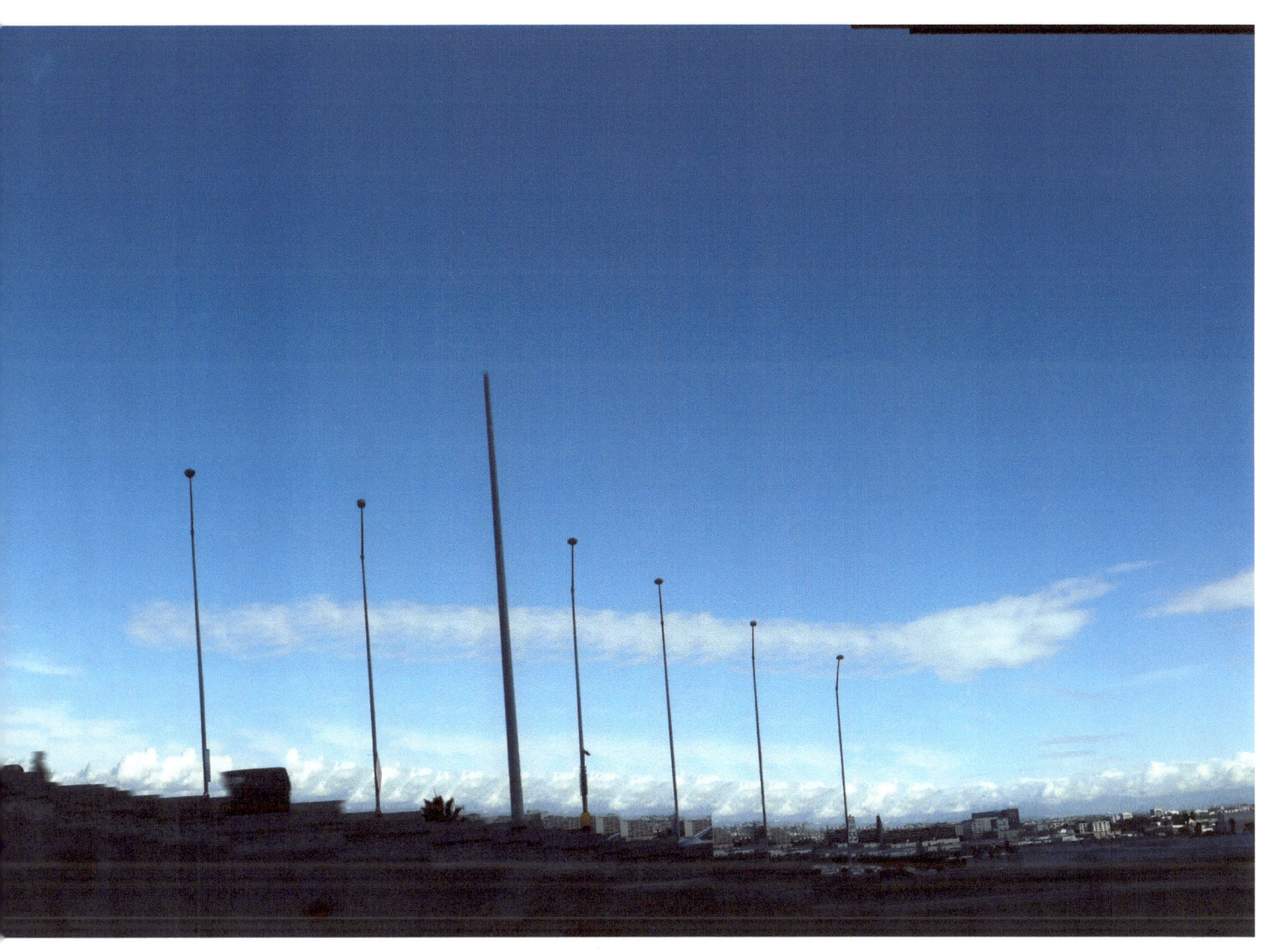

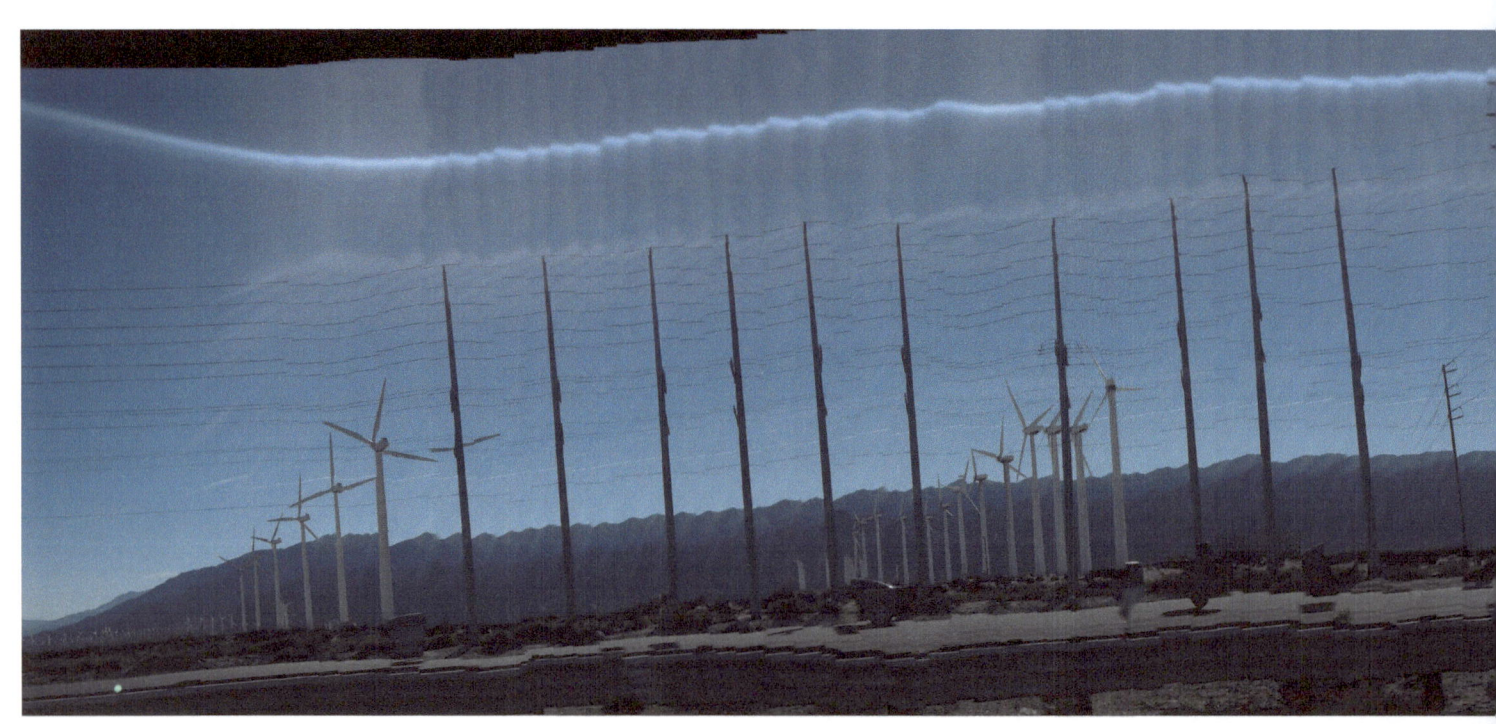

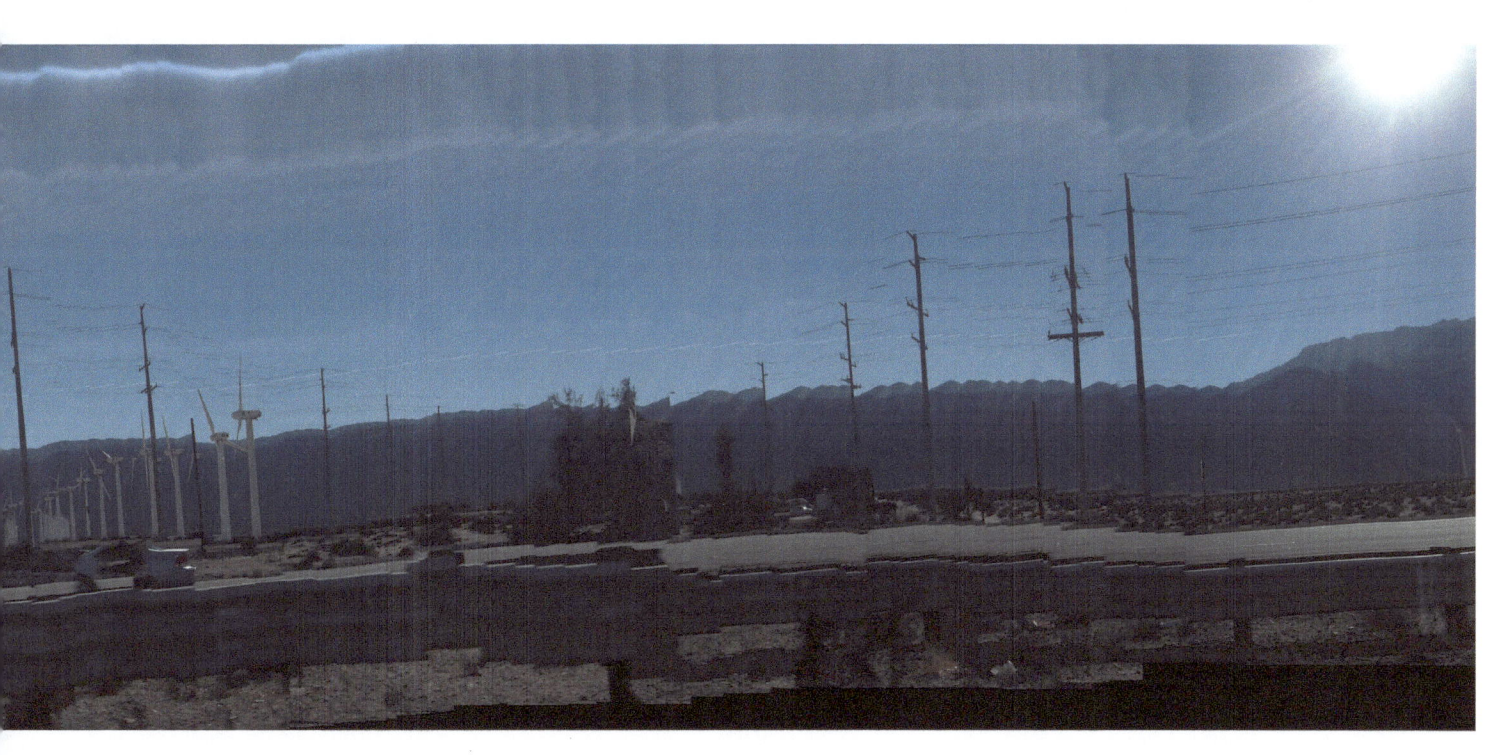

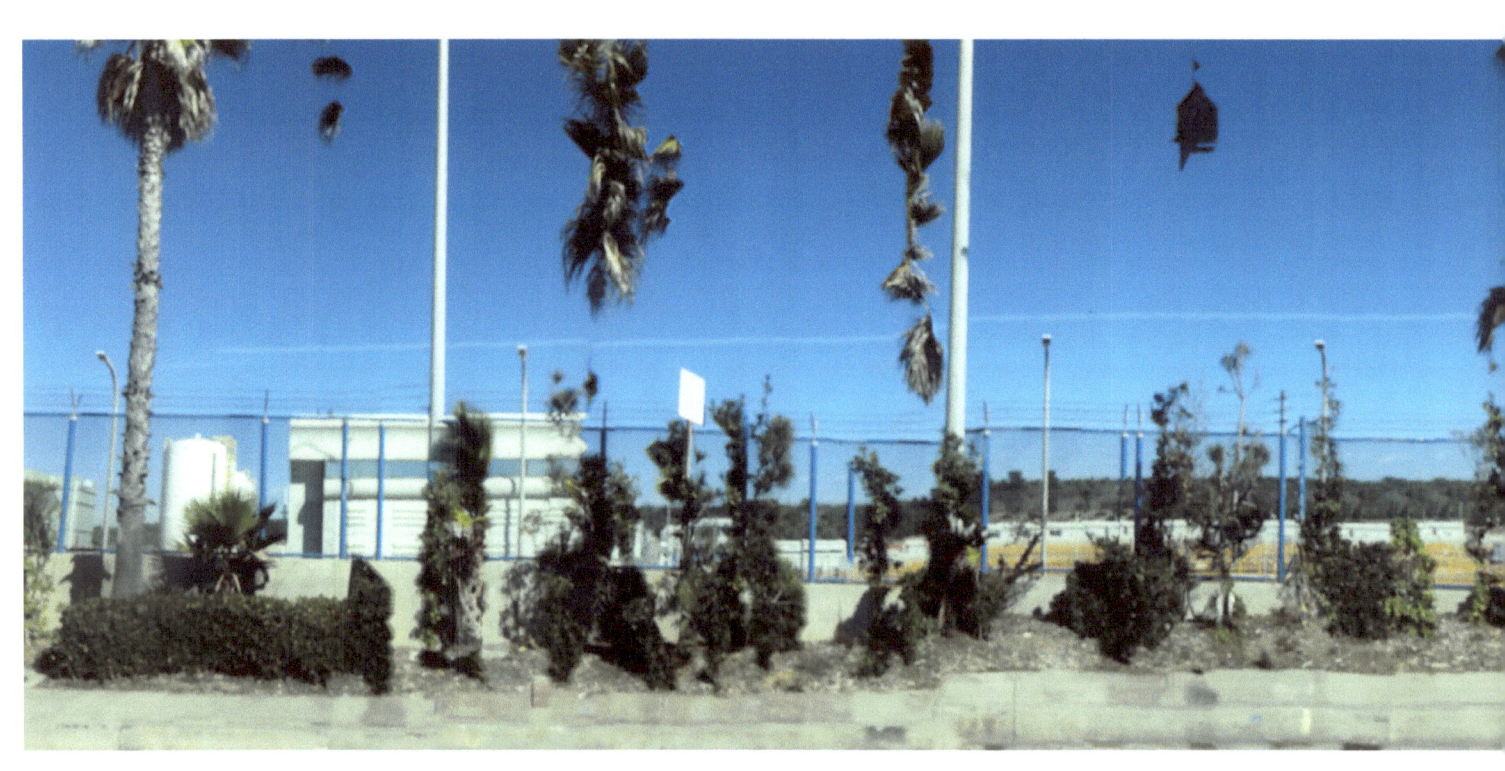

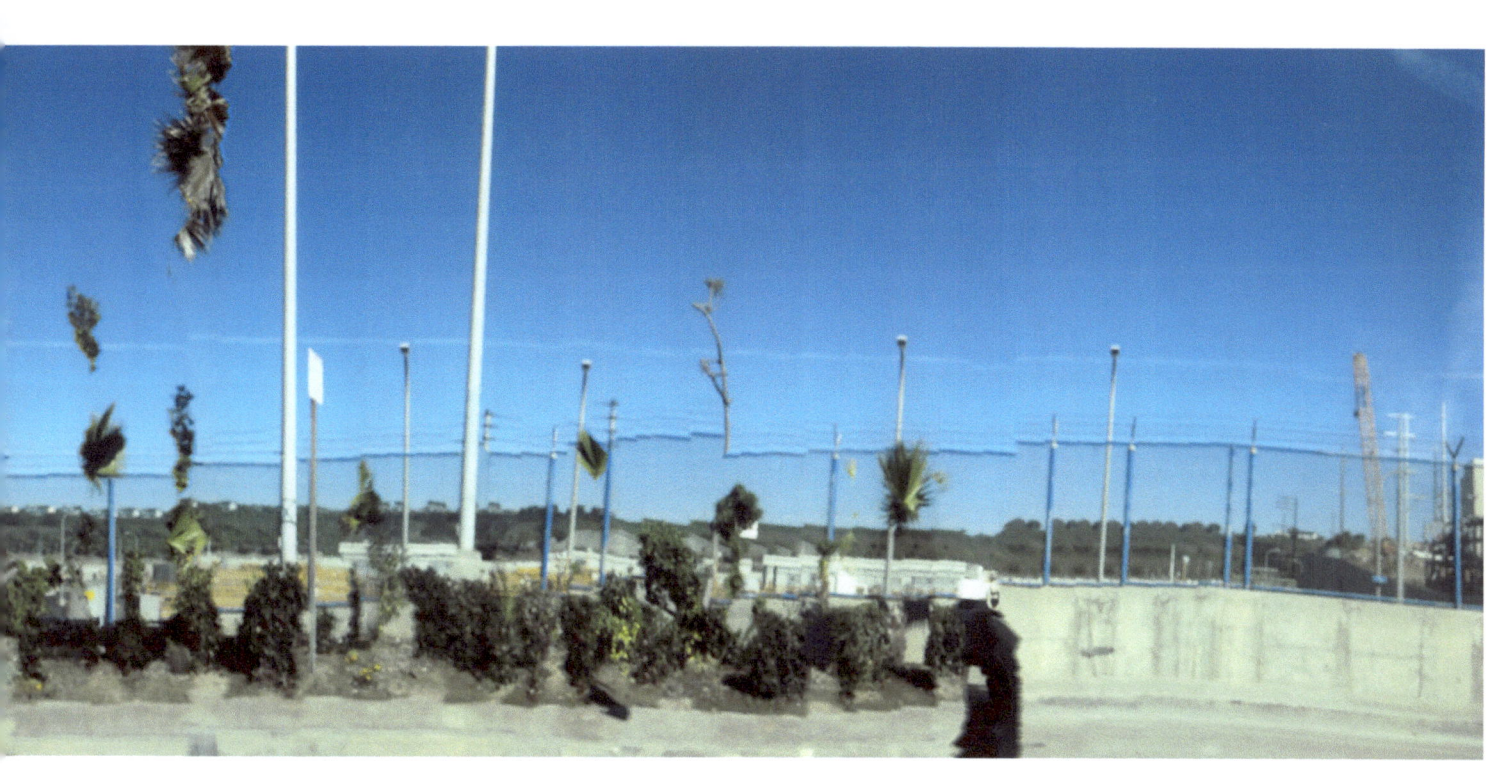

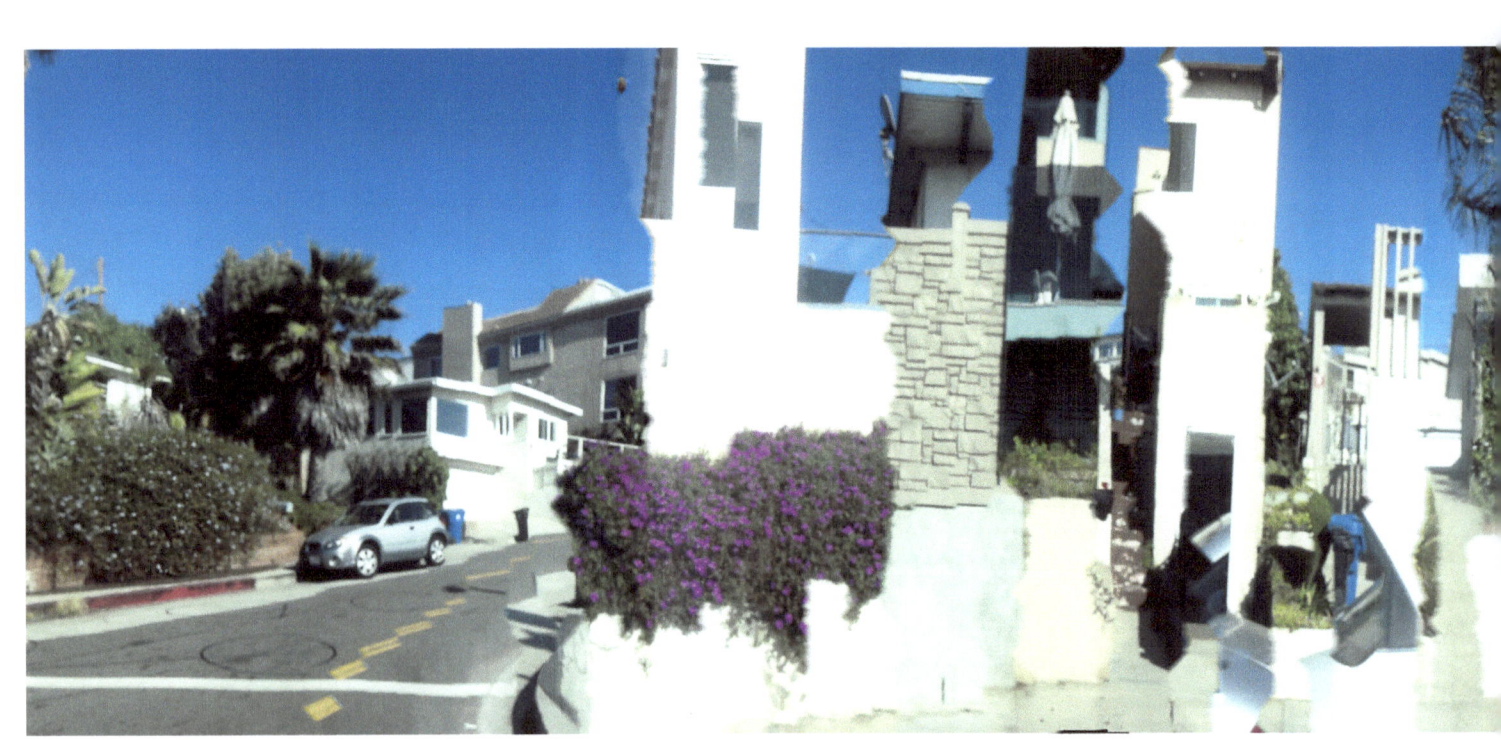

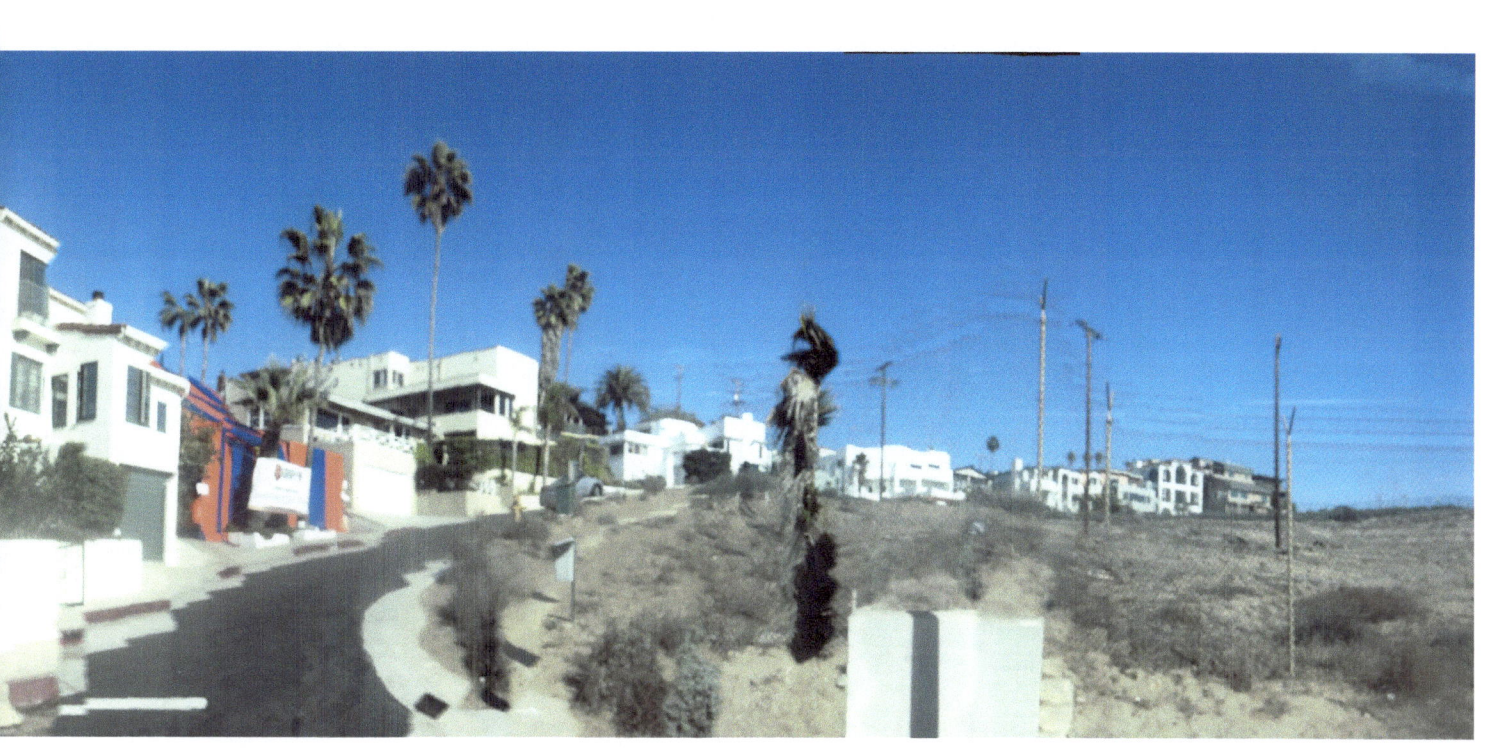

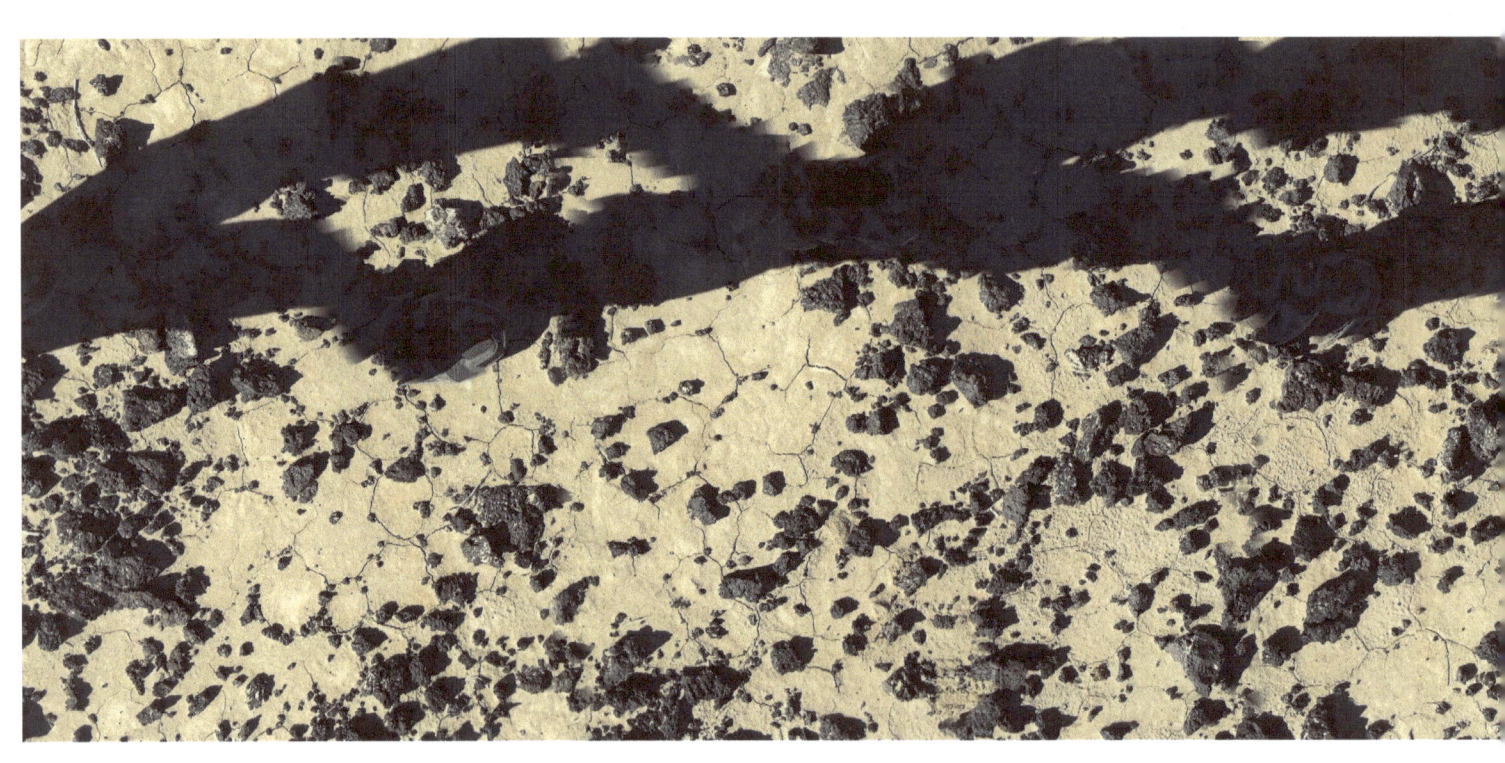

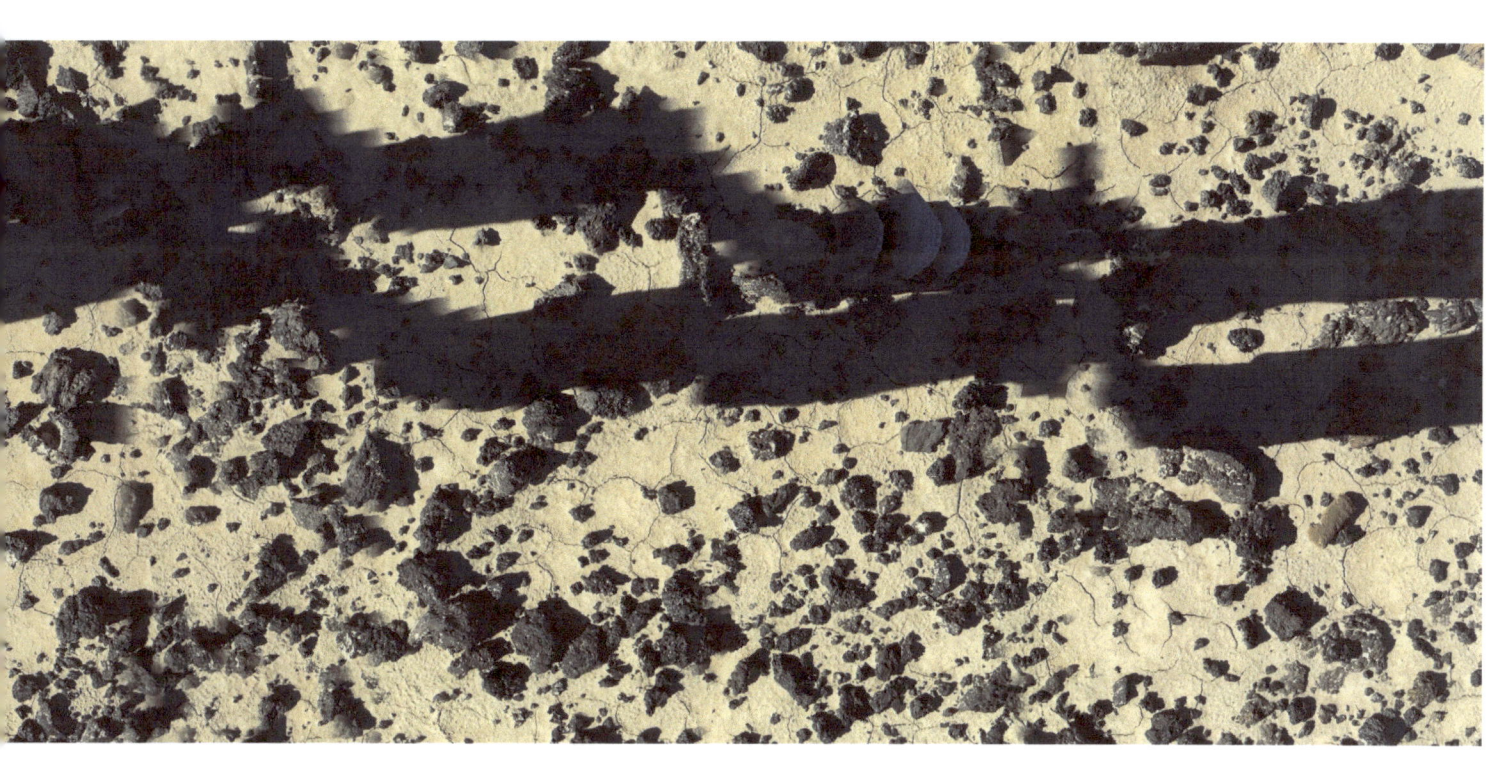

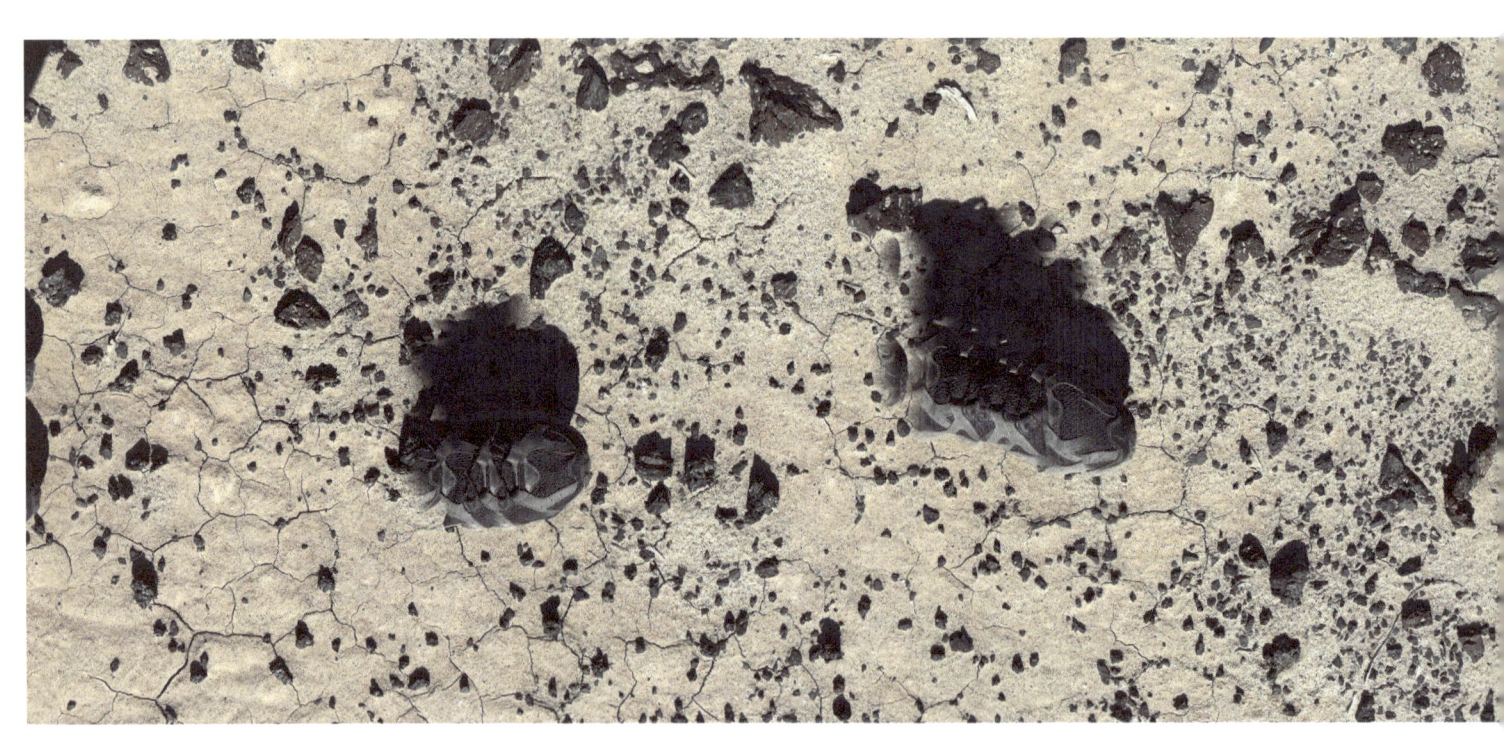

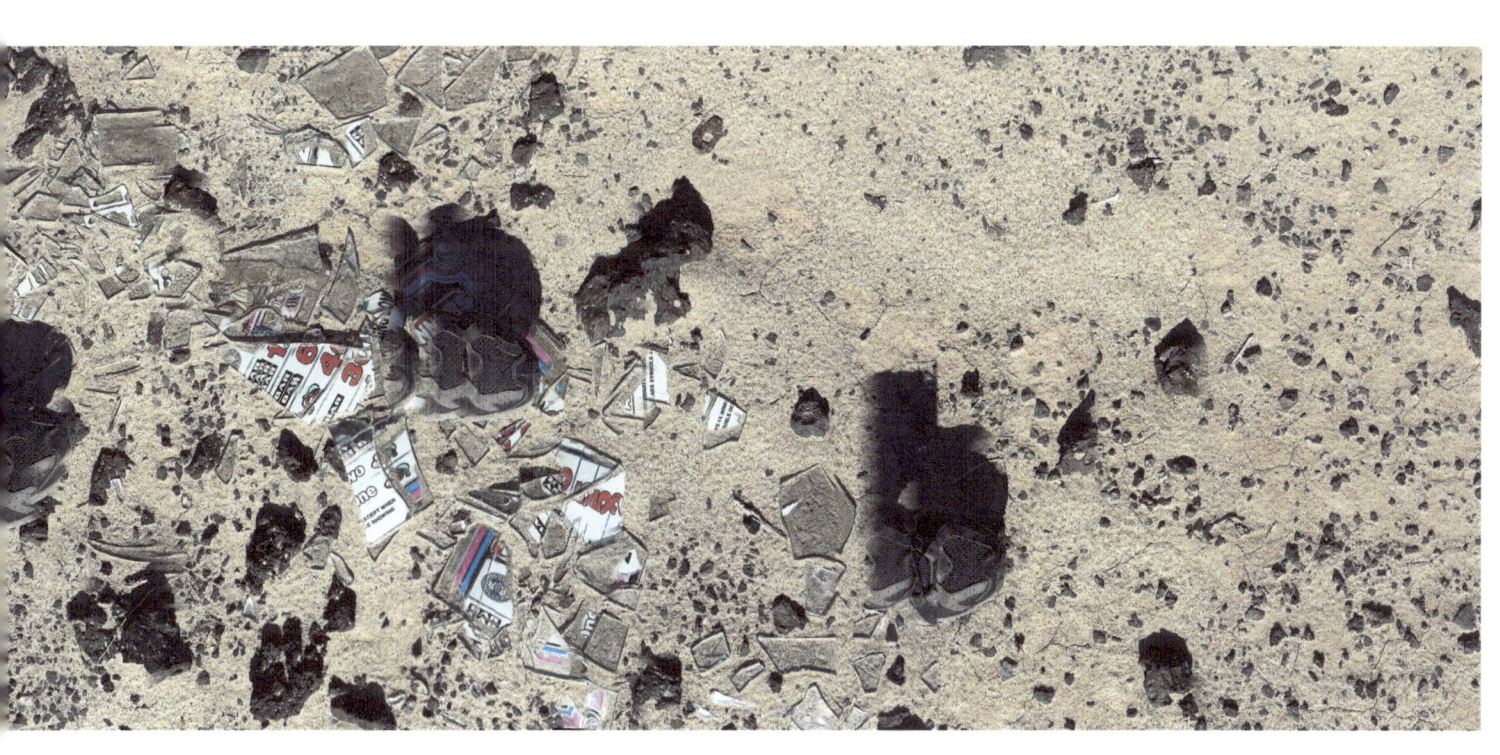

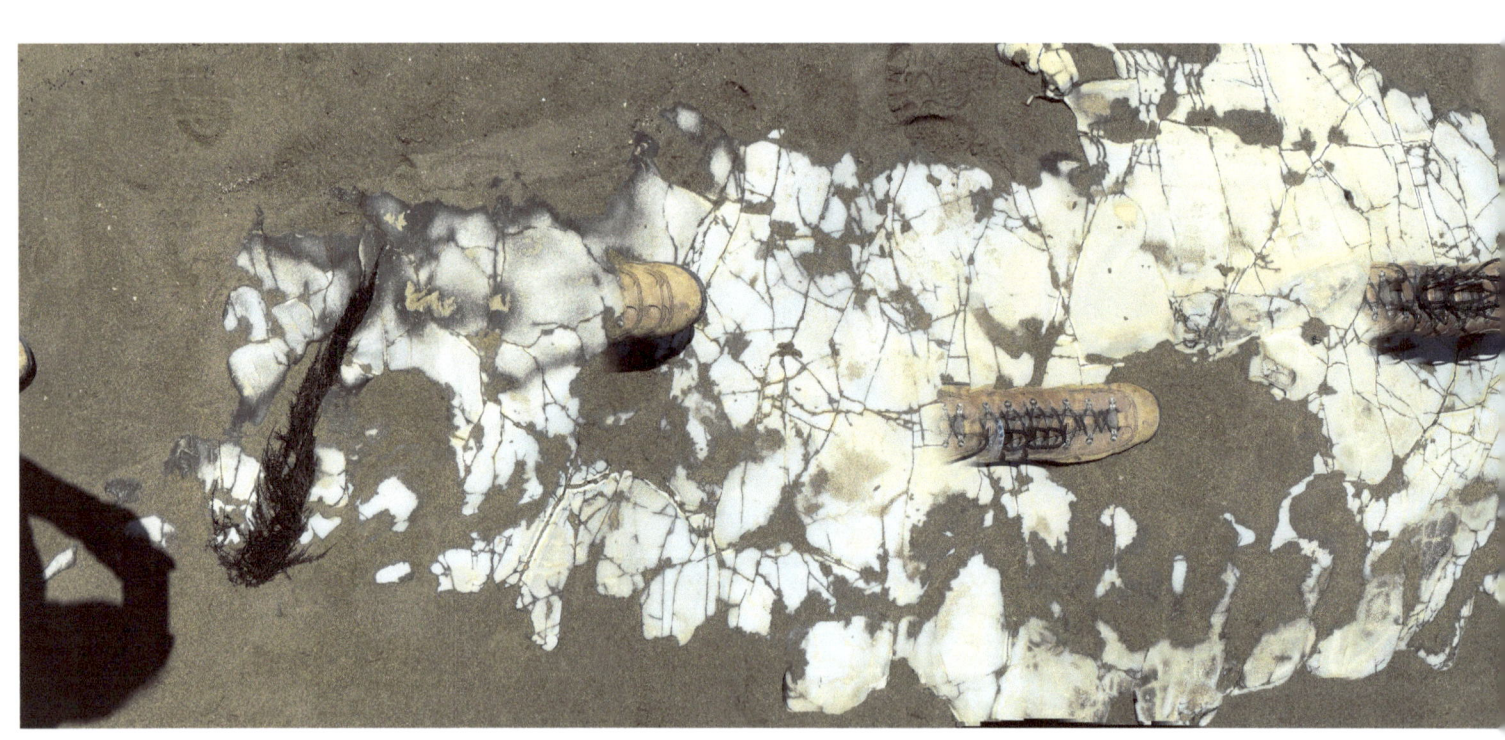

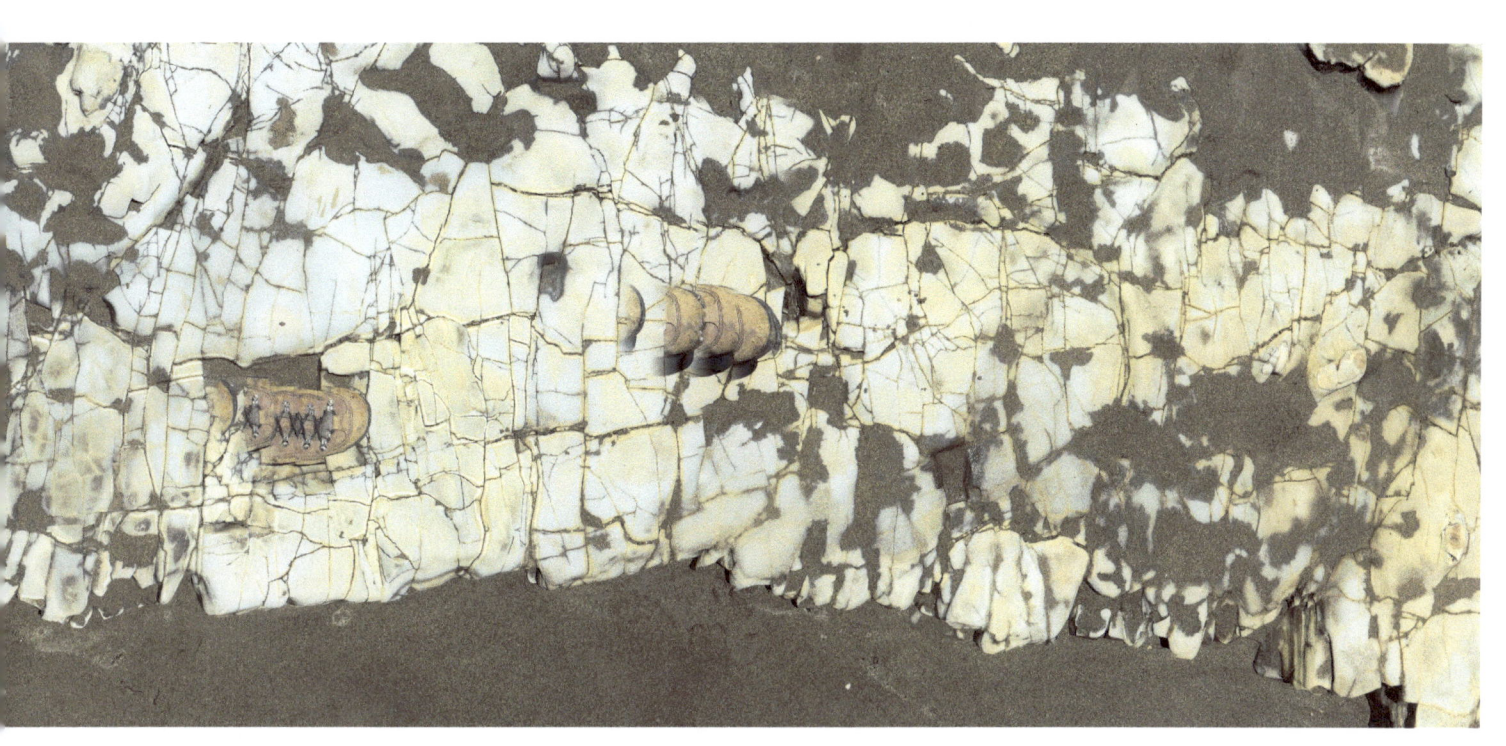

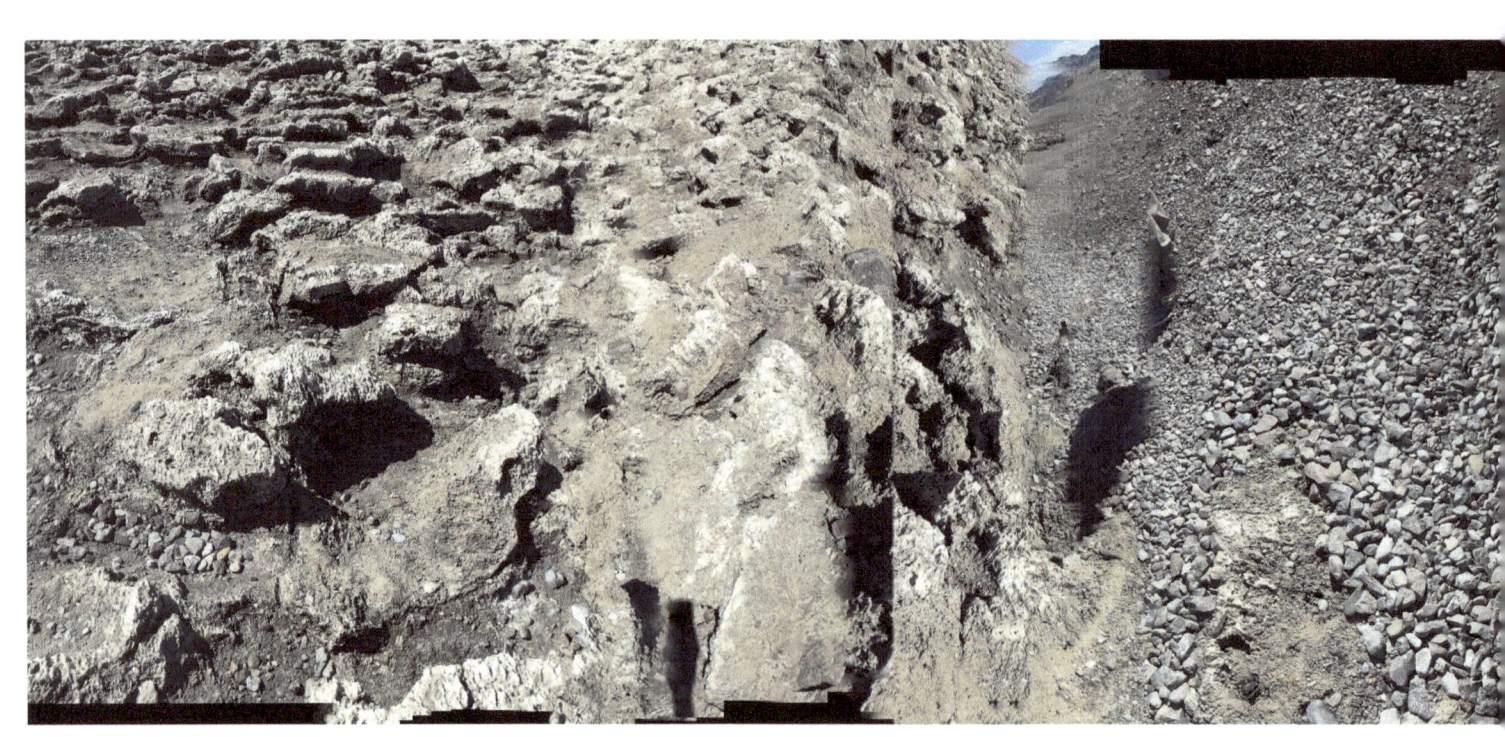

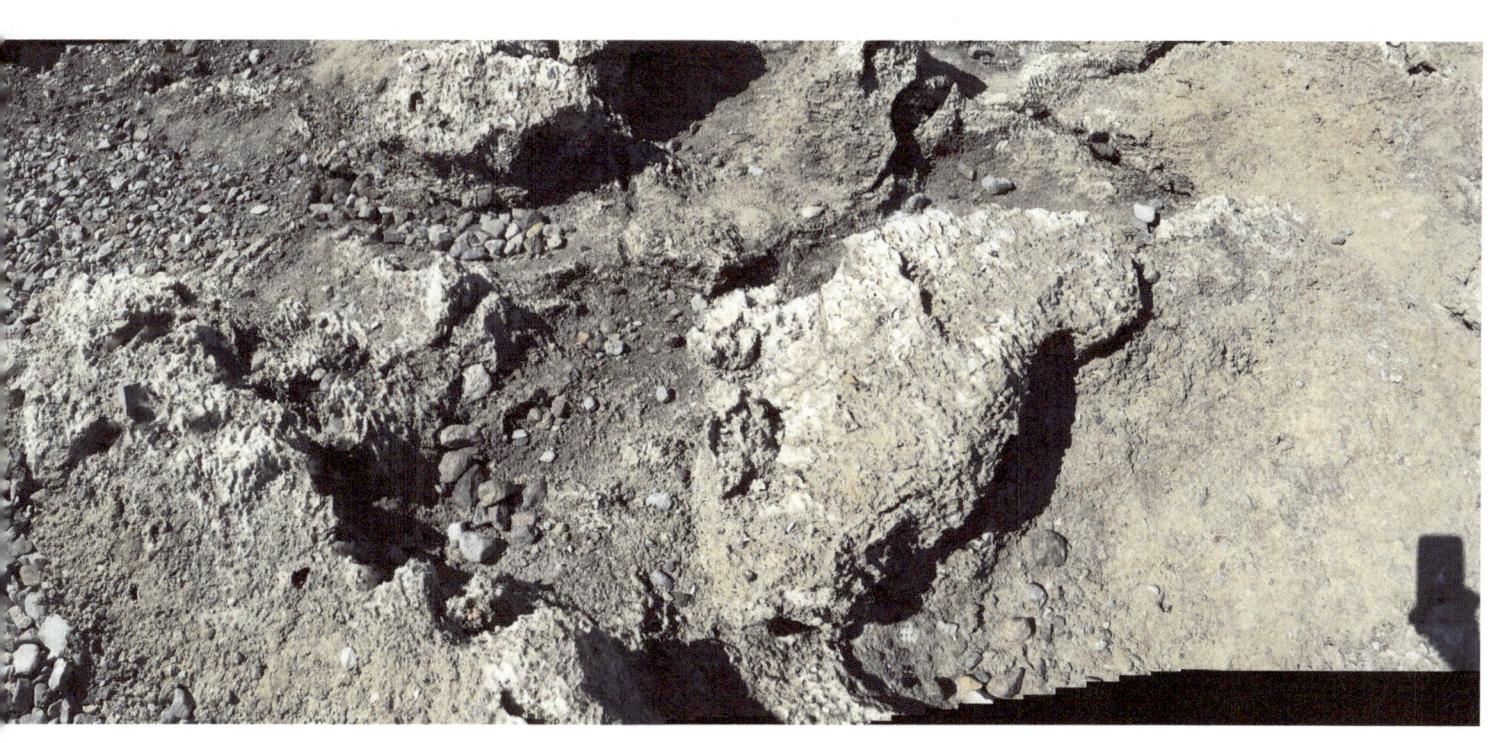

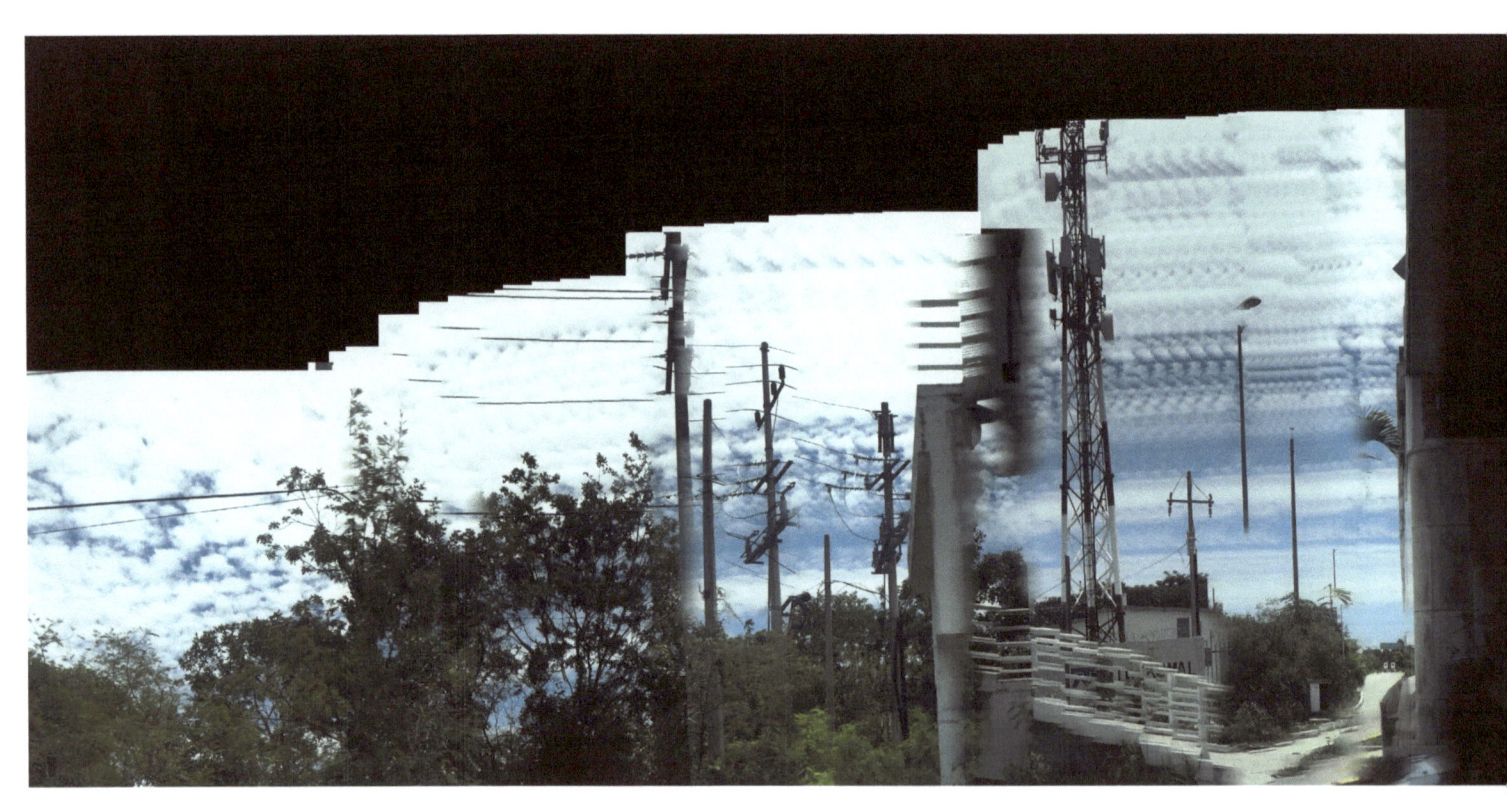

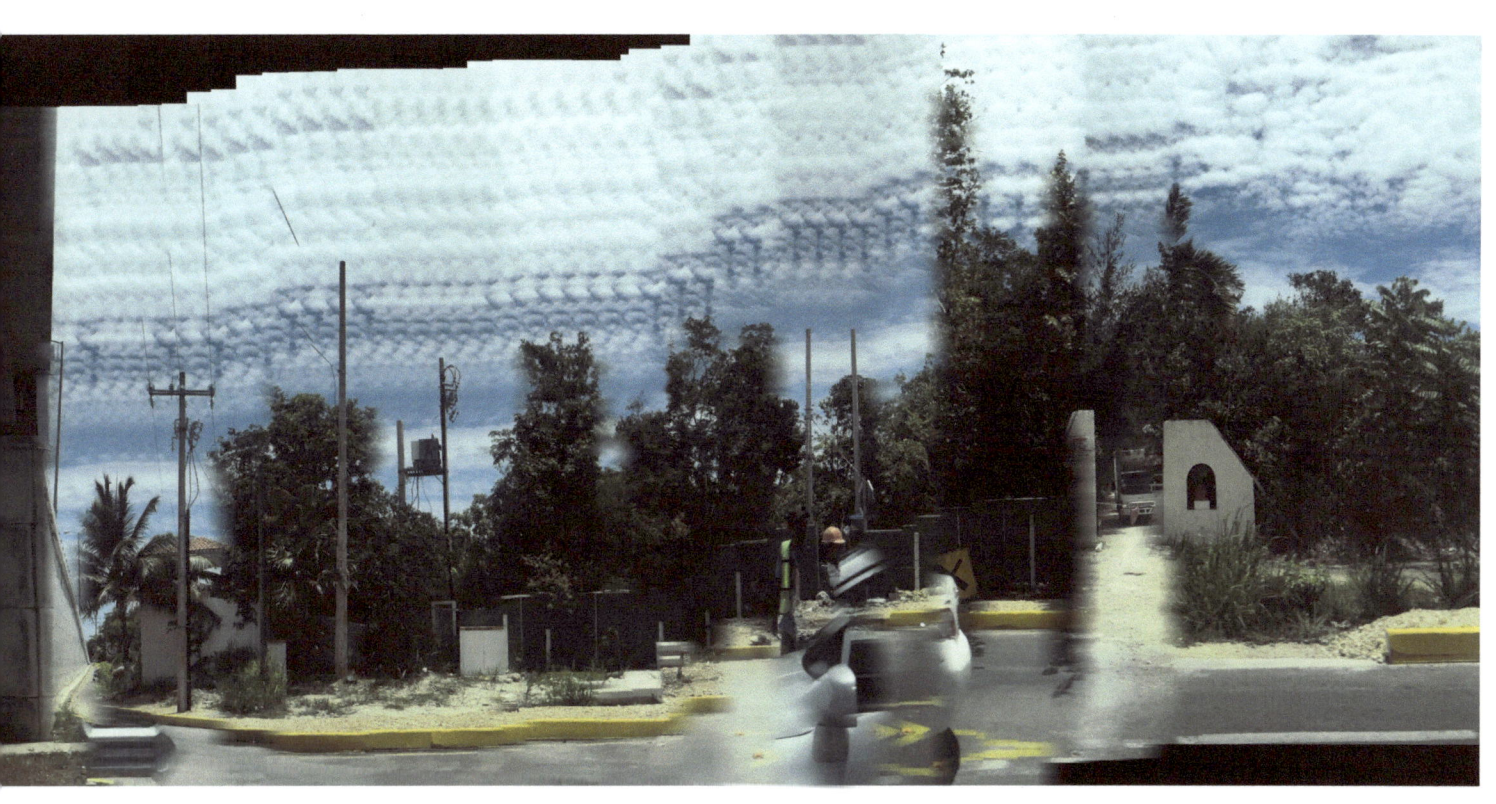

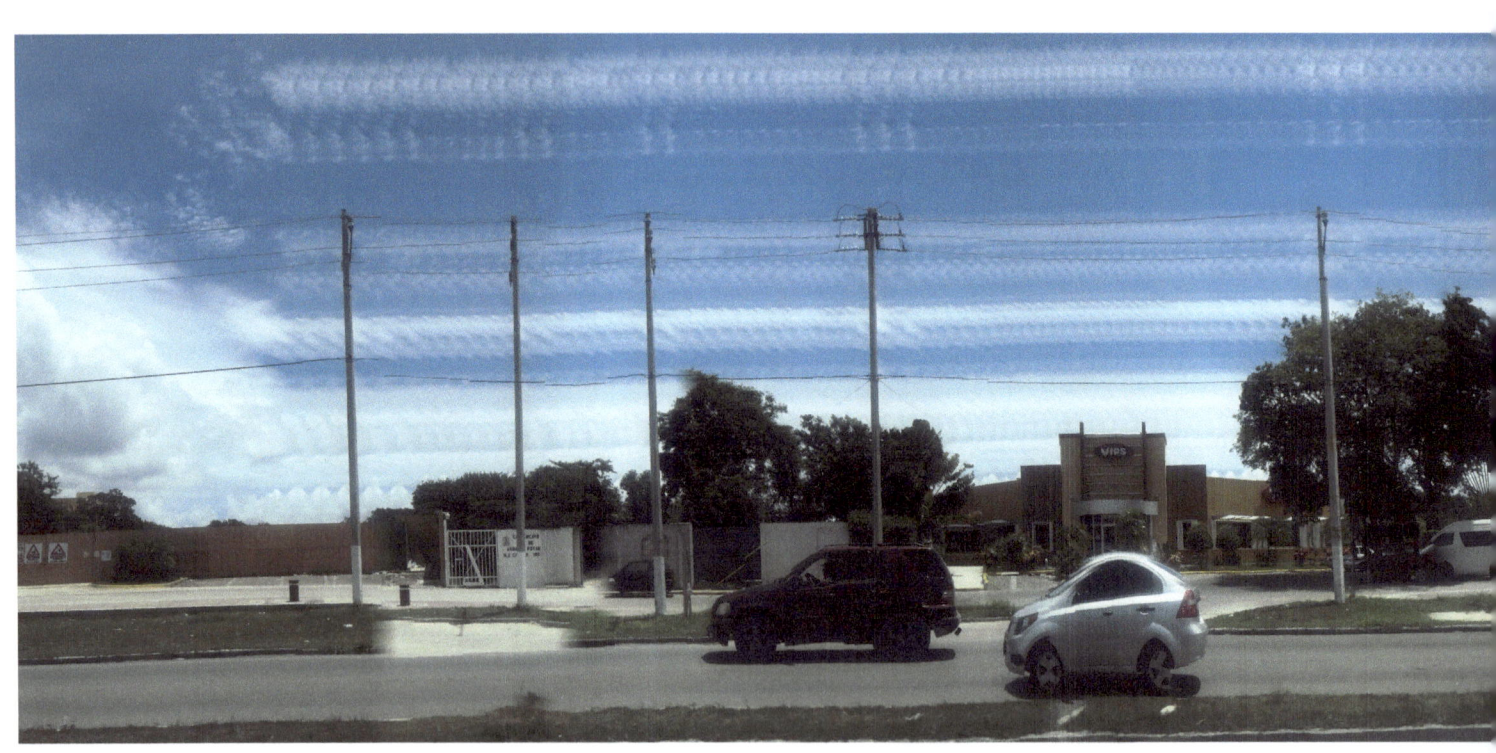

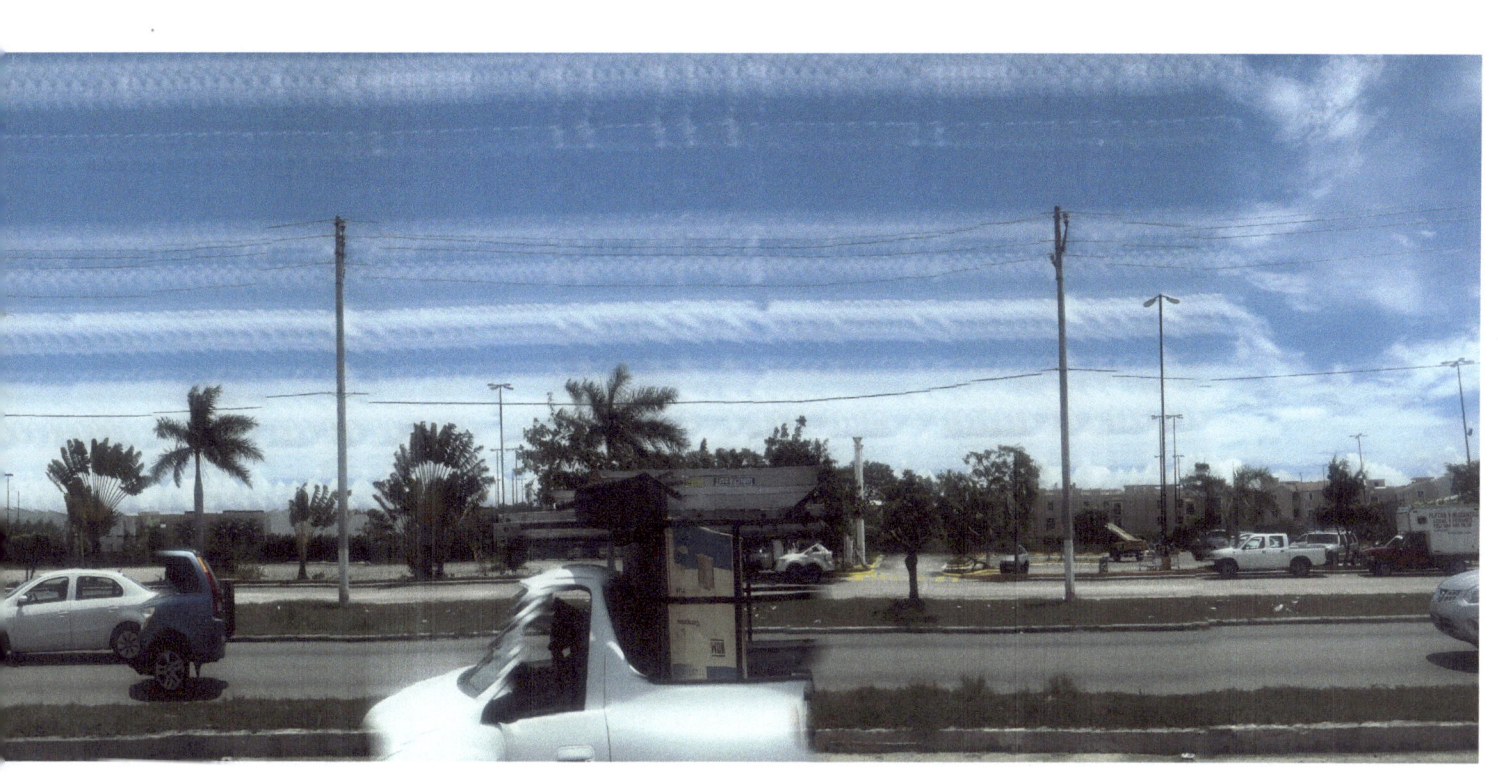

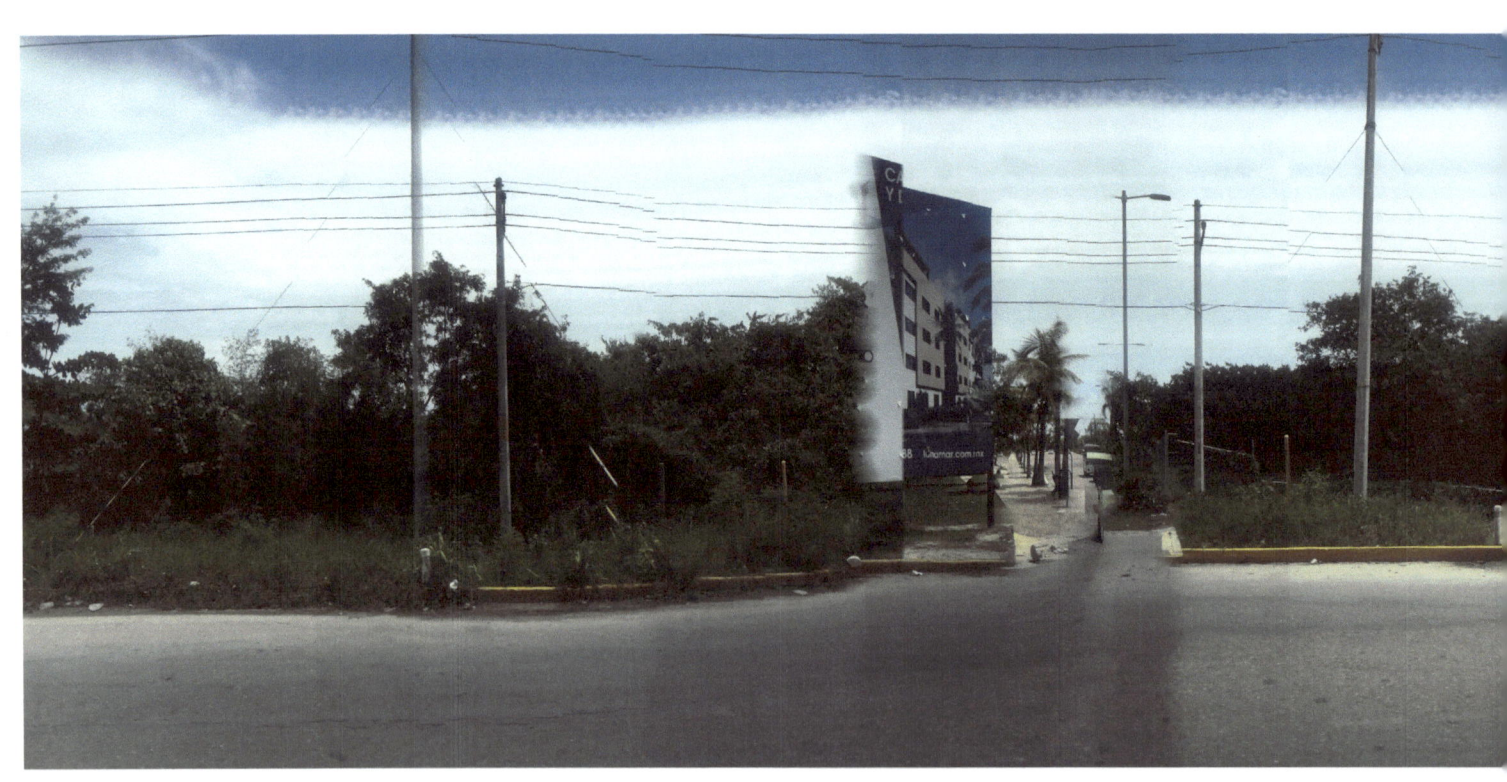

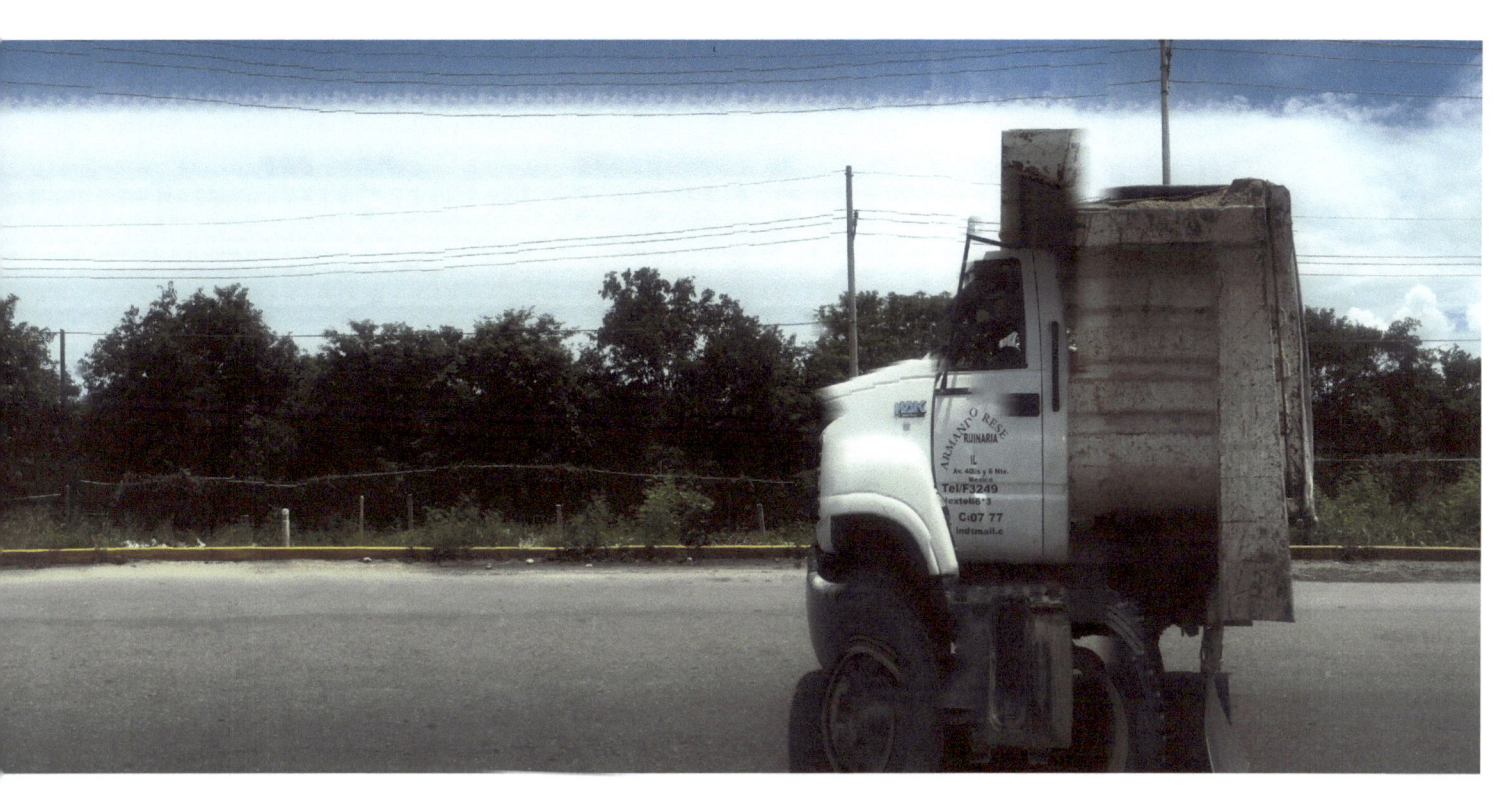

Acknowledgements

Thanks to Arvid, wherever you are. I only knew you for a few hours but you helped get this journey started. To my son, Riley Scaff, who accompanied me on some of these adventures and participated in the image-making. And loving gratitude to my editor, partner and wife Crystal Scaff, who helped me remove the glitches from my life and complete this project.

About the Author

Julian H. Scaff is a designer and futurist working in the fields of UX and Interaction Design. He is also a multidiscipinary artist, who has worked with experimental video and photography, sound, installation and environmental art. He is Design Director at the agency Interactivism and teaches Interaction Design at ArtCenter College of Design in Pasadena, California.

www.ingramcontent.com/pod-product-compliance
Lightning Source LLC
Chambersburg PA
CBHW050712180526
45159CB00003B/1007